Thailand Beyond the Crisis

Thailand Beyond the Crisis includes recent research to give an accurate and up-to-date picture of the status of Thailand's economic recovery. The Asian economic crisis began in Thailand, and ended a decade of sustained economic boom. This book identifies the role of policy errors that led to the crash of the fastest growing economy in the world. It addresses the consequences of the crisis, including increased poverty incidence and a backlog of non-performing loans which clogged the banking system, delaying recovery. This book also explores the political consequences of these events, including the emergence of the populist government of tycoon turned politician Thaksin Shinawatra. Featuring distinguished contributors, including many from Thailand, this survey concludes that Thailand's long term prospects depend on crucial economic reforms.

Key content includes:

- The causes of the crisis
- The social and political consequences of the crisis
- Dealing with bad debt
- Public sector reform
- Implications of a floating exchange rate
- Education
- Urbanization and the environment

Peter Warr is currently John Crawford Professor of Agricultural Economics at the Australian National University.

Rethinking Southeast Asia
Edited by Duncan McCargo
University of Leeds, UK

Southeast Asia is a dynamic and rapidly-changing region which continues to defy predictions and challenge formulaic understandings. This series will publish cutting-edge work on the region, providing a venue for books that are readable, topical, interdisciplinary and critical of conventional views. It aims to communicate the energy, contestations and ambiguities that make Southeast Asia both consistently fascinating and sometimes potentially disturbing.

This series comprises two strands:

Rethinking Southeast Asia aims to address the needs of students and teachers, and the titles will be published in both hardback and paperback.

Rethinking Vietnam
Duncan McCargo

RoutledgeCurzon Research on Southeast Asia is a forum for innovative new research intended for a high-level specialist readership, and the titles will be available in hardback only. Titles include:

1 **Politics and the Press in Thailand**
   Media machinations
   Duncan McCargo

2 **Democracy and National Identity in Thailand**
   Michael Kelly Connors

3 **The Politics of NGOs in Indonesia**
   Developing democracy and managing a movement
   Bob S. Hadiwinata

4 **Military and Democracy in Indonesia**
   Jun Honna

Thailand Beyond the Crisis

Edited by Peter Warr

RoutledgeCurzon
Taylor & Francis Group
LONDON AND NEW YORK

First published 2005
by RoutledgeCurzon
2 Park Square, Milton Park, Abingdon, Oxon OX14 4RN

Simultaneously published in the USA and Canada
by RoutledgeCurzon
270 Madison Ave, New York, NY 10016

RoutledgeCurzon is an imprint of the Taylor & Francis Group

Transferred to Digital Printing 2005

Typeset in Baskerville by Wearset Ltd, Boldon, Tyne and Wear

British Library Cataloguing in Publication Data
A catalogue record for this book is available from the British
Library

Library of Congress Cataloging in Publication Data
A catalog record for this book has been requested

ISBN 0-415-24447-1

Printed and bound by Antony Rowe Ltd, Eastbourne

In Memory of
H.W. Arndt
1915–2002

Contents

Contributors

Peter Warr is John Crawford Professor of Agricultural Economics and Director of the Poverty Research Centre at the Australian National University, Canberra. He is a former Visiting Professor of Economics at Thammasat University (1986 to 1987) and Chulalongkorn University (2000 to 2001), both located in Bangkok. His e-mail address is: Peter.Warr@anu.edu.au

Ammar Siamwalla is Distinguished Scholar and former President, Thailand Development Research Institute, Bangkok. His e-mail address is: ammar@tdri.or.th

Chris Baker is a freelance author and researcher resident in Bangkok. His e-mail address is: Pasuk.P@Chula.ac.th

Isra Sarntisart is Associate Professor in the Faculty of Economics, Chulalongkorn University, Bangkok. His e-mail address is: Isra.S@Chula.ac.th

Pasuk Phongpaichit is Professor in the Faculty of Economics, Chulalongkorn University, Bangkok. Her e-mail address is: Pasuk.P@Chula.ac.th

Stefan Koeberle is the former Country Economist for Thailand, World Bank, Bangkok, and is now Manager, Country Economics Unit, Operations Policy and Country Services Vice Presidency, World Bank, Washington. His e-mail address is: Skoeberle@worldbank.org

Pakorn Vichyanond is Research Fellow, Thailand Development Research Institute, Bangkok. His e-mail address is: yos@tdri.or.th

Bhanupong Nidhiprabha is Associate Professor in the Faculty of Economics, and Vice Rector, Thammasat University, Bangkok. His e-mail address is: bhanupong@econ.tu.ac.th

Sirilaksana Khoman is Associate Professor, Faculty of Economics, Thammasat University, Bangkok. Her e-mail address is: siri@econ.tu.ac.th

Douglas Webster is Consulting Professor in the Asia Pacific Research Center, Stanford University, Palo Alto, California. As of February 2004, he is also Head of Urban and Regional Planning, International Center for Geo-Information Science and Earth Observation, the Netherlands. His email address is webster@itc.nl

Mingsarn Kaosa-ard is Professor in the Faculty of Economics, Chiang Mai University, Chiang Mai, and former Vice-President, Thailand Development Research Institute, Bangkok. Her e-mail address is: csds@econ.cmu.ac.th

Preface

The world knows about Thailand's crisis of 1997–98 mainly through media reporting. The image conveyed was of an economy in collapse. Although it had been booming over the decade preceding the crisis, it was now in deep recession, a victim of evil Wall Street speculators and corrupt domestic politicians. According to these reports, poverty had increased massively, even among people who were previously wealthy. Countries as far away as Europe and the United States nervously anticipated negative effects on their exports. Japanese banks dreaded the prospect of massive non-repayment of loans to Thai banks and corporations. Many of the very commentators who had previously been so impressed by the Thai experience now called it an example to be avoided.

Some of this was correct, but much was not. Seven years after the crisis, it is timely to consider what really happened and its implications for Thailand's future. In 2004, the Thai economy is again booming. Will the same cycle of boom and bust be repeated? If not, what steps need to be taken to avoid this outcome? This book brings together the perspectives of some of Thailand's most distinguished economists and a group of well-informed foreign observers. The authors review not only what happened during the crisis itself but, more particularly, the route for Thailand to achieve a sustained recovery.

I thank all the contributors to this book for their professionalism, cooperativeness and patience during the production process. I am proud to have worked with them. In addition, I gratefully acknowledge the excellent research assistance provided by Colin Thompson and Arriya Mungsunti in helping assemble the manuscript. Financial assistance was provided by the National Thai Studies Centre at the Australian National University, which also sponsored a conference in Canberra at which initial versions of the papers were presented and discussed.

The book is fondly dedicated to the memory of Professor H.W. Arndt, who died in a tragic motoring accident in 2002, aged 87. Professor Arndt was a distinguished scholar, a founder of development economics in Australia and a true friend of Thailand. He was teacher, mentor, colleague and dear friend to many of the contributors to this book and participated actively in the conference that initiated it. He is missed.

Peter Warr

Note on referencing of Thai names

This book uses the Harvard system for citing the works of non-Thai authors. However, the Western convention of citing authors by their family names is awkward in the case of Thais. Thai custom is to refer to individuals by their first names. These are the names by which Thais are known to one another. Thai family names are often long and unfamiliar, even to other Thais. When Thai authors are cited by their family names, scarcely anyone knows who is being described until their first names are also known. In this book we have thus followed the Thai custom of citing Thai authors in the text by their first names. In the lists of references, first names and family names of Thai authors are provided, listed alphabetically by first name. Thus, a 2003 publication of Suthad Setboonsarng would be cited in the text as Suthad (2003) rather than Setboonsarng (2003) and would be listed in the references as Suthad Setboonsarng (2003).

Part I

Background to the crisis and the recovery process

Chapter 1

Boom, bust and beyond

Peter Warr

In the second half of 1997 and throughout 1998, Thailand experienced a deep economic contraction, interrupting 40 years of continuous growth. This contraction, now commonly known as 'the crisis', was in fact the consequence of two crises in one: first, there was a currency crisis, which then produced a banking crisis. These twin crises changed public affairs in Thailand permanently. Six years later, it is appropriate to review their significance. What caused 'the crisis'? How bad was it? How has it changed the priorities of economic and social policy? Has Thailand recovered fully from its effects? Are there any positive outcomes from the crisis? Is the country presently on a sustainable path of economic development? These matters are the focus of this book. The present chapter concentrates on the macroeconomic issues.

We begin with a sketch of the past half-century of Thai economic history.[1] Viewed from this long perspective, Thailand must surely be considered a great economic success story. At the end of World War II it was one of the world's poorest countries. Its economy had been stagnant for at least a century (Sompop 1989), it was seriously affected by the war itself, and most observers of the time rated its economic prospects very poorly (Ingram 1971). They were mistaken. By the mid-1990s Thailand was widely considered a champion of sustained development, having achieved a combination of rapid growth, macroeconomic stability and steadily declining poverty incidence, extending over several decades. Over the period 1965 to 1996, the average annual growth rate of Thailand's real GNP per person was well over 5 per cent (over 7 per cent per annum in total), compared with an average of 2.4 per cent for low- and middle-income countries (World Bank 1998).

Then came the boom. During the decade 1987 to 1996, the Thai economy was the fastest growing in the world. As we shall see below, this boom was driven by very high levels of investment, both domestic and foreign. Even more remarkable than the rate of growth over this long period was the stability of the growth. Not a single year of negative growth of real output per head of population was experienced over the four decades from 1958 to 1996, a unique achievement among oil-importing developing countries. Thailand's performance was often described as an example others might emulate. Its principal economic institutions, including its central bank, the Bank of Thailand, were cited as examples of competent and stable management.

The twin crises of 1997–98 changed all that. Domestically, the economy was in disarray: output and investment were contracting; poverty incidence was rising; the exchange rate had collapsed, following the decision to float the currency in July 1997; the government had been compelled to accept a humiliating IMF bailout package; the financial system was largely bankrupt; and confidence in the country's economic institutions, including the Bank of Thailand, was shattered. Internationally, Thailand was now characterized as the initiator of a 'contagion effect' in Asian financial markets, undermining economic and political stability and bringing economic hardship to millions of people.

Since the crisis, Thailand's economic recovery has been disappointing. Real GDP growth has been moderate, and it was not until 2003 that the level of real GDP per capita had recovered to its level of 1996; foreign direct investment had declined dramatically since 1998; and private domestic investment remained sluggish.

Figure 1.1 summarizes the above events, showing real GDP per capita and its growth rate from 1951 to 2003. In 2003, the level of real economic output per person was more than eight times its level 50 years earlier. The average annual rate of growth of real GDP per person over this entire period was 4.3 per cent. The figure divides this period into four phases.

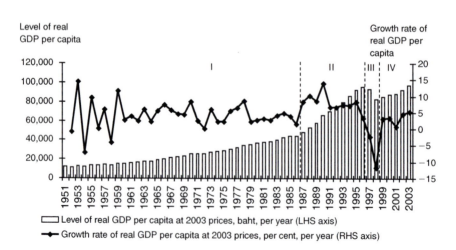

Figure 1.1 Thailand: real GDP per capita and growth of real GDP per capita, 2003 prices, 1951 to 2003 (source: author's calculations using data from National Economic and Social Development Board, Bangkok).

Table 1.1 Thailand: rates of growth of GDP and GDP per capita, 1951 to 2003

Period	Real GDP growth	Real GDP growth per capita
1951 to 1986 (Phase I) Pre-boom	6.5	3.9
1987 to 1996 (Phase II) Boom	9.2	8.0
1997 to 1998 (Phase III) Crisis	−6.1	−7.1
1999 to 2003 (Phase IV) Post-crisis	4.0	3.3
Whole period 1951 to 2003	6.2	4.2

Sources: Bank of Thailand: data for 1951 to 1986; and National Economic and Social Development Board: data from 1987.

Note:
Periods refer to Figure 1.1.

Their average annual rates of growth of real GDP and real GDP per person are summarized in Table 1.1. A fuller summary of Thailand's macroeconomic performance from 1985 to 2003 is provided in Table 1.2.

The crisis of 1997–98 eroded the economic gains that had been achieved in previous decades, but by no means erased them. In 1998, the level of real GDP per person was 14 per cent below its level in 1996, but this was still seven times its level in 1951. Positive growth was achieved in all subsequent years to 2003 (phase IV), but at an average rate of only 3.3 per cent (1999 to 2003).

Figure 1.2 places the last two decades in a comparative East Asian perspective. Data on real GDP are presented for eight East Asian economies, including Thailand. The pre-crisis period of 1986 to 1996 is covered in panel (a), with each country's 1986 level of real GDP indexed to 100. The crisis and post-crisis periods of 1996 to 2004 (data for 2003 and 2004 are projections from the Pacific Economic Cooperation Council) are shown in panel (b), with 1996 real GDP indexed to 100. Panel (a) shows that Thailand's boom was the largest of the countries shown, but only marginally so. Singapore, Malaysia, Indonesia, Korea and Taiwan were not far behind. Panel (b) shows that, in 1998, serious contractions occurred in Korea, Malaysia and Indonesia, but that, relative to 1996, Thailand's initial contraction was the most severe. Along with Indonesia, its contraction has also been the most long lasting. Thailand's crisis was initially more severe than Indonesia's, but Indonesia did not experience a comparable recovery in 1999. It is commonly said that Indonesia's economic crisis was more severe than Thailand's, but these data show that, as of 2002, the magnitude of their contractions of real GDP relative to their 1996 levels were almost identical.

This chapter is about the forces driving Thailand's experience, as summarized above. The structure of the chapter is as follows. We begin with an analysis of the long-term factors that produced the boom decade

Table 1.2 Thailand: macroeconomic summary, 1985 to 2003 (per cent annual growth rate, unless otherwise specified)

Year	Real GNP	Exports US$	Imports US$	Terms of trade (export/import unit value) (per cent, 1995 = 100)	Inflation (%)	Current account balance/GDP (%)	Real money supply (M1)	Total debt/ GNP (%)	Total debt service/ exports (%)	Exchange rate (baht/US$)
1985	3.0	−2.7	−8.8	100.7	2.5	−3.9	0.2	45.6	27.4	27.2
1986	4.6	23.9	1.1	112.4	1.9	0.7	13.2	42.9	24.7	26.3
1987	9.7	31.8	41.5	111.3	2.4	−0.6	22.8	40.0	19.8	25.7
1988	13.3	37.1	48.9	109.2	3.9	−2.4	18.5	34.4	15.0	25.3
1989	12.4	25.2	27.3	105.0	5.3	−3.3	19.7	31.6	12.9	25.7
1990	10.0	15.1	29.8	102.0	5.9	−8.3	16.8	34.8	10.8	25.6
1991	8.2	23.6	15.6	100.9	5.7	−7.5	2.4	38.8	10.6	25.5
1992	8.1	13.8	6.1	101.6	4.1	−5.5	19.7	39.8	11.3	25.4
1993	8.4	13.4	12.3	102.3	3.4	−4.9	10.1	42.3	11.2	25.3
1994	9.0	22.1	18.4	103.3	5.0	−5.4	20.1	45.7	11.7	25.2
1995	9.3	24.8	31.9	100.0	5.8	−7.9	17.1	61.0	11.4	24.9
1996	5.9	−1.9	0.6	98.0	5.9	−7.9	12.7	61.1	12.3	25.3
1997	−1.4	3.8	−13.4	102.3	5.6	−2.0	1.8	74.4	15.7	31.4
1998	−10.5	−6.8	−33.8	93.1	8.1	12.7	−2.0	97.3	21.4	41.4
1999	4.4	7.4	16.9	94.4	0.3	10.2	10.6	79.8	19.4	37.8
2000	4.6	19.5	31.3	85.8	1.6	7.6	9.8	66.1	15.4	40.2
2001	1.8	−7.1	−3.0	77.9	1.6	5.4	8.3	59.6	20.8	44.5
2002	4.9	4.8	4.6	76.7	0.7	5.5	12.3	47.8	19.6	43.0
2003	6.7	18.6	17.1	77.14	1.8	5.6	27.4	73.0	15.8	41.5

Source: All data from Bank of Thailand, Thailand's Macro Economic Key Indicators, http://www.bot.or.th/bothomepage/index/index_e.asp, except:
• Real Money Supply (M1), from CEIC database > Thailand Monetary > Table TH.KA03: Monetary Supply and Demand Deposits.
• Terms of trade: Bank of Thailand > Table 50: Trade Indices and Terms of Trade.
• Total Debt/GNP (%): Calculated from: Thailand's Macro Economic Key Indicators 1993–2003 and GNP from National Economic and Social Development Board.

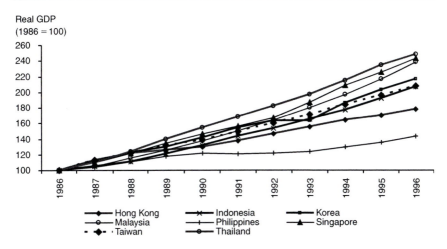

Figure 1.2a Real GDP in East Asia, 1986 to 1996 (source: ADB, *Key Indicators*, various issues).

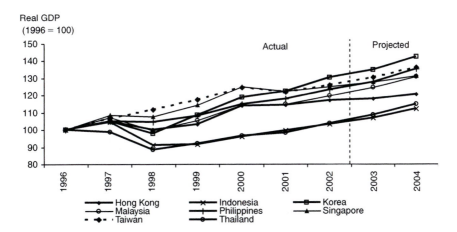

Figure 1.2b Real GDP in East Asia, 1996 to 2004 (source: ADB, *Key Indicators*, various issues; 2003 and 2004 projections from Pacific Economic Cooperation Council, *Pacific Economic Outlook 2003–04*).

following 1987, but which also left Thailand vulnerable to both a currency crisis and a banking crisis. This is contained in the following section (Boom). The next section (Bust) identifies the short-term trigger that led to the expectation of a devaluation, which then precipitated the currency crisis, and which in turn produced the banking crisis.[2] The final section (Beyond) reviews the prospects for the Thai economy following the crisis.

Boom

Thailand's crisis ended a long economic boom, unprecedented in its rate and duration – not only in Thailand, but almost any country. It is not possible to understand the crisis of 1997 except in the context of the boom that preceded it, because the crisis was the collapse of that boom. Over the pre-crisis period of 1988 to 1996, real GDP had grown at close to 10 per cent per annum. What fuelled this extraordinary growth?

Explaining the boom

Explaining long-term growth involves distinguishing between the growth of the factors of production employed and the growth in their productivity. We now discuss a growth accounting exercise for Thailand, covering the years 1981 to 2002, divided into the four periods indicated in Figure 1.1, and for the entire 1981 to 2002 period. The periods of greatest interest are the pre-boom years of 1981 to 1986 and the boom period of 1987 to 1996. The assumption being made is that during these periods, output was primarily supply-constrained; aggregate demand was not the binding constraint on output. As we shall see below, the crisis and recovery periods from 1997 onwards were characterized by a deficiency of aggregate demand. A growth accounting framework, which focuses on the determinants of aggregate supply, is therefore of limited relevance for such periods. The data are included here mainly for completeness.

Table 1.3 shows the growth rates of factors of production employed over the four periods indicated in Figure 1.1, beginning in 1981, and for the entire 1981 to 2002 period. The data are presented for the economy in aggregate and for the separate sectors – agriculture, industry (along with its manufacturing component), and services.[3] The data on labour inputs are adjusted for changes in the quality of the workforce by disaggregating the workforce by the educational characteristics of workers and weighting these components of the workforce using time series wage data for the educational categories concerned. Data on land inputs are similarly adjusted for the changing quality of land inputs by disaggregating by irrigated and non-irrigated land and aggregating these components using data on land prices.

In Table 1.4, these data are combined with information on GDP and its sectoral components, along with time series data on factor cost shares over time compiled from factor price data. These factor cost shares impose the assumption of constant returns to scale. The data on factor contributions shown in the table weight the growth rates of factors by their cost shares, producing an estimate of the degree to which growth of output is attributable to growth of the factor concerned. These data are then used to calculate total factor productivity growth as a residual. We will return to this

Table 1.3 Thailand: growth of factors of production, 1981 to 2002

Adjusted for factor quality	Growth of factors (per cent per annum)				
	Pre-boom 1981–86	Boom 1987–96	Crisis 1997–98	Recovery 1999–2002	Whole period 1981–2002
All sectors					
Capital stock	5.99	10.61	4.13	3.26	7.43
Labour	2.91	1.94	−0.10	0.75	1.80
Land	1.91	0.51	0.60	0.59	0.92
Agriculture					
Capital stock	1.41	4.49	−4.33	−1.70	1.72
Labour	1.96	0.07	−2.20	−4.19	−0.40
Land	1.91	0.51	0.60	0.59	0.92
Industry					
Capital stock	9.60	13.47	6.39	4.30	10.11
Labour	3.55	7.89	3.24	2.79	5.36
Manufacturing (component of industry)					
Capital stock	6.65	14.54	6.57	4.40	9.82
Labour	2.73	7.15	2.83	4.62	5.09
Services					
Capital stock	5.80	10.36	3.89	3.12	7.21
Labour	6.22	3.82	1.81	7.83	5.02

Sources: Data constructed from National Economic and Social Development Board capital stock data, from wage data from the National Statistical Office Labour Force Surveys. Land input data were from the Office of Agricultural Economics, Ministry of Agriculture and Cooperatives.

Note:
Periods refer to Figure 1.1.

table throughout this chapter. For now, we concentrate on the pre-boom and boom periods of 1981 to 1986 and 1987 to 1996, respectively.

The point that stands out most clearly from Tables 1.3 and 1.4 is the rapid growth of the physical capital stock in both periods, but especially during the boom. The capital stock grew more rapidly than output in both the pre-boom and boom periods. Table 1.4 indicates that this growth of the capital stock accounted for more than half of the growth of output in both periods. TFP growth was moderately important during both periods, but especially during the boom, accounting for 16 per cent and 21 per cent of output growth in these two periods, respectively. It is notable that the rate of TFP growth was highest in agriculture, where it accounted for most of the output growth. TFP growth in industry and services was much more modest.

Improvements in the quality of the labour force made only a modest

Table 1.4 Thailand: growth accounting, 1981 to 2002

	Pre-boom 1981–86	Boom 1987–96	Crisis 1997–98	Recovery 1999–2002	Whole period 1981–2002
All sectors					
Output growth	5.46	9.50	−5.93	4.11	6.01
Factor contributions					
Capital stock	3.22	4.80	1.81	1.04	3.42
Labour	1.35	2.68	1.29	1.88	2.05
Land	0.03	0.01	0.01	0.01	0.02
TFP growth	0.86	2.00	−9.03	1.17	0.54
Agriculture					
Output growth	3.61	2.67	−0.33	2.58	2.64
Factor contributions					
Capital stock	0.25	0.49	−0.37	−0.08	0.24
Labour	3.13	−0.46	−1.21	−0.53	0.44
Land	0.46	0.12	0.14	0.14	0.22
TFP growth	−0.22	2.52	1.10	3.04	1.74
Industry					
Output growth	6.72	12.77	−7.70	6.32	8.09
Factor contributions					
Capital stock	6.47	7.38	3.36	1.73	5.74
Labour	1.75	4.88	3.01	2.53	3.43
TFP growth	−1.50	0.51	−3.36	2.06	−1.08
Manufacturing (component of industry)					
Output growth	5.80	13.19	−4.82	7.06	8.42
Factor contributions					
Capital stock	4.11	7.44	3.21	1.59	5.08
Labour	1.54	5.08	2.65	2.26	3.38
TFP growth	0.15	0.67	−10.68	3.21	−0.04
Services					
Output growth	5.43	9.01	−5.44	2.45	5.53
Factor contributions					
Capital stock	4.07	5.93	2.11	1.18	4.21
Labour	2.79	2.05	1.77	3.06	2.41
TFP growth	−1.43	1.03	−9.32	−1.79	−1.10

Sources: Author's calculations using data from Table 1.3 along with factor share and output data explained in the text.

Note:
Periods refer to Figure 1.1.

contribution to Thailand's boom because the performance of its educational sector had been among the weakest in East Asia. Secondary school participation rates were low and did not improve greatly during the pre-boom and boom periods (see Sirilaksana 1993, and Chapter 9 of this volume). Similarly, since the 1960s, the expansion of the cultivated land area was small, so growth of the stock of land was not the source either. It is therefore not surprising that the explanation for Thailand's boom lies with the capital stock. Both foreign direct investment and domestic investment grew, but growth of foreign direct investment (FDI) was proportionately larger, from about 1987 (Warr 1993). This period of rapid growth of FDI coincides with the period of most rapid total factor productivity growth.

From annual rates of inflow varying between US$100 and US$400 million over the previous 15 years, the annual rate of FDI inflow rose more than fivefold in 1987, to over US$2 billion per year, and remained at roughly these levels over the next 8 years. Rates of domestic saving and investment were also high, but the stock of capital represented by foreign direct investment was increasing more rapidly than the stock represented by domestic investment. The proportion of the total capital stock that was represented by foreign direct investment was thus increasing.

To explain the boom we must take note of the massive inflow of foreign capital and abandon the notion that foreign and domestic capital are perfect substitutes. However, this inflow of foreign capital, along with the domestic investment boom that accompanied it, did not merely fuel the boom. Its magnitude and its changing composition, combined with the policy environment of the time, also created the foundations for the collapse of 1997.

Before turning to a more detailed examination of the sources of the growth of the aggregate capital stock it is helpful to review a further feature of the analysis underlying Tables 1.3 and 1.4. The data presented make it possible to distinguish between two components of aggregate total factor productivity (TFP) growth: the growth of productivity in individual sectors and the productivity effects of moving resources from sectors of low productivity to sectors of higher productivity. The theoretical basis for this decomposition was first presented by Jorgenson (1988), and its results are summarized in Table 1.5. Almost one half of the aggregate TFP growth that occurred during the boom was not due to productivity growth at the sectoral level but was the result of resource movement out of low productivity sectors (principally agriculture) and into higher productivity sectors within manufacturing and services.[4] This resource movement added 1 per cent per annum to aggregate growth.

How was the investment financed? Table 1.6 presents an accounting of this issue based on the identities that: (i) total investment = household savings + government savings + foreign savings; and (ii) foreign savings = long-term capital inflow (FDI) + short-term capital inflow − change in international reserves of the central bank. By far the most important source of finance, accounting for fully 93 per cent of total investment, was the private savings of Thais themselves. Contrary to the common perception that Thailand's boom was financed largely by FDI, this source

Table 1.5 Thailand: growth accounting (continued)

	Pre-boom 1981–86	Boom 1987–96	Crisis 1997–98	Recovery 1999–2002	Whole period 1981–2002
All sectors					
Growth	5.46	9.50	−5.93	4.11	6.01
TFP growth	0.86	2.00	−9.03	1.17	0.54
(TFP growth/growth) × 100	15.72	21.08	152.44	28.60	8.92
Agriculture					
Growth	3.61	2.67	−0.33	2.58	2.64
TFP growth	−0.22	2.52	1.10	3.04	1.74
(TFP growth/growth) × 100	−6.15	94.46	−332.46	118.11	65.97
Industry					
Growth	6.72	12.77	−7.70	6.32	8.09
TFP growth	−1.50	0.51	−3.36	2.06	−1.08
(TFP growth/growth) × 100	−22.24	4.00	43.62	32.65	−13.35
Services					
Growth	5.43	9.01	−5.44	2.45	5.53
TFP growth	−1.43	1.03	−9.32	−1.79	−1.10
(TFP growth/growth) × 100	−26.39	11.40	171.34	−72.89	−19.82
Manufacturing					
Growth	5.80	13.19	−4.82	7.06	8.42
TFP growth	0.15	0.67	−10.68	3.21	−0.04
(TFP growth/growth) × 100	2.57	5.05	221.76	45.45	−0.53
All sectors					
Aggregate sectoral TFPG	−1.22	1.02	−5.76	0.42	−0.70
Reallocation	2.08	0.99	−3.28	0.75	1.23

Sources: Author's calculations using data from Table 1.3 along with factor share and output data explained in the text.

Note:
Periods refer to Figure 1.1.

accounted for an average of only 4 per cent of total investment. Short-term capital inflows, consisting of borrowing from abroad plus portfolio inflows plus domestic bank accounts held by foreigners, were a much more important source, accounting for 23 per cent of total investment. Government dissaving (budget deficits) reduced the funds available for investment by 11 per cent, and increases in the international reserves of the Bank of Thailand reduced it by a further 9 per cent.

It is instructive to compare the boom period (1987 to 1996) with the pre-boom period (1973 to 1986). The major difference is in the proportion of total investment during the boom that was financed by short-term capital inflows. This proportion increased from 2 per cent before the boom to 23 per cent during the boom.

Table 1.6 Thailand: financing of aggregate investment, 1973 to 2003

| | Average share of each component (per cent) | | | | | | |
| | Household savings | Government savings | Foreign savings | | | | Total savings = total investment |
			Total	Long term capital inflow	Short term capital inflow	Decline in reserves	
1973 to 1986 – Pre-boom	112.9	−16.7	3.8	5.1	2.1	−3.4	100
1987 to 1996 – Boom	93.1	−11.4	18.2	4.1	22.8	−8.7	100
1997 to 1998 – Crisis	160.9	−23.2	−37.7	17.3	−70.4	15.4	100
1999 to 2003 – Post-crisis	134.3	−2.1	−32.2	10.3	−30.4	−12.1	100
1973 to 2003 – Whole period	116.4	−18.0	1.6	3.5	1.1	−3.0	100

Source: Author's calculations, data from Bank of Thailand and National Economic and Social Development Board, as follows:
Government and private investment: data from NESDB Quarterly GDP 2003, Table 11 Gross Fixed Capital Formation at Current Market Prices; http://www.nesdb.go.th/Main_menu/Macro/GDP/menu.html.
Long term capital flow (FDI): data from Bank of Thailand (BOT) Table 63 Net flow of Foreign Direct Investment Classified by Sector; http://www.bot.or.th/BOThomepage/databank/EconData/Econ&Finance/Download/Tab63.xls.
Government savings: data from Bank of Thailand (BOT) Table 85: Gross Investment and Savings at Current Prices; http://www.bot.or.th/bothomepage/data-bank/EconData/Econ&Finance/Download/Tab85.xls.
Current account: data from Bank of Thailand (BOT) Table 53: Balance of Payments (Summary) (Baht); http://www.bot.or.th/bothomepage/databank/EconData/Econ&Finance/Download/Tab53.xls.

Note:
Calculations are based on the identities that (i) total investment = household savings + government savings + foreign savings; (ii) foreign savings = long term capital inflow (FDI) + short term capital inflow − change in international reserves of the central bank; and (iii) change in reserves = current account balance + long term capital inflow (FDI) + short term capital inflow.

Bank of Thailand response: sterilization and liberalization

Thailand has a long and proud history of stable monetary policy and low inflation. The Bank of Thailand sees its major role as controlling inflation and for decades it had viewed the maintenance of a fixed exchange rate as central to achievement of that outcome.[5] Prior to 1990, financial capital movements into and out of Thailand had been subject to extensive controls, a policy that had allowed Thailand a significant degree of monetary independence in spite of its fixed exchange rate (Warr and Bhanupong 1996). But these controls were largely dismantled during the early 1990s. In part, it was hoped that Bangkok might replace Hong Kong as a regional financial centre following the restoration of Chinese sovereignty in Hong Kong in 1997, but the liberalization of capital controls was also apparently supported by the IMF.[6]

Following this liberalization, both the entry and exit of foreign funds was now very much easier. As foreign investment poured into the booming Thai economy, the Bank of Thailand attempted to sterilize its effects on the domestic money supply. This response was considered consistent with its objective of minimizing inflation. Domestic interest rates were bid up, despite the fixed exchange rate and the increased openness of the capital market, confirming that foreign and domestic assets were imperfect substitutes. The result was an increased level of short-term capital inflow, which entered the country in response to the increased rate of return.

Now suppose an inflow of long-term foreign investment was occurring. If sterilization was not occurring at all, the nominal prices of traded goods would not be affected, since they are determined (with lags) by international prices and the fixed exchange rate, but non-traded goods' nominal prices would be bid up by the increased domestic demand. That is, the capital inflow would produce a real appreciation – an increase in domestic non-traded goods' prices relative to domestic traded goods prices – the phenomenon now known as the 'Dutch Disease' (Corden 1984). The current account deficit would increase, but foreign exchange reserves would be unaffected, relative to what would otherwise have happened.

The outcome would be much the same if the monetary authorities were *attempting* to sterilize but where the exchange rate was fixed, capital movements were unimpeded, and foreign and domestic assets were perfect substitutes. Any attempt to sterilize by raising domestic interest rates, through the sale of bonds, would be defeated because it would produce an inflow of portfolio investment sufficient to drive the domestic interest rate down to its previous level. Demand would be increased by the monetary consequences of this inflow, producing the real appreciation described above. This is the familiar Mundell–Fleming model.

In the hypothetical case where sterilization was completely effective, the monetary effects of the capital inflow would be exactly offset by the sale of bonds. Bond prices would be forced down and domestic interest rates would rise relative to international rates. The money supply would not increase and relative domestic prices would not be affected. Reserves would increase by the amount of the capital inflow. This outcome assumes, however, that additional short-term capital inflow is not induced by the rise in domestic interest rates. For this reason, complete sterilization would be highly improbable in the Thai context of the early 1990s, because by then capital movements had been liberalized significantly. There was very little to prevent capital inflow in response to higher domestic interest rates.

Incomplete sterilization implies an intermediate outcome. This might be observed if the monetary authorities were attempting to sterilize but where domestic and foreign assets were imperfect substitutes, leading to capital inflows that only partially offset the attempts to sterilize, and/or where some residual controls on capital movements were limiting mobility. We would then expect coexistence of the following phenomena, relative to what would otherwise have occurred:

i   increased levels of foreign exchange reserves;
ii increased current account deficits;
iii increased domestic interest rates;
iv increases in prices of non-tradables relative to tradables – a real appreciation; and
v   increased inflows of foreign short-term capital.

This combination is what occurred. Items (i), (ii) and (iii) are obvious from inspection of Thailand's macroeconomic data. We can therefore concentrate on items (iv) and (v).

Real appreciation

A dramatic real appreciation was occurring throughout the 1990s. This real appreciation is indicated in Figure 1.3. We focus first on the series labelled 'Relative Price', an index of the relative prices of traded to non-traded goods. This series updates calculations presented in Warr and Bhanupong (1996), which used monthly domestic price data for Thailand to obtain an index of traded goods prices (using 33 individual wholesale prices which approximately match the analytical concept of traded goods) relative to non-traded goods (using 42 individual consumer prices which approximately match the analytical concept of non-traded goods).[7] In the earlier study, the data were presented for 20 years from 1968 to 1988. Over this period, the index took values between a maximum of 1.7 and a minimum of 0.68 (indexed to August 1973 = 1). At the end of the data series (January 1988) the value of this index was 0.7.

For convenience of comparison with the earlier series, the relative price series shown in Figure 1.3 is indexed to begin at 0.7 in January 1988 and its composition and construction are identical to the earlier study. Leaving aside short-term fluctuations, the index declined steadily from 1990 onwards. By April 1997 its value was 0.38. A very large real appreciation had occurred. The real exchange rate, so measured, had fallen to only 55 per cent of its lowest value over the two decades prior to the boom.

Do external exchange rate changes explain this outcome? The question arises because it is now well understood that the depreciation since 1995 of the Japanese yen and other currencies relative to the US dollar meant that any currency pegged to the dollar would suffer a real appreciation. But the answer is no.

The real appreciation within Thailand demonstrated in Figure 1.3 was not at all confined to the period since 1995, when the US dollar was appreciating. A large real appreciation within Thailand can also be seen in the first 5 years of the 1990s when the dollar was *depreciating* relative to the yen and other currencies. Most of the real appreciation from 1990 to mid-1997 was already evident by mid-1994, well before the appreciation of the US dollar began. External exchange rate changes were clearly relevant, but they were not the main causal factor.

The principal cause of Thailand's real appreciation resided in forces operating *within* the Thai economy – not external exchange rate adjustments. The principal source was the demand effects of very large foreign capital inflows, only partially sterilized. The effect of the real appreciation was that it undermined the competitiveness of Thailand's traded goods industries, meaning their capacity to attract resources within the domestic economy in competition with non-traded goods sectors.

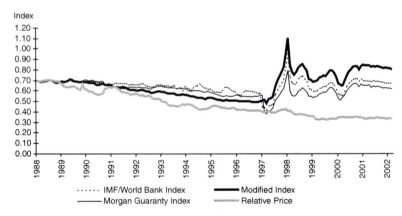

Figure 1.3 Thailand: real exchange rate indices, 1988 to 2002 (source: author's calculations using data from Ministry of Commerce and Bank of Thailand, Bangkok).

Figure 1.3 also shows three other measures of real exchange rates, also commonly called measures of 'competitiveness'. All three are based not on domestic relative prices but on nominal exchange rates adjusted by foreign and domestic price levels. The two most commonly used in the literature are labelled the 'IMF/World Bank Index', the export share weighted sum of trading partner consumer price indices, each multiplied by the bilateral exchange rate, divided by the domestic consumer price index; the 'Morgan-Guaranty Index', where the two consumer price indices described above are replaced by foreign and domestic wholesale price indices, respectively.

Finally, the series labelled 'Modified Index' replaces foreign consumer prices in the numerator of the 'IMF/World Bank Index' with foreign wholesale prices, but it retains the domestic wholesale price index in the numerator. This index is preferable to either of the other two as a proxy for traded goods prices relative to non-traded goods prices. The reason is that the share of traded goods in wholesale price indices is higher than its share in consumer price indices. Thus, the numerator of this index, the export share weighted sum of foreign wholesale price indices, each multiplied by the bilateral exchange rate, may be taken as a (very rough) proxy for domestic traded goods prices; and the denominator, the domestic consumer price index, may be taken as a (very rough) index of domestic non-traded goods prices.

For the reasons demonstrated in Warr (1986), all three of these exchange-rate-based measures – but especially the first two – may be expected to understate the magnitude of a real appreciation, compared with changes in the domestic relative prices of traded goods to non-traded goods.[8] This pattern is exactly borne out by the calculations shown in Figure 1.3. All four measures shown confirm that a real appreciation did occur but its magnitude is understated in particular by the 'IMF/World Bank' and the 'Morgan-Guaranty' measures.

Adequacy of reserves

The Bank of Thailand was attempting to maintain a (nearly) fixed exchange rate relative to the US dollar.[9] Were its reserves of foreign exchange adequate for this task? The conventional measure of reserve adequacy, the number of months of imports that reserves could finance, relates a financial stock, international reserves, to a trade flow, the monthly value of imports. Based on this measure, reserve adequacy increased steadily throughout the pre-crisis period, from 3 months of imports in 1988 to over 6 months in early 1997. This measure signalled no problem regarding reserve adequacy at the time of the crisis. On the contrary, it suggested a steady improvement in the adequacy of Thailand's reserves as the boom progressed. But this indicator is conceptually of little relevance as an indicator of vulnerability to a financial crisis.

At a time of financial panic it does not matter how many months of imports could be financed from reserves. What matters is whether reserves can withstand a capital outflow. Under a fixed exchange rate regime the relevant magnitudes are: (a) the *stock* of foreign currency available to the central bank to finance transactions that convert domestic currency to foreign currency, namely its international reserves, relative to (b) the *stock* of financial capital that could be presented to the central bank at short notice for such currency conversion. The accumulated stock of foreign-owned, short-term capital is a major component of the latter. It is not the only component, in that it does not include volatile capital held by domestic residents, but it is one of the most volatile and focusing upon it has the advantage that it can be isolated using balance of payments data.

Figure 1.4 compares the stock of the Bank of Thailand's reserves, on the one hand, with the estimated cumulative stock of short-term, foreign-owned capital, on the other. The latter includes foreign-owned portfolio capital, short-term bank loans and non-resident accounts held in Thai banks. This short-term capital is to be distinguished from long-term, foreign-owned capital, which includes foreign direct investment and long-term loans from abroad. The accumulated stock of long-term capital is also shown in Figure 1.4. Monthly balance of payments data from the Bank of Thailand on net flows of financial capital are used to construct

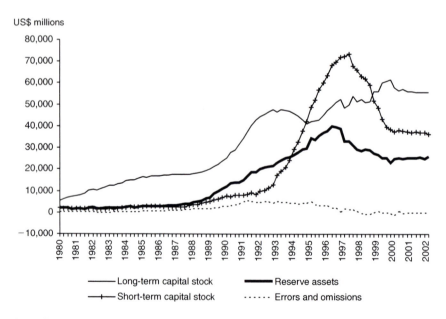

Figure 1.4 Thailand: stocks of long- and short-term capital and international reserves, 1980 to 2002 (source: author's calculations using data from Bank of Thailand, Bangkok).

these stocks. The data are accumulated from January 1970, prior to which flows of foreign-owned capital were very small.

The longer the boom continued, the greater the accumulated stock of mobile funds became, relative to long-term capital and, much more significantly, relative to reserves. Figure 1.4 reveals a significant increase in vulnerability to a crisis in the years preceding 1997, especially from 1993 onwards. From 1994 onwards, the stock of short-term foreign capital exceeded the value of reserves and the discrepancy between them increased steadily. By early 1997 the stock of short-term, foreign-owned capital exceeded reserves by 80 per cent. Both portfolio capital and non-resident accounts increased significantly in the years prior to the crisis, but the most significant component of the increase was in bank loans from abroad.

Clearly, the adequacy of Thailand's reserves had declined dramatically, when these reserves are measured in relation to the stock of volatile funds that could be presented against them in the event of a loss of investor confidence. Moreover, this vulnerability did not develop suddenly, immediately prior to the crisis, but steadily, over a period of several years. That the subsequent outflow of this stock of short-term foreign-owned capital was the cause of the decline in reserves that accompanied the crisis, is confirmed by comparing the decline in reserves during 1997 and 1998 (shown in Figure 1.4) with the decline in the stock of short-term foreign capital during the same period. The flight of this short-term, foreign-owned capital was clearly the principal source of the loss of reserves.

The growth of volatile foreign capital relative to reserves had left Thailand increasingly vulnerable to a speculative attack on its reserves, but few observers, if any, were looking at the appropriate indicators. Prior to the crisis, both the absolute value of reserves and the number of months of imports they could finance had been increasing, but the growth of reserves was far exceeded by the growth of volatile foreign capital. This was the key to Thailand's vulnerability to a financial crisis.

The bubble economy

What caused the massive inflow of volatile foreign capital in the years preceding the crisis? Large returns were being made by investing in Thailand and this situation had been sustained over several years. Euphoria induced by almost a decade of high growth produced over-confidence. In addition, the government was assuring the public that reserves were adequate to maintain the fixed exchange rate and the IMF also seemed satisfied, judging from its public statements. Investing in Thailand seemed both safe and profitable. Not to participate was to miss out.

Through the first half of the 1990s, investment in real estate and commercial office space soared. The rate of investment was so large that the quality of the investment inevitably declined, much of it proving to be financially non-performing, destroying the companies that had financed it. But why had investors acted so imprudently? Over-confidence was an important part of the story, but the underlying real appreciation was another. The classic bubble economy is one in which real estate prices continue to rise well beyond levels justified by the productivity of the assets; but, so long as the prices continue to rise, existing investors are rewarded and collateral is created for new loans to finance further investment, and so on – until the inevitable crash.

Unrealistic expectations of a continued boom are the underlying fuel for this process. These expectations are generally possible only after several years of sustained boom. The boom therefore generates the mechanism for a crash. This is why economic booms almost never peter out gradually. They collapse. In these respects, Thailand's financial panic was similar to many previous examples around the world, including the Mexican crash of 1994 (Edwards 1998).

In the Thai case, there were three other, less well understood causes for over-investment, each of which was policy-induced. First, as described above, the Bank of Thailand was attempting to sterilize the monetary consequences of capital inflows, despite its own relaxation of capital controls. By increasing domestic interest rates this encouraged further short-term capital inflows.

Second, beginning in 1993, the Thai government encouraged banks to borrow short-term through its establishment of the Bangkok International Banking Facility (BIBF), again with the apparent approval of the IMF. This development made short-term borrowing from abroad easier and more attractive for domestic banks and, from the point of view of the foreign lender, these loans were protected by implicit guarantees from the Bank of Thailand. The dramatic increase in short-term bank loans began at this time. In addition to new short-term loans, significant substitution of short-term loans for longer-term loans also occurred. Beginning in 1993, the stock of long-term loans actually declined for around two years while short-term loans accelerated.

Third, the Bank of Thailand also indirectly encouraged short-term borrowing by non-bank financial institutions. For many years prior to the crisis, banking licences in Thailand had been highly profitable. The issuance of new licences is tightly controlled by the Bank of Thailand but it had become known that the number of licences was to be increased significantly. Thai finance companies immediately began competing with one another to be among the lucky recipients. To project themselves as significant players in the domestic financial market, many companies were willing to borrow large sums abroad and lend domestically at low margins, thereby taking risks they would not ordinarily contemplate. With lenders eager to lend vast sums, real estate was a favoured investment because pur-

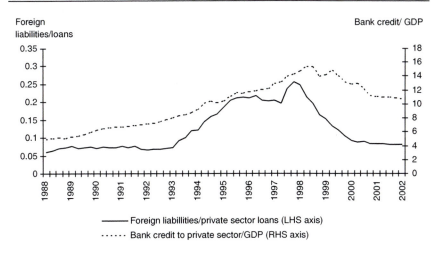

Figure 1.5 Thailand: bank exposure, 1988–2002 (source: author's calculations using data from Bank of Thailand, Bangkok).

chase of real estate requires almost no specialist expertise, only the willingness to accept risk.

Bank exposure

The implication of the above phenomena was a large increase in the exposure of the Thai banking sector to both exchange rate risk and to domestic default. This is indicated in Figure 1.5. First, the increased level of banks' foreign indebtedness relative to the lending base of the banks increased their exposure to exchange rate risk. Second, the increased level of bank credit to GDP increased their exposure to a domestic contraction.[10] Poor supervision of Thai banks has been widely blamed for their difficulties. There seems little doubt that standards of prudential control were indeed lax, a product of the over-confidence on the part of monetary authorities that also characterized the private sector. Nevertheless, the increased exposure of the Thai banks must be seen primarily as the consequence of the macroeconomic events described above and not as a separate event that could have been corrected by tighter supervision alone.

Bust

The trigger: export slowdown in 1996

The underlying causes of the crisis were long-term, as discussed above. The trigger that actually undermined confidence sufficiently to set a speculative attack on the baht in process was the collapse of export growth in 1996. Export growth declined from over 20 per cent per year in previous years, a performance which made the high current account deficits of the time seem (almost) sustainable, to around zero in 1996. This provoked capital outflow and speculation against the baht because it produced the expectation of a devaluation. Once this expectation developed and portfolio capital headed for the exit, the process was unstoppable. Table 1.7 shows the levels of exports and their growth rates for the years 1994 to 1996. The slowdown was widespread among Thailand's export destinations but was greatest in exports to Japan, NAFTA and the Chinese economies. By looking at the composition of exports by commodity it can be seen that the slowdown was concentrated in manufactured exports from labour-intensive industries.[11]

The export slowdown of 1996 did not *cause* the crisis. In normal circumstances a temporary slowdown in exports would be met by an increased current account deficit, financed by a combination of reduced reserves and temporary borrowing from abroad. The slowdown coincided with an already high current account deficit, equivalent to around 8 per cent of

Table 1.7 Thailand: sources of the 1996 export slowdown – export growth, 1994 to 1996

	1994	1995	1996
Total exports (million baht)	1,137,602	1,406,310	1,401,392
Growth rate (%)	20.9	23.6	−0.35
Growth rate by commodity (%)			
1 Computer and parts	44.9	38.7	31.3
2 Garments	12.4	1.3	−21.9
3 Rubber	43.3	46.5	1.4
4 Integrated circuits	27.5	28.4	3.4
5 Gems and jewellery	8.3	11.5	8.4
6 Rice	18.9	24.1	8.4
7 Sugar	41.2	67.2	11.7
8 Frozen shrimps	29.9	2.3	−17.8
9 Television and parts	26.2	12.7	14.1
10 Shoes and parts	40.5	37.0	−40.9
11 Canned seafood	24.7	4.1	−0.3
12 Air conditioner and parts	62.1	49.6	33.6
13 Plastic products	−29.1	102.2	51.4
14 Tapioca products	−13.6	−2.8	16.7
15 Textiles	4.5	22.1	−4.4
Above 15 commodities value (million Baht)	611,536	765,734	740,683
Growth rate (%)	20.7	25.2	−3.27
Share in total exports (%)	53.8	54.4	52.9

Source: Bangkok Post, *Year-end Economic Review*, December 1996.

GDP. Given this, and the high level of vulnerability to a crisis which had developed by 1996, as outlined above, the export slowdown of 1996 affected confidence sufficiently to trigger the expectation of a devaluation. This expectation produced a self-reinforcing capital outflow.

Evidence of the erosion of business confidence that occurred during 1996 is provided by the behaviour of equity prices. The Stock Exchange of Thailand index of stock prices declined dramatically during the second half of 1996, as shown in Figure 1.6, beginning fully one year before the exchange rate crisis of July 1997. Between June 1996 and January 1997, the index declined from 1247 to 788. By June 1997 it had declined further to 527. As these data show, most of the decline had already occurred six months before the crisis.

The export slowdown of 1996 has attracted many attempted explanations from observers of the Thai economy. Arranged in what would seem to be increasing order of importance, the causes of the export slowdown included: the political events of the previous two years; monetary policy; Thailand's trade liberalization; the congestion of the industrial infrastructure; falsification of export data to receive value added tax rebates; increasing competition in international markets from China since the latter's devaluation in 1994; a slowdown in demand in importing countries; and effective appreciation of the baht through pegging to the dollar while the latter appreciated relative to the yen from late 1995 through 1997. Each of the above probably played some role in 1996, especially the last, but two other factors appear to have been more important. These were the long-term real appreciation within Thailand resulting from the

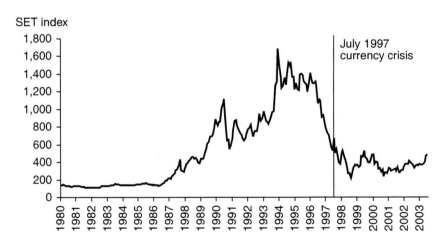

Figure 1.6 Thailand: stock exchange index, 1980 to 2003, monthly (source: Stock Exchange of Thailand).

demand effects of foreign capital inflow, discussed above, and a closely related phenomenon, a large increase in real wages.

Real wages

Data on real wages provide a powerful explanation for Thailand's export slowdown and its concentration in labour intensive industries. Research at the Thailand Development Research Institute has recently produced a reliable series of wage data for Thailand's manufacturing sectors. When these data on average nominal wages in manufacturing are deflated by the consumer price index they indicate that, over the 15 years from 1982 to 1996, real wages roughly doubled, but this increase was heavily concentrated in the years since 1990. Over the years 1982 to 1990, the increase was from an index of 100 to 117, an average compound rate of increase of 2 per cent. But over the following six years to 1996 the same real wage index increased to 202, an average annual rate of increase of real wages of 9 per cent.

Both supply and demand side forces played a role in the real wage increases.

First, the supply side. During the early stages of Thai economic growth, the rising industrial and services sector demand for labour could be satisfied from a very large pool of rural labour with relatively low productivity. The potential supply of unskilled rural labour was so large and so elastic that as workers moved from agriculture to more productive jobs in the manufacturing and services sectors, it was possible for these sectors to expand their levels of employment without significantly bidding up real wages. Thailand, at this time, was apparently a classic Lewis 'surplus labour' economy. But as this process continued, that pool of 'cheap' rural labour was largely used up, so that by the early 1990s labour shortages were becoming evident. Labour supply was no longer as elastic as it had been. Agricultural industries were themselves experiencing serious problems of seasonal labour shortages. Further increases in the demand for labour outside agriculture then led to rising wages.

Changes in the demand for labour also played a role, as a consequence of the real appreciation described above. Non-tradables are, on average, more labour-intensive in their production than tradables. As non-tradables prices rose, relative to tradables, wages were bid up relative to both tradables and non-tradables prices (the Stolper–Samuelson effect) and wages therefore rose relative to the consumer price index.

With the end of the era of 'cheap labour', the competitiveness of Thailand's labour intensive export industries declined. The importance of this point is confirmed by the fact that the export slowdown shown in Table 1.7 was concentrated in labour-intensive industries such as garments, footwear and textiles.[12] Thailand's export industries are especially vulnerable to increases in real wages for two basic reasons. First, many of Thailand's most successful export industries are highly labour intensive, implying that a given increase in real wages has large effects on their costs. Second, these export industries face highly competitive international markets for their products, where they must act as price-takers. This means that cost increases cannot be passed on in the form of increases in product prices, whereas producers for the domestic market may have greater scope for doing so.

Onset of the crisis

Through late 1996 and the first half of 1997, the Bank of Thailand struggled to maintain the stability of the baht/US dollar exchange rate against speculative attacks. The speculation was fuelled by expectations of a devaluation. Despite the insistence of the government and the Bank of Thailand that the exchange rate could be defended, market participants did not believe them. They were right. The level of official foreign exchange reserves declined from US$40 billion in January 1997 to well under US$30 billion six months later. On 2 July, the Bank of Thailand announced a float of the currency. The rate moved immediately from 25 baht per US$ to 30. By January 1998 it was 55, subsequently moderating by February to 45. These exchange rate movements are summarized in Figure 1.7. Late in 1997, IMF assistance was requested, and a stringent package of financial measures was required by the Fund.

The crisis had political casualties. In November 1997, a year after it came into government, the administration of Prime Minister Chavalit

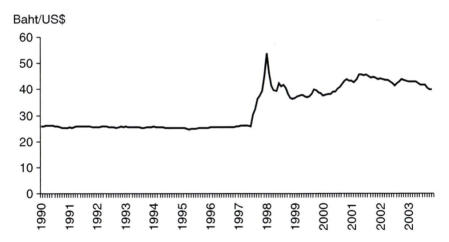

Figure 1.7 Thailand: exchange rate, baht/US$, 1990 to 2003, monthly (source: Bank of Thailand).

Yongchaiyudh was forced to surrender office as its coalition of political parties unravelled. It was replaced by a new coalition government led by Democrat Party leader and former Prime Minister, Chuan Leekpai, who had led the parliamentary opposition to the Chavalit government. The Chavalit government had lost public confidence, appearing unable to cope with the developing crisis. Chapter 3 of this volume, by Chris Baker, analyses these political events in greater depth.

The change of government gave Thailand a major political advantage in responding to the crisis, which some of its neighbours lacked. The new government did not need to defend itself against blame for the crisis itself. Notwithstanding the parliamentary efforts of the new Opposition, now led by General Chavalit, there seemed little political necessity for debate as to whether foreigners, domestic businessmen or the domestic government were ultimately responsible for the nation's problems. Full attention could be given to instituting the reform package that might resolve the emergency.

There was considerable debate as to what the most appropriate reform package could be. The government felt constrained to implement the IMF package and to announce public commitment to it. The package was widely criticized within Thailand, however, and behind the scenes the government was lobbying to have the package modified. The economic crisis produced a contraction of domestic demand that was much larger than expected by most observers, including the IMF. Private consumption and investment spending declined significantly. Inflation remained low, in spite of the mid-year depreciation of the baht.

The IMF programme seemed a copy of packages the Fund had previously devised for Latin American countries burdened with external imbalances associated with massive public sector debt, hyperinflation and low rates of private saving. The external imbalance in Thailand, like most of its neighbours, lacked any of these features. Inflation was relatively low, debt was primarily a private sector problem (US$72 billion out of US$99 billion total external debt) and saving rates remained high. The crisis produced a massive contraction in private spending. The IMF package added a public sector contraction by initially requiring a budget surplus equivalent to 1 per cent of GDP, but this was subsequently relaxed. Moreover, at a time when confidence in the financial sector was essential, the IMF required that problem institutions be closed. Given the circumstances of the time, this requirement seemed to many observers to be ill advised.

While the IMF rescue package was handled poorly, it was not the main failure. That occurred *before* the crisis, not after it. The main failure was that the developing crisis had apparently not been foreseen in time and was thus not averted. Some IMF officials have subsequently stated that the Thai government was indeed properly warned during 1996 about the impending danger. If so, the warnings were made only in secret and cannot be verified. They were also inconsistent with published IMF commentary on Thailand during the immediate pre-crisis period, including Kochhar *et al.* (1996) and the Fund's Annual Reports.

The economic boom since the late 1980s had encouraged the Bank of Thailand to remove almost all of its earlier restrictions on movement of financial capital into and out of Thailand. What surprised all observers was the rate at which funds could flow out of the country in response to what seemed small changes in market sentiments, putting irresistible pressure on the Bank of Thailand's foreign exchange reserves. The crucial point was the very large volume of short-term capital that had entered Thailand during the boom. To attract this capital, Thailand had removed most of the capital controls that had made maintenance of its fixed exchange rate policy consistent with a degree of monetary independence. But the liberalization meant that speculative attacks on the baht were now much easier than previously. To attract large volumes of financial capital into Thailand it had been necessary to demonstrate not only that entry was open, but that the exit was unobstructed as well. When market expectations moved in favour of a devaluation, the rate of financial outflow was so great that the expected depreciation became inevitable. In January 1998 the influential *Bangkok Post Year-end Economic Review* commented (p. 18) that:

> Liberalized capital flows but a fixed exchange rate proved to be the undoing of the Thai economy.

The impossible trinity

Thailand was not alone in this. During the boom decade preceding 1997, all of the countries that subsequently succumbed to the crisis were growing rapidly and were enjoying large inflows of foreign direct investment (FDI). However, some basic lessons of economics were ignored. Most important was the 'impossible trinity' demonstrated by Robert Mundell more than three decades earlier. During the pre-crisis decade, all of the crisis-affected economies were:

a   pegging their exchange rates to the US dollar;
b   opening their capital markets, where they were not already fully open; and
c   attempting to use domestic monetary policy to 'sterilize' the domestic monetary effects of inflows of FDI.

Mundell's Nobel Prize-winning contribution to economics was in showing that these three policies cannot be implemented simultaneously.

The fact that it was possible to raise domestic interest rates above foreign rates at all reveals that capital mobility was incomplete and, more importantly, that domestic debt was an imperfect substitute for foreign debt. However, the effect of the attempted sterilization in the presence of a high degree of capital market openness was to encourage the inflow of short-term capital from abroad. This took the form of bank loans, as a substitute for more expensive domestic borrowing, portfolio investment from abroad in search of high returns and foreign holding of domestic bank accounts, in response to the high domestic interest rates.

As the discussion above has demonstrated, the principal source of increased vulnerability to a currency crisis was precisely the accumulation of this stock of mobile foreign-owned capital. Eventually, its size dominated the level of the country's international reserves, leaving it vulnerable to a currency crisis. The two other sources of vulnerability identified above are also attributable to the excessive inflow of short-term capital: over-exposure of the domestic banking system and a 'Dutch disease' appreciation of the real exchange rate, which undermined the profitability of traded goods industries.

Ignoring the 'impossible trinity' laid the foundations for the crisis. In 1962, Mundell showed that, under a pegged exchange rate with an open capital market, the effects of domestic monetary contractions or expansions will be undone by the international movement of short-term capital. This is indeed what happened. In these circumstances, monetary policy is ineffective in cooling a boom. In recognition of the impossible trinity, the overheating that characterized the boom decade preceding the crisis could only have been controlled by implementing some combination of:

- fiscal contraction,
- capital controls, and
- floating exchange rates.

Fiscal contraction alone may not have been enough by itself, because the booms in East Asia were so large. Therefore, the central contradiction was between the opening of the capital account and the maintenance of pegged exchange rates.

The economic contraction

Figure 1.8 tracks the path of the crisis using data on quarterly real GDP and its growth rate. Table 1.8 shows the contributions to annual GDP growth of the various components of GDP on both the expenditure and production side, covering the years 1994 to 2003. The major macroeconomic change that is apparent for 1997 and 1998 is the collapse of private investment demand and, to a lesser extent, private consumption. The net outcome was a contraction in aggregate demand, especially in durables-producing industries such as construction, which contracted very severely. The critical importance of the private investment component of aggregate

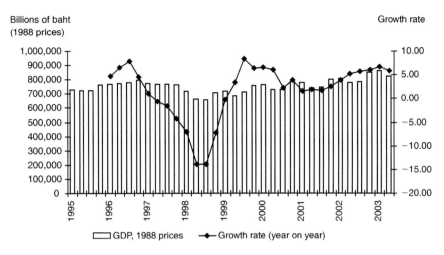

Figure 1.8 Quarterly real GDP growth, 1995 (Q1) to 2003 (Q2), monthly (source: National Economic and Social Development Board).

demand is shown more clearly by Table 1.9, which shows the composition of the level of aggregate demand (rather than its growth, as in Table 1.8, above) as a share of GDP. Between 1996 and 1998, private investment declined from 33 per cent of GDP to 10 per cent. We shall refer to this table again in the discussion of the recovery period.

The crisis undermined investment for two key reasons. First, the balance sheets of banks and other financial institutions were severely affected by the exchange rate depreciation that followed the floating of the baht. To the extent that these institutions had borrowed abroad, in foreign currency, to lend domestically, in baht, their ability to service these loans was diminished. Further, to the extent that their customers had themselves borrowed abroad, their ability to service their existing loans with the banking system was damaged because the cost of servicing their foreign currency denominated loans had increased markedly. The share of loans that were non-performing increased dramatically. The banks' response to this situation was to be extremely cautious about any new lending. The second effect was that, as demand contracted, the utilization of existing capacity similarly contracted. Firms were unwilling to invest in new capacity when existing capacity was under-utilized. This compounded the loss of business confidence. In short, both the supply of loanable funds and the demand for them contracted. Since interest rates fell, the latter effect was probably the more important. These financial market issues are analysed further by Ammar Siamwalla in Chapter 2 and by Pakorn Vichyanond in Chapter 7 of this volume.

Table 1.8 Thailand: contributions to growth, 1994 to 2003 (per cent per year) of real GDP

	1994	1995	1996	1997	1998	1999	2000	2001	2002	2003
Expenditure side										
Private consumption	4.3	4.3	3.2	−0.7	−6.3	2.3	2.7	2.1	2.7	3.5
Government consumption	0.7	0.4	1.0	−0.2	0.3	0.3	0.2	0.3	0.2	0.1
Gross fixed investment	4.6	4.6	3.0	−8.7	−15.2	−0.7	1.1	0.2	1.3	2.3
Private	2.9	3.6	0.0	−9.8	−11.8	−0.4	1.9	0.6	1.7	2.5
Public	1.7	1.1	0.0	1.1	−3.3	−0.3	−0.8	−0.4	−0.4	−0.1
Exports of goods and services	6.1	6.9	−2.6	3.0	3.8	5.0	10.1	−2.6	7.3	4.2
Imports of goods and services	−6.6	−9.5	0.3	5.6	9.6	−4.1	−11.2	2.7	−6.3	−3.7
Change in inventories	−0.2	1.3	−0.7	−0.7	−2.2	2.3	1.1	0.3	0.1	0.2
Statistical discrepancy	0.2	1.2	1.8	0.5	−0.5	−0.7	0.8	−0.9	0.0	0.1
GDP	**9.0**	**9.2**	**5.9**	**−1.4**	**−10.5**	**4.4**	**4.8**	**2.1**	**5.4**	**6.7**
Production side										
Agriculture	0.4	0.4	0.4	−0.1	−0.1	0.2	0.7	0.4	0.3	0.7
Manufacturing	3.0	3.8	2.1	0.5	−3.7	4.0	2.2	0.5	2.5	3.8
Construction	0.9	0.4	0.4	−1.6	−1.8	−0.2	−0.3	0.0	0.1	0.1
Wholesale and retail trade	1.7	1.7	0.3	−0.5	−2.2	0.6	0.6	−0.2	0.3	0.5
Transportation	0.9	1.0	1.0	0.4	−0.8	0.6	0.7	0.6	0.7	0.5
Hotels and restaurants	0.1	0.2	0.1	−0.1	−0.2	0.2	0.2	0.2	0.2	−0.1
Financial intermediation	1.1	0.5	0.3	−0.8	−1.9	−1.7	−0.3	0.1	0.3	0.4
Other	1.0	1.3	1.2	0.8	0.2	0.8	0.8	0.6	1.1	1.0
GDP	**9.0**	**9.2**	**5.9**	**−1.4**	**−10.5**	**4.4**	**4.8**	**2.1**	**5.4**	**6.7**

Source: Author's calculations from NESDB tables, *Quarterly Gross Domestic Product* at: http://www.nesdb.go.th/Main_menu/Macro/GDP/menu.html; expenditure side: Tables 2 and 12, production side: Table 4.

Table 1.9 Thailand: composition of aggregate demand, 1994 to 2003 (per cent of GDP)[a]

	1994	1995	1996	1997	1998	1999	2000	2001	2002	2003
Private consumption	55.2	54.4	54.4	54.4	53.8	53.7	53.8	54.8	54.5	54.3
Public consumption	8.2	7.9	8.4	8.2	9.6	9.4	9.3	9.3	8.9	8.5
Private investment	32.9	34.5	32.1	22.7	12.1	11.2	12.5	12.8	13.8	15.2
Public investment	8.7	8.9	10.4	11.6	9.2	8.5	7.4	6.8	6.1	5.6
Exports	44.6	47.1	42.0	45.7	55.3	57.7	64.8	61.0	64.3	64.5
Imports	−47.8	−52.5	−49.2	−44.3	−38.8	−41.0	−49.9	−46.3	−48.9	−50.0

Source: Author's calculations from NESDB tables, Quarterly Gross Domestic Product 2003, online at: http://www.nesdb.go.th/Main_menu/Macro/ GDP/menu.html, Tables 2 and 12.

Note:
a Shares may not add exactly to 100 due to statistical discrepancies.

The contraction in spending led to an improvement in the current account balance, but this was due almost entirely to a reduction in imports, a consequence of reduced demand for consumer goods and capital goods rather than a response of exports. The contraction of output was largest in manufacturing and services. Agricultural production did not show the rapid response to the depreciation that was expected, but this should not have been a surprise. Studies of agricultural supply response in Thailand indicate very low elasticities of supply response for the principal crops.[13] Nevertheless, agricultural output did not decline at a rate comparable with the rest of the economy, illustrating a stabilizing role of the agricultural sector of developing economies which development economics has not fully recognized. Tourist numbers were affected only marginally, if at all, by the crisis but were later badly affected by the SARS crisis of 2002.

Beyond...

By late 2003, the Thai economy had gone a considerable way towards recovery from the effects of the crisis. For the first time, real GDP per person had recovered to its level of 1996 (Figure 1.1, above). In that limited sense, Thailand was indeed 'Beyond the Crisis'. But major problems remained. The crisis produced an economic contraction because it undermined aggregate demand: the sum of private consumption demand, private investment demand, government demand and export demand. The central problem of Thailand's economic recovery from the crisis has been the continued insufficiency of aggregate demand. The slowness of Thailand's recovery has not been due to a deficiency of productive capacity (aggregate supply) because excess capacity has been evident throughout the economy. Table 1.10 presents data on this matter for the manufacturing sector. Relative to the pre-crisis period, the crisis and post-crisis years (1997 onwards) have been characterized by widespread excess capacity. The problem of restoring aggregate demand provides the organizing framework for our discussion of the post-crisis economic environment.

Investment

The decline in investment demand was not unique to Thailand. Figure 1.9 shows investment to GDP ratios for several East Asian countries from the first quarter of 1997 (ratios indexed to 1 for this period) to the first quarter of 2003. Severe and protracted declines have occurred in Indonesia and Malaysia, but Thailand's investment crisis is the most severe of all, extending into 2003. Although, in 2002 and 2003, it was popular to say in Thailand that 'the crisis is now behind us', in the words of the Governor of the Bank of Thailand, these data do not support that view, at least in so far as private

Table 1.10 Thailand: industrial capacity utilization, 1995 to 2003 (per cent)

	1995	1996	1997	1998	1999	2000	2001	2002	2003
Total	77.5	72.5	64.8	52.8	61.2	55.8	53.5	59.3	66.3
Food	42.4	38.1	37.7	33.5	42.6	44.1	42.1	45.1	54.0
Beverage	82.3	83.0	79.1	77.2	101.9	32.6	36.4	50.5	56.6
Tobacco	75.2	84.2	75.8	60.4	54.4	53.7	52.1	53.8	55.8
Construction materials	97.3	78.7	72.9	44.6	49.8	50.1	52.3	56.9	57.6
Iron & steel products	64.2	65.2	51.9	35.9	39.6	47.0	50.0	60.6	64.4
Vehicles and equipments	81.4	67.6	48.5	23.4	35.6	40.1	44.5	54.6	69.4
Petroleum products	93.2	85.7	90.1	84.0	85.7	83.9	74.8	76.2	79.5
Electronic and electrical products	63.9	67.8	62.2	47.5	53.4	65.4	47.5	55.4	62.1
Others	80.0	77.7	66.1	68.9	72.9	75.4	77.0	71.4	73.9

Source: Bank of Thailand. (BOT): Capacity Utilization Table http://www.bot.or.th/BOTHomepage/databank/EconData/Econ&Finance/download/tab71.xls.

Note:
The above categories account for 44.5 per cent of 1995 manufacturing sector value added.

investment is concerned. In 1996, private investment was 32 per cent of GDP and, in 1998, it was 12 per cent, but by 2002 and 2003 it had risen to only 13.8 and 15.2 per cent, respectively (Table 1.9). The trend is in the required direction, but this aspect of the recovery remains far from complete.

Thailand's collapse of investment demand had a curious feature. It was concentrated in demand for domestically produced capital goods, rather than imported capital goods. This is indicated by Figure 1.10, which shows data for gross fixed investment and capital goods imports. Until the crisis

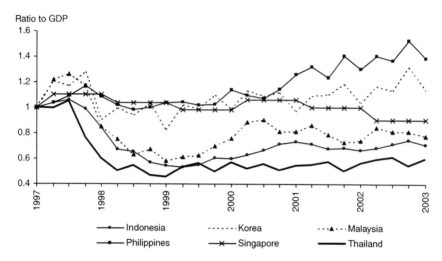

Figure 1.9 East Asia: investment to GDP ratios, 1997 to 2003 (source: Data from Roong *et al.* (2003), available at: http://www.bot.or.th/bothomepage/index/index_e. asp).

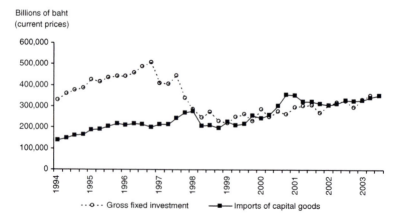

Figure 1.10 Thailand: gross fixed investment and imports of capital goods, 1994 to 2003 (source: Bank of Thailand).

Table 1.11 Thailand: financing of aggregate investment, 1995 to 2003

Average share of each component (per cent)

	Household savings	Government savings	Foreign savings				Total savings = total investment
			Total	Long-term capital inflow	Short-term capital inflow	Decline in reserves	
1995	90.2	−14.9	24.8	2.9	31.9	−10.1	100
1996	90.1	−16.8	26.8	3.2	22.4	1.1	100
1997	105.8	−10.5	4.6	6.2	−70.4	68.7	100
1998	216.0	−36.0	−80.0	28.4	−70.4	−38.0	100
1999	227.6	−61.4	−66.2	20.9	−65.8	−21.3	100
2000	118.7	12.8	−32.8	8.4	−41.7	0.4	100
2001	108.7	11.8	−20.5	12.5	−3.0	−30.0	100
2002	114.3	11.1	−25.4	3.3	−5.4	−23.3	100
2003	112.3	13.0	−25.3	5.0	−7.2	−23.1	100

Source: Author's calculations, data from Bank of Thailand and National Economic and Social Development Board. For further details, see Table 1.6.

Note:
Calculations are based on the identities that (i) total investment = household savings + government savings + foreign savings; and (ii) foreign savings = long-term capital inflow (FDI) + short-term capital inflow − change in international reserves of the central bank.

of 1997, the magnitude of the former was about double the latter. But from 1998 onwards the two series move closely together. Imports of capital goods have continued on roughly their pre-crisis trend, but purchases of domestically produced capital goods have collapsed.

Table 1.11 applies the same method to analyse the financing of investment since the crisis as was applied in Table 1.6, above. Whereas short-term capital flows were a net source of financing of investment prior to 1997, this item has been negative in each year since. Until 2000 it was a large source of capital outflow. Holders of mobile capital, both foreign and domestic are choosing to relocate it outside Thailand. Before the crisis, foreign savings were a net addition to the funds available for investment in Thailand. Since the crisis, foreign savings have been a net drain on the resources available for investment. However, when allowance is made for additions to the Bank of Thailand's foreign exchange reserves, this effect disappears.

Net foreign direct investment did not decline immediately with the 1997–98 crisis, but by 2003 it had contracted to around one fifth of its 1998 level. This is indicated in Figure 1.11. Putting the decline of FDI together with the decline in domestic investment, it is clear that the confidence of investors in the Thai economy has not yet recovered. Restoring investor confidence is an ongoing task of the Thaksin government. The sustainability of economic growth depends upon it. Maintaining the momentum of economic reform and upgrading Thailand's governance is necessarily the path forward.

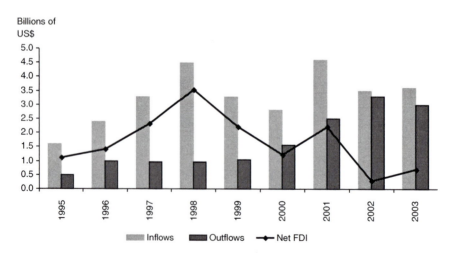

Figure 1.11 Thailand: FDI inflows and outflows, 1995 to 2003, US$ (source: Bank of Thailand).

Exports

Tables 1.8 and 1.9 above show that, in the immediate post-crisis years 1997 and 1998, consumer demand and, more particularly, investment demand declined. In 1999 and 2000, real GDP grew moderately, at 4.4 and 4.6 per cent, respectively, but this was not due to recovery of consumer or investment demand, which remained sluggish. In these years, expansion of aggregate demand was led by exports. This qualitative story also applied to the other crisis-affected East Asian countries, as is shown in Table 1.12. In Korea and Malaysia, where impressive recovery occurred over the 1999 to 2000 period, it was led by growth of exports. In Indonesia especially, export demand failed to provide this impetus and recovery was weak.

In 2001, Thailand's recovery stalled, with real GDP growth of 1.9 per cent. Both investment demand and export demand declined, but as Table 1.8 above shows, the decline of export demand was more important. The decline in investment reflected a lack of investor confidence in Thailand – partly, but not entirely, reflecting internal events, but the decline in export demand was externally driven.

In 2001, continued recession in Japan, a slowdown in Europe, followed by a recession in the United States, produced a serious deterioration in Thailand's external environment. The contraction of export demand was particularly severe in the IT and semiconductor sectors. According to the Bank of Thailand's classification, high technology items (including automobiles) account for 60 per cent of Thailand's exports and these exports slowed markedly. With total exports exceeding 60 per cent of GDP, the Thai economy is particularly vulnerable to contractions in external demand. Not surprisingly, several of Thailand's Southeast Asian neighbours were also suffering from the global slowdown. Thailand's real growth rate was 1.7 per cent in 2001, compared with 3.2 per cent in Indonesia, 0.8 per cent in Malaysia and 2.7 per cent in the Philippines. In

Table 1.12 East Asian countries: contributions to aggregate demand, 1999 to 2000

	Indonesia 1999–2000	Korea 1999–2000	Malaysia 1999–2000	Philippines 1999–2000	Thailand 1999–2000
Real GDP Growth rate	2.8	9.9	7.2	3.6	4.2
Consumption	3.2	4.7	4.4	2.7	2.6
Investment	−1.9	4.3	2.7	−0.1	2.0
Export	−3.7	8.7	15.8	4.2	7.2
Import	−5.3	7.3	15.8	−0.2	6.2

Source: World Bank (2001): http://www.worldbank.or.th/monitor.

Note:
Consumption and investment include both public and private expenditures.

Singapore, more export-dependent than any of the above, real GDP contracted by 3 per cent. Korea, also badly affected by the Asian currency crisis, grew at 2 per cent.[14]

The deterioration in the global economic environment reduced the demand for Thailand's exports, causing both export volumes and export prices to decline. In discussions of the current state of the Thai economy, the magnitude of this price effect has not been sufficiently appreciated. From the pre-crisis year of 1996 until 2001, Thailand's terms of trade (the ratio of the average international prices of Thailand's exports to those of its imports) declined from an index of 100 to 79 (see Figure 1.12). That is, over this period, the volume of imports that could be purchased from a given volume of exports declined by about one fifth. Taking account of the share of exports in GDP, this deterioration in export prices, relative to constant external terms of trade, is equivalent to 12.3 per cent of GDP. The decline in the terms of trade was particularly severe in the year 2000 to 2001, when the index fell from 87.4 to 79 (where 1996 = 100), a decline of almost 10 per cent in a single year, which was equivalent to 6.5 per cent of GDP. In this year, exports measured in US$ declined by over 3 per cent.

The significance of these calculations is that, holding domestic output constant, the level of real national income – defined here as the level of real expenditure (private consumption plus private investment plus government spending) that is consistent with the current account balance – declines as the terms of trade deteriorates. But measured 'real' GDP

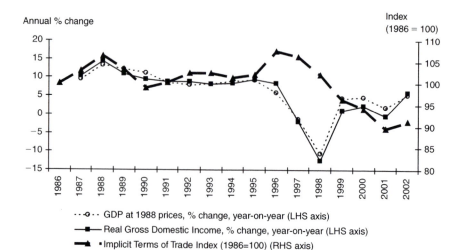

Figure 1.12 Thailand: terms of trade, GDP growth and real gross domestic income growth, 1986 to 2002 (source: Author's calculations as described in Table 1.13).

makes no allowance for this fact. It captures only changes in domestic output, evaluated at constant prices. The meaning of 'real GDP' is that base period prices (1988 prices in the Thai data) are used to evaluate all components of domestic output, including exports. When the international prices of Thailand's exports decline, as in this example, 'real' GDP does not change, even though the true purchasing power of Thai consumers, firms and government may have fallen considerably. Since 'real' GDP takes no account of this effect, the slow growth of real GDP *understates* considerably the degree to which the global slowdown of 2001 reduced economic welfare within Thailand.

The national income accounting concept that allows for this effect is called *Real Gross Domestic Income* (RGDI). Thailand's national income statistics do not include calculations of RGDI, but the relevant calculation is presented here to show its significance for an open economy like Thailand. These calculations are shown in Table 1.13, with real GDP and RGDI indexed to be the same in 1988. When exports constitute a large share of national income, changes in the terms of trade can cause large differences to arise between real GDP and RGDI. Terms of trade changes were not

Table 1.13 Thailand: GDP at 1988 prices and real gross domestic income, 1986 to 2002 (millions of baht)

	GDP at 1988 prices	Real gross domestic income	GDP at 1988 prices, % change, year-on-year	Real gross domestic income, % change, year-on-year	Implicit terms of trade index (1986 = 100)
1986	1,257,177	1,237,459	–	–	100.0
1987	1,376,847	1,364,020	9.5	10.2	102.9
1988	1,559,804	1,559,804	13.3	14.4	106.3
1989	1,749,952	1,731,941	12.2	11.0	103.2
1990	1,945,372	1,897,031	11.2	9.5	99.1
1991	2,111,862	2,065,884	8.6	8.9	100.3
1992	2,282,572	2,248,622	8.1	8.8	102.4
1993	2,470,908	2,431,766	8.3	8.1	102.3
1994	2,692,973	2,636,438	9.0	8.4	101.3
1995	2,941,736	2,885,045	9.2	9.4	102.0
1996	3,115,338	3,128,614	5.9	8.4	107.4
1997	3,072,615	3,070,629	−1.4	−1.9	106.2
1998	2,749,684	2,690,096	−10.5	−12.4	102.1
1999	2,871,980	2,716,813	4.4	1.0	96.4
2000	3,005,394	2,780,947	4.6	2.4	94.1
2001	3,063,705	2,768,276	1.9	−0.5	89.5
2002	3,224,633	2,929,091	5.3	5.8	91.1

Source: Author's calculations with data from: 1993–2002: NESDB: Quarterly Gross Domestic Product 4/2002, Tables 1 and 2; http://www.nesdb.go.th/Main_menu/Macro/GDP/menu.html; 1986–92; ADB, Key Indicators 2002; http://www.adb.org/Documents/Books/Key_Indicators/2002/default.asp.

particularly significant between 1988 and 1996 and the two series move closely together. However, the terms of changes that followed 1998 caused RGDI to fall below real GDP. Relative to 1996, the data on real GDP over-state the *level* of real national income (defined as RGDI, as above) in 2001 and 2002 by about 10 per cent. Whereas real GDP per person declined between 1996 to 2001 by 7 per cent, our calculations indicate that RGDI declined by almost 20 per cent.

Obviously, the growth rates of real GDP and RGDI similarly diverge when the terms of trade are changing. These growth rates are shown in Figure 1.12, above. When the terms of trade declines, as it did from 1996 to 2001 the growth rate of the former exceeds that of the latter. When the terms of trade improve, as occurred in 2002, the opposite occurs. From 1999 to 2002 the average annual growth rates of real GDP and RGDI were 3.9 and 2.5 per cent, respectively. Of course, for a small trading economy like Thailand, the terms of trade are almost entirely outside its control. There is virtually nothing that the government could have done about this (hidden) component of Thailand's economic experience. But this does not mean that the government is following the best course.

The Thaksin government

The '*Thai Rak Thai*' (Thais love Thais) political party led by Thaksin Shi-nawatra won a record number of seats in the March 2001 general elec-tions. Mergers with lesser parties have subsequently increased its parliamentary majority even further, giving the present regime powers unprecedented for a non-military government. These and further planned mergers with opposition parties will give the ruling coalition suffi-cient numbers in the lower house and senate to amend the Constitution at will and to block any censure motions against the government.

Who and what does *Thai Rak Thai* (subsequently TRT) represent? Ideo-logically, TRT is a populist party which has drawn on the widespread per-ception that the lesson of the 1997 crisis is that Thailand's liberalization during the 1987 to 1996 boom went too far, creating the circumstances that led to the crisis.[15] The TRT ideology is inward-looking in that it insists that solutions to Thailand's problems must be sought from within the country. The question is how this translates into economic policy. Thaksin's first major speech as Prime Minister, addressed to an inter-national audience, was delivered at the United Nations Economic and Social Commission for Asia and the Pacific (ESCAP) meetings in April of 2001. Mr Thaksin said that Thailand had to look for 'original strengths, unique local know-how and mix them with new marketing and communi-cations technology'. He also noted that the newer technologies were developed in advanced countries, 'based on physical and intellectual property accumulation possessed by the West' and which the developing countries such as Thailand could not match. The Prime Minister also said that 'the country could no longer rely on adopting or importing discarded industries or products of low value, or on promotion of export industries requiring high import contents and low cost labour with low domestic value added'.[16]

It was unclear what policy conclusions Prime Minister Thaksin wished to draw from these remarks, but they were interpreted in the local and foreign press as foreshadowing a hostile environment for foreign investors and an end to support for the liberalization of international trade. 'Inward-looking' was the descriptive phrase most often appearing in these accounts and it was taken as a euphemism for protection of domestic business elites against foreign competition. The Prime Minister spent much of the next several months disowning such interpretations of his speech, but the damage had been done. Foreign direct investment and domestic investment both declined sharply during 2001.

Whereas its predecessor government, led by the Democrat party, had strong middle class support, especially in Bangkok, TRT represents two very different groups: first, a broad coalition of low-income rural people, mobilized by rural power brokers, and second, big business. The Prime Minister himself, reputedly the richest individual in the nation, has extensive business interests, especially in telecommunications, where he and his immediate family own the largest single company, Shin Corp. Monopolies granted by previous governments have enabled Shin Corp, and Thaksin himself, to accumulate massive wealth. This dual nature of TRT's political base – the rural poor and the corporate elite – helps explain much of the *Thai Rak Thai* economic policy agenda. Major parts of the package redistribute incomes in favour of these two groups.

The super-rich are few in number and successful electoral campaigns are not built on promises to assist them. TRT won office by offering the rural poor three seemingly significant benefits:

- *Low cost health care*
  Low-income people were to be provided with health care at public hospitals at a fixed charge of 30 baht (US$0.75) per visit.
- *Village revolving fund*
  Each of Thailand's villages was to be provided with 1 million baht for community development purposes.
- *Farmer debt relief*
  Farmers unable to repay loans owing to the government-owned Bank for Agriculture and Agricultural Cooperatives (BAAC) were to be provided with a three-year repayment moratorium.

The TRT website has included estimates of the cost of these programmes, even at the time of the election campaign, along with qualifications as to the coverage of the programmes and restrictions on eligibility. During the campaign, most of these details were overlooked by TRT's marketing managers but, in the post-election environment, the details came to light, substantially reducing the benefits poorer Thais can expect to receive.

The low-income health card turns out to be available only to people who have been previously paying 100 baht or more per month. Moreover, public hospitals – lacking sufficient funding for the costs the 30 baht scheme would otherwise impose on them – have found it necessary to reduce the services provided under the scheme. The net value of the 30 baht minimum charge is therefore substantially reduced. The government has announced that putting an effective health insurance system in place will require three years. Although this reduces the benefits that might have been expected from the scheme, it does make sense. A poorly designed health insurance system could easily be worse than none at all. In the meantime, the benefits from the 30 baht health card are small, but not negligible. Researchers at Naresuan University have estimated the cost of universal health insurance at 90 to 100 billion baht. The present scheme falls far short of that. A generous estimate of its value might be around 20 billion baht.

The 1 million baht village fund is not recurrent funding but a one-off benefit. Even so, if it were really a grant of 1 million baht, the total value would be considerable. Spread across Thailand's 63,000 rural villages, the total of 63 billion baht would be equivalent to around US$1.4 billion, quite a sum. However, this amount is not to be a net increase in funding for rural development, but is to be diverted from other rural programmes of a similar nature, spread over three years and with various restrictions on eligibility. The net gain to rural people, if any, depends on whether the value of the money allocated in this way exceeds the benefits that would have been derived from the forms of expenditure that will be eliminated to finance it. For the poor to gain, reduced corruption in the expenditure of the funds would seem essential and this is an aspect of the scheme that has been underemphasized. Even making optimistic assumptions about improved accountability and monitoring of these expenditures, it seems unlikely that the net value to poor people could exceed 10 billion baht.

The farmer debt relief is potentially more significant. The BAAC is by far the largest lender to farmers. Private banks have been reluctant to extend loans to farmers, partly because of the high cost of doing business with very large numbers of small loans and partly because Thailand's inadequate system of land titling makes farm land an insecure form of collateral. BAAC also has commercial problems of this kind and its loans are not concentrated among the poorer farmers. Of the 230 billion baht farmers owe to the BAAC, TRT says that only 50 billion is trouble-free. It is therefore proposed that the remaining 180 billion be subject to a three-year repayment moratorium. Farmers pay about 7 per cent for BAAC loans, so suspension of interest repayments on 180 billion baht worth of loans would be worth around 13 billion baht per year for three years, a total of say 40 billion baht.

This proposal raises severe practical problems. First, are farmers who have sacrificed consumption in order to maintain payments to BAAC to be rewarded by being excluded from the moratorium? Apparently so. Second, what is to happen after the three years? The TRT proposal implicitly assumes all problem loans will thereafter be paid at the scheduled rates. But the moratorium would hardly encourage such behaviour. Even if farmers were able to pay, the manner in which the moratorium is to be implemented would encourage non-payment in the hope of a further moratorium, and so forth. That is, the moratorium system contains features that may undermine the possibility of a workable system of agricultural credit in the future.

Are these amounts large? The combined annual value of the above three schemes, from the point of view of rural Thais, each estimated generously, is something less than 70 billion baht (US$1.6 billion), spread over three years, or around 23 billion baht (US$525 million) per year. This annual amount is about 2.5 per cent of the Thai government's budget for Fiscal Year 2002 or about 0.5 per cent of GDP. The amount may not seem large but the package does involve an element of income redistribution from taxpayers to poor people.[17] In contrast, other aspects of the TRT economic package involve redistributions from taxpayers to the richest Thai people, which may far exceed this amount. Two examples follow.

TELECOMMUNICATIONS

WTO rules require that monopolistic arrangements within the telecommunications industry be opened up to international competition. The profits generated by the past arrangements have been enormous and, not incidentally, have been the principal source of Thaksin's wealth. An intense battle has occurred over the new arrangements and a great deal of money has been at stake. Previously agreed transition arrangements involved revenue sharing between the privately owned companies (including Thaksin's company, the largest) and the state-owned telecommunications enterprises.

The government commissioned a review of these arrangements from the Intellectual Property Institute at Chulalongkorn University, which recommended that the revenue sharing simply be dropped. The government has provisionally approved the proposed changes, but a public outcry has ensued. Independent analysts, including researchers from the respected Thailand Development Research Institute (TDRI), have suggested alternative arrangements and have estimated that the revised arrangements, which are proposed by the government, would involve a windfall gain to the private telecommunications companies, at the expense of public revenue, of around 300 billion baht (approximately US$6.7 billion), of which about one third would accrue to Thaksin's Shin Corp. Government spokesmen have heatedly disputed the details of these calculations, and have attempted to justify the proposed arrangements. But even if the TDRI calculations were overestimated by several-fold, the amount of transfer from taxpayers to rich Thai people which these arrangements involve would still far exceed the magnitude of the pro-poor redistributions that the government is implementing.

THAI ASSET MANAGEMENT CORPORATION

The 1997/98 crisis left Thai banks with large levels of non-performing loans (NPLs). The volume of these loans is of the order of 800 billion baht (US$18 billion). As discussed above, the high level of NPLs has left the banks undercapitalized and reluctant to lend. For the government, there are two possible solutions to this dilemma. First, be tough on the non-paying borrower through strengthened bankruptcy and foreclosure procedures. Second, be gentle with them by having a government agency buy them out, even if this entails a loss to taxpayers.

The justification for the second solution is that this measure will rid the banks of the NPLs and enable them to return to the business of financing new investment. The owners of indebted firms, including wealthy Thais whose equity was eroded and perhaps even eliminated by the crisis, are strongly attracted to this second solution. TRT has been strongly attracted to it as well and the Thai Asset Management Corporation (TAMC), established by the Thaksin government, is based on this line of reasoning.

So far, the TAMC has been successful only in acquiring the NPLs of state-owned banks. It has had very little success in purchasing non-performing loans from the private banks, even though they account for the largest stock of NPLs. The purchase of the NPLs of state-owned banks is essentially a transfer from one government agency to another and does little to change the lending behaviour of the banks concerned. There are two reasons for the lack of success, so far, with private banks. First, the private banks have typically been wrestling with the firms concerned for the past four years in an effort to recover their loans. These banks know a great deal more about the firms concerned than do the managers of the TAMC. The TAMC rightly takes this lack of information into account in the price it is willing to offer for the NPL concerned, a problem known as an informational asymmetry. Consequently, the offer price of the TAMC is generally below the price that is acceptable to the bank, and few such transactions occur. Those that do occur are likely to be ones in which the TAMC has overestimated the value of the loan, in which case losses are likely. The second reason is that private banks have been more successful in recovering bad loans than state agencies. Other things being equal, an NPL in the hands of a private bank is likely to be worth more than the same loan in the hands of the TAMC.

The TAMC can make major inroads into the NPLs of the private banks only if the policy decision is taken to raise the subsidy provided by the taxpayer to the TAMC. There is support within TRT for just that. It is unclear whether this will prevail but, if it does, a very large transfer from taxpayers to rich Thais will result.

The theory behind the argument for a greatly expanded role for the TAMC is that undercapitalization of banks is the reason for the low level of lending and, hence, the low level of investment. This argument ignores two central facts. First, the entire corporate sector of Thailand – and not just the banks – is undercapitalized, due to the erosion of equity resulting from the crisis. An undercapitalized corporate sector is reluctant to borrow, even at the very low interest rates prevailing in Thailand today. Recapitalizing the banks alone will not change this fact. Second, firms do not wish to invest when their level of capacity utilization is low, as it is today. With low levels of capacity utilization and poor prospects for increased sales within the immediate future, firms do not wish to incur additional debt.[18]

The economic analysis used to justify the TAMC is faulty. The TAMC is not a likely vehicle for stimulating investment in Thailand, but it is a potential vehicle for transferring very large amounts of public funds into the hands of the corporate sector. There is a danger that it will be used for that purpose.

Decentralization

Thailand's new Constitution, promulgated in 1997, and the Decentralization Act that followed it, specify an ambitious programme of decentralizing of government expenditures. The share of total government expenditures disbursed by local government authorities is scheduled to increase from around 8 per cent in 2000 to 35 per cent in 2006. The programme involves both transfers of revenue from the central government to the local level and also the transfer of some taxing powers to the local level. The programme was conceived before the 1997/98 crisis, during a period of rising prosperity and (regrettably, unfounded) economic optimism. The motivation for the programme was political and little attention was given to its economic consequences. The assumption was that if there were costs, Thailand could afford them. Unfortunately, that pre-crisis assumption has continued into current decision-making, even though the economic environment is very different. Thailand's decision-makers should now be taking the possible economic consequences of decentralization much more seriously.

Because some forms of expenditure *cannot* be decentralized – obvious examples include defence and foreign affairs – the degree of decentralization of those expenditures which could, in principle, be decentralized will necessarily exceed the overall level of 35 per cent. Crucial examples include education, health, agricultural extension and social safety nets. For centuries, Thailand's system of government has been highly centralized and reducing the concentration of public spending at the central government level has been on the policy agenda for some time – at least since Thailand's political crisis of 1992. The desire to reduce the power of the central government was a reaction to a long series of political dictatorships and military coups.

The declared purpose of the decentralization is to increase the extent to which local communities have control over the way public expenditures are disbursed and thus to increase the degree of local accountability for them. Beyond this, it is hoped that the bias in public expenditures towards urban areas and, in particular, towards the urban rich might be reduced by placing expenditures directly in the hands of local communities. For example, the crucial issue of raising secondary school participation rates in rural areas, where Thailand's poor are heavily concentrated, has not been addressed satisfactorily by Thailand's highly centralized educational bureaucracy. Decentralizing control over expenditures may be the only available way to get the money to the areas where it most needed.

Despite these laudable goals, preliminary indications suggest that the programme is overly ambitious in the degree of decentralization that is planned. There is a danger that the programme will fail because of this. The nature of Thailand's decentralization process is made clearer by comparison with Indonesia, which is also embarked on an ambitious decentralization programme. In Indonesia, a high proportion of government expenditure is to be reallocated to the district (*kabupaten*) level. This means decentralization to about 350 local level government authorities, with average population size over half a million. Considering that Thailand's population is one quarter of Indonesia's, a similar degree of decentralization would mean devolving a large proportion of expenditures to around 80 local administrative units, corresponding roughly to the number of provinces (*changwat*).

At present, Thailand's 76 provincial governments are not democratically elected (provincial governors are appointed from Bangkok) and the decentralization programme is not aimed at increasing expenditure significantly at this level. Rather, it is aimed at the *tambon* level, meaning the 7,000 or so Tambon Administrative Councils. In rural areas, the average population size of these entities is about 5,000. They are just too small. The average *tambon* cannot support a high school, an appropriately equipped hospital or the professional administrative staff needed to account properly for the way a large increase in funds is actually being spent.

Massive wastage of public expenditures could result if the Tambon Administrative Councils are unable to manage large increases in expenditures well. Local level corruption will also increase in many areas if effective programmes of monitoring cannot be implemented in time. Some cynics have labelled the entire programme 'Decentralizing corruption'. But cynicism is not required to see that the basic problem of low levels of participation in secondary education among Thailand's rural population could not be addressed by the decentralization programme unless local Tambon Administrative Councils are able to group themselves into larger units. This will probably happen if the programme proceeds but it will take time and, meanwhile, serious disruption could occur. As the central government transfers revenue to the local level it necessarily transfers functions as well. The education, health and other services now provided by the central government may not be forthcoming from the *tambon* level if the Tambon Administrative Councils are inadequately prepared.

According to the World Bank, international experience indicates that decentralization works best when decentralization of functions precedes reallocation of revenues.[19] In Thailand, the opposite has occurred. The result may be that local administrative units receive substantially increased revenue from the central government but are, for some time, unable to supply the services that are no longer provided by the central government.

There are many desirable features to Thailand's decentralization programme, but its failure could be socially disruptive on a large scale and would jeopardize the long-awaited recovery from the 1997 crisis. The main difficulties impeding recovery have been restoring the functioning of a financial system burdened by high levels of non-performing loans and restoring investor confidence. Both have been much more difficult than was appreciated. To avoid large-scale disruption, it may be necessary to rethink major components of the current decentralization strategy. This may require democratizing the provincial governments and then according them a larger role in the planned decentralization. These matters are highly controversial and none of it could be done quickly; but delay to the schedule of decentralization may be better than failure.

Recovery and the poor

The discussion of this chapter has concentrated on economic growth and the means to restoring it. But is economic growth really so important? Do the poor actually benefit from it, or only the rich? Within Thailand, as elsewhere, there is much debate about these matters. Before turning to the relationship between poverty incidence and economic growth in Thailand, some characteristics of poverty in Thailand will be reviewed.

Characteristics of poverty in Thailand

Despite much dispute about measurement and conceptual issues, all major studies of poverty incidence and inequality in Thailand agree on some basic points:

- Absolute poverty has declined dramatically over the last four decades, but inequality has increased.
- Poverty is concentrated in rural areas, especially in the Northeastern and Northern regions of the country.
- Large families are more likely to be poor than smaller families.
- Farming families operating small areas of land are more likely to be poor than those operating larger areas.
- Households headed by persons with low levels of education are more likely to be poor than others.

The following discussion draws upon the official poverty estimates produced by the Thai government's National Economic and Social Development Board (NESDB) which, like all other available poverty estimates, are based upon the household incomes data collected in the Socio-economic Survey (SES). Despite their imperfections, these are the only data available covering a long time period. These survey data have been collected since 1962. The early data were based on small samples, but their reliability has improved steadily, especially since 1975. Table 1.14 and Figure 1.13 summarize all of the available official data for the four decades from 1962 to 2002.

Table 1.14 focuses on the familiar headcount measure of poverty incidence: the percentage of a particular population whose household incomes per person fall below the poverty line. The table confirms that most of Thailand's poor people reside in rural areas. The SES data are classified according to residential location in the categories: municipal areas, sanitary districts and villages. These correspond to inner urban (historical urban boundaries), outer urban (newly established urban areas) and rural areas, respectively. Poverty incidence is highest in the rural areas, followed by outer urban, and lowest in the inner urban areas. When these data are recalculated in terms of the share of each of these residential areas in the total number of poor people and then the share of the total population, as in the last two rows of the table respectively, a striking point emerges. In 2000, rural areas accounted for 93 per cent of the total number of poor people but only 68 per cent of the total population.

The final column of Table 1.14 shows the Gini coefficient of inequality. This index takes values between 0 and 1, with higher values indicating greater inequality. The index has risen significantly over the 40 years

Table 1.14 Thailand: poverty incidence, 1962 to 2002

	Poverty incidence (headcount measure, per cent of population)			Inequality Gini coefficient
	Aggregate	Rural	Urban	Aggregate
1962	88.3	96.4	78.5	0.423
1969	63.1	69.6	53.7	0.430
1975	48.6	57.2	25.8	0.425
1981	35.5	43.1	15.5	0.432
1986	44.9	56.3	12.1	0.482
1988	32.6	40.3	12.6	0.482
1990	27.2	33.8	1.6	0.520
1992	23.2	29.7	6.6	0.541
1994	16.3	21.2	4.8	0.522
1996	11.4	14.9	3.0	0.518
1998	12.9	17.2	3.4	0.515
1999	15.9	21.5	3.1	0.520
2000	14.2	19.1	3.6	0.525
2001	13.0	16.6	5.1	0.518
2002	9.8	12.6	3.8	0.511
Poverty share 2000	100	92.6	7.4	–
Population share 2000	100	68.4	31.6	–

Source: Development Evaluation Division, National Economic and Social Development Board, Bangkok, and Medhi (1993).

Notes:
Poverty incidence means the number of poor within a reference population group expressed as a proportion of the total population of that group. The headcount measure of aggregate poverty incidence is the percentage of the total population whose incomes fall below a poverty line held constant over time in real terms; rural poverty is the percentage of the rural population whose incomes fall below a poverty line held constant over time in real terms, and so forth. Poverty share means the number of poor within a reference population group expressed as a proportion of the total number of poor within the whole population. Population share means the population of a reference group expressed as a proportion of the total population of that group.

The data shown are identical to the most recent data from the National Economic and Social Development Board (NESDB) for the years 1988 to 2002, except that the published data for Municipal Areas and Sanitary Districts have been aggregated to an 'urban' category using their respective population shares in the total for urban areas (the sum of the two) as weights. The data for the earlier years have been spliced together with this series from published sources so that the resulting series matches the NESDB series for the year 1988. The data from 1962 to 1988 are summarized in Medhi (1993).

shown. Combined with the reduction in absolute poverty, which also occurred, this means that the real incomes of the poor increased with economic growth, but the incomes of the rich increased even faster. Another way of representing this increase in inequality is shown in Figure 1.14. The figure shows the share of total national household income received by the poorest 20 per cent of the population (Quintile I), the second poorest 20 per cent (Quintile II), up to the richest 20 per cent (Quintile V), using

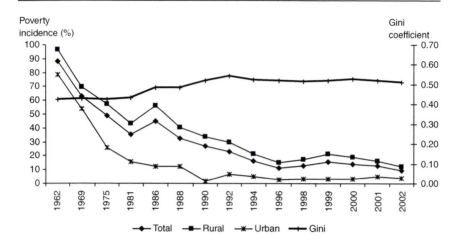

Figure 1.13 Thailand: poverty incidence and inequality, 1962 to 2002 (source: Author's calculations as described in Table 1.14).

Note:
Poverty incidence means the headcount measure and inequality means the Gini coefficient.

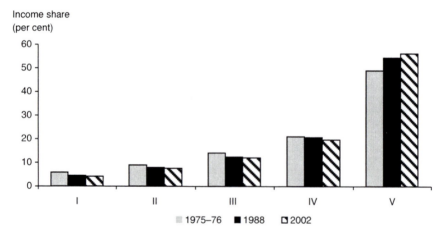

Figure 1.14 Thailand: income shares of quintile population groups, 1975–76 to 2002 (source: National Economic and Social Development Board).

Note:
Quintile I is the poorest: Quintile V is the richest.

data for 1975–76, 1988 and 2002. Over this quarter of a century, the poorest quintile's share of total household income declined from 6 per cent to 4.2 per cent. Only one quintile's share increased – the richest, whose share increased from 49 to 56.3 per cent.

The data reveal a very considerable decline in poverty incidence up to 1996, a moderate increase to 1998 and a further increase over the following two years. Over the eight years from 1988 to 1996, measured poverty incidence declined by an enormous 21.4 per cent of the population, an average rate of decline in poverty incidence of 2.7 percentage points per year. That is, each year, on average, 2.7 per cent of the population moved from incomes below the poverty line to incomes above it. Over the ensuing two years ending in 1998, poverty incidence increased by 1.5 per cent of the population. Alternatively, over the eight years ending in 1996, the absolute number of persons in poverty declined by 11.1 million (from 17.9 million to 6.8 million); over the following two years the number increased by 1 million (from 6.8 million to 7.9 million). Thus, according to the official data, measured in terms of absolute numbers of people in poverty, the crisis reversed 9 per cent of the poverty reduction that had occurred during the eight-year period of economic boom immediately preceding the crisis. Chapter 4 of this volume, by Isra Sarntisart, argues that the official data overstate the increase in poverty that actually occurred.

During periods when incomes are steadily increasing, lags in reporting changes in household incomes may not be important. But during periods when past trends are suddenly reversed, as with the crisis of 1997 and beyond, these reporting lags can be very significant. For this reason, for assessment of the impact that the economic crisis had on poverty incidence, the 1996 data should best be compared with the 2000 data, not 1998. This comparison roughly doubles the poverty impact of the crisis.

From Table 1.15, it is apparent that one region, the Northeast, accounted for 61 per cent of Thailand's poor people in 2000, but only 34 per cent of the total population. Every other region's share of the total

Table 1.15 Thailand: poverty incidence by region, 1988 to 2002

Period	North	Northeast	Central	South	Bangkok and vicinity
1988	32.0	48.4	26.6	32.5	6.1
1990	23.2	43.1	22.3	27.6	3.5
1992	22.6	39.9	13.3	19.7	1.9
1994	13.2	28.6	9.2	17.3	0.9
1996	11.2	19.4	6.3	11.5	0.6
1998	9.0	23.2	7.7	14.8	0.6
2000	12.2	28.1	5.4	11.0	0.7
2002	9.8	18.9	4.3	8.7	1.4
Poverty share 2000	17.8	60.6	8.3	11.9	0.6
Population share 2000	18.8	34.2	23.3	13.3	10.4

Source: See Table 1.14.

number of poor is smaller than its share of the total population. Combining Tables 1.14 and 1.15, it is clear that poverty is an especially important issue for rural people, especially in the Northeast. In 2000, rural people in the Northeast accounted for 59 per cent of all poor people in Thailand, but only 29 per cent of the total population.

More dramatic than any of these data, however, are recently released data on the relationship between poverty incidence and education. According to the National Economic and Social Development Board's data, of the total number of poor people in 2002, 94.7 per cent had received primary or less education. A further 2.8 per cent had lower secondary education, 1.7 per cent upper secondary, 0.48 per cent had vocational qualifications and 0.31 per cent had graduated from universities. Thailand's poor are overwhelmingly uneducated, rural and living in large families. But they are not necessarily landless.

Poverty reduction and economic growth

As Tables 1.14 and 1.15 above indicate, reductions in poverty incidence were not confined to the capital, Bangkok, or its immediate environs, but occurred in rural areas as well. Since 1988, the largest absolute decline in poverty incidence occurred in the poorest region of the country, the Northeast. What caused this reduction in poverty? Long-term improvements in education have undoubtedly been important, but despite the limitations of the underlying SES data, a reasonably clear statistical picture emerges on the relationship between poverty reductions and the rate of economic growth. The data are summarized in Table 1.16, which divides the periods shown into high, medium and low growth categories.

It is obvious that, over the long term, sustained economic growth is a necessary condition for large-scale poverty alleviation. No amount of redistribution could turn a poor country into a rich one. But what does the evidence indicate about the short run relationship between aggregate economic growth and poverty reduction? When the rate of economic growth during the intervals between SES data points is graphed against measured changes in poverty incidence over the same periods, we obtain the relationship shown in Figure 1.15.

Although the number of data points is small, the implications seem clear. Economic growth was strongly associated with reduced levels of absolute poverty incidence. Moderately rapid growth from 1962 to 1981 coincided with steadily declining poverty incidence. Reduced growth in Thailand caused by the world recession in the early to mid-1980s coincided with worsening poverty incidence in the years 1981 to 1986. Then, Thailand's economic boom of the late 1980s and early 1990s coincided with dramatically reduced poverty incidence. Finally, the contraction following the crisis of 1997–98 led to increased poverty incidence. The

Table 1.16 Thailand: GDP growth, poverty reduction and inequality, 1962 to 2002

Year	Annual GDP growth	Annual change in poverty incidence	Annual change in Gini coefficient
Rapid growth periods			
1986–88	9.75	−6.15	0.0
1988–90	10.27	−2.7	1.95
1992–94	7.01	−3.45	−0.45
Average	9.01	−4.1	0.5
Medium growth periods			
1962–69	5.08	−3.6	0.2
1990–92	6.47	−2.0	0.6
1994–96	6.44	−2.45	−0.6
1975–81	4.86	−2.18	0.23
Average	5.71	−2.56	0.11
Slow growth periods			
1969–75	4.15	−2.42	−0.15
1981–86	3.67	1.88	0.88
1996–98	−6.5	0.8	−0.2
1998–2000	4.65	0.65	0.01
2000–02	3.63	−2.2	−0.01
Average	1.92	−0.26	0.11

Source: Poverty and inequality data, as with Table 1.14. GDP data, National Economic and Social Development Board, Bangkok.

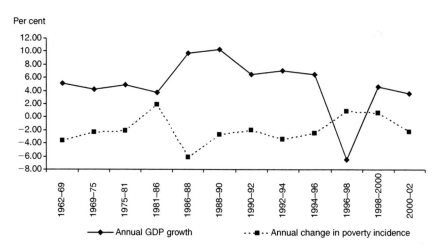

Figure 1.15 Thailand: poverty incidence and economic growth, 1962 to 2002 (source: Author's calculations using inequality data as in Table 1.13 and GDP data from National Economic and Social Development Board).

recovery since the crisis has been associated with significant poverty reductions.

Does the rate of economic growth also explain the long-term increase in inequality which accompanied the reduction in absolute poverty? The relationship between the change in inequality over time and the rate of growth is plotted in Figure 1.16. No consistent correlation emerges. Whereas Figure 1.15 indicates a clear relationship between the rate of growth and changes in the level of poverty incidence, the rate of growth does not seem to be a significant determinant of short-term changes in the level of inequality. Other social factors are presumably playing a role, but research on this issue remains inconclusive.

In summary, the evidence from Thailand indicates that the rate of aggregate growth is an important determinant of the rate at which absolute poverty declines, even in the short run. However, the statistical relationship is far from perfect. Reduction of poverty incidence must depend on more than just the aggregate rate of growth, but the rate of growth is undeniably important.

The Ninth Five-Year Plan

Medium-term economic planning was institutionalized in Thailand in 1959 with the formation of the (then named) National Economic Development Board – subsequently renamed the National Economic and Social

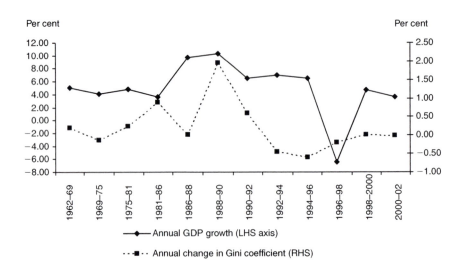

Figure 1.16 Thailand: inequality and economic growth, 1962 to 2002 (source: Author's calculations using inequality data as in Table 1.13 and GDP data from National Economic and Social Development Board).

Development Board (NESDB). The NESDB is assigned the task of coordinating the activities of the various government ministries and for producing, every five years, a medium-term development plan. The latest such plan, the ninth, covers the years 2002 to 2006 and was released in late 2001. These Plan documents are indicative only and have no legal status. Nothing compels the various Ministries to adhere to the Plan, and it is well known that some Ministries do not even read it. In a rapidly changing world, the assumptions on which these plans are based become irrelevant before the document has left the printers, but the plans do indicate the direction that the bureaucracy thinks is most appropriate for economic policy. The distinction between the views of the bureaucrats and the government was particularly important in the preparation of the Ninth Plan. The government rejected the draft version of the Ninth Plan more than once before it was finally approved. Once the Plan was approved, the Secretary General of the NESDB resigned, reportedly at the government's request.

Poverty alleviation is a central objective of the Ninth Plan. The Plan sets a target for the level of poverty incidence to be achieved by 2006, along with other, closely related, economic objectives. The latter include targets for the growth of aggregate real GDP, growth of sectoral outputs, inflation, export growth, growth of tourist arrivals, and so forth. The major elements of these targets include:

- Poverty incidence, 2006 – 12 per cent of total population;
- growth rate of real GDP, 2002 to 2006 – 4 to 5 per cent;
- growth rate of agricultural output, 2002 to 2006 – 2 per cent;
- growth rate of industrial output, 2002 to 2006 – 5.5 per cent;
- inflation (growth rate of the average price level), 2002 to 2006 – 3 per cent.

The target for poverty incidence refers to the headcount measure of poverty incidence – the proportion of the total population whose incomes fall below a poverty line held constant over time in real terms. Using the government's official poverty line, poverty incidence in 1999 was 15.9 per cent. The target thus means that, by 2006, poverty incidence is to be reduced by at least 4 per cent of the population; by 2006, the proportion of the population in poverty – defined in terms of the government's poverty line – is to be no more than three quarters of the proportion obtained in 1999.

As Table 1.14 above indicates, according to the official poverty incidence data, the target was already reached by 2002. A close inspection of Figure 1.15 above shows that the reduction in reported poverty incidence between 2000 and 2002 (from 14.2 to 9.8 per cent) is well in excess of the reduction that would be predicted from the rate of growth of GDP that occurred. The reasons for this larger than expected reduction in poverty are not yet well understood, but independent researchers have confirmed that the Socio-economic Survey data do indeed indicate reductions in poverty incidence of about this magnitude. Seemingly encouraged by this statistical outcome, the Prime Minister announced during 2003 that poverty would be eliminated completely within 6 years; that is, by 2009. The logic behind this projection may be that if poverty could be reduced at the rate of 2.2 per cent of the population per year between 2000 and 2002, as the official data report, then projecting this rate of reduction, six years should be sufficient to eliminate it completely.

The Prime Minister's goal is commendable, but it seems unlikely that the large reduction in poverty incidence that occurred between 2000 and 2002 could be replicated in this way. The large reduction that apparently occurred may have resulted from large numbers of people, forced just below the poverty line level of income by the effects of the crisis, emerging just above the poverty line between 2000 and 2002. Once these people are removed from the stock of poor households, those who remain include a higher proportion of chronically poor households, who are not so easily reached by economic growth. However, suppose the past relationship between poverty and economic growth was used to project poverty incidence. How much growth would it take to achieve the Prime Minister's announced goal?

The effects of this statistical exercise are reported in Table 1.17. If the past statistical relationship between poverty reduction and economic

Table 1.17 Thailand: projected poverty incidence in 2009 (per cent of population)

Assumed growth rate of real GDP from 2002 to 2009 (% p.a.)	Assumed inflation rate from 2002 to 2009 (% p.a.)					
	0	2	4	6	8	10
−2	27.6	29.8	32.1	34.3	36.5	38.8
−1	24.5	26.8	29.0	31.3	33.5	35.7
0	21.5	23.8	26.0	28.2	30.5	32.7
1	18.5	20.7	23.0	25.2	27.4	29.7
2	15.4	17.7	19.9	22.2	24.4	26.6
3	12.4	14.7	16.9	19.1	21.4	23.6
4	9.4	11.6	13.9	16.1	18.3	20.6
5	6.4	8.6	10.8	13.1	15.3	17.6
6	3.3	5.6	7.8	10.0	12.3	14.5
7	0.3	2.5	4.8	7.0	9.3	11.5
8	0.0	0.0	1.7	4.0	6.2	8.5

Source: Author's calculations using data from Table 1.14 and estimated equation relating poverty reduction to economic growth reported in Warr (2002).

Note:
The projections begin with assumed poverty incidence of 9.8 in 2002.

growth continued to apply, then to eliminate poverty incidence completely by 2009 at the current poverty line level of income, and assuming continued low inflation, would require growth of 8 per cent or more. This seems improbable, but growth of 6 per cent per year could reduce poverty incidence in 2009 to less than half its level in 2002. Clearly, reduction of poverty does not depend on the rate of economic growth alone. For example, it is shown in Warr (2003) that pro-poor reforms to Thailand's fiscal policies have the potential to enhance the poverty reducing power of Thailand's economic growth significantly without increasing the size of the budget deficit.

Conclusions

In 2003, Thailand finally emerged from its crisis of 1997–98. National income per person at last surpassed its pre-crisis (1996) level, and the Thai economy was again performing well, with good immediate prospects. But the fact that the crisis is over does not mean that it should be forgotten. Its causes and consequences must be understood thoroughly to prevent a recurrence and to chart the appropriate path ahead.

It is vital to recognize that Thailand's crisis was the collapse of a boom. It was not caused primarily by avaricious speculators or by corrupt politicians, although both of these played a role, but by errors of macroeconomic policy. These policy errors occurred during the *boom* period and arose from the complacency, and to some extent, arrogance, produced by a decade of unprecedented economic growth. Central among these policy mistakes was the insistence on retaining a fixed exchange rate when circumstances no longer suited it. The extended boom also produced a euphoria – some would say greed – which led business decision-makers and others to take risks they would not ordinarily have accepted.

The prolonged boom that preceded the crisis was fuelled by high levels of investment in physical capital. This investment was financed primarily by domestic household savings, but capital inflows from abroad were also important. These inflows consisted of long-term capital inflows, in the form of foreign direct investment, but more importantly of short-term capital inflows, in the form of bank loans from abroad, portfolio investment from abroad, and domestic bank accounts held by foreigners. As the boom developed, these high levels of foreign-owned capital inflow, combined with Thailand's fixed exchange rate policy, set in train a 'Dutch disease' real appreciation, in which real wages increased unsustainably, undermining the competitiveness of the traded goods sector. In 1996 this produced a slowdown in export growth, which provoked the expectation of a devaluation.

Over the same pre-crisis period, the vulnerability of the country's foreign exchange reserves to a financial panic had increased very substantially. The vulnerability derived from a greatly increased stock of volatile capital within Thailand, which could be presented for conversion into foreign exchange at short notice. The growth of this stock of volatile capital relative to reserves was itself the outcome of macroeconomic policies. First, the attempt to sterilize capital inflows raised domestic interest rates and induced very large inflows of short-term foreign capital. Second, controls on capital movements were largely eliminated in the early 1990s. Third, the Bangkok International Banking Facility, established by the government in 1993, encouraged domestic banks to borrow abroad, short-term. Finally, non-bank financial institutions were also encouraged to borrow from abroad, in the hope of qualifying for highly profitable domestic banking licences.

A recurrence of a currency crisis like that of 1997 is not impossible but it is unlikely within the foreseeable future. There are three basic reasons for this assessment. First, and most important, Thailand is no longer attempting to defend a fixed exchange rate. Second, the analysis presented above indicates that the conditions of foreign exchange reserve vulnerability that existed in 1996 and 1997, and which laid the foundation for the currency crisis, do not exist to a comparable extent at present. Third, the Bank of Thailand is a competent institution which has learned from the 1997 crisis and is unlikely to repeat the policy errors that led to it. If another macroeconomic crisis occurs in Thailand, it will be different from the 1997 currency crisis.

The crisis brought suffering to many Thai people, but not all of its effects were negative. A reconsideration of the appropriate relationship between the government and the citizenry has led to reforms that have already made Thai society more democratic and its government more transparent and responsive to public concerns. Although its consequences are less predicable, a healthy reconsideration of basic values has also been stimulated, drawing upon Thailand's unique cultural and religious traditions. The boom both fed upon and stimulated a high level of greed. Thailand's Buddhist traditions have rightly led to a re-evaluation of this aspect of the boom period. In Buddhist terms, it is only to be expected that greed will culminate in suffering. The 'growth at any cost' mentality that accompanied the boom period has been discredited, among Thai intellectuals if not the current government. There is much truth in this interpretation of the lessons of the crisis, but there remains a danger that its central message could be taken too far.

Continued economic growth is important for Thailand. It reduces poverty and provides the resources that can be used to finance improvements in the nation's health, education and physical infrastructure and for dealing with environmental problems. There seems every reason to expect that with the steady restoration of business confidence, Thailand can maintain moderate rates of economic growth. In this author's view, the goal should not be to return to the 9 per cent growth rates of the pre-crisis boom, because growth at this rate has been shown to be unmanageable. Rather, the objective should be a restoration of the 6 to 7 per cent growth of the three decades that preceded the boom. Sustained recovery along these lines will be dependent on continuation of the reforms on which restoration of confidence depends. Substantial problems of structural change and policy reform must be confronted.

Many observers have said that the 'fundamentals' for Thailand are good and that rapid growth will soon be restored, at rates resembling those of the pre-crisis boom decade. It is seldom specified what these 'fundamentals' actually are. The Thai economy grew at over 6 per cent in 2003 and prospects for 2004 seem good. Prime Minister Thaksin has promised a period of rapid growth from 2004 onwards, even reaching double-digit levels. Nevertheless, there are reasons to doubt whether the rapid growth of the boom period could be achieved again for any sustained period, even if it was desired.

First, cheap unskilled labour, which fuelled the boom, will no longer be abundant once the unemployed workers released by the current recession are re-absorbed. Once these workers re-enter the work force the era of cheap labour will be over for Thailand. The evidence for this view is the dramatic increase of real wages over the early 1990s, as described above. The capacity of the Thai education system to supply the skilled labour required to facilitate movement to more skill-intensive modes of production, especially for export production, will then be critical. As Sirilaksana Khoman explains in Chapter 9 of this volume, the central problem is the low rates of secondary school participation and the poor quality of secondary education, rather than failure at either the primary or tertiary levels. Education is clearly the most important reform issue facing Thailand today. Progress is too slow.

Second, private domestic investment, the driving force for the growth of the capital stock that made the output boom possible, remains sluggish. The current recovery is, in this respect, quite different from the pre-crisis boom. Third, foreign investment contributed to the boom to a degree that is not fully captured by the volumes of capital involved because it brought with it advanced technology and skills. It seems doubtful that foreign investment will return to the levels experienced during the boom because foreign investors are now much more cautious. Finally, public infrastructure, especially transport, was badly congested by 1996. The severe cutbacks in public investment that followed the crisis will mean that, after the recovery, that constraint will operate again.

In the short-term, an expansion in aggregate demand is badly needed, but Thailand's policy options are limited. The scope for monetary expansion is constrained by the existence of a 'liquidity trap', in which banks are already flush with cash but are nevertheless reluctant to lend and most firms are reluctant to borrow. Pushing Thailand's already low interest rates even lower is unlikely to stimulate investment. The scope for fiscal expansion is limited by the fact that legal limits exist for both the level of the budget deficit as a share of GDP and the size of the public debt. A moderate fiscal expansion is already underway, and the legal limits are already being stretched. The present government has the political power to amend these limits, but the level of the public debt as a share of GDP (at 65 per cent) already exceeds the level the government had promised as its maximum (60 per cent). A moderate fiscal expansion is desirable, but would be more beneficial if targeted to the poorest groups, rather than the political allies of the current government.

The bad news is that, in the short-term, Thailand is dependent on a revival of export demand and investor confidence, which in turn require a revival of global demand. The good news is that the present period of moderate growth, combined with the government's large parliamentary majority, provides an opportunity for lasting reform. Regrettably, the Thaksin government shows little interest in such matters. Indeed, a rolling back of recent reform measures seems more probable. Education reform, discussed above, is a principal example as are competition policy and trade policy. While substantial progress in trade policy reform occurred between 1995 and 1999 (Warr 2000), that momentum has been lost since the crisis.[20] The Thaksin government has aggressively pursued Free Trade Agreements with Thailand's trading partners, including China, USA, India and Australia, but shows little interest in trade policy reform beyond that.

The Thaksin government has expressed a welcome concern for the welfare of Thailand's poor, but its favoured solutions consist mainly of handing out relatively small amounts of public revenue in disguised forms of income support. This is politically rewarding in the short-term but does not provide a lasting solution to poverty. It ignores the underlying issue – the low productivity of large numbers of people, especially rural people. Raising the productivity of poor people is the long-term answer to poverty. Raising labour productivity is also the key to ending Thailand's dependence on labour-intensive forms of production, which the Prime Minister rightly identifies as being inconsistent with rising prosperity in the increasingly competitive international environment that Thailand faces. Reform of the education system should therefore be recognized as the most urgent long-term issue. The Prime Minister's own rhetoric suggests that he agrees, but little is happening.

The rural population receives markedly inferior education to urban Thais, both in quality and quantity. As young adults, these people may migrate to urban areas, but the damage has already been done. The poor standards of education they received in rural Thailand doom them to menial work and low incomes. The dropout rates at the secondary level are very much higher in rural areas than in the cities and, perhaps more important, the quality of teaching is lower as well. The central government's Education Ministry has resisted reform and Thaksin's successive Ministers of Education have apparently not wished to fight this battle, seemingly being captured by the educational bureaucracy, and even defending the system of rote learning which is prevalent in Thailand's schools.

Thailand's governments have historically been known for an inability to get things done because of the large numbers of small political parties usually needed to make up a coalition large enough to hold office. Disunity within the fragile coalitions that result normally prevents any long-term agenda from being implemented. The political success of Prime Minister Thaksin Shinawatra has enabled his government to avoid that familiar dilemma, affording him a unique opportunity to implement lasting reform. Thaksin is, moreover, a decisive, energetic and popular leader, fully capable of implementing an agenda of reform if that was his desire. The present indications are not all positive. There is a danger that the political capital earned by Thaksin's electoral success may be dissipated on pork-barrelling and short-term political point scoring. The opportunity may not recur soon.

Appendix: some useful websites on the Thai economy

Asia Recovery Information Center (ARIC), Asian Development Bank
http://aric.adb.org/

Asian Development Bank (ADB)
http://www.adb.org/

Research School of Pacific and Asian Studies, Australian National University
http://rspas.anu.edu.au

Bank of Thailand (BOT)
http://www.bot.or.th/bothomepage/index/index_e.asp

Bangkok Post newspaper
http://www.bangkokpost.net/

Chulalongkorn University
http://www.chula.ac.th/

Governments on the WWW Thailand
http://www.gksoft.com/govt/en/th.html

International Monetary Fund, *International Financial Statistics* (IMF, IFS) http://www.imf.org/external/pubs/cat/longres.cfm?sk=397.0

Ministry of Education (MOE)
http://www.moe.go.th/English/

Ministry of Science, Technology and Environment
http://www.moste.go.th/moste_eng/index.htm

National Economic and Social Development Board (NESDB)
http://www.nesdb.go.th/nesdb4-eng.html

National Statistical Office of Thailand (NSO)
http://www.nso.go.th/eng/index.htmv

National Thai Studies Centre, Australian National University
http://www.anu.edu.au/asianstudies/thaicen/

Office of the National Education Commission (ONEC)
http://www.edthai.com/

Organization for Economic Co-operation and Development (OECD)
http://www.oecd.org/EN/home/0,,EN-home-0-nodirectorate-no-no-no-0,
FF.html

Overseas Economic Cooperation Fund (OECF)
http://www2.dgsys.com/~oecfwsh/

Royal Forest Department of Thailand
http://www.forest.go.th/default_e.asp

School of Oriental and African Studies, University of London (SOAS)
http://www.soas.ac.uk/

Thai Customs Department
http://www.customs.go.th/

Thailand Board of Investment (BOI)
http://www.boi.go.th/

Thailand Development Research Institute (TDRI)
http://www.info.tdri.or.th/

Thammasat University
http://www.tu.ac.th/default.tu/default.eng.html

The Nation newspaper
http://www.nationmultimedia.com/

Tourism Authority of Thailand (TAT)
http://www.tourismthailand.org/

United Nations Development Programme (UNDP)

http://www.sdnp.undp.org/

United Nations Educational, Scientific and Cultural Organization
(UNESCO)
http://whc.unesco.org/

United Nations Human Settlements Programme
http://www.unchs.org/

World Bank Group
http://www.worldbank.org/

World Bank Office, Thailand
http://www.worldbank.or.th/

World Resource Institute (WRI)
http://www.wri.org/wri/

Notes

1 For an earlier review of the long-term performance of the Thai economy, see Warr (1993). The account presented here updates that discussion.
2 Chapter 2 of this volume, by Ammar Siamwalla, provides a complementary, but not identical, perspective on these critical events.
3 The data underlying Tables 1.3 and 1.4 update the data set and expand on the analysis presented for the period 1981 to 1995 by Chalongphob and Pranee (1998). The author is grateful to these authors for providing access to their original data set.
4 These resource movements have social consequences, not all of which are necessarily favourable, as Chapter 5 of this volume, by Pasuk Phongpaichit, convincingly argues.
5 Until it was floated on 2 July 1997, the baht had been loosely pegged to the US dollar since the 1950s, except for devaluations of 10 and 15 per cent in 1981 and 1984, respectively. For a detailed account of this period, see Warr and Bhanupong (1996).
6 See the IMF reports by Robinson *et al.* (1991) and Kochhar *et al.* (1996) for favourable accounts of this policy change. On the other hand, see Warr and Bhanupong (1996, p. 204), for a warning of the dangers inherent in this programme of capital market liberalization in combination with a fixed exchange rate. Warr and Bhanupong recommended that if the capital market liberalization was to be maintained, Thailand would require a more flexible exchange rate system.
7 For a full discussion of this index and its composition, see Warr and Bhanupong (1996, pp. 221–6).
8 All three also greatly exaggerate the gain in export competitiveness resulting from a depreciation and distort the pattern of its changes over time. See Warr (1986) for a theoretical demonstration of these points.
9 See Warr and Bhanupong (1996, Ch. 9), for a detailed discussion of exchange rate management over the period ending in 1991, and also Robinson *et al.* (1991).
10 See Sachs *et al.* (1996) for a fuller discussion of these concepts.

11 The 15 commodities represented in Table 1.7 comprised between 52 and 54 per cent of total exports in each of the three years shown.
12 The frozen shrimp industry is a special case, where US import restrictions were important, effectively banning imports of non-farm shrimps from Thailand. These restrictions were lifted in the following year.
13 See, for example, Ammar and Suthad (1991) and Somporn and Nipon (1995).
14 The above real GDP growth rates are derived from: http://www.adb.org/ Documents/Books/ADO/2001/Update/tha_update.pdf.
15 For an account of Thailand's boom, which supports this assessment in so far as capital market liberalization is concerned, see Warr (1999).
16 The above quotations are taken from the Bangkok Post, April 24, 2001. See: http://scoop.bangkokpost.co.th.
17 The redistribution to poor people is far less than this total. The largest component, the moratorium on BAAC loan repayment, is not concentrated on poor farmers because the BAAC loans themselves are not concentrated on small farmers.
18 For further discussion of these issues, see Ammar Siamwalla, 'Picking up the pieces: bank and corporate restructuring in post 1997 Thailand' and 'AMC: an idea whose time has gone', available at http://www.info.tdri.or.th/reports/ ammar/as_paper.html.
19 See World Bank, *Thailand Economic Monitor*, July 2001. This and previous issues are available at http://www.worldbank.or.th/monitor.
20 For a recent discussion of Thailand's trade policies, see the World Bank's October 2003 *Thailand Economic Monitor*, available at http://www.worldbank.or. th/monitor.

References

Ammar Siamwalla and Suthad Setboonsarng (1991) Thailand, in: A.O. Krueger, M. Schiff and A. Valdes (eds) *The Political Economy of Agricultural Pricing Policy: Vol. 2, Asia*, Baltimore: Johns Hopkins University Press.
Chalongphob Sussankarn and Pranee Tinakorn (1998) *Productivity Growth in Thailand, 1980 to 1995*, Bangkok: Thailand Development Research Institute.
Corden, W.M. (1984) Booming sector and Dutch Disease economics: a survey, *Oxford Economic Papers*, 36, pp. 359–80.
Edwards, Sebastian (1998) *Real Exchange Rates, Devaluation and Adjustment: Exchange Rate Policies in Developing Countries*, Cambridge, MA: MIT Press.
Ingram, James C. (1971) *Economic Change in Thailand: 1850–1970*, California: Stanford University Press, Stanford.
Jorgenson, Dale W. (1988) Productivity and postwar U.S. economic growth, *Journal of Economic Perspectives*, 2, pp. 23–42.
Kochhar, Kalpana, Louis Dicks-Mireaux, Balazs Horvath, Mauro Mecagni, Erik Offerdal and Jianping Zhou (1996) Thailand: the road to sustained growth, *Occasional Paper* No. 146, December, Washington, DC: International Monetary Fund.
Medhi Krongkaew (1993) Income distribution and poverty, in: Peter G. Warr (ed.) *The Thai Economy in Transition*, Cambridge: Cambridge University Press, pp. 431–462.
Robinson, David, Yangho Byeon and Ranjit Teja (1991) Thailand: adjusting to success, current policy issues, *Occasional Paper* No. 85, Washington, DC: International Monetary Fund.

Roong Poshyananda Mallikamas, Yunyong Thaicharoen and Daungporn Rod-pengsangkaha (2003) Investment cycles, economic recovery and monetary policy. Monetary Policy Group, Bank of Thailand, August. Available at: http://www.bot.or.th/bothomepage/index/index_e.asp.

Sachs, J., A. Tornell and A. Velasco (1996) Financial crises in emerging markets: the lessons from 1995, *Brookings Papers in Economic Activity*, 1, pp. 147–215.

Sirilaksana Khoman (1993) Education policy, in: Peter Warr (ed.) *The Thai Economy in Transition*, Cambridge: Cambridge University Press, pp. 325–54.

Sompop Manorungsan (1989) *Economic Development of Thailand, 1850–1950*, Institute of Asian Studies Monograph No. 42, Chulalongkorn University.

Somporn Isvilanonda and Nipon Poapongsakorn (1995) Rice supply and demand in Thailand: the future outlook. Thailand Development Research Institute, Bangkok, January.

Vines, David and Warr, Peter (2003) Thailand's investment-driven boom and crisis, *Oxford Economic Papers*, 55, pp. 440–64.

Warr, Peter (1986) Indonesia's other Dutch Disease: economic effects of the petroleum boom, in: J.P. Neary and S. van Wijnbergen (eds) *Natural Resources and the Macroeconomy*, Oxford: Basil Blackwell, pp. 288–320.

Warr, Peter (1993) The Thai economy, in: Peter Warr (ed.) *The Thai Economy in Transition*, Cambridge: Cambridge University Press, pp. 1–80.

Warr, Peter (1999) What happened to Thailand?, *The World Economy*, 22, pp. 631–50.

Warr, Peter (2000) Thailand's post-crisis trade policies: the 1999 WTO trade policy review, *The World Economy*, 23, pp. 1215–36.

Warr, Peter (2002) Economic recovery and poverty reduction in Thailand, *Thailand Development Research Institute Quarterly Review*, 17, pp. 18–27.

Warr, Peter (2003) Fiscal policies and poverty incidence: the case of Thailand, *Asian Economic Journal*, 17, pp. 32–56.

Warr, Peter and Bhanupong Nidhiprabha (1996) *Thailand's Macroeconomic Miracle: Stable Adjustment and Sustained Growth*, Washington and Kuala Lumpur: World Bank and Oxford University Press.

World Bank (1998) *World Development Report, 1998*, New York: Oxford University Press.

Chapter 2

Anatomy of the crisis

Ammar Siamwalla

I truly believe ... that we, more than any other country are also trying to change the rules of the game and the basic structures of the economy because there is a lot more recognition of this problem in Thailand – that it was the rules and regulations which broke the economy and not the lack or the excess of money. The bubble did not just create a void. During the bubble, a lot of new structures were put up in capriciousness, in over-confidence, and in ignorance. I think we have learnt our lessons and we are trying to change back to the rule of sensibility, logic, and conservatism.

M.R. Chatumongkol Sonakul, former Governor of the
Bank of Thailand[1]

The bubble

Until the crash of 1997, the Thai economy had performed exceptionally well. Economic growth averaged 7.6 per cent over the two decades from 1977–96. The rate dipped in the early 1980s when an adverse shift in the terms of trade (high oil prices and low agricultural prices) depressed growth between 1980–85 to 4.5 per cent. In the meantime, Thailand also adjusted its production structure to reflect its changed comparative advantage towards labour-intensive industries and away from agriculture, thus creating the conditions that led to the export-led manufacturing boom beginning in the second half of the 1980s and which continued until 1996.

The basis of the boom in its earlier and middle stages – that is until about 1993 – was sound, with rapid investments in manufacturing capacity brought about by the relocation of industry from East Asia following the appreciation of the yen. As a result, economic growth accelerated sharply, reaching double-digit rates towards the end of the 1980s. Such high growth rates naturally led to severe pressures on the capacity of the infrastructure. Consequently, major investments had to be made in telecommunications, power generation, and urban expressways. Together with the investments in manufacturing, there was a sharp acceleration in the country's gross capital formation.

This growth in demand for investment funds coincided with the decision of the Bank of Thailand to liberalize Thailand's financial system, particularly in its relationship to the rest of the world. There were two important milestones in this process. The first was acceptance of the obligations under Article VIII of the International Monetary Fund in 1990. This required the lifting of all controls on all foreign-exchange transactions on the current account, most of which had already been removed. The second was the gradual opening of the capital account in a long process, capped by the launching of the Bangkok International Banking Facility (BIBF) in 1993. This facility was designed to make Bangkok a centre for financial services by encouraging foreign financial institutions to set up operations in Thailand. These financial institutions were to make loans to domestic borrowers and to borrowers in other countries in the region, although in the end BIBF proved to be more efficient as a conduit for domestic borrowers.

Following the logic of these two milestone decisions, most remaining foreign-exchange control measures were removed. Although Thai residents who wished to acquire assets abroad had to obtain the approval of the central bank, this was readily granted. Similarly, it became easier for foreigners to hold non-resident baht accounts.

On the domestic front, all ceilings on interest rates were removed in 1992, and the requirement for banks to direct a certain proportion of their loans to the agricultural sector was gradually loosened until it became almost meaningless. The rules relating to non-performing assets were changed to conform to those defined by the Bank for International Settlements (BIS). But the Bank of Thailand chose to use the loosest of the rules. For example, a loan was deemed to be non-performing only if principal and interest were overdue for 12 months.

At a time when the country was growing rapidly and had major capital requirements, financial liberalization fuelled an investment boom and later an asset price bubble which grew out of control. With foreign money available at the low interest rates prevailing in the developed world, and with an exchange rate perceived to be fixed forever, borrowers perceived their cost of capital to be considerably reduced. This stimulated the investment boom, which in turn nurtured a high growth rate. Side by side with the investment boom, the high growth rate of the economy, and the low perceived cost of capital, an asset price bubble emerged. The benchmark SET index for stock prices rose from 613 at the end of 1990 to peak at 1410 at the end of January 1996.

A similar bubble in property prices was to have wider repercussions. The property boom went back to the late 1980s, when Thailand was enjoying double-digit growth. The high growth rate led to a shortage of office and residential space, particularly in Bangkok. The resulting construction spree was only to be expected and, in the beginning, justified by demand, at least until about 1992–93 (Renaud *et al.* 1998). By 1994 it was becoming obvious that supply was overshooting requirements. There was an Indian summer of construction activity, when everyone raced to complete their projects before the impending crash, helped along by the cheap money available at the time.

Lenders collaborated closely in fuelling the property boom. Bank of Thailand data indicate that the share of real estate lending in the overall portfolio of the banks went up from 6.3 per cent at the end of 1988 to 14.8 per cent at the end of 1996. Over the same period, the share of real estate in the portfolios of the finance companies went up from 9.1 per cent to 24.3 per cent (cited in Renaud *et al.* 1998).

These figures actually underestimate the role of property in the financial system. The majority of Thai bank loans are based on collateral, and property is the usual form of collateral. With rapidly rising prices, property placed as collateral could be used to raise more loans, which could in turn be used to purchase yet more property, fuelling asset price rises even further. The difficulties that banks and finance companies are currently experiencing are in no small measure due to the close nexus between property and bank loans.

However, while the bubble arose in large part out of private decisions, there were also major policy and regulatory failures. One should not fault the Bank of Thailand simply for having liberalized the financial regime, a decision which set in train the events that caused the bubble to grow and then burst. Liberalization under the right circumstances can be beneficial. But the right circumstances were not present. First, domestic financial institutions were not ready for a liberalized market – managers in the financial sector still used the old methods of employing collateral as security and did not try to assess cash flows and their risks carefully. With these weaknesses among the financial institutions, the Bank of Thailand was at fault, because it failed to adopt strict prudential measures in tandem with the liberalization and failed to take firm action when it was needed.

First of all, the central bank should not have continued with an essentially fixed exchange rate regime. An open capital account has repeatedly been shown to be incompatible with such a regime (unless there is a very strong currency board that strictly eschews the use of monetary policy). The crises in Chile in 1982, in Sweden in 1990 and in Mexico in 1994 can be cited as examples of the failure to heed this rule. The insurance against exchange rate movements offered by the central bank tended to encourage excessive movements of capital, both inwards and outwards. The outward movement would also be bound to be more violent if associated with a fear of devaluation, which is what happened in the first half of 1997.

Second, given the central bank's decision to keep the exchange rate fixed, the authorities are also responsible, because they did not take appropriate action to control excessive demand. True, the Bank of Thailand began to apply monetary brakes starting from mid-1994 onwards; but under a fixed exchange rate regime with an open capital account, monetary policy is not very effective, which soon became tragically apparent. As the central bank's policy pushed domestic interest rates upwards, the flow of foreign money into Thailand surged. The current account deficit rose to 8 per cent of gross national product (GNP) in 1995 and 1996. This high current account deficit was primarily due to the capital inflow, which in turn fuelled high domestic investment. The investment rate eventually reached 42 per cent of GNP in 1996.

With monetary policy ineffective, fiscal policy should have become the central instrument to limit aggregate demand. While Thai fiscal policy appeared conservative, with a string of budget surpluses going back almost a decade, it was not so by design. Rather, it was an outcome of the strong growth, combined with an excessive caution in revenue estimates. In any case, the surplus as a percentage of GNP steadily declined and turned into a small deficit in 1996. The 1996 deficit was in fact a conscious decision to loosen fiscal policy at a time when monetary policy was already quite tight. Given the overheated economy, however, this was definitely a mistake.

Irrespective of these policy mistakes, the primary cause of the bubble was the high growth rate itself and expectations that this growth rate would continue. With the economy growing rapidly, asset prices continued to appreciate, revenues continued to grow, and the burden of any debt incurred then could be expected to decline relative to income in the future. With an open capital account and the economy performing miraculous feats of sustained high growth, debt could be increased seemingly without limit. As foreign money continued to pour in, output growth continued, confirming the expectations of high growth that had initially generated the state of euphoria.

The crisis that finally occurred was felt in many different markets at different times. The following analysis will examine events in each of the following markets (credit, currency, goods, labour markets). The stress on markets emphasizes the fact that it was market failings which led to the crisis. There were, of course, policy failures as well, many of which pertain directly to government action and inaction in each individual market and will be covered in the relevant section. There were also other, more general, policy issues, which will be addressed in the final section.

Financial institutions and markets

The flotation of the baht on 2 July 1997 is now conventionally designated as the start of the crisis in Thailand and, more broadly, throughout East

Asia. This is because it was this dramatic event that hit the headlines in the international media. Actually, Thais had been aware for some time that their economy was entering a stormy period. What triggered that awareness was the suspicion that the balance sheets of many financial institutions were extremely shaky, with some institutions close to insolvency. Many of the loans, particularly to the property sector, were already non-performing, but with the economy spiralling downwards and, after the float, with the baht rapidly depreciating, the total size of the non-performing loans was increasing. In the past, the government had often bailed out the depositors of insolvent banks, but there was no automatic guarantee. Considerable uncertainty existed, and this is an important backdrop to developments in the critical year, 1997.

Finance companies

The Bank of Thailand, as the supervisor of these institutions, began to move on some of the worst cases, first asking ten finance companies to increase their capital (on 3 March 1997), and encouraging them to merge. Strangely enough, the names of these companies were announced. This action shows, at the same time, too tough a stance (by announcing the names of the problematic firms) and too mild a stance (in hoping that there would be investors willing to put up the capital). The result was to precipitate a run on these and other finance companies, which were kept going only by loans from the Financial Institutions Development Fund (FIDF). The amount lent by FIDF during March shot up by 80 billion baht from the total of 50 billion baht outstanding at the end of February (Nukul Commission 1998, paragraph 343). At that point, the total deposits of businesses and households with all finance companies stood at 995 billion baht.

As seepage from the finance companies continued, more finance companies came to FIDF for funds, this time joined by a bank. On 28 June, the government suspended the operations of 16 finance companies, including the 10 that were required to increase their capital. These 16 included what was then the largest finance company in Thailand. Depositors at these institutions were asked to have their promissory notes replaced by those issued by a finance company, Krung Thai Thanakit, which was in turn owned by a state bank, Krung Thai Bank. The maturity for deposits was extended: for deposits greater than 1 million baht the maturity was three years and for deposits greater than 5 million baht the maturity was five years, at floating interest rates somewhat below market rates. Creditors to these suspended financial institutions were not protected.

The depositors were thus not quite fully protected – at the very least, the forced extension of the maturity created problems for them. This prompted a huge run on all remaining financial institutions, which only a few large banks managed to escape. An announcement by the Prime Minister one day after the suspension of the 16 firms assured the population that the government would not suspend any more financial institutions and that deposits and loans at the remaining ones would be guaranteed. The first part of the announcement was falsified on 5 August when 42 more finance companies were suspended, bringing the total to 58. After the suspension, the managements of these companies were asked to submit rehabilitation plans. The authorities eventually decided (in December 1997) that only two of these were satisfactory, and the remaining 56 were closed down permanently, their assets transferred to the newly instituted Financial Restructuring Authority. By the end of the year, the FIDF had on its books a total of more than 700 billion baht (18 per cent of GDP) owed by these and other financial institutions including a number of banks (Nukul Commission 1998, paragraph 346).

Until July 1997, the decision with respect to the financial institutions was entirely in the hands of Thai authorities. The International Monetary Fund (IMF) was not yet involved. The extent of the IMF's involvement in the August decision to suspend 42 firms, however, is less clear. The suspension preceded Thailand's formal entry into the IMF programme, and it was said at the time that this was the entry price into the programme. In the first letter of intent submitted by the Thai authorities to the Fund (dated 14 August 1997), the measures taken with respect to the finance companies were outlined:

> The first part, which has already been set in train, begins by isolating fundamentally unviable finance companies from the rest of the financial system. We have made clear the principle that the public costs of this intervention will be strictly minimized through burden sharing among the claimants of unviable institutions, starting with a capital write-down of existing shareholders and losses for the creditors of finance companies.

The depleted funds at these institutions were made up by loans from the FIDF, which in turn borrowed from the Bank of Thailand.[2] All these actions led, in effect, to the transfer of a very large chunk of the financial institutions' assets to the FIDF – assets whose value was highly dubious. To finance these transfers, the Financial Institution Development Fund began to issue notes that promptly ballooned in size, so that eventually they totalled nearly a trillion baht. Worse than that, when there was a severe run and high demand for FIDF loans by the finance companies, the Bank of Thailand took up many of the FIDF notes that could not be sold in the money market.

The assets acquired by the FIDF from the 56 closed finance companies were passed on to the newly instituted Financial Sector Restructuring

Authority (FRA) to be auctioned off. Until 13 September 1999, the FRA was able to sell core assets (loans) whose face value was 584 billion baht for 147 billion baht, implying a recovery rate of 25 per cent. Additional revenue of 34 billion baht was raised from the sale of non-core assets, mostly securities of unknown face value.[3]

Commercial banks

The problems with the finance companies did not end with the closure of the 56 companies. The remaining ones continued to worry the authorities, and several were closed in 1998. These problems were submerged under far more serious difficulties with the commercial banks. One bank, the Bangkok Bank of Commerce – a subject of numerous fraud investigations – had already been taken over in 1996, two others were taken over at the end of 1997, and another two in 1998. The takeover of the last two banks was in conjunction with an overall programme to rehabilitate the entire banking sector.

The central problem with the banks that were taken over, and indeed of the banking system as a whole, was a frighteningly rapid deterioration in the quality of bank assets. The single most important cause of this deterioration was the fall in the value of the baht. The net exposure of the banks (and finance companies) to exchange risk had been regulated by the Bank of Thailand to be less than 20 per cent of the banks' capital. However, most local banks belong to the BIBF. As such, they were permitted to act as conduits for cheap dollar loans to Thai companies. As liabilities and assets for these loans were both in dollars, technically they did not increase the banks' exposure to exchange risks. But as their customers were so exposed, the banks' *credit* risks certainly increased. Therefore, in addition to the problems created by the property sector, which before 2 July had already weakened the financial institutions, the banks now faced the far more serious consequences of the baht depreciation. The sharp decline in economic activities after July 1997 added a further impetus to the rate of loan non-performance.

After July 1997, the Bank of Thailand no longer accommodated the banks' loan problems by practising regulatory forbearance. It steadily tightened the definition of non-performing loans (NPL), as a result of which the NPL figures climbed to the incredible rate of more than 40 per cent for the whole system, and as much as 70 per cent for the state-owned banks.

The huge volume of non-performing loans and the resulting recapitalization requirement under the more stringent rule froze the entire financial system. Banks were increasingly reluctant to lend, even for working capital. As a result, firms began to hoard cash rather than repaying their loans or even paying interest, merely to maintain their operations, thus pushing the NPL figures even higher. Some firms began to reduce prices, particularly on sales overseas, to generate cash flow (Suthep 1999). This hoarding of cash in preference to loan repayment was the mildest form of what came to be known as the 'strategic NPL' problem. Other borrowers were less strategic and more opportunistic. This adds to the financial institutions' balance-sheet problems, causing them to require further increases in their capital.

The depreciation of the baht wreaked such havoc with the balance sheets of most Thai firms that no rational lender would lend to them. Many firms were able to continue operating by adopting strategic NPL practices. The freezing up of the credit market appeared to have relatively little impact on the firms' ability to obtain working capital, as indicated by the fact that Thai exports *in baht terms* expanded considerably, indicating that exporters had no trouble processing their orders.[4] Of course, any expansion or modernization plans had to be shelved.

The banks, even those that had not been taken over by the government, needed to increase their capital to make up for deteriorating assets. At first, the government encouraged the banks to do so on their own. In March 1998, two of the largest banks, Bangkok Bank and Thai Farmers' Bank, successfully raised capital overseas. As it turned out, they luckily floated their new shares during a very narrow window of opportunity. Soon after, the yen was facing severe problems, Russia defaulted, and Asia went out of fashion once more. The NPL figure in the Thai banking system grew relentlessly, further depressing banking share prices (see Figure 2.1). Those who put their funds in the two banks lost a great deal of money. After that, it became impossible for any other bank to raise equity in the markets.

Eventually, the government had to step in. On 14 August 1998 it announced a series of measures to facilitate the recapitalization of banks, by means of public funds if necessary. Two more banks were taken over by the government and, together with two of the banks that had been taken over earlier in the year, were to be merged into two government banks. The two banks taken over earlier had their FIDF debts converted into equity, to the point where their NPLs were adequately covered by reserves up to the year 2000. These were to be sold to investors, most likely foreign. One bank, the Bangkok Bank of Commerce (BBC) was to be closed down altogether.

The 14 August measures eased the recapitalization burden by shifting the required proportions of tier-1 and tier-2 capital in favour of the latter. They also provided government funding for both these capital tiers. Those commercial banks committing themselves to comply with new rules of loan loss provisioning by the end of 2000 were to be entitled to issue new preferred shares to the government in exchange for tradable government bonds. To encourage banks to restructure debts with their clients, the government stood ready to provide them with non-tradable government bonds equal to the losses incurred during the restructuring. These bonds would be exchanged for the banks' subordinated debentures, which could count as the banks' tier-2 capital (Thailand Development Research Institute 2000). Parliamentary approval was sought for the issuance of 300 billion baht worth of government bonds.

Although all banks except the larger ones have come to the government, the total offtake of the government bonds to date has been less than 100 billion baht. Only banks that already had large government holdings asked for and received tier-1 capital. The government had plans to sell off its remaining banks, except the largest, Krung Thai Bank, most likely to foreigners. Several of them have been taken over. Consequently, foreigners' share of the Thai banking business is now much larger than before and looks set to expand further.

These recapitalization efforts merely tackled the consequences of the loan non-performance, but they did not get at the root cause of it. The figures for NPLs soared, peaking in June 1999 (Figure 2.1). To obtain a full picture of the NPL problem, one has also to look at the demand side of the story.

Corporate finance

Thai corporations have always been highly leveraged. In an international comparison of debt/equity ratios among publicly listed non-financial companies, Thailand ranked quite high, even among Asian countries; exceeded only by Japan and Korea (Claessens and Djankov 1999). The reasons for this have not been well analysed.[5] Rapidly growing firms have

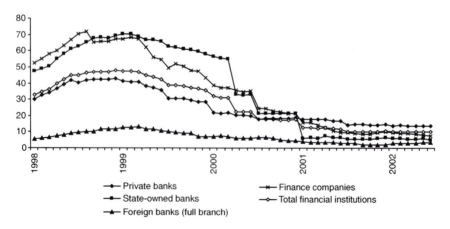

Figure 2.1 Non-performing loans in Thai financial institutions, June 1998 to November 2002 (source: Bank of Thailand).

to depend on external sources of capital for their expansion. Among these sources, loans from banks and the finance companies have been the preferred option because, in Thailand, the founding families still exert overwhelming control over their firms, and they are reluctant to dilute their equity holdings too much.

Furthermore, the finance sector is quite narrowly based, with banks and finance companies capturing most of the household financial savings. Other financial intermediaries (such as insurance companies or pension funds) are not only much smaller relative to the banks, but are also ineffective in generating risk capital. As a result, the equity market before 1997 was dominated by small investors, dealing in shares of companies where the founding families exert overwhelming control. Such an environment is hardly conducive to good corporate governance, a fact which further discourages equity financing.

From the corporations' point of view, the high leverage and dependence on the banks meant that they were extremely vulnerable to the kind of crisis that occurred. Moreover, that vulnerability had been steadily increasing, because the heavy investments they had been making were yielding progressively lower returns throughout the 1990s. From high teens in the early 1990s, the median rate of return (in nominal dollars) on assets of publicly-listed non-financial companies had sunk to 13.2 per cent in 1995 and 11.5 per cent in 1996. In real baht terms the rate of return on these assets sank from around 11 per cent in the early 1990s to 7.8 per cent in 1995 and 7.4 per cent in 1996 (Claessens and Djankov 1999).

When the crisis began, Thailand's business sector was populated by vulnerable companies, which owed large debts denominated in dollars. The price of the dollar rose enormously – far more than anybody had expected. During the crisis, when the exchange rate was at its peak, even a blue-chip company such as the Siam Cement group became technically insolvent. In fact, the balance sheets of almost all the major companies were askew, because these companies had the easiest access to dollar loans, some through their Thai banks, some directly contracted with foreign banks, and some through both channels. Only a small minority of firms hedged their dollar loans.

The high level of non-performing loans was thus inevitable. Unfortunately, resolution of these debts is turning out to be very difficult and time-consuming, largely because of poor legal infrastructure and incentive incompatibility among key actors.

Debt workouts

Decades of continuous growth before 1997 meant that the problems posed by the bankruptcy of firms were never serious enough to warrant a close examination of Thai bankruptcy laws. Never modern to begin with, they had become increasingly irrelevant over time. There was only one option for creditors faced with an insolvent debtor – liquidation. For troubled companies, this would mean a mutually unprofitable race for the remaining assets. This was no doubt a wasteful way of handling bad debts, but while such companies constituted a small portion of the economy, no one thought of changing it.

Worse than the bankruptcy laws were the foreclosure procedures – an important consideration, given the important role that collateral played in Thai banking. It could take from three to five years to foreclose on a mortgage. Again, in the era of high growth, this created little problem, because the carrying cost caused by the delay would be partly, and sometimes more than, compensated by the appreciation of the land price. With the onset of serious corporate insolvency problems, reforms became necessary. These were undertaken with the enactment of wide-ranging legislation that instituted Chapter 11-type procedures, as an alternative to liquidation for insolvent firms. Foreclosure procedures were also made more rapid.

In addition to these judicial procedures, lenders and borrowers had another option with the establishment of the Corporate Debt Restructuring Advisory Committee (CDRAC) under an agreement signed by the Thai and foreign bankers' associations, the Association of Finance Companies, the Federation of Thai Industries and the Board of Trade. The Bank of Thailand provides the secretariat and acts as a facilitator for CDRAC. The CDRAC process entailed a prior agreement among lending institutions (its members) to abide by certain rules in their negotiations with debtors. For example, they agree not to seek recourse to the Bankruptcy Courts until the avenue of negotiations within CDRAC, with its strict time frame, is closed.

The CDRAC process is similar to a Chapter 11 proceeding, with some exceptions. Because it is based on a voluntary agreement among creditors, the majorities required for the CDRAC process to take effect are larger than in the new bankruptcy law. In any case, the agreement reached through this process would ultimately have to be ratified by the court in order to bring the dissenting creditors into line. As it is a quasi-policy body and not a judicial one, it could – and did – negotiate with the tax authorities to change tax rules for transactions within the framework of a CDRAC agreement. As it is more flexible than the Bankruptcy Court, CDRAC has become the preferred venue for debt negotiations, and has had some success in restructuring debt.

The process was not easy. Like bankruptcy proceedings everywhere, it faces the problem that creditors' incentives differ greatly among themselves as well as with those of the debtor. In addition to the usual conflict between secured and unsecured creditors, the financial institutions' incentives to write off debts also differ greatly, as will be discussed below.

This issue has broader macroeconomic implications, which warrant elaboration.

In a crisis arising from overinvestment, the book values of many firms' assets and net worth would have to be written down. Where such reductions threaten the solvency of the firms, reductions on the liabilities side of the balance sheet must also take place to accommodate reductions on the asset side.[6] All bankruptcy proceedings and the CDRAC process entail negotiations to that end. The aim is to ensure that the collection of assets that together form the company can again function as a unit and yield a return that is compatible with its new value. The process of writing down the assets and liabilities of the debtor company should be as speedy as possible, so that the firm can continue business without the disruption caused by a credit constraint. If too many companies are stuck in the limbo of debt renegotiations for too long, macroeconomic recovery from the crisis may be delayed or even put in jeopardy.

Certain peculiarities of Thai business practice as well as the nature of the crisis and the recapitalization rules introduced by the government combine to slow this process considerably. The first problem is with respect to the shareholders of the debtor firms. In advanced countries, this normally causes the least trouble. When a reduction in the value of assets and liabilities becomes necessary, it is customary that the shareholders' interest takes the first cut. When the shareholders' equity is reduced to zero, this means their ejection from the company. In Thailand, nearly all companies are family-owned and managed. To eject the owners would raise many problems for the creditors, as they would lose the management as well, thereby losing part of the value of the company. The creditors' bargaining power, vis-à-vis the owners of the debtor firms, is therefore less than in Western companies, where management is usually separate from the owners and can continue functioning independently of them.

Turning now to the creditors, we find different types of financial institutions facing different incentives, and a willingness to conclude deals with their debtors. Most foreign banks do not lend on collateral, but on the basis of cash flow. This method means that foreign banks have less NPL problems to begin with. In addition, when problems do arise, they have a greater understanding of their clients' business prospects. They have been far readier to write down problem loans where necessary. Ironically, despite their reputation for close connections with their customers, Thai banks turned out to be much less understanding of their customers' prospects and problems both before and after the crisis hit them.

Thai banks also had to recapitalize, so taking losses on the value of the debt would mean a much greater burden. Hence, their preference for rescheduling rather than write-offs. But rescheduling is insufficient to put the affected companies on a solid financial footing, and re-enable them to move aggressively in their markets. Worse, because in many cases, minimizing write-offs means that the residual earnings kept by the firms are also minimal. These firms are therefore extremely vulnerable to any adverse changes in their environment, for example, an increase in the interest rate. If this happens, the debts will have to be renegotiated all over again, and the recovery would be jeopardized. Above all, it means that firms' balance sheets remain fragile and access to new capital for future investments is limited.

Table 2.1 shows the achievements of the restructuring, both through the CDRAC process and through various alternative mechanisms, including bilateral negotiations, as of late 1999, the different incentives led to different results. Thai private banks managed to restructure 66.1 per cent of the value of the total, when their share of the NPLs on the books was only 46.1 per cent. This may suggest their greater willingness to negotiate. In fact, they chose the easier route by rescheduling the debts. State-owned banks performed poorly. Their managers are subject to government regulations that hold them (as public employees) liable for any decision that entails loss of public money. They have thus been excessively rigid in renegotiating their loans. The figure for foreign full branch banks in Table 2.1 does not represent those of all foreign banks, most of which have merely a representative or a BIBF office. It does, however, reflect their behaviour, that is the greater willingness to remove the NPLs from the books. Not visible from these figures is their greater willingness to write off rather than to reschedule the debts.[7]

Working out the debt problems of a company requires a projection of economic trends so as to assess the firm's future earning capacity. The

Table 2.1 Total loans outstanding, non-performing loans and restructured debts, classified by types of financial institutions, end of October 1999

Types of financial institutions	Total loans outstanding	Non-performing loans	Restructured debts
	Billions of baht		
Private bank	2,984.72	1,132.84	546.08
State-owned banks	1,744.50	1,138.55	174.04
Foreign full branch banks	687.04	78.89	61.44
Finance companies	188.65	105.84	45.18
Total financial institutions	5,604.90	2,456.12	826.73
	Per cent		
Private bank	53.25	46.12	66.05
State-owned banks	31.10	46.36	21.05
Foreign full branch banks	12.26	3.21	7.43
Finance companies	3.37	4.31	5.46
Total financial institutions	99.98	100.00	100.00

Source: Bank of Thailand.

economic trend can be thought of as given, as long as we confine our attention to the firm level. I have argued above that the future trend of the economy is itself a function of how quickly the debt problem is resolved for the corporate sector as a whole. The Thai approach has been conservative, with the problems being resolved largely by the debtors and creditors themselves and the government involved only marginally in securing favourable tax treatment for the debt transfers.

This strategy has led to a period of trench warfare, which will continue for some time. The alternative could have been one of blitzkrieg. The government could have bought out and managed the non-performing loans from the banks, allowing the banks to get on with the business of generating new loans for new investments. Arguably, growth would have resumed faster and the recovery rate on the NPLs would have been better under the blitzkrieg approach.

Adopting such an approach in Thailand would be risky, and, from a polit- ical point of view, difficult. Sales by the FRA of the assets of the 56 defunct finance companies (which included loans that were still performing) had given a very low yield of only a quarter of their face value. Admittedly, this low yield was predicated upon the assumption of low or negative growth. For the finance minister to adopt the blitzkrieg approach would have involved an estimate of the incremental yield from the resulting higher growth (which also had to be guessed). Given the large uncertainties involved, the charac- teristically conservative approach of Thai officialdom triumphed.

The future of bank-based capitalism in Thailand

In the past, Thai banks had been phenomenally successful in gathering savings, and investing them productively. Thais apparently trusted these institutions, as shown by the high M2/GNP ratio compared with other developing countries (Table 2.2).

Consequently, banks occupied the dominant role in the economy, and played a central role in channelling savings to firms. In investing these savings, the banks relied on a close relationship of mutual trust with their clients, to the point where banking families had acquired equity interest in many of their clients' businesses. Insider lending was thus quite wide- spread. At the same time, banks performed the important task of coordinating investment by firms. In this respect, their importance sub- stantially overshadowed that of government agencies. By relying on tradi- tional methods of lending, Thai banks tended to eschew modern (that is, Western) reliance on financial analysis and risk management. While growth was strong, such alien techniques appeared unnecessary. Such tried and tested methods of mobilizing capital had worked over the course of three decades. Companies had expanded, and the economy had grown at more than 7 per cent throughout this period.

Table 2.2 Ratios of money and quasi-money (M2) to
GNP in selected countries, end of 1996

Chile	0.41
Korea, Republic of	0.2
Malaysia	0.93
Mexico	0.28
Thailand	0.81
Turkey	0.32
Japan	1.12
United Kingdom	1.09
United States	0.59

Source: International Monetary Fund, International Financial
Statistics, 1997.

Note:
Turkey's figure is for 1995.

When foreign money began pouring in, in large quantities in the
1990s, the delicate nexus joining lenders and borrowers began to unravel.
With access to rival sources of credit, corporate clients were no longer
captive to the banks. When the crash came and companies' debt had to be
restructured, it was revealed that many of them had a very large number
of creditors. The largest problem company, the Thai Petrochemical Industries Company (TPI), with debts of close to 100 billion baht, had 140 creditors from among the financial institutions. A much smaller debtor, with
only 3 billion baht of debts, had 29 creditors.

Both local and foreign banks and the corporate borrowers appeared to
settle on the use of short-term credit to finance much of their investment.
The banks were further encouraged in this practice by the rules on capital
requirements (taken from the Bank for International Settlements) that
class short-term loans as less risky and therefore requiring less capital to
cover the risks. While banks could thus get clear of the problem of maturity mismatch – they obtained short-term funds and lent short-term – their
customers did not. They were borrowing short-term and investing in
longer-term projects. But no one appeared concerned, least of all the borrowers. The heady atmosphere of the bubble assured them that they could
easily refinance their loans.

The Thai authorities did not ignore the need for a market for long-
term risk capital. The equity market was developed and encouraged to
grow during the 1980s and the 1990s with that segment in view. The
outcome of that development has been to draw in individual investors,
mostly from the growing Thai middle class, rather than the institutional
investors based on life insurance companies or pension funds, for
example. The problem with relying on individual investors to power the
equity market is that monitoring of corporate officers has been less than

satisfactory, a problem compounded by the lack of protection afforded to minority shareholders against majority family interests.

The crisis probably means the end of traditional Thai-style capitalism. Resuscitating the past is not among the options available. With the devastation wreaked on the capitalist class as a whole, it is clear that the banks, at the very least, will begin to look distinctly different from now on. The multinational presence in the financial sector will be much more strongly felt than before. More significantly than would be implied by their share of the market, they will be the standard-setter for banking practices. And with a different banking culture, practices that were once taken for granted among borrowing corporations will have to give way to something different. What form that will take, no one can foresee. What can be predicted is that, because the changes required would be institutional and even cultural, the process will take time. Meanwhile the saving–investment nexus will remain frayed and this is yet another reason why growth will be stunted.

The currency market

I have suggested that, by the middle of the 1990s, Thai economic growth was increasingly based on self-fulfilling expectations, and its tie with the fundamentals justifying such growth was becoming increasingly tenuous. By 1996, the assumptions on which growth was premised were being exposed as false one by one. The problems with the financial system have already been discussed. In the foreign sector, export growth rates fell dramatically in mid-1996 from a level in the upper teens to a negative level. The cause of this collapse is still not understood. It is natural, particularly for economists, to link this decline to the misaligned exchange rate, in particular to the rise in real effective exchange rate, consequent on the higher inflation rate relative to other countries. I shall return to the issue of real exchange rates as indicators of disequilibria in the goods markets. Other forces, however, appeared to be at work in 1997, and had a larger impact on the currency markets than the goods market disequilibria.

Indeed, the emphasis on the current account was misplaced. With capital account liberalization, movements of capital have become the dominant factor in the balance of payments. Expectations play a major role in these movements and, to that extent, export competitiveness matters only inasmuch as it affects expectations. But export competitiveness was only one among many influences on expectations. At least of equal importance is the state of the Thai financial institutions, discussed earlier. From the currency market's point of view, these problems increased the probability that the contingent liabilities of the government would become actual liabilities. Although deposits in financial institutions were not explicitly insured by the government, past practice and political considerations suggested that, should these institutions fail, the government would not stand idle and let depositors take the fall. These contingent liabilities of the government began to cause concern in the market, and may have been a contributing factor in the speculative attacks on the baht.[8]

In addition to these underlying weaknesses, Thailand's external debt situation made it particularly vulnerable to attack. Its total foreign debt at the end of 1995 was US$90.5 billion, or just under 50 per cent of GDP at the exchange rate at the time. Of this, US$37.6 billion or 42 per cent had a maturity of less than one year. Buffering against this was US$38.7 billion in gross official reserves, which would be adequate in normal times, but could not withstand serious capital flight.

These weak fundamentals were sufficient to trigger waves of speculative attacks against the baht. It is important to recognize that, while Thailand was vulnerable to sudden capital withdrawals because of the large amounts of short-term debt, it was not the lenders who were heading for the exit door in the beginning. Indeed, capital inflows remained positive throughout the entire first half of 1997, although the rate of inflow began to ebb markedly in the second quarter. It was only in the third quarter that the outflow became substantial (Table 2.3). The outflow of most of the capital account items was small and could be handled with adequate foreign currency reserves at the beginning of the year.[9] In the end, the collapse of the baht came about because of speculation by parties who originally did not hold any position in Thai assets. This activity was only partially recorded in the balance of payments accounts.

Imagine a foreign speculator as he surveyed the problems of the Thai economy at the end of 1996. It did not require particular astuteness to realize that asset prices were considerably misaligned. The prices of land, property, and stocks were well above what was justified by their future returns, particularly now that growth could no longer be assumed to be automatic. Even the value of deposits in some financial institutions would be less than their face value, if proper consideration were given to the assets backing these deposits. For the speculator, such expectations, verging on certain knowledge, could in theory be converted into profit.

But there is a problem in the working of the asset markets. When an asset price is expected to rise, profit can be made by buying the asset and waiting until the price actually rises. On the other hand, when the asset price is falling, the matter is more complicated. Here, profit can only be made by short-selling the asset. Now, short sales are possible only in very few markets. The one important market where short sales can be easily made is the currency market.

Thus, the only way our foreign speculator could make a profit in Thailand was to short-sell the baht. It is thus not surprising that, beginning in

Table 2.3 Current account and net flows of private financial account, 1996 to 1999

Year/ Quarter	Current account balance	Bank		Non-bank							Total
		Commercial banks	of which recapitalization	BIBFs	Direct investment	Other loans	Portfolio investment	Non-resident baht accounts	Trade credits	Others	
1996											
Q1	−86,365	−58,704	n.a.	44,206	12,277	23,291	28,742	93,466	2,760	303	146,341
Q2	−123,667	14,914	n.a.	47,888	7,778	44,424	23,037	5,281	639	62	144,023
Q3	−91,884	42,050	n.a.	3,665	8,625	42,571	21,017	−30,437	−5,520	53	82,024
Q4	−70,243	12,583	n.a.	20,169	8,143	27,736	15,446	5,454	−1,581	217	88,167
1997											
Q1	−54,268	39,132	n.a.	22,086	13,649	−2,971	13,191	−43,773	6,523	−1,723	46,114
Q2	−81,178	−7,054	n.a.	7,989	14,707	−21,881	31,775	−46,583	−1,766	335	−22,478
Q3	−23,024	−146,919	n.a.	−44,152	37,798	−28,266	78,246	−127,196	438	7,575	−222,476
Q4	118,163	−61,795	n.a.	−62,313	39,112	−80,107	15,768	61,277	−17,874	3,281	−102,651
1998											
Q1	196,988	29,329	39,444	−98,700	47,866	−96,661	21,037	−102,971	−8,733	8,093	−200,740
Q2	112,836	−70,811	46,313	−85,762	59,721	−32,575	1,914	45,944	−3,712	−2,111	−87,392
Q3.p	139,798	−100,350	0	−79,450	49,996	−30,257	−696	32,375	−6,557	6,550	−128,390
Q4.p	142,461	−26,515	0	−128,496	35,962	−25,210	2,286	−90,782	−2,106	−1,554	−236,415
1999											
Q1.e	127,083	−125,372	783	−71,189	33,514	−45,934	8,196	−11,675	67	−1,350	−213,744

Source: Bank of Thailand

November 1996, three waves of attacks (the other two were in February and May 1997) were made against the baht, in the expectation that the central bank would be forced to devalue it. The original baht currency used by the speculators to mount their attacks was acquired by short-selling stocks, by borrowing in the local inter-bank markets and, more importantly, by borrowing in the offshore baht market, and by drawing down on the non-resident baht accounts. However, these were basically used to prime the speculative pump. As the attacks continued, much of the baht was actually supplied by the Bank of Thailand because of the method it was using to defend the currency.

In addition to buying baht for dollars from the speculators, the Bank would engage in a 'swap'. In the swap transaction, it would sell baht for the dollars in the spot market in exchange for a forward purchase of baht for dollars. These transactions, in effect, allowed the Bank to postpone the release of the dollar reserves. From the point of view of the Bank, the swap had two attractions. First, because it was considered 'off-balance-sheet', the loss of reserves was hidden from the markets and from the public. Second, another means by which the market could have become aware of the size of the attacks was by its impact on the money market. Without the swap transactions, as more and more baht were withdrawn from the market and sold to the Bank of Thailand, interest rates would climb. By engaging in the swap operation (remember that this entails sale of baht in the current period), the Bank would sterilize the speculators' sales of baht and thus lessen the impact on interest rates. The downside of this operation, of course, was that the speculators were able to obtain fresh supplies of baht continuously from the spot sales by the Bank during the swap transaction (Nukul Commission 1998, paras. 105–117).

The fiercest attacks came in May 1997. On 14 May it lost US$10 billion in 24 hours. Within days, the Bank had almost run out of net reserves, which had stood at US$33.8 billion at the beginning of 1997, although this fact was not known at the time, because only gross reserve figures are reported. It barely avoided devaluing the baht then, but only by sharply reversing the policy of opening the foreign exchange market that it had been conscientiously following for the previous decade. It told Thai commercial banks to stop loans to non-residents. This sharply curtailed the flow of baht overseas, and caught those who short-sold the baht in a squeeze. A gap arose in the baht exchange rates onshore and offshore, with the latter commanding a premium of as much as 10 per cent at times.

This closing-off of the flow of baht overseas was undertaken too late, and extended the life of the old baht exchange rate by only six weeks. In June, the problems of the baht worsened. This time it was a run by the Thais themselves, not by outside speculators. Finally, on 2 July, the baht was floated, whereupon its value deteriorated, slowly at first, but then, as other countries joined Thailand in allowing their currencies to depreciate, sharply, particularly between November 1997 and January 1998. This rapid depreciation was caused primarily by a sudden exodus of money (Table 2.3), which previously had flowed so easily into the country. The motive behind this exodus was panic, fed in part by the revelation in August 1997 of the extent of the swap commitments of the central bank, in part by the spread of the crisis throughout Asia, and in part by the rapidly collapsing financial system.

In January 1998, the exchange rate reversed itself, and has settled at a level around 37–40 baht to the dollar from April 1998 onwards. At that point, the nominal effective exchange rate vis-à-vis trading partners stood at a level 40 per cent above that in June 1997 and fluctuated in the range between 35 and 40 per cent. The nominal rate vis-à-vis Thailand's competitors had increased by 20 per cent.

After April 1998, stability returned to the currency markets. Foreign lenders' rush to withdraw credit appeared to have ceased. Although the capital account still remained in substantial deficit (Table 2.3), this was mostly due to the repayment of loans by the larger banks wishing to take advantage of the lower domestic interest rates. Throughout the post-float period, the Bank of Thailand has constantly claimed (with one exception[10]) that it allows the baht to float freely without any intervention. The Bank, however, had one policy instrument at its disposal – the pace with which it unwound the vast swap positions built up when it was defending the baht peg, and of its build-up of reserves. Each transaction to this end was no doubt timed with an eye towards maintaining exchange rate stability.

There is now, if anything, a danger that exchange rates may have become too stable, leading to built-in expectations of further stability, which, if disappointed, will again lead a disastrous surge in volatility as occurred in 1997–98.

The real sector

Before the crash in 1997, there were two disequilibria in the real sector. The first was in the property sector, which I have already discussed. The second, less obvious disequilibrium, arose out of overinvestment in the manufacturing sector, particularly that part which supplied the export trade. The problem made itself felt in the sudden drop in exports in 1996. At that time the causes of this drop were shrouded in some mystery.

Dasgupta and Imai (1998) and the World Bank (1998) have since thrown light on this matter by looking at the problem in some detail, within an East-Asia-wide framework. This broader framework is essential because the export slowdown was not confined to Thailand, but extends to nearly all countries in East Asia. They attributed the reasons for the decline to the following facts.

- World trade in nominal dollar terms and in real terms fell in 1996 owing to the appreciation of the dollar.
- Japanese growth, which used to be the main engine of East Asian growth, was sluggish.
- The prices of major East Asian exports declined.

Of these, the first two suggest a cyclical phenomenon. In the case of the first, it is of interest that, since 1990, Asian trade volumes had finally begun responding to world trade cycles, whereas, in the past, they have ridden above the world cycles. The decline of export prices, however, reflects something that may not disappear easily.

The World Bank study (1998, p. 21) cites data from US import prices, which show that prices were falling for a wide spectrum of manufactured goods. When classified by sources of goods, import prices for the United States for goods from the Asian newly industrialized economies fell more deeply than those from other sources, suggesting that Asians were concentrating on the 'wrong' products to sell. The same study shows that the decline in the prices of electronic equipment and computer equipment – items on which the Asians were concentrating – was the sharpest. But other prices were falling as well, such as machinery, transport equipment and electrical machinery, though not as sharply. In addition, throughout 1996–97, *The Asian Wall Street Journal* reported on various studies that forecast impending excess capacity in a number of industries, such as petrochemicals, automotive and steel, based on projections of the growth rates as expected before the crisis hit Asia.

The changes in relative prices described above are Asia-wide. The impact on Thailand of these developments can be first seen in the changes in Thailand's real exchange rates. Three different concepts of the real exchange rate are used here. Figure 2.2 shows the first of these, the ratio of the prices of traded goods to non-traded goods (this ratio will henceforth be abbreviated to TNT). The method used to recalculate and update this set of data is as in Warr and Bhanupong (1996). This ratio has shown a steady decline from 1988 until 1997. The implied real value of the baht rose by as much as 50 per cent (TNT has fallen by a third) from 1988 to the eve of the baht flotation on 2 July 1997. It could be argued that the fall in the real exchange rate is due to the secular growth of the economy, pushing TNT downward (see Bhagwati, 1984, and the literature cited therein). But the demand pressure brought about by the bubble and induced by the capital inflow was at least partially responsible. In the case of non-tradables, this extra demand cannot find release through trade, causing their prices relative to tradables to shift upwards.

However, the rise in the prices of non-tradables also reflected a rapid rise in wages (discussed below). The consequence of this increase was a decline in the competitiveness of the more labour-intensive sectors. Thus,

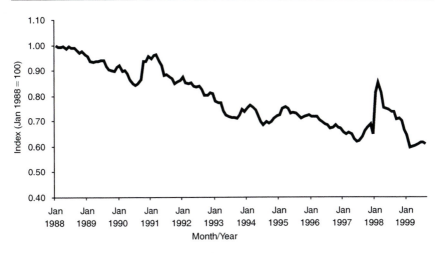

Figure 2.2 Relative prices of traded to non-traded goods January 1988 to August 1999 (source: data from Warr and Bhanupong (1996) and Ministry of Commerce).

1996 saw sharp declines in the exports of garments (21.9 per cent relative to 1995), footwear (40.9 per cent) and textiles (4.4 per cent) (Warr 1999).

Figure 2.3 shows two real effective exchange rates (REER), one vis-à-vis trading partners, and the other vis-à-vis trade competitors.[11] The list and the weights for countries considered as Thailand's competitors (all of whom are in Asia) are from Mathinee (1999), although the calculation of the results reported in Figure 2.3 is mine. The results for the pegged exchange rate period are dramatically different from the results for

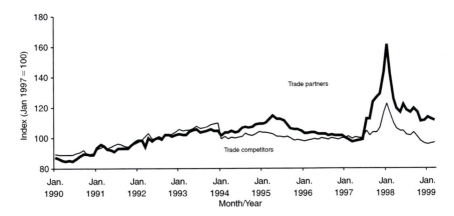

Figure 2.3 Real effective exchange rate vis-à-vis trade partners and trade competitors, 1990 to 1999 (source: data from Bank of Thailand).

TNT.[12] Until 1995, the baht was actually depreciating in real terms, but thereafter it appreciated until the float in mid-1997. With respect to Thailand's competitors, the results are similar, at least for the period before 1994. The sharp appreciation of the REER vis-à-vis competitors at the beginning of 1994 reflected the 'depreciation' of the yuan.[13]

Incidentally, the data on REER are significant for the exchange rate policies discussed earlier. The Bank of Thailand's decision to defend the baht in 1996 and 1997 at the then current peg was based partly on its calculations of the REER against trading partners (Nukul Commission 1998, paragraph 24). These data, which do not show an overwhelming case in favour of a devaluation of the baht, led the Bank to pursue its policy of resistance.

After the crisis, domestic demand in Thailand fell sharply, as can be expected when a country that had been running an 8 per cent current account deficit was suddenly forced to run a 12 per cent current account surplus by the massive capital exodus.

Because the crisis was Asia-wide and not confined to Thailand, the export growth that had been expected in the wake of the baht depreciation did not materialize. Other Asian countries went through similar experiences, and therefore added to one another's decline, feeding through a multiplier process which resulted in severe economic declines for all.

Figure 2.4 indicates monthly figures for the non-food manufacturing production index (MPI) from the beginning of 1997 onwards, and Figure 2.5 indicates quarterly figures for non-agricultural GDP.[14] The sharp deterioration in both sets of figures can be seen. Between its peak in January 1997 and the same month one year later, the non-food MPI declined by 23 per cent. Between the third quarter of 1997 and the same period one year later, non-agricultural GDP declined by 14 per cent. Such a decline is

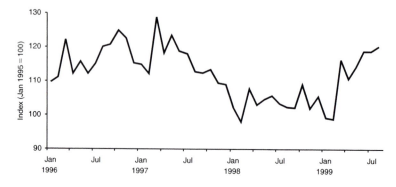

Figure 2.4 Manufacturing production index, excluding food, January 1996 to August 1999 (source: Bank of Thailand).

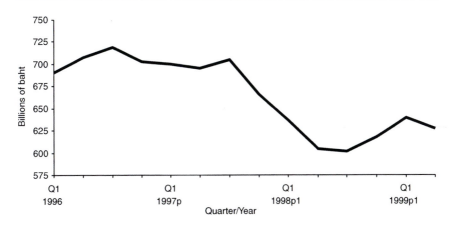

Figure 2.5 Quarterly non-agricultural GDP, 1996Q1 to 1999Q2 (1998 = 100) (source: Data from National Economic and Social Development Board).

unprecedented in the postwar economic history of Thailand, and is largely responsible for the sorry state of the financial system.

The biggest surprise from the crisis, apart from its severity, is the low level of price inflation following the strong depreciation of the baht. Explaining the moderate level of inflation is, of course, the massive fall in output and the consequent excess capacity. This moderate level of price inflation has meant that REER should have increased considerably. Ignoring the spike at the end of 1997 and beginning of 1998, the REER vis-à-vis trading partners (shown in Figure 2.3 above), only increased by 15–20 per cent. Of even greater significance, however, is the finding that the REER vis-à-vis competitors has reverted to the pre-devaluation level, suggesting that Thailand, probably along with its Asian neighbours, faced very severe competitive pressure in selling its goods overseas. It is for this reason that, in 1998 and early 1999, despite the depreciation of the baht and the presence of excess capacity at home, the dollar value of exports showed little movement relative to the previous year, even though there was a strong improvement in the quantity exported.

Figures 2.4 and 2.5 show that output stopped falling in the third quarter of 1998 and appears to have begun recovering at the beginning of 1999. There are also signs that the rate of recovery is quite slow compared with the earlier rate of decline. Just why the recovery took place has not yet been well studied and documented. The policy of rapid fiscal loosening and rapid expansion of the government deficit is usually cited (by the government itself) as the reasons for the recovery. But, as will be discussed below, there are grounds to dispute this claim. Since the beginning of 2000, there has also been a strong export recovery, which contributed to the general recovery of the Thai economy. This has been spurred by strong growth in other countries affected by the East Asian crisis.

The labour market

The labour market was very tight during the bubble, and may have played a role in its bursting. Wages were rising very rapidly, reducing the competitiveness of the more labour-intensive sectors, such as textiles and footwear (Warr 1999). At the time, the wage increase and falling competitiveness of certain sectors were thought to be a normal part of the process of development, but the sectoral shifts that were taking place may have been premature and a direct consequence of the bubble. Thus, the supposedly cheap foreign loans that were readily available during the bubble led to heavy investments in capital-intensive industries, such as petrochemicals, refining, automotives and steel.

For the Thai labour force, such investments required improved quality as well. In the past, Thailand had been a notorious laggard in human capital investment, with a secondary school enrolment ratio lower than even its poorer ASEAN neighbours, such as Indonesia and the Philippines. While the Thai public education system did successfully increase enrolments at levels higher than primary, the labour force itself is still burdened with large numbers of older people educated only at the primary level. Consequently, wage differentials for people with different levels of education increased significantly during the bubble. My calculations from the labour force survey data indicate that, between 1990–97, real wages for university graduates increased at an annual rate of 7.0 per cent, while those of secondary school graduates and lower increased at only 4.6 per cent.

Unemployment in Thailand has traditionally been low. In August, in the middle of the agricultural season, this would amount to less than 2 per cent of the labour force. In February, an additional 2–4 per cent of the men and 6–8 per cent of the women would become seasonally unemployed. Altogether, seasonally unemployed workers amount to about 1 million persons. As there was no major change in what the labour force surveys record as seasonal unemployment,[15] we shall exclude this group from the discussion. Nevertheless, even with this exclusion, one should still expect the remaining numbers to be influenced by the seasonal component.

The three panels in Figure 2.6 report changes in unemployment and underemployment during the last years of the bubble and the crisis period. Because the term 'unemployment' is defined very restrictively in the labour force surveys (a person is deemed to be unemployed only if he or she has not worked at all during the week preceding the survey), I have included data on the severely and moderately underemployed. People are

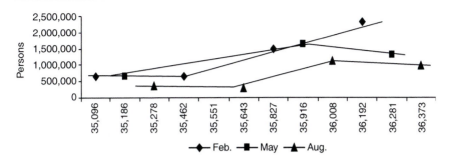

Figure 2.6a Unemployed persons (excluding seasonal) 1996 to 1999 (source: Labour Force Survey data tapes, National Statistical Office).

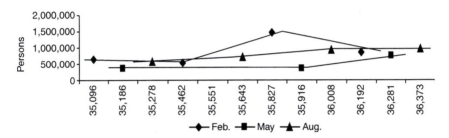

Figure 2.6b Severly underemployed persons 1996 to 1999 (source: Labour Force Survey data tapes, National Statistical Office).

Note:
Severely underemployed means that the workers work less than 20 hours per week.

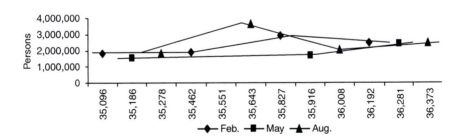

Figure 2.6c Moderately underemployed persons 1996 to 1999 (source: Labour Force Survey data tapes, National Statistical Office).

Note:
Moderately underemployed means that the workers work 20–34 hours per week.

deemed to be severely underemployed if they work less than 20 hours a week, and moderately underemployed if they work between 20 and 34 hours a week. Those working more than 35 hours a week are considered fully employed.[16]

The data clearly show a rapid rise in unemployment. This is particularly noticeable in the February 1998 figure, but probably started in the last quarter of 1997, during which, unfortunately, the National Statistical Office (NSO) did not conduct a labour force survey.[17] Unemployment rose dramatically through 1998, continuing until February 1999, although the continued rapid rise in that month was mostly among women. Then, following May 1999, there was some – but not much – improvement in the unemployment picture.

The data for underemployment showed a slight trend upward over the entire period, although this was interrupted by a spike in the immediate aftermath of the crisis, which continued until the beginning of 1999. These data suggest that, initially, employers reduced workers' hours and later were compelled to dismiss these workers. Anticipation of an increase in the severance pay rates, which was due in August 1998, caused the employers to start dismissing workers in the first half of 1998, reducing the level of underemployment in the second half of the year.

This kind of unemployment is unprecedented in Thailand, although, at its peak in February 1999, it totalled 'only' 4.1 per cent of the labour force. For countries with a functioning unemployment insurance system, this figure may not appear high, but Thailand does not have such a system. In its place it does have, for workers in the formal sector, a rather generous severance pay system – before August 1998, workers who had worked for an employer for at least three years had a right to six months' pay from the employers. After 1998, this rate was made higher, on a sliding scale according to the length of employment.

The lack of unemployment insurance and, more generally, of a publicly financed social safety net system has now been isolated by the government and the multilateral lending agencies as a major shortcoming of the Thai economic system. In the past, it was claimed that the economy's strength has been its resilience, and that resilience has rested on the flexibility of the labour market in particular. When the crisis developed, it was widely hoped that the agricultural sector would act as a shock absorber. This hope was not unreasonable in view of the fact that the overwhelming proportion of the industrial workers were first-generation, had just left their rural homes and could resume rural employment relatively easily.

There were two assumptions implicit in this belief – that the workers would return and that there would be employment prospects in agriculture. The first was true, but the second turned out to be unrealistic. Agricultural employment was disappointingly unresponsive. Before reporting the figures for agricultural employment, I need to point out that the first impact of the crisis was a dramatic rise in crop prices when the 1997 harvest came in at the end of the year, mostly as a result of the sharp spike in the exchange rate. Agricultural activity in 1998 was therefore quite high. By the end of 1998, agricultural prices were again falling worldwide, and the exchange rate had come down again, so that the brief respite at the end of 1997 quickly came to an end.

Between August 1997 and August 1998, male employment in agriculture went up by less than a quarter of a million, from 8.31 to 8.54 million, but female employment fell by half a million, from 7.23 to 6.74 million, leading to a fall in total agricultural employment of about 220,000 (Table 2.4). Roughly the same was true for the dry season. This was particularly disappointing in that the sector hardest hit by the crisis was construction, which shed 980,000 (45 per cent) of its workers between February 1997 and February 1998 and 720,000 workers between August 1997 and August 1998. Traditionally, employment in this sector, being largely in the dry season, dovetailed nicely with agricultural employment. Its collapse has thus affected rural incomes adversely.

The recovery of agricultural employment in February 1999 proved short-lived, and August 1999 showed a resumption of the decline, this time with male employment also falling by as much as 400,000. As the workers from urban areas returned, and employment in the rural sector proved inadequate to absorb the influx, rural unemployment increased. This increase was particularly severe in the Northeast, the traditional exporter of labour within Thailand, with the unemployment rate there rising as high as 8.1 per cent (Ammar and Orapin 1998). Overall employment had not regained its pre-crisis level by August 1999.

The full consequences of the crisis on the incomes of rural households

Table 2.4 Employed persons by industry 1995 to 1999 (thousands)

	1995	1996	1997	1998	1999
February					
Employed persons by industry	29,055	30,099	30,266	29,413	30,025
Agriculture	11,849	12,146	11,938	11,640	12,553
Industry (excl. construction)	5,098	5,188	5,229	5,174	5,100
Construction	2,649	3,125	2,984	2,042	1,560
Services	9,460	9,639	10,116	10,557	10,812
August					
Employed persons by industry	32,575	32,232	33,162	32,138	32,087
Agriculture	16,929	16,127	16,691	16,472	15,564
Industry (excl. construction)	4,591	4,524	4,517	4,408	4,605
Construction	1,846	2,172	2,021	1,280	1,286
Services	9,209	9,409	9,933	9,979	10,633

Source: National Statistical Office, Labour Force Survey, data tapes.

are not fully known. Estimates indicate that the incidence of poverty increased from 6.8 to 7.9 million between 1996–98. In percentage terms it increased from 11.4 to 12.9 per cent. Given the severity of the crisis, the increase observed must be considered relatively mild.

There are many plausible reasons for this. First, analysis of the labour force surveys shows that the wage differential between the more highly educated and the less educated appears to have narrowed after the crisis. Nominal wages among the males in the educated group fell by about 6–8 per cent between August 1997 and August 1998, and by about 4–7 per cent among females. Among the less educated, the fall was less than 2 per cent. The fall in nominal wages continued into August 1999, at a slightly reduced rate. For some reason, the labour market seems to have provided more protection for the relatively worse off.

Second, one should bear in mind that the SES, which generated the poverty figures, was collected in 1998, but with questions that asked for incomes partially back to 1997. Now, at the end of 1997 and the beginning of 1998, rural households, which include most of the poor, were benefiting from the windfall brought about by a rapidly depreciating baht, which in turn caused agricultural commodity prices to rise rapidly. That windfall subsequently disappeared.

It seems that, helped by factors such as the rise in commodity prices, rural households could draw on their reserves throughout much of 1998. However, anecdotal evidence indicates that the slowness of the recovery in employment may have added to the strain on poor households in 1999.

Stabilization strategy

Thailand entered the International Monetary Fund programme in August 1997, having just floated the baht after a very costly defence, and concurrently experiencing a financial meltdown of massive proportions. It obtained loans totalling US$17 billion from myriad sources.[18] Both the government and the Fund perceived the primary task to be the restoration of confidence, to put a stop on the massive capital flight that began in the wake of the devaluation and continued through the rest of the year and much of 1998.

Faulty policy strategies were in place prior to the full emergence of the crisis in July 1997, most notably the failure to follow a sufficiently stringent fiscal policy to sop up the excess demand arising from the large capital inflows between 1994–97. As 1997 began, a fall in government revenue presaged the emergence of the full-blown crisis. Year-on-year growth in government revenues turned negative, at which point the government began to make the first moves to contain expenditure in order to maintain its fiscal balance. As government revenues continued to fall, further cuts were made, with the same objective in mind, consistent with the dictum that, with a fixed exchange rate, fiscal policy is the more efficient means to contain an overheated economy.

After Thailand floated its currency and entered into the IMF programme, however, the policy of fiscal austerity continued. The Fund demanded tax increases and reductions in state enterprise investments in order to achieve a surplus of 1 per cent in the consolidated public sector account. It was expected that this surplus would provide a 'full offset to estimated implicit financial restructuring costs in 1997/98'.

As well as the series of measures on the fiscal side, the government was also to follow a stringent monetary policy, primarily in order to stabilize the exchange rate. The broad money aggregate M2A (M2 plus deposits with finance companies) was not to expand by more than 7 per cent (compared with 18 per cent in 1994 and 1995 and 12 per cent in 1996).

As outlined in the memorandum attached to the first letter of intent, the primary task of the earlier measures was to restore stability and confidence. 'The package is focused on upfront measures that are expected to restore confidence early, stabilize the currency, stem capital outflows, and strengthen the financial system'. With the floating of the exchange rate, tightening monetary policy to prevent a massive drop in the value of the baht is perhaps understandable, particularly since many financial institutions and their customers were heavily exposed to dollar debts.

Tight monetary and fiscal policies were thus maintained through the end of the year. The second letter of intent (dated 25 November 1997) said that, notwithstanding the slower pace of economic activity leading to a large revenue shortfall equivalent to 2.5 per cent of GDP, 'we [that is, the Thai authorities] are determined to maintain the fiscal goal of keeping the consolidated public sector in a surplus of 1 per cent of GDP in 1997/98'. Further cuts in government expenditures were made, and some minor tax increases (involving luxury products, beer, spirits and tobacco) were implemented. Monetary policy was made even more stringent, with M2A growth to be kept at 1 per cent. (For key quantitative estimates and targets in the various letters of intent, see Table 2.5.)

The backdrop to the drafting of the second letter of intent is of some interest. Within Thailand, the Minister of Finance who signed it had just entered office after the previous Cabinet resigned, and the letter opened with the statement that the new government reconfirmed its full commitment to the programme as outlined in the first letter of intent. Unlike finance ministers under the previous government, the new one had total support from his prime minister, and also had a much clearer, if orthodox, vision of what needed to be done. Consequently, from this point of view, it is more accurate to view the programme as a joint one between the IMF and the Thai government. In addition, at the time the second letter of intent was signed, South Korea was just entering its period of crisis –

Table 2.5 Key policy variables and expected outcomes in various letters of intent, 1997 to 1999

Letter of intent no.	Date	Policy variables						Policy outcomes								
		Public sector balance			M2A growth			GDP growth			Current account			CPI inflation		
		1997	1998	1999	1997	1998	1999	1997	1998	1999	1997	1998	1999	1997	1998	1999
1	8/97	−1.5	1.0	—	7.0	11.0	—	2.5	3.5	—	−5.0	−3.0	—	7.0	8.0	—
2	11/97	−1.5	1.0	—	1.5	6.8	—	0.6	0 to 1	—	−3.9	−1.8	—	6.0	10.0	—
3	2/98	−1.5	−2.0	—	3.1	5.1	—	−0.4	−3 to −3.5	—	−2.2	3.9	—	5.6	11.6	—
4	5/98	−2.1	−3.0	—	2.1	9.0	—	−0.4	−4 to −5.5	—	−2.0	6.9	—	5.6	10.5	—
5	8/98	n.a.	−3.0	—	n.a.	n.a.	—	−0.4	−7.0	—	−2.0	10.0	—	5.6	9.2	—
6	12/98	n.a.	n.a.	—	n.a.	n.a.	—	—	−7 to −8	1.0	—	11.0	8.0	—	8.0	2.0 to 3.0
7	3/99	n.a.	n.a.	—	n.a.	n.a.	—	—	−8.0	1.0	—	12.0	9.0	—	8.0	2.0
8	9/99	−2.1	−3.0	−5.5	2.0	6.1	6.0	−1.3	−9.4	3.0 to 4.0	−2.0	12.8	9.0	5.6	8.1	0.5

Source: Various Letters of Intent.

Note:
Growth and inflation are in per cent per annum, public sector and current account balances are expressed as per cent of GDP.

the final Asian country to be subject to the contagion let loose by the floating of the baht in July.

The period between the second and third letters of intent was probably the worst in the post-crisis period. The exchange rate lurched upwards to reach 54 baht to the dollar at the end of January before stabilizing slightly. With the value of the baht dropping rapidly, interest rates soared and the economy continued to deteriorate. It is thus not surprising that the third letter of intent (dated 24 February 1998) showed the first signs of a turn-around in policy, particularly in fiscal policy. Because of a further revenue shortfall and a rise in expenditure on account of the baht depreciation, a deficit of 2 per cent instead of a 1 per cent surplus was projected. Nevertheless, 'at this juncture, a complete offset of the projected deterioration would be unnecessary ... because current account adjustment is already exceeding substantially our earlier goals'. Interestingly, no mention was made of the fiscal cost of the financial restructuring that featured so prominently in the two earlier letters of intent. Conversely, the need to achieve a comfortable current account surplus, whose attainment was now mentioned as allowing fiscal relaxation, was not explicitly stated as a reason for fiscal stringency in the earlier letters.

Deficit spending as a stabilization strategy was finally embraced in the fourth letter of intent (dated 26 May 1998). Given the stabilization of exchange rates and the reduction of interest rates, 'the immediate priority under the programme is to minimize any further decline of the economy and bring about early recovery, while sustaining stabilization gains'. Additionally, the need to strengthen the existing arrangements for the social safety net was also mentioned.

In the second half of 1998 and in 1999, the government, in its letters of intent to the IMF, continued with its policy of fiscal relaxation, expanding the size of the deficit to 6 per cent for the fiscal year October 1998– September 1999. Part of the rationale was, of course, the need to shore up the stricken economy further, but another part was the fall in interest rates, which was felt to lessen the cost of financial restructuring.

Interest rates fell from the second half of 1998 onwards because, at that point, the outward rush of foreign capital had subsided. But by then, relaxing monetary policy was futile. It did not increase investments, partly because the economy was suffering from an excess capacity, but more importantly, the financial meltdown had so devastated corporate balance sheets and so disrupted the relationship between banks and borrowers that the former had become unwilling to lend money for any project. Luckily for the banks, the government entered the market and floated large amounts of bonds, which went some way towards absorbing the rising liquidity, which would otherwise have swamped the system.

Did the International Monetary Fund and the government blunder badly in their approach to stabilizing the Thai economy? A stringent monetary policy was defensible in the immediate aftermath of the baht float with net official reserves close to zero. The very tenuous position of the baht under these circumstances demanded high interest rates to prevent a drastic outflow of money. If the baht had been allowed to sink, Thai borrowers of dollar loans would not be able to repay their debts. It must be admitted, however, that these debtors and the Thai authorities were caught in a dilemma. To prevent the baht from falling, the domestic interest rate had to be kept high, but the high interest rate was no less damaging to the Thai borrowers than the falling value of the baht. Given this choice, it would have been surprising if the Thai authorities and the IMF had escaped criticism, whatever choice they made.

On the fiscal policy side, however, the decision by the IMF and the government to run a fiscal surplus was deservedly criticized. Max Corden, one of the gentler critics had said of this fiscal policy position: 'initially the IMF went off the rails' (Corden 1999: 14). It is only fair to add that this was said in the context of an exposition of a simple Keynesian model. Corden fully recognized the complications that arise from the implementation of the Keynesian pump-priming strategy.

When exchange rates are flexible and capital mobile, the use of fiscal deficits as a pump-priming mechanism has been shown to be ineffective. Mundell (1963) points out that when the two conditions are met, any fiscal stimulus will lead to an influx of foreign capital, triggering an appreciation of the home currency. This appreciation will in turn cause a rise in imports and a fall in exports. The contractionary effect through the trade balance will exactly offset the expansionary effect of the fiscal policy. Conversely, if the government was to adopt a strategy of fiscal contraction, then the effect will be a depreciation of the home currency and an improvement in the balance of trade.

In Thailand, this analysis can only be applied bearing in mind the large capital exodus that took place in the aftermath of the baht float in July 1997. That exodus was already causing the currency to depreciate substantially, leading to an almost immediate improvement in the current account. In the beginning, this improvement in the current account was due much more to the absorption (income) effect rather than the expenditure-switching (price) effect. The sharp fall in investment owing to the capital exodus, as well as to the increase in country-risk premium, which increased domestic interest rates, was causing a sharp reduction in economic activity.

In this scenario, a fiscal surplus would, and did, reduce economic activity further. The fiscal surplus, however, had a second impact in that it would tend to depreciate the currency, particularly as the extra saving from the public sector had no other place to go but abroad given the fall in domestic investment demand. This extra depreciation can be defended on the grounds that it was necessary to improve the current account situation, but, if that were the case, it would flatly contradict the main objective of the monetary policy.

The IMF in particular has been criticized for applying the lessons of Latin America to Asia. Most Latin American crises reflected weaknesses in public finances. Their (theoretical) nature and occurrence are well captured by Krugman (1979). The Thai fiscal position in 1997, however, was quite strong – the stock of public debt was less that 15 per cent of GDP.[19] True, the looming fiscal cost of the deposit guarantee given to financial institutions may give the Thai crisis a Latin American flavour. The first two letters of intent gave this fiscalization problem as the main reason for the fiscal stringency. That problem has not hit Thailand yet, but in the meantime the stringent fiscal policy has cost the country a great deal in lost output, and indeed increased the cost of financial restructuring.

When the IMF reversed itself and agreed to the government's expansionary fiscal expansion policy, this was greeted as the point at which the IMF had learnt its lesson. However, by the time that turnaround was actually implemented in the second quarter of 1998, fiscal relaxation was probably no longer of any use. Exchange rates had stabilized. A fiscal expansion financed by direct government borrowing from abroad would lead to a currency appreciation, which would bite into export growth. Mundell's analysis shows that this cut in export growth (plus some import expansion) would exactly negate the stimulus provided by the fiscal expansion.[20]

In addition, as the increasing cost of financial sector restructuring began to loom, worsened by the economic contraction, which was partly caused by fiscal and monetary stringency, allowing larger deficits to add to the burden of future public debt was no longer appropriate.

In summary then, the fiscal stance of the IMF and the Thai government has been mistimed. In the immediate aftermath of the crisis, it should have been expansionary in order to counter the steep fall in investment and negative absorption effect of the sharp currency depreciation. Instead it was contractionary. Six to nine months later, a fiscal stimulus would have less of an impact on economic activity, adversely affect exports and add to the debt burden, yet that was the policy followed.

Using more stringent capital controls to slow down the massive capital outflow, which in the final analysis was the cause of the crisis, was never considered as an option. Given that most of the outflows after July 1997 were repatriations of short-term credit back to the lending banks, for the government to put a stop to this outflow would have smacked of a debt moratorium, or worse. Thailand may potentially have been severely punished in the currency and other markets. However, given the markets' reluctant acceptance of Dr Mahathir Mohammed's move towards capital controls in September 1998, and later admiration when the move proved successful, the Thai government's caution may well have been misplaced.

In all fairness, it has to be admitted that for Thailand to follow the capital control strategy successfully, two conditions would have been necessary. First, the measures would have needed to be well crafted and their implementation firm and decisive. Before Thailand's entry into the IMF programme, the Chavalit government was too disorganized and the Bank of Thailand too demoralized to initiate such a strategy.

Once Thailand entered the IMF programme, a second condition was required – the Fund had to agree to the strategy. In 1997 and early 1998, when such a strategy could have been useful, the Fund was still resolutely opposed to it. Indeed, the government had imposed a mild form of capital control to fend off the currency speculators in May 1997, but the Fund wanted to have these measures removed, and required that a promise to do so be included in the first two letters of intent. After confidence had been painfully gained in 1998, it is not clear what capital control could have achieved.

Conclusions

The Thai economic crisis had its origin in the private sector – a fact that has been widely recognized. That individual agents' behaviour led to such a disastrous outcome is *prima facie* evidence for market failure. Hence, I have organized the above presentation to emphasize the functioning and the dysfunctioning of the various markets.

Pride of place has to be given to the failures of the financial system and the financial markets as the major cause of the Thai crisis. The problems here are manifold, but I would emphasize the inadequate markets for risk and, related to this, a grossly inadequate legal framework underpinning market-based risk sharing. The over-reliance on debt as a means of financing new investments – and these investments were, relative to the size of the economy, massive – has made companies and the financial institutions extremely vulnerable.

Nearly four decades of relatively stable growth had lulled everyone into complacency regarding the risks that they were taking. In the past, those who made mistaken investments had almost always been rescued by growth. Market-supporting institutions and arrangements that could sort out the consequences of these mistakes, such as bankruptcy laws or deposit insurance, were either not developed or, when proposed, always put on the backburner. The process of supervision and regulation of financial institutions was not overhauled to take account of the new environment opened up by financial market liberalization.

Financial market liberalization without adequate preparation thus turned out to be extremely detrimental to the economy. As Thailand emerged painfully – and fitfully – from the crisis, it had to take stock (literally) of its position. The flow variables showed clear signs of recovery, fuelled in the beginning by large fiscal deficits and later by strong export performance. But the balance sheets of firms and financial institutions were still in a parlous state, and debt/equity ratios for most of the larger corporations had become even higher, mostly as a result of heavy foreign exchange losses. Many of these companies remained technically bankrupt. As a result, non-performing loans form a very large fraction of the total loans outstanding to financial institutions, which – as a consequence – largely remained non-functional. As long as the recovery is based on using up excess capacity, the economy can still move forward. Once all this excess capacity is brought into use again, growth will grind to a halt because of problems with the financing of new investments.

The dismal balance sheets of the Thai non-financial corporations are due to the lack of any rapid mechanism through which they can be adjusted to reflect new realities and, where necessary, changes in owner-ship can take place. Since these adjustments have implications for the financial institutions' balance sheets, and their health, the channels from savings to investment will remain clogged for some time, and firms will remain starved of funds for new investment, while the financial institu-tions are awash in money.

As can be easily surmised, the changes and adjustments that have already taken place have wrought considerable changes to the wealth of many individuals, and probably to the overall distribution of wealth in Thailand. Surprisingly, while there has been an increase in the incidence of poverty, that increase has been small and, judging by the size of the observed impact, probably less than the undoubtedly large impact on the very rich. This is true, despite the fact that there is very little in the way of a social safety net for the poor. The fact that most of the industrial workers laid off from their jobs are still first-generation migrants from the rural areas may explain the relatively mild consequences for the poor. Their ties to their families and the informal social security thus provided are still strong.

Good fortune, however, is no excuse for complacency in constructing a proper social safety net, rather than the jerry-built one put in place during the crisis. At the very least, the resources that have been, and will be, put up by the taxpayers to cushion the blow to investors and lenders in miscon-ceived investments have been out of all proportion to the safety net provided to the poor. And that should be an offence to anyone's sense of justice.

Notes

1 From 'Thailand: what happened and has anything really changed?'. Speech given at the ASEM Conference in Copenhagen, Denmark, 8–9 March 1999.
2 Although a separate legal entity from the Bank of Thailand, FIDF is in reality a part of it – almost all of its personnel are drawn from the Bank.

3 The figures are from FRA's home page (www.fra.or.th).
4 Dollar *et al.* (1998) find in the sample of firms they surveyed in the last quarter of 1997 and first quarter of 1998 that these firms perceived the credit constraint to be much less of a problem than was generally assumed in policy circles at the time. The credit problem was swamped by others, such as the fall in domestic demand. Ito and Pereira da Silva (1999) argued that there was a 'credit crunch', in the sense that many firms that should be able to get access to credit were being denied it. The two views are not incompatible. The position I expound in this part of the text (in terms of impact on firms and of export performance) is broadly in agreement with Dollar *et al.* (1998) but the existence of a 'credit crunch' in the sense used by Ito and Pereira da Silva is documented further below.
5 To pick on only one of many possible explanatory hypotheses, La Porta *et al.* (1998) proposed legal tradition as an important determinant of forms of corporate finance. The common law tradition is supportive of both equity investors as well as of lenders to corporations. The civil law tradition is less supportive of equity investors in general, while the German branch of civil law is more supportive of creditors – hence the traditionally strong role of banks in Germany. Thailand has a body of codified civil law. Its commercial law is derived from Germany via Japan. The fact that most of Thailand's judges are trained in the common law tradition is probably an important factor.
6 The baht depreciation has meant that the book value of foreign debts must also be increased.
7 My evidence for the last assertion is limited to interviews with individuals involved with the workout process.
8 Paul Krugman (1979) argues that continued government deficits can lead to a speculative attack on the currency. Although the Thai government had been running fiscal surpluses continuously for almost a decade before 1997, the contingent liabilities arising out of the need to support financial institutions may lead to similar attacks.
9 The one item where considerable activity could be observed is in the non-resident baht accounts. These may have been caught up in the speculative activity of the baht.
10 The exception was in October and November 1999, when the baht/dollar exchange rate suddenly surged from the normal 37–40 baht range to 42 baht. The Bank of Thailand later admitted to some intervention to bring the exchange rate back down again.
11 The real exchange rate vis-à-vis another foreign currency is defined as the exchange rate divided by the home inflation rate and multiplied by the foreign country's inflation. The real effective exchange rate (an index) is then the weighted average of the indices of the real exchange rates. The weights for the real effective exchange rate against trading partners are in proportion to their (two-way) trading volumes with Thailand. The weights for the real effective exchange rate vis-à-vis competitors are drawn from an unpublished study from the Bank of Thailand. They are as follows (in per cent): China 18.6, Hong Kong 21.1, South Korea 9.2, Singapore 14.2, Taiwan 19.9, Malaysia 8.6, Indonesia 6.4, Philippines 1.9. Because of lack of data, Indonesia is not included in the result shown in Figure 2.3.
12 The REER measure will always show less movement than TNT. Normally, as in the data presented here, the REER would be obtained by using aggregate price data, including tradables and non-tradables to deflate the nominal exchange rate, when only the non-tradable price should be used. The effect is to dilute the movement.

13 Some scepticism concerning this 'devaluation' must be expressed, as the Chinese authorities merely unified what had been multilateral exchange rates, with relatively little impact on the actual prices paid and received by both parties involved in the trade (World Bank 1998: 24, Box 2.1).

14 Food and agriculture have been excluded in the two sets of figures because they introduce a strong, and distracting, seasonality into the data. For the non-food manufacturing production index and non-agricultural GDP, seasonally adjusted series have been estimated, but are not reported, because the adjustment made little difference to the figures.

15 The surveys classify unemployed persons into three groups: those actively seeking work, those ready to work but not actively seeking work, and finally those waiting for seasonal work. It is the last group for which we use the term 'seasonally unemployed'.

16 The terminology and definition of 'severely' and 'moderately' underemployed are idiosyncratic to this paper. The 35-hour borderline for full employment is the standard adopted by the National Statistical Office, which conducts the surveys.

17 Starting from 1998, the NSO intends to conduct four labour force surveys a year: in February, May, August and November. Prior to 1998, there was no November survey and since, in addition, the May survey was conducted every other year, there was also no May 1997 figure.

18 The lenders were Japan, $4 billion; the central banks of Australia, China, Hong Kong, Malaysia and Singapore, $1 billion each; the central banks of South Korea and Indonesia, $0.5 billion each; the World Bank, $1.5 billion, and the Asian Development Bank, $1.2 billion. Since then, Japan has taken up the contributions of South Korea and Indonesia.

19 Including guarantees for state enterprises.

20 Mundell's analysis does not require the government to go out and raise funds from abroad – it can raise them domestically – but then the private sector will be crowded out of the domestic market into foreign borrowing, with the same end result. However, in the world financial markets that Thailand was facing in 1998–99, this was unlikely to happen. In the event, the government had to raise the funds itself, mostly from official sources.

References

Ammar Siamwalla and Orapin Sobchokchai (1998) Responding to the Thai economic crisis, *UNDP Working Paper*, Bangkok: UNDP.

Bhagwati, J.N. (1984) Why are services cheaper in the poor countries?, *Economic Journal*, 94, pp. 279–86.

Claessens, S. and Djankov, S. (1999) Publicly-listed East Asian corporates: growth, financing and risks. Paper presented at the Conference on Asian Corporate Recovery: corporate governance and government policy, Bangkok, March.

Corden, W.M. (1999) *The Asian Crisis: is There a Way Out?*, Singapore: Institute of Southeast Asian Studies.

Dasgupta, D. and Imai, K. (1998) The East Asian Crisis: understanding the causes of export slowdown, and the prospects for recovery. Background paper presented at the World Bank study on *East Asia: the Road to Recovery*, Washington, DC: World Bank.

Dollar, D., Hallward-Driemeier, M., Iarossi, G. and Chakraborty, M. (1998) Short-term and long-term competitiveness issues in Thai industry, in: J. Witte and

S. Koeberle (eds) *Competitiveness and Sustainable Economic Recovery in Thailand*, Bangkok: National Economic and Social Development Board and World Bank Thailand Office.

Ito, T. and Pereira da Silva, L.A. (1999) The credit crunch in Thailand during the 1997–98 crisis: theoretical and operational issues with the JEXIM Survey, *EXIM Review*, 19, pp. 1–40.

Krugman, P. (1979) A model of balance-of-payments crises, *Journal of Money, Credit and Banking*, 11, pp. 311–25.

La Porta, R., Lopez-de-Silanes, F., Shleifer, A. and Vishny, R.W. (1998) Law and finance, *Journal of Political Economy*, 106, pp. 1113–55.

Mathinee Subhaswadikul (1999) Datchanee kha ngoen thi thae jing (Real effective exchange rate: REER): Naew Khid Withee Karn Khamnuan lae Karn Prayook Chai Koranee Prathet Thai, *Rai Ngarn Setthakit Rai Duen*, 39, pp. 11–29 [in Thai].

Mundell, R. (1963) Capital mobility and stabilisation policy under fixed and flexible exchange rates, *Canadian Journal of Economics and Political Science*, 29, pp. 475–85.

Nukul Commission (1998) *Analysis and Evaluation on Facts behind Thailand's Economic Crisis*, English translation by Nation Multimedia Group, Bangkok.

Renaud, B., Zhang, M. and Koeberle, S. (1998) How the real estate boom undid financial institutions: what can be done now? In: J. Witte and S. Koeberle (eds) *Competitiveness and Sustainable Economic Recovery in Thailand*, Bangkok: National Economic and Social Development Board and World Bank Thailand Office.

Suthep Kittikulsingh (1999) Non performing loans (NPLs): the borrower's viewpoint, *TDRI Quarterly Review*, 14, pp. 19–30.

Thailand Development Research Institute (2000) *Financial Reforms in Thailand*, Bangkok: Thailand Development Research Institute.

Warr, P.G. (1999) What happened to Thailand?, *The World Economy*, 22, pp. 631–50.

Warr, P.G. and Bhanupong Nidhiprabha (1996) *Thailand's Macroeconomic Miracle: stable adjustment and sustained growth*, Washington, DC and Kuala Lumpur: World Bank and Oxford University Press.

World Bank (1998) *East Asia: the Road to Recovery*, Washington, DC: The World Bank.

Part II

The social and political context of the recovery process

Chapter 3

Pluto-populism
Thaksin and popular politics

Chris Baker[1]

> You can be proud of me because I am not bad, I just have too much.
> Prime Minister Thaksin Shinawatra[2]

In February 2001, Thaksin Shinawatra, one of Thailand's richest business-men, became prime minister and appointed a Cabinet studded with other leading business figures. This was new. Although businessmen had domin-ated Thailand's parliament as electoral politics developed over the previ-ous two decades, the biggest business figures had remained slightly aloof. Thaksin had won the election on a platform of measures appealing directly to the rural mass. This too was new. Previous elections had been won by local influence, and party platforms had not been taken seriously (Arghiros 2001; Callahan and McCargo 1996). Thaksin's party had won just short of an absolute majority. In no previous election since 1979 had any party reached one third. Over the coming year, Thaksin implemented (or tried to implement) all the major elements of his electoral platform. This was very new indeed. By mid-2002, Thaksin was predicting he would remain in power for 16 years. No previous elected premier had survived one 4-year term.

What sort of change in Thai politics does Thaksin represent? According to one interpretation, Thaksin is just another business politician, and the ground rules of Thai politics have not changed (McCargo 2002b). However, some commentators detected powerful new forces of populism and nationalism generated by the Asian crisis.

The *Far Eastern Economic Review* (18 January 2001) concluded that Thaksin 'won by embracing populism on a grand scale', and by 'his pop-ulist policies', 'populist spending programmes', 'populist pledges', 'pop-ulist sheen', 'populist election campaign' and 'populist brand of government'. This phrasing also was new. The term populism had been occasionally applied to earlier Thai politicians (Samak, Chamlong), but not on this scale. It was taken up by the local press, but with difficulty. Some newspapers used a transliteration, *poppiwlit*, which was vague.

Others translated it as *prachaniyom*, which was rather neutral (roughly, people-ism). Thai academics helpfully wrote press articles to explain the word and its history (e.g. Kasian 2001).

The term populism is notoriously imprecise, and is used with a variety of meanings to serve various agendas. The *Review*'s usage highlighted Thaksin's direct appeal for popular support, with an implicit accusation that the popular appeal was 'buying' support to gain power with other objectives. Populism has also been used in another sense in the context of the Asian crisis. The shock of such a sharp and unprecedented economic downturn provoked a confused array of reactions. Some advocated a retreat away from modernity, industrialization and global forces, towards tradition, agriculture and the locality. Marxists identify this tendency as 'populist' because it obfuscates class interests, and disengages from the struggle within capitalism (Hewison 2002; Brass 1995). Particularly after the King spoke in endorsement of localism, this agenda was seen as an attempt to preserve old social bases of power. In his election campaign, Thaksin had support from some localists and borrowed some of their vocabulary. In one of his first public speeches in English as prime minister, he talked of 'looking inward'. While Thaksin is clearly a populist in the sense of appealing for popular support, how far is he a populist in the sense of promoting conservative localism?

Thaksin was also identified as a nationalist, rising on reactions stirred up since the 1997 financial crisis. His party's name, Thai Rak Thai (Thai love Thai), is patently nationalistic. He criticized the previous Democrat government for being too passive with the IMF and foreign business. During the election campaign, he revelled in the antagonism of the foreign press because it lent him an image of defiance. But at the same time he insisted, 'I am very international'. His education, language skills, experience, and demeanour marked him as more worldly than his election rivals – indeed, than any previous elected Thai premier. He celebrated his election victory, not by the traditional visit to make merit at a *wat*, but by driving his wife in their Porsche to have coffee at Starbucks. In what way is Thaksin a nationalist?

This chapter examines the significance of Thaksin's rise to power, and the meaning of his rich–poor, pluto-populist alliance, in the aftermath of the crisis. The next section sketches the background of political change in the 1990s. The three following sections look at the components of Thaksin's support, and a fourth shows how these came together in the election of January 2001. Thaksin led a group of big business interests, which saw the need to control state power to protect and promote domestic capital. They looked for support among small businessmen who bore the main brunt of the collapse of the banking system. They also gained the support of rural groups who were stirred up in the short term by the impact of the crisis, but who were also engaged in a longer-term struggle to overcome their exclusion from politics.

The final two sections reflect on the meaning of Thaksin's victory for Thai politics by looking at his first year in power, and the development of his alliance between big business leadership and rural electoral support. He deployed nationalistic appeal, but within limits imposed by the lack of any popular nationalist tradition. Although he tapped both localists and modernizers in the pre-election phase, his speeches and actions in power identify him clearly as a modernizer. His rural policies have more to do with deepening capitalism than with agrarian reform. His rise reflects both the growing political importance of big capital, and the growing political assertiveness of the rural mass. But it is uncertain how long these two very different political forces will remain aligned.

Background: money politics, reform and crisis

> Any attempt at predicting the future, based either on existing economic text-books or on number-crunching, to try to establish a trend, will be futile. I ask my critics to go back and check the first book by Microsoft's Bill Gates. That shows the makeup of the past and the components of the future have very little in common.
>
> Thaksin (*The Nation*, 19 November 2001)

Although the 2001 election result was new in many respects, it was an extension of trends that had developed over two decades of rapid economic change and political development.

Thailand moved to government by an elective parliament over the 1980s, as the army was pushed back to the barracks. But the Cold War left behind suppressive controls and a hegemonic antagonism to popular political organization. Parliament was monopolized by businessmen, especially provincial businessmen able to control elections through cash, intimidation, and pork-barrelling. These businessmen quickly negotiated a *modus vivendi* of power and profit sharing with the formerly dominant bureaucracy. The resulting 'money politics' came under attack in the early 1990s from an alliance of conservatives (businessmen, political scientists, bureaucrats) and liberal social activists. This alliance constructed a new draft constitution aimed at upgrading the quality of politicians, and creating more stable governments, while retaining some strong limits on popular participation.[3] The constitution was passed in 1997 after the financial crisis persuaded businessmen and the urban middle class that politics had to be reformed to achieve better economic management. The general election that brought Thaksin to power was the first under this new charter.

The most successful party of the 1990s was the Democrat Party which headed the governing coalition for all but 28 months from September 1992 to the 2001 election. In the early 1990s, the Democrat Party had re-engineered itself to reflect the needs and aspirations of a society under-going an economic boom and rapid urbanization. It brought in tech-nocrats who promised to manage and modernize the economy. It showcased a new generation of young urban professionals who symbolized urban aspirations for modernization. It attracted electoral support from the capital and from the more urbanized southern region.

In 1994, the Democrats were pushed out of power by provincial-based parties. But after the advent of the financial crisis in mid-1997, business-men and the urban middle class clamoured for the Democrats to return and manage the economy. In December 1997, their return was manoeu-vred without either coup or election. Over the next three years, the Democrats were closely identified with the IMF programme of crisis man-agement. In fact, the programme was in place before they resumed office, and the Democrats pressed the IMF for modifications. But Demo-crats also fiercely defended the programme and resisted arguments that it damaged Thai business and society for the benefit of international finance. As the crisis lingered and the IMF's approach was widely discred-ited, the Democrats suffered from the association (Pasuk and Baker 2002, Ch. 12).

Layer one: Thaksin the businessman

In my business, we have to understand politics and political direction in order to survive. I might have the advantage in that I was a civil servant before and know what ought and ought not to be. Politics and business are inseparable, like the earth which would get too hot if it moves closer to the sun and too cold if it moves too far away.

Thaksin (said in 1991, quoted *The Nation*, 27 December 2000)

Thaksin Shinawatra was the single most successful entrepreneur during Thailand's boom from 1986 to 1997. He is a fourth-generation member of a Chinese-immigrant family that settled in Chiang Mai. The family started as tax-farmers, later switched to various businesses including silk trading and cinema management, and gradually moved through education into bureaucracy and politics. Thaksin's father was prominent in the local poli-tics of Chiang Mai, while his uncle entered parliament and became minis-ter of transport and communications in the mid-1980s (Sorakon 1993).

Thaksin went to university in the US (MA from Eastern Kentucky Uni-versity, doctorate from Sam Houston State University, both in criminal justice) and returned to join the police. In 1980, he married the daughter of a powerful police general, and began selling computers to this general's department. He secured government concessions to start a cable TV network in 1985 and a paging service in 1986, and quit the police two years later. Neither the cable, paging nor computer business was especially profitable. In 1988, the shift from a military to an elected premier began a process of partial liberalization in telecommunications (Sakkarin 1995). Thaksin secured another concession for paging (1989), the first concession to operate a mobile phone network (1990), and four lesser projects (data transfer services and card phones). After a military coup in 1991, Thaksin won the project to launch Thailand's first satellite. He listed his four main companies on the stock exchange between 1990 and 1994 when inflows of portfolio capital boosted the index from 600 to a peak of 1753. The asset value of the Shinawatra companies increased from 0.6 to 56.0 billion baht over five years (Sakkarin 1995: 162–3). By the mid-1990s, Thaksin was estimated to be worth 60–80 billion baht.[4]

All Thaksin's businesses started from a government concession or licence. To secure these projects, Thaksin had to gain favour from politicians (especially military) and senior bureaucrats. Some of these contacts later became executives and directors of his companies.[5] He presented a Daimler to a military politician in gratitude for help offered. When the satellite was launched, he said 'I could not have this day without Big Jod', meaning General Sunthorn Kongsompong, the head of the 1991 coup junta (quoted in *The Nation*, 28 March 2001).

When this junta fell in 1992, the military lost influence not only over the Cabinet but over many state enterprises, including the telephone and telecommunication authorities (Sakkarin 1995: Ch. 4). Politicians took over. Soon after, Thaksin crossed the boundary between business and politics. In November 1994 he joined the Cabinet as a non-MP and foreign minister under Chamlong Srimuang's *Palang Tham* Party, which happened to control the Ministry of Transport and Communications in the current coalition. But the party withdrew from the coalition three months later. In 1995, Chamlong nominated Thaksin to succeed him as party leader. Thaksin was elected MP in Bangkok, projecting an image as a new-style politician for the globalized era. He served as deputy prime minister under Banharn Silpa-archa, but withdrew the party from the coalition in August 1996. In 1997, he joined the Chavalit Yongchaiyudh government as deputy prime minister for its last four months.

Over this period, he extended his business into government-granted highway concessions, and manoeuvred for a fixed-line telephone contract. Despite serving in the Chavalit Cabinet, he lost influence over the Ministry of Transport and Communications to his main rival, the Charoen Pokphand (CP) group.[6] He failed to secure the fixed-line contract; CP was awarded a mobile phone concession, which threatened Thaksin's most profitable business;[7] and Chavalit laid plans for the army to launch a satellite (Ukrist 1998). In addition, the government committed to the WTO to liberalize service businesses including telecommunications by 2006. The future success of his business depended on political decisions. He needed political power for commercial survival.

When the financial crisis struck in 1997, Thaksin and his rivals pooled resources for survival. Thaksin and CP merged their cable TV networks, and agreed to cooperate in other areas. In 1998, Thaksin re-entered politics, started the Thai Rak Thai party (TRT), and launched his bid for the premiership. Pitak Intrawitayanunt, who served as a political ambassador of the CP group, was among the early members.[8]

Thaksin's party became a magnet for other leading businessmen. Shortly before the 2001 election, he was publicly endorsed by the heads of the largest Thai conglomerate (CP) and the largest bank (Bangkok Bank). Chatri Sophonpanich of Bangkok Bank explained that he supported Thaksin as prime minister 'because as a businessman, he understands business' (*The Nation*, 28 November 2000). Dhanin Chearavanont of CP emphasized the need for Thailand's businessmen, in the wake of the crisis, to draw on the power and protection of the state: 'This is an age of economic war. It's crucial that we have a prime minister who understands business and the economy' (*Bangkok Post*, 31 October 2000).

Two people with close associations to the CP group were included in Thaksin's Cabinet, appointed in February 2001: Pitak as a deputy prime minister and Sombat Uthaisang, a former telecommunications bureaucrat, as deputy interior minister. Another telecoms entrepreneur, Adisai Potharamik of the Jasmine group, became minister of commerce. Pracha Maleenon, head of a television and entertainment conglomerate, became deputy minister of communications. Suriya Juengrungruangkit, head of the largest local producer of auto parts, became minister of industry. In addition, Thanong Bidaya of Thai Military Bank (TMB) was appointed to several key economic roles, including heading up the Thai Asset Management Corporation established to take over banks' bad debts. Thaksin had been a client of TMB during his entrepreneurial rise, and had bought a stake in the bank when it desperately needed capital during the crisis. Other lesser business interests formed a penumbra around this core group. These included the Srivikorn family, the M. Thai property group, Italthai construction, and the Grammy entertainment group (Ukrist 2000).

There had not been such a concentration of leading capitalists in the Cabinet since the early 1980s. Partly, they had been squeezed out over the 1980s when provincial bosses learnt how to manipulate elections. Partly, they had not seen the necessity of taking a direct role in politics. Their reappearance in 2001 was made possible by the party-list system[9] and was motivated by the effects of the economic crisis. They needed the state.

The companies they headed were among the survivors of the crisis. Often they had come through the experience with considerable difficulty. CP had sold off many ancillary businesses, both in Thailand and China. Bangkok Bank had sold 49 per cent of its shares to foreigners and downsized. In the aftermath, however, the survivors were in some ways strengthened (Hewison 2000). Many of their competitors had disappeared. Many dominant conglomerates of the pre-crisis period had been crippled, making space for new leaders. The Maleenon family had not earlier been placed in the front rank of conglomerates, yet in 2000 it had the largest family holding of shares on the stock exchange (*Matichon*, 19 December 2000; Hewison 2001).

Many of these firms were in service industries. Several domestic conglomerates based in manufacturing had either been squeezed out by the influx of foreign capital in the late 1980s, or bought out in the crisis. But some service industries still enjoyed state protection through licensing arrangements (telecoms), or the alien business law (entertainment). These service sectors represented the future source of profit and growth for Thai domestic capital.

Several of these business leaders had a history of tapping political power for business benefit. Bangkok Bank's pre-eminence was created by its association with military dictators in the 1950s, and was sustained by persistent lobbying to maintain the protected banking cartel up to the crisis. The Maleenon family won their television concession from military leaders, and secured an extension on the eve of threatened liberalization of the market. The telecoms players depended on government concessions. The auto parts industry was protected by local content rules until the mid-1990s.

In sum, Thaksin's venture into the political world over the 1990s was the logical extension of his business success based on state concessions. His new party attracted other big business families, which survived the crisis, which knew the value of state protection, and which were convinced by the experience that they needed closer control over state power to develop the profit potential of the service sector. When Thaksin launched the TRT party in July 1998, his founder members included the pioneers of this business grouping, and a motley collection of reformers.[10] A year later, when the party announced a sort of shadow cabinet to monitor the government, most of the members were representatives of business families, or former bureaucrats who had been their sympathetic connections inside government (Phak thai rak thai 1999).

Over the next 18 months, however, the party changed. Only eight of the 43 members listed in this shadow cabinet were appointed ministers in Thaksin's cabinet in February 2001. The party was changed by the realities of electoral politics, but also by other social forces intruding on the political system in the context of the financial crisis.

Layer two: Thaksin and the small businessman

> A lot of my brothers and sisters are still enduring great suffering and my business friends still cannot find money from banks ... Don't worry for me but for the country.
>
> Thaksin (*Bangkok Post*, 27 December 2000)

The rapid capital outflow from mid-1997 onwards rendered most Thai companies either illiquid or bankrupt or both. The banks that had inter-mediated between foreign lenders and local borrowers were especially hit, and the banking system effectively collapsed (Pasuk and Baker 2000: Ch. 3). Small and medium companies were deprived of credit. Over 1998–99, Thaksin appealed to small businessmen with proposals to stimulate entre-preneurship as a route to recovery.

The IMF, which arrived in July 1997 to dictate crisis policies, blamed the crisis on Thai companies for excessive borrowing and poor invest-ments. This interpretation was corroborated by the international media and academic analysis, which attributed the crisis to an 'Asian model' of development marked by 'crony capitalism'. The IMF strategy assumed that debtor companies (including financial intermediaries) would have to go bankrupt in large numbers, and the economy would regenerate through a 'fire sale' of cheap distressed assets to foreign buyers. Under IMF dicta-tion, financial firms were closed down, restrictions on foreign ownership removed, and asset sales orchestrated to favour foreign bidders. Over the next three years, more foreign capital flowed into Thailand than over the 11 years of the preceding boom, mostly to buy up the wreckage of col-lapsed domestic firms (Pasuk and Baker 2000: Ch. 9).

Most local businessmen interpreted the crisis quite differently. The typical urban Thai enterprise had been started by an immigrant who arrived between the wars, and was accumulated over two to four genera-tions by hard work, thrift, mutual cooperation, and investment in educa-tion. A few became sprawling conglomerates. Most were small businesses relying on family labour, or medium enterprises with 10–20 employees. All but a handful were family concerns. Less than 400 out of the total of over 100,000 registered businesses entered the stock market. Most businessmen did not see themselves as proponents of any 'Asian model' or as 'crony capitalists'. Rather, they felt they had made two mistakes that brought about their downfall: they had followed market forces by seeking credit from the lowest-cost supplier (foreign loans), and they had believed their government when it promised the baht would remain pegged to the dollar. They did not feel inclined to take both the blame and the pain for the crisis. As one leading businessman explained in 1998, 'our priority is survival' (*Bangkok Post*, 28 November 1998). Their reactions to the crisis, including an unprecedented readiness to break the bonds of trust that usually made loan repayment a near-religious duty, were 'a scheme to counter the threat of extinction' (Suthep 1999: 24).

They perceived the IMF-inspired policies towards the crisis as an abdi-cation of the government's usual relationship to domestic capital. Since the 1950s, when Thai governments – under US tutelage – committed to a strategy of development led by private enterprise, successive governments had created a protective environment for domestic capital. The Democrat government, implementing the IMF's crisis package, was perceived to have abandoned that stance.

From late 1997, indebted businessmen organized opposition to the crisis strategy of the IMF and the Democrat government. While one or two of the business activists came from the large conglomerates, most were from medium-size firms. They attempted to raise support against forces which they described as 'neo-colonial'. New organizations appeared, such as the Alliance for National Salvation (*Phanthamit ku wikrit chat*), National Salvation Community (*Prachakhom kop ban ku muang*), and United Thai for National Liberation Club (*Chomrom ruam jai thai ku chat*) (Kasian 2000). But these groups were small and their efforts gained only a narrow base of support. An attempt to hold an anti-IMF rally, in cooperation with other protest groups, drew only 1,500 people. The formal business associations gave no endorsement. One of the leaders failed to get re-elected to a post in the Chamber of Commerce because of his activism. The press was luke-warm. The attempt by the largest bad debtor, Prachai Liaophairat of TPI, to portray his own plight as a nationalist cause, gained precious little support from press, colleagues, or politicians. From mid-1998, these activities declined. The indebted businessmen failed to persuade a broader public that their decline was a public cause.

Debate among academics and public intellectuals developed separately. While there were some early attempts to blame Soros for precipitating the crisis, and some complaints against the IMF for making it worse than necessary, there was a general acceptance that, even if the crisis was somehow a product of globalization, the solution would have to be found locally. This soul-searching split into two main camps. On the one hand, some argued that Thailand would have to make a strategic retreat from modernity on grounds that the society was patently not yet ready. This discourse found legitimacy from the King's speech of December 1997, which advocated a partial retreat to a 'sufficient' or more 'self-reliant' economy. The King's proposal was essentially a practical anticipation of what had happened in previous, less severe downturns – namely, that the burden was passed back to the villages. However, it prompted a wider discussion on the need to reform and strengthen *traditional* and *local* institutions – family, community, school, village economy, *wat* – in order to have stronger foundations for facing or evading globalization (Pasuk in this volume; Hewison 2002; Kasian 2000).

On the other hand, others argued that Thailand must respond to the crisis by reforming and strengthening its *modern* institutions. Arguably, this discourse was the stronger and the most productive. In 1999, the government passed a major educational reform that had been gestating for years. The Civil Service Commission produced blueprints for reform, again after years of debate. The armed forces followed suit. Businesses struggled to modernize.

Mass reaction to the crisis developed more slowly and in a diffuse form. Over 1998–99, the Thai economy shrank sharply, and the hopes for a rapid and moderately painless recovery were abandoned. International criticism of the IMF handling of the crisis rose. A sense of resentment against outside forces (globalization, the IMF) developed, but faced difficulties finding a clear expression. Thailand had no mass nationalist movement in its history. The elite had fended off colonialism, the nation had been formed top-down, and national symbols had remained 'official property', not easily appropriated for mass action.[11] The early inchoate attempts to express mass concern over the crisis in 1998 adopted metaphorical symbols such as the elephants that had been relocated to work in the city and which suffered in this unnatural, modern environment (Pasuk and Baker 2000: Ch. 7). In 1999–2000, television dramas began to reflect this resentment, but they struggled because of the lack of a local nationalist tradition. The first drama to adopt a defend-the-homeland theme, *Khon khong phaendin* (People of the Country), was set in a mythical pan-Asian country, its foreign rulers were modelled on a Latin American junta, and its nationalist heroes were drawn from Indian models, including representations of Gandhi and Nehru.[12] The homeland was rather far from home.

These expressions moved closer to classic nationalism by borrowing stories from schoolbook national history. The shorthand for the fall of the old capital of Ayutthaya to the Burmese in 1767 (*sia krung*, the fall of the city) transferred easily to the modern crisis. In 1999, a film based on one of the most popular stories from this history enjoyed unprecedented popular success. *Bang Rajan* told the story of a village that resisted the Burmese invasion without help from the capital's elite. In 2001, the film of *Suriyothai*, a 16th-century queen who died fighting the Burmese, extended this theme. While these dramas expressed the sense of being under attack, they dramatized the pain without defining any active and successful resistance. The stories all ended in tragedy and defeat.

In 1999, the business critique of crisis management re-emerged. The parliamentary opposition launched a no-confidence debate, which criticized the Democrat government for being subservient to the IMF, biased in favour of foreign capital, and negligent in its duty to foster Thailand's 'real economy'. The opposition New Aspiration Party (NAP) took this message on a stump tour. Compared with a year earlier, the message about the government's duty to protect domestic capital was more acceptable now that the crisis had become worse, and now that the message was delivered by politicians rather than indebted businessmen.

Against this background, Thaksin began to present himself and his party as the saviour of the small and medium entrepreneur. In June 1999, he stated his difference from the Democrats' finance-led strategy with the remark, 'I wouldn't solve this crisis just from a commercial banker's point of view' (*Far Eastern Economic Review*, 17 June 1999). In September, he described the Democrat leader Chuan Leekpai[13] as a bureaucrat-like 'salary man who cannot even buy a house of his own' in contrast to Thaksin's own status as a self-made businessman of great wealth. He went on: 'If I'm the government, I will open things up for people who have the leaning and ability to be entrepreneurs to have that choice so that people who earn salaries now will have the opportunity to quit and become entrepreneurs without facing excess risk' (*Matichon Sutsapda*, 11 September 1998).

This public bickering with Chuan defined the difference between Thaksin and the Democrats as entrepreneur vs. bureaucrat. Thaksin now promoted recovery from the crisis through growth in small and medium enterprises (SMEs) on an Italian or Tuscan model, achieved by the marriage of traditional craft skills and high technology. The party staged an SME exhibition which showcased examples of successful small Thai businesses. The idea appealed so successfully to the entrepreneurial aspirations, local pride, and sense of abandonment among small businessmen, that the government and other parties rushed to form their own SME policies (*The Nation*, 6 November 2000). Shortly before the spat with Chuan, Thaksin was talking about coming 'third or fourth' in any future election (*The Nation*, 24 March 1999). Shortly after, he was talking about becoming premier.

In March 2000, the TRT party announced its plan for economic recovery. It dropped the 'Italian' inspiration of the concept, but retained the emphasis on SMEs, and the combination of local skills and inputs with high technology in production and marketing. It added a business school model which divided sectors into rising stars, cash cows and sunset industries, and boosted the stars with capital injections and other government aid. It emphasized the need to revive the banking system (*Bangkok Post*, 20 March 2000).

In sum, the initial attempt by businessmen to rally domestic capital against the IMF programme was a failure. But over 1998–2000, the crisis impact deepened, debates on self-strengthening proliferated, and a diffuse resentment of external forces spread. Thaksin responded to these trends by crafting a political platform that made government support for small businesses a route for recovery from the crisis.

Layer three: Thaksin and rural discontents

> Nothing will stand in my way. I am determined to devote myself to politics in order to lead the Thai people out of poverty . . . I think the people want Thai Rak Thai to take the government's reins and solve the country's problems.
>
> Thaksin (*The Nation*, 23 December 2000)

Business support was not enough. The majority of the Thai electorate still lived in the villages (the 2000 census classified 69 per cent of the population as non-municipal). In his electoral campaign, Thaksin made a direct appeal to the rural voter on a platform of measures to spread wealth and help local economies. No previous political leader had done anything similar.

Thaksin was exploiting a trend of rising rural dissidence. In 1978, the government counted 42 incidents of protest. In 1994, the figure was almost 1,000. Most of these were rural, and around half about the control over natural resources (Praphat 1998: 27, 30, 39). In 1992, farmers marched on Bangkok like an invasion, and repeated the same tactic in most years following. Over the 1990s, many new rural organizations were formed, including the Small-scale Farmers of the Northeast, the Northern Farmers Network, the Thai Farmers Federation, and the Assembly of the Poor.

This upsurge of rural protest was a function of agrarian decline and political liberalization. Until the 1980s, agriculture was still growing because of an expanding land frontier, heavy investment both public and private, and rising international prices. At the same time, rural society was kept under firm political control. The army destroyed political organizations, and rural leaders simply got shot. Farmers were expected to wait passively for the government to help them. Over the 1980s, all this changed. Agriculture lost its buoyancy because the land frontier ran out, investment was diverted to industry, and the world terms of trade turned against agricultural goods. With the ending of the Cold War, the army's role in Thai politics diminished, and the attempts to suppress rural politics relaxed.

By the early 1990s, two streams of rural protest emerged. The first was located among more market-oriented farmers who protested against falling crop prices and rising rural debt. In short, they complained that market-oriented agriculture was no longer profitable. The second stream of protest was located among marginal farmers at the edge of the land frontier whose access to land, water, and other natural resources was threatened by dams, government forest policies, and industrialization. They protested to defend their own *withi chiwit*, way of life (Baker 2000; Pasuk 2002; Somchai 2001).

The financial crisis increased the intensity of these protests. Initially, farmers did well because agricultural prices (in local currency) rose. But from mid-1998 onwards, the impact of the crisis spread through rural society. The international price of rice dropped sharply. The cost of imported inputs rose. Remittances from family members working in the city shrank. Rural migrants lost their jobs and were thrown back on the support of the rural family. The number in poverty rose by 3 million, virtually all rural (World Bank 2001).

In early 1998, when the government wanted to implement IMF meas-ures for the financial sector, farmers' groups demanded the government help the poor rather than the rich through agrarian debt relief. This protest was repeated in 1999 and 2000. Farmer's groups also protested for price support. Paddy growers invaded Bangkok's northern suburbs and blocked roads. Cattle raisers started marching on the capital with herds of cows. Cassava farmers threatened to build a bonfire in the city centre. During an UNCTAD conference in late 1999, the police had to block radial roads to prevent sugar trucks invading the city. Displaced villagers and unemployed workers occupied empty land – both land in forests and unused land held by speculators. By 2000, every large infrastructure project that needed to appropriate resources of land, forest, or water was blocked by some form of protest. These included two power plants, a gas pipeline on the Malaysian border, several dams, an experimental nuclear project, an industrial waste scheme for Thailand's most polluted province, and urban waste schemes for the two largest cities. The Democrat-led government branded such protests as illegitimate and usually refused to negotiate.

This growing rural movement engaged in an internal debate on polit-ical strategy (Somchai 2001: 87–90, 149–54). Some advocated working at the local level, strengthening local communities, and organizing local protests (the community culture approach). Others argued that farmers had to engage more both with the wider economy through greater com-mercialization, and with national politics through negotiation with government and politicians (the political economy approach). Through the mid-1990s, this debate was resolved by experience: rural organizations found they had to combine protests to get attention along with negotia-tions to gain concessions. The debate then focused on the nature of polit-ical involvement. Rural organizations negotiated packages of concessions from the government in 1996 and 1997, only to see these agreements col-lapse when the Cabinet changed. Some argued this experience showed that farmers needed their own political party. Over 1999–2000, this pro-posal was debated at several meetings; an attempt was made to revive the Farmers' Federation from the 1970s; and proposals were floated to launch a 'green party' (*The Nation*, 26 March 2000). However, most rural leaders believed forming a party would worsen factional conflict, and provoke attempts to co-opt or suppress rural organizations. They preferred to bargain their support to political parties in return for specific concessions.

At the launch of TRT, Thaksin espoused the principle of rural uplift, but initially had no rural programme at all. His early recruitment efforts focused on urban groups. A prominent student activist from the 1970s, now turned orchard farmer, faxed him a three-page rural programme but received no response. In early 1999, however, the rural protests for debt relief, price support, and land reached a peak. Thaksin's team now began to consult with rural leaders and NGO workers. He took up the activist's three-page plan (*The Nation*, 23 March 2001). His team did some research to test and refine the content. Some NGO activists who advocated a localist opposition to the crisis contributed ideas. Thaksin adopted some of their vocabulary about strengthening communities and building recovery from the grassroots. In March 2000, Thaksin announced that the main feature of his rural platform would be a moratorium on rural debts (*The Nation*, 28 March 2000). In August, TRT revealed a fuller rural programme, including the debt moratorium, a revolving fund of 1 million baht for every village, and a 30 baht-per-visit scheme of health care (*Bangkok Post*, 17 August 2000).

In December 2000, farmer groups in the Northeast resolved to 'drive the Democrats to extinction' at the polls in revenge for their antagonism to rural protest and their revocation of the Assembly of the Poor's concessions (*Bangkok Post*, 11 December 2000). The following week, Thaksin held a meeting with the leaders of the Assembly (*Bangkok Post*, 19 December 2000). While these groups gave no direct endorsement of Thaksin and TRT, the meaning was evident.

Thaksin had distanced himself from the Democrats who collaborated with the IMF's destructive strategy, abandoned the government's duty to protect business, and treated rural protest with contempt. He bidded for the support of small businessmen and farmers by adopting these groups' own demands.

The 2001 elections: campaign and result

We dream of making big changes, but in reality it is not the way things are. Half the MPs are old-timers, so it takes time to replace them with fresh faces ... I don't know what they [Thaksin's Cabinet ministers] did in the past, but I will give them all a chance... If any of them are found to be corrupt while working for me, I will get rid of them.

Thaksin (*Bangkok Post*, 18 February 2001)

The election of January 2001 was a complex mix of the old and the new. Thaksin campaigned in a totally new style and secured a dramatically different result – a simple majority in the house after a little bit of juggling.[14] At the same time, however, the deployment of money and influence was similar to previous polls, and about half of Thaksin's victorious party consisted of old-fashioned elements in Thai politics.

The January 2001 polls had a prologue. In March 2000, elections were held for the Senate. Although the rules differed from those for the lower house,[15] the Senate elections served as a test run for the 1997 constitution, and for the mood and preferences of the electorate. The results were instructive. In Bangkok and some other urban areas, the electorate returned social activists and media figures of a new style in Thai politics. However, these were a minority of around 30–40 within the overall complement of 200 senators. The remainder were ex-bureaucrats or local businessmen connected to local political bosses (some by marriage or kinship). Money and influence were as much in evidence as ever. The Election Commission cancelled 78 of the victories for malpractice, and eventually held seven polling rounds, totalling 306 contests, before every victor was approved (Gothom 2001). The old politics were still alive.

Around this time, Thaksin agreed to admit Snoh Thienthong and his faction into the TRT party. Snoh was a trucking magnate from the eastern border who had proved the most enduring of the political 'godfathers' of the 1990s. He led a faction of provincial MPs into the Samakkhitham party in 1992, then to Chat Thai in 1995, and to New Aspiration in 1996. In both 1995 and 1996, his support helped to decide who became premier. After Chavalit's fall from the premiership in November 1997, Snoh eased away and formally entered TRT in mid-2000. Thaksin's decision to admit Snoh appears to have been taken shortly after the Senate elections emphasized the surviving importance of the old politics. Snoh's shift started the process of log-rolling that had preceded all recent elections. By August 2000, it was estimated that around 100 sitting MPs from other parties were expected to run under TRT at the coming election.[16] The Democrats publicly accused Thaksin of 'sucking' in MPs with money.

The TRT electoral campaign was also emphatically new in several ways. The party spent two years setting up a local network, and used the principles of pyramid selling in an attempt to sign up enough party members in each constituency to deliver an electoral victory. By the election it claimed 8 million members (*The Nation*, 18 December 2000). The party highlighted its three-point platform of measures targeted at the rural mass (debt moratorium, village funds, 30-baht health care) on election posters throughout the country. In previous elections, party platforms had never been taken seriously. The impact of the TRT rural programme and particularly of the three-point posters was so strong that other parties scrambled to produce their own rural platforms (*The Nation*, 14 October 2000; *Bangkok Post*, 6 October 2000). The NAP campaigned under the slogan: 'To help a tree grow we have to water its roots. To revive the country we must help the poor' (*Bangkok Post* 23 November 2000). Chat Thai chose 'Reform agriculture thoroughly to solve the country's problems'. The Democrats held a conference to protest that they were misunderstood and really had a rural programme (*Bangkok Post*, 24 April 2000).

The TRT campaign focused heavily on the party leader. From two years ahead of the poll, TRT erected large posters all over Thailand showing Thaksin with the party motto, 'Think new, act new, for every Thai'. During the run-up to the polls, TRT posters in every constituency were produced in a uniform format showing Thaksin with the constituency candidate.

The author of a recently acclaimed biography was hired to write Thaksin's life-story, serialized in *Matichon* weekly news magazine and then assembled as a book. The biography portrayed Thaksin rising from modest origins to outstanding commercial success through hard work, persistence, and daring (Sanlaya 2001). The essence of the book was distilled into a press ad and posters headlined: 'Let me use my life's knowledge and experience to solve the problems of the people'. The following excerpt conveys something of the village-to-world story and the homely style:

> I was a village kid. I started my schooling in a village school. I became a coffee dealer; helped my dad on his farm; delivered newspapers; got into mining; then computers. I once had a company with seven employees. Now it's over 60,000 and a turnover of billions of baht. I put a satellite up in the sky. I invested overseas. I had to chase after customers to collect checks. I got into debt to the banks and became an NPL.[17] I almost went bankrupt three times but now I have more wealth and property than I could ever have imagined. Even today, my friends range from hired motorcycle drivers to the presidents of great countries.[18]

The various incidents in his life were then linked to his policies: his rural origins dictated his rural uplift policies; his small business origins explained his interest in SMEs; his experience as an NPL led to his focus on the capital market; and so on. The policies of TRT emerged from the life of its leader.

At the polls themselves, the deployment of money and influence appeared little different than in previous elections. Indeed, the uncertainty of this election may have tempted some candidates to invest more than usual, and to experiment with new tactics. Policemen and military officers were allegedly hired to threaten voters (*Bangkok Post*, 13 December 2000). Two campaign cars were discovered with trunks full of small denomination notes and campaign materials (*The Nation*, 19 December 2000, 6 January 2001). In a tapped telephone conversation, an ex-minister and Chat Thai leader instructed campaign managers how to direct their 'ammunition' in the final stages of the campaign. In many constituencies, the vote counting developed into a secondary battle, with officials and election monitors accused of malpractice. The Election Commission cancelled some candidatures before the polls (*Bangkok Post*, 5 January 2001), refused to register 62 of the 400 victors in the first round, and eventually conducted a total of 486 contests over six polling rounds (Gothom 2001).

The results reflected the mix of old politics and new. Local influence still counted, but party affiliation was more important than before. Many candidates from influential local families which failed to enter TRT were massacred at the polls;[19] those that did enter TRT had a high chance of victory.[20]

In some cases, the failure of influential people was directly linked to tighter election controls. In Samut Prakan, the Asavahame clan had dominated politics for two decades. In 2001, however, the patriarch's two sons, brother, and daughter-in-law (a popular singer) all lost at the polls, while the patriarch himself failed on the party list. After the previous polls in 1996, a judge ruled that the patriarch and his two allies had stuffed 20,000 votes into the ballot boxes, but had to acquit them on a technicality. Television cameras had filmed ballot stuffing when the patriarch's son contested the election for mayor. Without these tactics and without the TRT stamp, the clan lost.

The result redrew the political map (see Table 3.1 and Figure 3.1). Several parties disappeared. The Solidarity and Muanchon parties retired before the contest. The Prachakon Thai, Ratsadon, and Social Action parties were obliterated at the polls. The Seritham party secured 14 constituency MPs, but its leaders lost on the party list, and Seritham agreed to merge into TRT. Three of the largest parties of the 1990s were reduced to a few isolated clusters of seats which represented the local networks of their leaders. The Chat Thai party won three such 'islands', representing the networks of the Silpa-archa family around Suphanburi (A on the map), Chidchob family around Buriram (B), and Khunpleum (Kamnan Po) clan around Chonburi (C). New Aspiration Party won two areas corresponding to the bases of Chavalit around Nakhon Pathom (D) and Wan Muhammed Noor in the far south (E). Chat Phatthana won just one (F) around the Khorat base of its late founder-leader, Chatichai Choonhavan.

Outside these islands and Bangkok (which for the first time voted close to the national pattern), the electoral map was starkly divided by an arc drawn east–west through the capital. South of this line, in the region that had long been the party's heartland, the Democrats won 61 seats and lost

Table 3.1 Election results by party and region, January 2001

	North	Northeast	South	Centre	Bangkok	Total	Party list	Grand total
Thai Rak Thai	54	69	1	47	29	200	48	248
Democrat	16	6	48	19	8	97	31	128
Chat Thai	3	11	–	21	–	35	6	41
Chat Phatthana	2	16	–	4	–	22	7	29
New Aspiration	1	19	5	3	–	28	8	36
Seritham	–	14	–	–	–	14	–	14
Ratsadon	–	1	–	1	–	2	–	2
Social Action	–	1	–	–	–	1	–	1
Thin Thai	–	1	–	–	–	1	–	1
Total	76	138	54	95	37	400	100	500

Source: Results as announced by the Election Commission on 2 February 2001 to inaugurate the parliament.

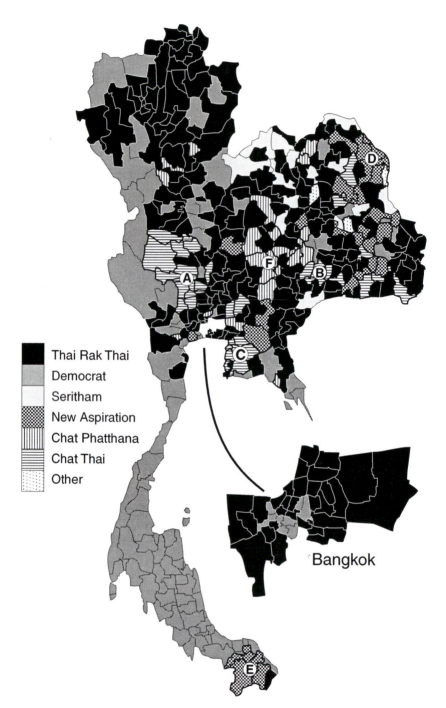

Thai Rak Thai
Democrat
Seritham
New Aspiration
Chat Phatthana
Chat Thai
Other

Bangkok

Figure 3.1 Election result, January 2001.

only seven. North of this line, TRT won 166 and lost 75. Voting had followed party lines as never before.

The TRT parliamentary party consisted of two groups of roughly equal size. The first consisted of first-time MPs, with an average age in their late 30s. The second consisted of defectors from other political parties, including the Snoh Thienthong group, with an average age in the mid-50s.[21] Thaksin mixed the old and new still further by forming a coalition with the Chat Thai party of Banharn and New Aspiration party of Chavalit.

Thaksin in power

> We have to ask ourselves what kind of person we really need to solve the country's problems... If your answer is an absolutely clean man and it doesn't matter if he has never done anything at all, then we need one type of [anti-corruption] law. But if you prefer efficiency and experience, the prerequisites they use when selecting a company's president, then we need another type of law.
>
> Thaksin (*The Nation*, 24 November 2001)

Thaksin had risen to power with the backing of three constituencies: the business interests of himself and his business allies; the aspirations for recovery of small and medium entrepreneurs; and the expectations aroused among the rural mass by the TRT electoral platform. These three shaped his actions in his first year in office.

Thaksin's Cabinet consisted of three groups. The first included big businessmen and a handful of close personal associates of Thaksin.[22] This group took control of all the main economic portfolios including finance, commerce, and industry. The second group consisted of reformers who Thaksin had recruited among committed technocrats and civil society activists, including several former 1970s student activists such as Praphat Panyachartrak who had suggested the rural plan. These were allocated to the two main areas of the TRT electoral platform, agriculture and health, and to education and labour. The third group consisted of the old political bosses, both from within TRT and its allied parties in the coalition.

Ten days before the election, the National Counter Corruption Commission (NCCC) ruled that Thaksin had failed to report his full assets on three occasions over 1997–98 when he had to make a statutory declaration as a minister. The concealed assets, amounting to between 0.6 and 2.4 billion baht, were registered in the names of Thaksin's cook, maid, gardener, and driver. The NCCC surmised that the concealment was 'part of a dishonest scheme, or there would have been no need to use the nominees in the first place' (*The Nation*, 27 December 2000). If the Constitutional Court decided that Thaksin had *intentionally* concealed the assets, he would be banned from politics for five years.

Thaksin fought the case with legal argument: his lawyers tried many strategies, but settled on the claim that the concealment was an 'honest mistake' committed by one of the women in Thaksin's entourage (wife, secretary etc). But the case was also fought by building popular support, especially by rapidly implementing his electoral agenda for the rural mass.

Some 2.4 million farmers took up options of either a debt moratorium or interest rate reduction (*Bangkok Post*, 18 October 2001). The 30-baht-a-visit health care scheme began rolling out province by province before mid-year. For the scheme to allot one million baht to each village as a rolling fund, the local administrative mechanisms took longer to devise, but disbursement began in the fourth quarter. The government also quickly launched a 'People's Bank' offering micro-credit loans through a new window into the existing Government Savings Bank (*The Nation*, 26 June 2001), and adopted the Japanese campaign of 'One Village, One Product', offering another source of credit for community enterprise; 6,340 villages applied to join the scheme (*Bangkok Post*, 9 November 2001). Finally, the government negotiated directly with rural organizations. Thaksin spent his first lunch in office at the Assembly of the Poor's protest encampment outside Government House. After agreement to set up committees to negotiate the Assembly's demands, the encampment dissolved some weeks later (*Bangkok Post*, 4 April 2001).

Policies to help small businessmen remained more rhetorical than real. The government created an SME bank by repackaging an existing state financial institution, but attempts to revive the commercial banking system moved slowly. Thaksin's team held a brainstorming conference with the bankers during its first weeks in office, and subsequently made several small adjustments to banking rules. But neither these measures, nor government urging, convinced the banks to halt their strategy of reducing credit.

Measures that directly affected the telecoms industry and other interests of Thaksin's business allies were more concerted. Immediately on taking office, Thaksin suspended a state-owned mobile phone project designed by the previous Cabinet to undermine the sector's oligopolistic pricing.[23] Thaksin also tried to deter the entry of Hutchison into the mobile phone market by publicly ridiculing their technology. However, throughout 2000, Hutchison continued with their entry, CP began a project in association with UK Orange, and Norwegian Telenor invested in TAC, converting it into a serious competitor. In 2001, the parliament passed a Telecommunications Bill that placed a maximum of 25 per cent on foreign shareholding in telecoms ventures. (This clause was not in the original bill, but was inserted as an amendment in the Senate, and then rapidly approved at a final reading in the lower house.) This provision had important implications for the liberalization of the telecoms sector designated for 2006 under commitments to the WTO. It also embarrassed the new competitors to Shinawatra (particularly Telenor-TAC), which exceeded this shareholding limit. After a storm of complaint, the government agreed to revoke the clause, but this required time to prepare and pass the legislation.

The establishment of independent commissions, mandated in the 1997 constitution, to regulate both the telecoms and media industries became deadlocked after the press and senators challenged the procedure followed in the selection of members. The government showed little interest in untangling the deadlock. It began to privatize the Telephone Organization of Thailand (the body that granted and still managed the Shinawatra concessions) in a way that, rivals feared, would allow Shinawatra to acquire the body.

The government set up the Thailand Asset Management Corporation (TAMC) to manage the bad debts clogging the financial system. Commercial banks were lukewarm to the project because they doubted that officials could manage debts better than the banks themselves, and because the banks would incur any resulting loss. Hence, the TAMC became mainly a device for handling the debts of state and semi-state banks, including the Thai Military Bank, which was part of the Thaksin network. The TAMC had wide powers to rescue debtors. It wrote off 75 per cent of the debts of a company in the Manager media group whose head had become an enthusiastic supporter of Thaksin (*The Nation*, 20 August 2002). Government funds were used to stimulate the property and stock markets. The central bank abandoned most of the court cases launched against financiers for malpractice before and during the 1997 collapse. One of those reprieved was the elder brother of the finance minister (*The Nation*, 15 August 2001).

These measures provoked a rising trend of criticism, particularly within academia and NGOs. However, the government paid close attention to the management of the media. The four older TV channels and most radio stations still operated under ownership or licence from government or army. Some TV and radio programmes on these media were cancelled (*The Nation*, 16 and 24 August 2001). Others were subject to surreptitious censorship or stern warnings (*The Nation*, 13 July 2001). The Defence Ministry instructed radio stations operating its licences to run two minutes of pro-government material at the head of news bulletins. The country's first independent TV channel, ITV, had appeared in 1996. In 1997, Thaksin bought a minority stake. Shortly before the 2001 election, 23 ITV employees were summarily sacked after complaining that the management was biasing election coverage in favour of TRT. The Shinawatra group subsequently raised its stake in ITV to a 64 per cent majority share (*The Nation*, 6 October 2001).

The press had a tradition of independence and criticism, which the Thaksin group managed with money and spin (Kavi 2001a, 2001b).

Advertising revenue from government projects and from companies in the Shinawatra and allied groups was denied to papers that were critical of the regime. Editors were approached to cooperate. Foreign embassies were instructed to question foreign papers that printed critical material (*The Nation*, 29 May 2001). Domestic journalists covering the political beat were provided with facilities (food, computers, Internet links) which they were unlikely to jeopardize. Thaksin's staff expertly prepared news stories to make the journalists' jobs easier. Five PR companies were engaged to arrange government events and manage the prime minister's image.[24]

In sum, Thaksin rushed to implement his election promises, in part to build popular support before the Constitutional Court decision on his asset concealment. This tactic worked. In August, the Court decided in Thaksin's favour by an 8–7 split decision, with at least three judges admitting their decisions were based more on political expediency than law. The Thaksin government also used state power to favour the business interests of its members and friends. To manage the resulting criticism, the government took a firmer grip on the news media, but it was able to do little for small and medium businessmen without the cooperation of the banks.

Thaksin, big business, and the poor

> We are open for business... We are very international. My business background is international.
>
> Thaksin (*The Nation*, 26 July 2001)

TRT's election strategy, and its actions over its first year in power, signalled a new alignment in Thai politics – big business leadership voted into power after making a direct appeal for the support of the rural mass. Over 2001, Thaksin and his allies gave speeches which clarified how these two components fitted together.

To begin with, Thaksin linked his pro-business policies and pro-poor policies by attributing them to a common origin. At a speech in April 2001, he blamed banking reforms and other crisis measures for creating 'massive financial cleanup costs and major roadblocks, leaving a severe and unfair burden for the poor' (*Bangkok Post*, 24 April 2001; *The Nation*, 24 April 2001). In other words, the IMF's policies had inflicted damage on domestic capitalism which ended up hurting the poor.

Over this and a subsequent speech in April, Thaksin signalled the outline of his government's new direction. Thailand would have to turn away from an 'Asian model' of growth, which relied on exporting cheap products to the advanced economies. Instead, 'We are looking inward to our original strengths, our unique local know-how, and matching them with new marketing and communications technology'. The aim was to create 'a new class of entrepreneurs' who could marry local skills and products with international technology and hence move 'up the value chain'. This strategy, Thaksin claimed, was appropriate not just for Thailand but for Asia:

> Asian capabilities, aesthetic skills, unique local know-how, knowledge and dedication, when combined with world-class modern design, cutting-edge technology, appropriate cost-effective engineering, modern packaging, advanced marketing and Internet capabilities, will be the key to the new Silk Road and the new spicy life styles.
>
> (*The Nation*, 10 May 2001)

The rejection of an 'Asian model', however, extended only as far as the export emphasis. Indeed, the task of rebuilding the entrepreneurial class would require considerable cooperation between government and business. The core of 'Thaksinomics' was government stimulation of domestic private enterprise.

This policy, Thaksin continued, had to be matched by measures to 'solve the problem of poverty of the majority' and 'reduce the socio-economic gaps between the poor and the well-to-do, and, especially between the rural and urban sectors'. These were needed 'to ensure social cohesion and political stability, which will enable economic recovery and growth' (*The Nation*, 10 May 2001). In Tokyo, in November 2001, Thaksin emphasized that his social policies were designed 'to create a stable social platform for investment... Improving the quality of life at the grass-roots level will create a stable social platform – a cushion. This social harmony protects and enhances your investments from the volatility of the global economy'.[25] In other words, social policies were needed to prevent political problems destabilizing entrepreneur-led growth; the rising tide of rural protest, and the blockage of so many large-scale investment projects, had to be overcome. Thaksin clarified that most of the rural policies – micro-credit, village revolving funds, one village one product – were attempts 'to encourage Thais to be more entrepreneurial' (*The Nation*, 24 August 2001). Thaksin had no strategy to empower farmers or change their structural position. Rather he wanted to convert them into businessmen. Localist advocates who had cooperated with TRT before the election became openly hostile.[26]

Through mid-2001, as the export-led partial recovery of the previous two years faltered in the face of a global downturn, Thaksin presented his rural policies as a way to stimulate domestic demand to compensate for falling exports: 'The objective is to strengthen domestic demand and production so as to serve as a cushion to immunize the Thai economy against the adverse effects of global volatility and the forces of globalization' (*The Nation*, 24 August 2001). Thaksin and his team also clarified that the domestic policy emphasis did not exclude export promotion and foreign investment. Rather, Thailand was pursuing a 'dual track policy'. Speaking to businessmen in New York in December, finance minister Somkid insisted that 'many foreign investors read these two goals as contradictory, when in fact these twofold goals are concurrent and complementary'. The support for SMEs would build 'supporting industries for your investments'. The domestic demand stimulus would 'expand the buying power of 62 million Thais' for the benefit of investors targeting the domestic market. The cheap health care scheme would 'ensure a strong and healthy workforce' so that 'production need never be put on hold by disruptions in supply of utilities, or by sick-leave' (*The Nation*, 19 December 2001).

In sum, Thaksin's economic strategy was the stimulus of business entrepreneurship across the whole spectrum of society. This was the route to a recovery from the crisis led by domestic capital. It might even attract foreign capital. It would overcome the problems of poverty and inequality that threatened to create political barriers to business success.

Conclusions

We used to have so many political parties that we could not remember all their names. We used to set up parties only to see them collapse later. We are now sending a message to the world that there will be continuity in politics and we can run the country for the next ten years.

Thaksin (*Bangkok Post*, 28 January 2002)

In early 2001, Thaksin Shinawatra led a group of the major domestic capitalists who had survived the financial crisis to capture state power, with the explicit aim of using it to protect and promote domestic capital. This group was mobilized in reaction to the damage inflicted by the 1997 Asian crisis. It gained support from the large base of small business families that had suffered from the collapse of the banking system, and which were attracted by the promise of government assistance for entrepreneurship. Thaksin's rise was a logical extension of Thailand's business-dominated 'money politics', but also a dramatic change of scale. It brought some of the wealthiest elements of domestic capital into the seat of power. It superseded 'money politics' with 'big money politics'.

The extent of Thaksin's electoral success in January 2001 can be partly attributed to the constitution, which changed the electoral system with the aim of reducing the fragmentation of political parties and the instability of coalitions (Hicken 2001). However, Thaksin magnified this by the deployment of his own wealth to log-roll old politicians, and by the construction of a party platform that appealed to social forces stirred up by the crisis.

Until 1998, there was no sign that Thaksin would attempt to change the style of Thai politics. Until then he projected himself as a more modern version of the modernist model, which worked well for the Democrats. The founder members of his party, and its first 'shadow cabinet', were a conventional mix of businessmen, bureaucrats, and intellectuals. The party's policies, and Thaksin's rhetoric, changed over 1998–2000 as the social and political responses to the crisis became better defined.

TRT asked small businessmen and the rural mass what they wanted from the state, campaigned on this electoral platform in a way that partially circumvented old structures of local influence, and delivered probably more of its promises than its supporters expected.[27] His appeal to the rural mass succeeded because of the nature of rural politics. Over the previous decade, rural groups had become more organized, and had experimented with agitation for political demands. But they did not feel strong enough to overcome the structural barriers (the degree requirement for MPs) or the hegemonic barriers (the legacy of past suppression of rural organization) to full participation in parliamentary politics. They responded to the TRT platform because it offered something rather than the nothing available in the past. But by remaining outside organized politics, these rural groups remained imprisoned by the old paternalist relationship between the political elite and the rural mass.

This pluto-populist alliance between rich and poor was glued together by nationalism. Thaksin drew on the resentment of outside forces (IMF, globalization) stirred up by the 1997 crisis. He tapped a widespread impression that the Democrat government, under IMF auspices, had abandoned its responsibility to promote private business. He cited a Harvard professor (R. Greenfield) 'who suggested that for a country to succeed in the capitalist world, nationalism was a vital ingredient' (*The Nation*, 10 January 2002).

However, Thaksin's nationalism was bound by some constraints, as the reactions to the crisis had revealed. The indebted businessmen's attempt to raise nationalist opposition to IMF policies failed to gain any significant support. Public intellectuals were disunited and talked to minority audiences. Mass resentment against outside forces grew slowly and remained diffuse.

Thaksin's nationalism was interestingly different to the Cold War version, represented by the Chat Thai party, whose name translates as 'Thai Nation party' and whose logo uses the two strong national symbols of the map outline and the flag. TRT's party name plays on the ethnic signifier, Thai, and echoes one of the self-help organizations, *Thai chuai thai* (Thai helps Thai), which emerged during the crisis. The party symbol uses the T letter, which is the initial of both Thaksin and Thai, and the red–white–blue spectrum, but not the flag itself. TRT election rallies were not festooned with national flags, as American party rallies or UK Tory party conferences. The party's slogan ends with 'for every Thai' rather than statements like 'to cure the country's/nation's problems' used by Chat Thai and other parties. In speeches, Thaksin prefers the word *ban-muang* (literally 'village-town', roughly meaning 'people' or 'society') to forms like *chat* (nation) and *phaendin* (country, realm). Talking on the subject of nationalism, Thaksin said: 'I am not calling for people to become nationalistic, but to have a sense of nationhood' (*The Nation*, 10 January 2002). Thaksin's nationalism evokes a community of 'Thai people' without fully embracing the vocabulary and symbols of nation and state.

There may be several reasons for this delicately soft approach. The hesitant emergence of *mass* nationalist sentiment in 1997–99 (as distinct from intellectual positions or business self-defence) suggests the limitations in a society without a historical experience of mass nationalism. Given that TRT claimed to have used research to choose its name and refine its campaign, it is likely that this soft approach reflects popular preference against a more militant form.

Besides, Thaksin did not represent a retreat from globalization behind national barriers, but a strategic readjustment so that Thailand might become a stronger global competitor. He has presented himself, by virtue of his 'international' qualities, as the best leader to manage the globalizing forces which enveloped Thailand in the 1990s.

In addition, the mobilization of nationalism may have limitations in a country where the monarchy serves as the focus of national sentiment. In December 2001, the King chided Thaksin in the presence of the massed Thai elite on live television. The King talked about 'double standards', excess ego, and national 'catastrophe'.[28] The *Review* (10 January 2002) explained that the King had spoken 'because of Thaksin's perceived arrogance and his alleged attempts to meddle in royal family affairs'. But was there a wider significance? Thaksin had not only projected himself as the saviour of the nation, but also as the friend of the poor, a technology-aware modernizer, and the head of a close, modern, nuclear family.

What finally is the content of Thaksin's 'populism'? Because of the novelty of his bid, the confusion created by the crisis, and the anti-rural bias of the Democrats, Thaksin was able to appeal to a broad swathe of rural groups and activist agendas. But once in power, the nature of Thaksin's articulation between big business and rural activism became more clearly defined. Big business' main motivation for redrawing the social contract was to stem the rising tide of political dissent. Social policies were simply a 'cushion' to protect profit making. Thaksin's main strategy for rural change was to pump in capital funds. He had no interest in land reform, land-to-the-tiller programmes, tax reforms, or other policies to shift the structural position of peasants within the national economy. He placed much less emphasis on agriculture than on the urban economy. His approach was not so much to help the farmer, as to convert him into something else – a businessman. He adopted some of the language of community culture and localism, but none of the content. As a whole, his strategy was to deepen capitalism in order to reverse the growing division – both economic and cultural – between city and village.

Similarly, Thaksin's programmes have not followed the Latin American populists' emphasis on benefits for labour. Indeed, TRT's policies scarcely mention labour as a category.

How far is this pluto-populism a real change in Thai political culture, and how far is it specific to Thaksin? Certainly, the TRT victory immediately rendered obsolete the old Thai politics of alliance between provincial businessmen and bureaucrats. In August 2001, Thaksin was cleared of his asset case by the Constitutional Court, and immediately began talking of a second term.[29] In January 2002, TRT absorbed its main coalition ally, NAP, giving his party almost 300 seats in the 500-member house. Thaksin immediately projected that TRT would rule for a decade. As the economy improved in mid-2002, he predicted he would remain in power for four terms, totalling 16 years (*The Nation*, 23 August 2002).

Thaksin's rise has probably brought two lasting changes. First, big domestic capital has come right into the core of Thai politics. This trend, replicated in countries such as Italy and Mexico, reflects a renewed awareness of the importance of state power for promoting domestic capitalism in the context of globalization. Second, the rural mass has gained some bargaining power through the ballot box. Again, this reflects a broader trend whereby rural groups gain greater political space while facing greater economic exploitation under globalization. But how long can these two elements of Thaksin's pluto-populism coexist?

Notes

1 Thanks to Ukrist Pathamanand, Sakkarin Niyomsilpa, Kevin Hewison, Duncan McCargo, Michael Nelson, Pasuk Phongpaichit, John Sidel, and audiences of preliminary versions of this paper at Columbia University and Johns Hopkins SAIS.

2 Quoted in *The Nation*, 19 April 2001.

3 The main reforms of parliament were as follows. Constituencies were broken down from multi to single member. Vote counting now prevented candidates from tracing how individual villages or wards had polled. The conduct of the elections was transferred from the Ministry of Interior to an independent Election Commission, which has stronger powers to penalize candidates for malpractice. As well as 400 territorial constituencies, 100 MPs were elected from a 'party list' by a national vote. Constituency MPs selected as ministers had to resign their seats. All MPs were required to hold a tertiary degree. On the evolution of the constitution, see Connors (1999), McCargo (2002a), Pasuk and Baker (2000, Ch. 5).

4 At that time the exchange rate was roughly 25 baht to 1 US dollar.

5 Notably Paibul Limphaphayom, who was sacked as head of the telephone organization (TOT) following corruption allegations shortly after the TOT had allotted Thaksin the mobile phone concession and other projects (Sakkarin 1995: 204).

6 CP is the largest Thai conglomerate. It rose with an integrated chicken business, then expanded into a range of agribusinesses in Thailand and other countries of the region. From the 1980s, CP became a major investor in China (especially Shanghai), and selected telecommunications as its priority for future expansion.

7 Thaksin never had a total monopoly on mobile phones. UCOM/TAC received a second concession a year after Thaksin. But, because of better terms, Thaksin was able to gain almost double UCOM/TAC's subscribers (Sakkarin 1995: 235). The CP project was threatening because it used technology that had succeeded in Japan. In fact, the system ran into technical problems (probably caused by Thailand's humidity), but this was not known until later.

8 Sarasin Viraphon, CP executive and son-in-law of the CP patriarch, was expected to be a founder member, but withdrew at the last moment (*The Nation*, 15 July 1998).

9 The 1997 constitution added 100 MPs chosen by a party vote. Adisai, Pitak, Pracha, and Suriya all came in through the TRT party list where they were positioned 5, 8, 10 and 12.

10 The 23 founder members are listed at www.thairakthai.or.th/about/list/founder.htm. Ten became MPs and/or ministers in the 2001 government.

11 Except by right-wing groups such as Apirak Chakri, or in a limited and defensive form by others, popular demonstrations habitually carry flags and pictures of the royal family in order to affirm that their actions should not be construed as an attempt to overthrow the state or the traditional order.

12 It was followed by a drama set in a mythical northern Tai hill state, oppressed by a powerful neighbour, which seemed to be Thailand itself.

13 Chuan was a lawyer by training, but his public demeanour recalled traditional bureaucrats, and his strategy as premier was to refer everything to the bureaucracy.

14 At the initial polls, TRT secured 248 of the 500 seats (see Table 3.1). The Seritham party, which won 14, merged with TRT shortly after the results were known.

15 Provinces served as multi-member constituencies, with up to eight seats (18 in Bangkok); candidates were not allowed to be members of political parties and were not allowed to campaign, only to announce their candidature.

16 Including 58 from NAP, 16 from Chat Phatthana, 11 from Social Action, nine from Chat Thai, and six from the Democrats (*The Nation*, 30 August 2000).

17 A 'non-performing loan', meaning a defaulting debtor.

18 This ad appeared in most newspapers in the first week of December 2000.

19 The old political families which lost included: Asavahame in Samut Prakan, Angkinan in Phetchaburi, Moolasartsathorn in Surin, Manasikarn in Phitsanulok, Iasakul in Nong Khai, Harnsawat in Pathumthani, Lik in Kamphaeng Phet, Yubamrung in Thonburi, Lertnuwat in Chiang Rai, Khamprakorb in Nakhon Sawan, Wongwan in Lamphun.

20 The most glaring loss by an old politico who had joined TRT was Yingphan Manasikarn in Phitsanulok. His wife won the neighbouring seat as a TRT candidate by a large majority.

21 Among the 200 TRT MPs from territorial constituencies, 110 were new MPs with an average age of 42, and 90 were old MPs with an average age of 51.

22 The latter group included Purachai Piemsombun (interior), Somkid Jatusripitak (finance), Suvarn Valaisathian (deputy finance), and Pongthep Thepkanchana (justice). Interestingly, this group had jurisdiction over every issue which arose out of Thaksin's assets declaration case, including whether the concealment was intended to avoid tax or cover up stock-market irregularities, as the National Counter Corruption Commission surmised.

23 The project later resurfaced, heavily under the influence of the Shinawatra family.

24 This management of the media was generally effective, but within certain limits. The *Nation* group refused to cooperate and remained strongly critical. It recognized that the government's management of the press created a market opportunity because people bored easily of reading pro-government news. It launched a Thai-language daily, *Khom Chat Luk* (Sharp Clear Deep), which criticized government policies, and which quickly gained a large readership. The market leader *Thai Rath* had to moderate its support for the government in order to recover market share.

25 'Thailand: Invest in Our Future', speech in Tokyo, November 20, 2001, at www.thaigov.go.th/news/speech/thaksin/sp20nov01.htm.

26 'But immediately dumping money in unprepared villages will divide communities. Top-down, unaccountable management through state mechanisms will encourage corruption'. Songkhla village leader, quoted by Sanitsuda Ekachai (*Bangkok Post*, 25 May 2001). See also, 'Message to Thaksin from Prawase Wasi' (*Bangkok Post*, 19 May 2001), an open letter advocating the community approach which Thaksin pointedly ignored.

27 Polls after the election showed that many voters believed the TRT platform was 'too good to be true' (*Bangkok Post*, 12 February 2001).

28 'At present everyone knows that the country faces a catastrophe ... because now everything seems to be in decline. The prime minister is making a long face. He's not pleased I talked about catastrophe. But that's the truth, because whatever is done seems to be a problem. The prime minister is happy but only on the outside, not the inside. I don't know what is to be done, because nothing is progressing'. 'Phraratchathan nai luang [King's speech]', *Matichon*, 5 December 2001.

29 This was ambitious given that no previous elected premier has ever survived even one full 4-year term. But it makes sense when you consider that Thaksin and his allies need the second term to ensure they are in charge through the critical period of WTO telecoms liberalization in 2006.

References

Arghiros, Daniel (2001) *Democracy, Development and Decentralization in Provincial Thailand*, Richmond: Curzon.

Baker, Chris (2000) Thailand's assembly of the poor: background, drama, reaction, *South East Asia Research*, 8, pp. 5–29.

Brass, Tom (1995) Postscript: populism, peasants and intellectuals, or what's left of the future?, in: T. Brass (ed.) *New Farmers' Movements in India*, London: Frank Cass, pp. 246–86.

Callahan, William A. and McCargo, Duncan (1996) Vote-buying in Thailand's Northeast, *Asian Survey*, 36, pp. 376–92.

Connors, Michael K. (1999) Political reform and the state in Thailand, *Journal of Contemporary Asia*, 29, pp. 202–25.

Gothom Arya (2001) Participation in Thai politics. Paper presented at the conference on Thailand: The Next Stage, SAIS, Johns Hopkins University, Washington, DC, November.

Hewison, Kevin (2000) Thailand's capitalism before and after the economic crisis, in: Richard Robison *et al.* (eds) *Politics and Markets in the Wake of the Asian Crisis*, London: Routledge, pp. 192–211.

Hewison, Kevin (2001) Pathways to recovery: bankers, businessmen and nationalism in Thailand, SEARC Working Papers 1, City University of Hong Kong, April.

Hewison, Kevin (2002) Responding to economic crisis: Thailand's localism, in: D. McCargo (ed.) *Reforming Thai Politics*, Copenhagen: NIAS, pp. 247–60.

Hicken, Allen D. (2001) From Phitsanulok to parliament: multiple parties in pre-1997 Thailand, in: Michael H. Nelson (ed.) *Thailand's New Politics: KPI Yearbook 2001*, Bangkok: King Prajadhipok's Institute and White Lotus, pp. 145–76.

Kasian Tejapira (2000) Post-crisis economic impasse and political recovery in Thailand: the resurgence of economic nationalism. Paper presented at Fifth Shizuoka Asia-Pacific Forum, December.

Kasian Tejapira (2001) Pisat poppiwlisam [The populism devil], *Matichon*, 20 January [in Thai].

Kavi Chongkittavorn (2001a) Captured by the spin: media manipulation, *Nation*, 20 August.

Kavi Chongkittavorn (2001b) Media reform in Thailand: new prospects and new problems. Paper presented at the conference on Thailand: The Next Stage, SAIS, Johns Hopkins University, Washington, DC, November 2001.

McCargo, Duncan (2002a) Introduction: understanding political reform in Thailand, in: D. McCargo (ed.) *Reforming Thai Politics*, Copenhagen: NIAS, pp. 247–60.

McCargo, Duncan (2002b) Thailand's January 2001 general elections: vindicating reform?, in: D. McCargo (ed.) *Reforming Thai Politics*, Copenhagen: NIAS.

Pasuk Phongpaichit (2002) *Withi chiwit witi su: khabuankan prachachon ruam samai* [Ways of Life, Means of Struggle: Contemporary Popular Movements], Chiang Mai: Silkworm Books [in Thai].

Pasuk Phongpaichit and Baker, Chris (2000) *Thailand's Crisis*, Chiang Mai: Silkworm Books.

Pasuk Phongpaichit and Baker, Chris (2002) *Thailand: Economy and Politics*, 2nd edn, Kuala Lumpur: Oxford University Press.

Phak thai rak thai (1999) *Khana tham ngan phu tit tam kan patipat ngam ratthaban* [Working groups to monitor the government], undated pamphlet, around August.

Praphat Pintobtaeng (1998) *Kanmuang bon thong thanon: 99 wan samatcha khon jon* [Politics on the Street: Ninety-Nine Days of the Assembly of the Poor], Bangkok: Krirk University [in Thai].

Sakkarin Niyomsilpa (1995) The political economy of telecommunications liberalization in Thailand, unpublished PhD thesis, Australian National University.

Sanlaya [Phumtham Vetchachayacha] (2001) *Thaksin Chinnawat: ta du dao thao tit din* [Thaksin Shinawatra: Eyes on the Stars, Feet on the Ground], Bangkok: Matichon [in Thai].

Somchai Phatharathananunth (2001) Civil society in Northeast Thailand: the struggle of the Small Scale Farmers' Assembly of Isan, unpublished PhD thesis, University of Leeds.

Sorakon Adulyanon (1993) *Thaksin shinnawat asawin khloen luk thi sam* [Thaksin Shinawatra, Knight of the Third Wave], Bangkok: Matichon [in Thai].

Suthep Kittikulsingh (1999) Non-performing loans (NPLs): the borrower's viewpoint, *TDRI Quarterly Review*, 14, pp. 19–30.

Ukrist Pathmanand (1998) The Thaksin Shinawatra group: a study of the relationship between money and politics in Thailand, *Copenhagen Journal of Asian Studies*, 13, pp. 60–81.

Ukrist Pathmanand (2000) From Shinawatra group of companies to the Thaksin Shinawatra government: the politics of money and power merge. Paper presented at conference on Crony Capitalism, Quezon City, January.

World Bank (2001) *Thailand Social Monitor: Poverty and Public Policy*, Bangkok: World Bank.

Chapter 4

Socio-economic consequences of the crisis

Isra Sarntisart

From the beginning of the 1960s and through the first half of the 1990s, Thailand's rate of economic growth was very impressive, with the average real rate of growth fluctuating between 8 and 12 per cent during this period. It dropped to approximately 6 per cent in 1996, and to a slightly negative rate for the first time in many decades in 1997. In 1998, the Thai economy contracted severely. This chapter asks what these macroeconomic events meant for the living conditions of the Thai people.

The results of many past studies indicate that during the period of economic boom the benefits of growth trickled down to most Thais and their economic well-being improved substantially. During the long period when the rate of economic growth exceeded 8 per cent per annum, the proportion of the poor in the total population decreased continuously and significantly. Based on Oey (1979), this proportion (known as the head-count measure of poverty incidence) declined from approximately 57 per cent in 1962/63 to 33 per cent in 1975/76. Using comparable measures of poverty, Isra (1995) adds that it declined further to 22 per cent in 1988 and to 14 per cent in 1992. Further impressive reductions in poverty incidence occurred between 1992 and 1996, and these will be discussed in subsequent sections.

However, the benefits of economic growth were not distributed equally. During the same period, income inequality, as measured by the Gini index,[1] increased from 0.426 in 1975/76 (Suganya and Somchai 1988) to 0.493 in 1988 and 0.531 in 1992 (Isra 1995). There was a slight decline until 1996, when the index was 0.511 (see Table 4.2, below). It is widely believed that the crisis produced significant changes in poverty incidence and income inequality. These changes are the principal focus of this paper.

Many policy measures have been adopted by the government in response to the crisis. In addition to the floating of the exchange rate and other macroeconomic measures, the government's decision to increase the value added tax (VAT) rate on 16 August 1997 from 7 per cent to 10 per cent also had significant implications for aggregate demand, inflation and social welfare. The decision to reduce the VAT rate back to 7 per cent on 1 April 1999 was, conversely, expected to reduce the burden on Thai households, to increase domestic demand, and thereby to boost output. Efforts were also made to identify disadvantaged groups and to assist them in dealing with hardships caused by the crisis, by expanding existing social safety programmes and developing new programmes. These efforts involved not only government agencies but also NGOs, local communities and others.

This chapter explores the socio-economic consequences of the crisis and the effectiveness of policy measures adopted in response to it. Following this introductory section, the chapter is organized into six sections. The first explores the conceptual issues involved in analysing the effects that an event such as the 1997 crisis had on incomes, poverty incidence, and income inequality. The second section focuses on the socio-economic consequences of the crisis, especially its effects on poverty incidence. As well as effects on overall poverty incidence, we also consider effects on poverty decomposed by region, rural–urban location, farm and non-farm employment and by the gender of the household head.

The third section examines changes in household economic welfare and the profile of households that experienced a decline in economic welfare following the crisis. The fourth and fifth sections review the impact of the crisis on employment, and income from labour earnings, respectively. The educational impact is discussed in the sixth section. The last section draws conclusions. Data and definitions are summarized in an appendix at the end of the chapter.

Consequences for poverty incidence

Conceptual issues: measuring 'crisis impact'

Two recent studies discuss the short-term changes in poverty incidence that occurred during the crisis. Although both conclude that the crisis increased poverty incidence, they do not reach the same conclusion on the magnitude of the impact. These studies are Warr (1998) and Kakwani (1999). Both of these studies are based on the official data on poverty incidence, assembled by the government's National Economic and Social Development Board (NESDB). A comparison of these two studies helps illustrate the conceptual and empirical problems involved in estimating the effects of an event like the 1997 crisis.

Warr analysed changes in poverty incidence in four Southeast Asian countries, including Thailand. In the case of Thailand, the study points out that the economic crisis was a setback in the trend of poverty reduction, but argues that the number of people falling below the poverty line following the crisis may have been less than was often suggested at the time. The increase in poverty incidence was estimated to be around 1.5 per cent of the total population or approximately 0.9 million people.

Warr's estimate was based on a comparison of (a) his estimate of actual poverty incidence at the end of 1998 (the same time that his estimates were presented) with (b) official estimates of actual poverty incidence in 1996. The estimates in (a) were based on an econometrically estimated projection model that related changes in poverty incidence to the rate of economic growth, which he combined with data on the actual rates of growth in 1997 and 1998. A projection was necessary because official data on poverty incidence are not published until some time after the event and Warr was discussing the *current* level of poverty incidence.[2] Warr also used this model to estimate the degree to which future rates of poverty incidence might depend on the rate of growth.

Based on the official (NESDB) poverty line, Kakwani reported a reverse in the trend of poverty incidence in 1998. According to the study, approximately 32.6 per cent of the Thai population were classified as poor in 1988. The percentage of the population in poverty decreased to 27.2 per cent in 1990, 23.2 per cent in 1992, 16.3 per cent in 1994, and 11.4 per cent in 1996. Based on data for the first three quarters of 1998, Kakwani's estimate of poverty incidence rose to 12.9 per cent of the total population. Surprisingly, estimated poverty increased in all regions except the North, where it decreased from 11.2 per cent to 9.2 per cent of the total population in that region. The overall increase in actual poverty incidence between 1996 and 1998 was 1.5 per cent of the total population, or approximately 0.9 million, exactly the same as Warr's earlier, model-based projection.

However, Kakwani takes a further step. He argues that if the crisis had not occurred, the expected number of poor people in 1998 would have been 6.4 million. This is based on a simple projection to 1998 of the (pre-crisis) declining trend in poverty incidence over the period 1988 to 1996. Thus, comparing (a) his estimate of actual incidence in 1998 (7.9 million) with (b) his counterfactual estimate of what poverty incidence *would have been* in 1998 without the crisis (6.4 million), Kakwani concludes that the impact of the crisis was an increase in the number of poor of 1.5 million, or 2.5 per cent of the population.

Clearly, the difference between the estimates of crisis impact in the Warr and Kakwani studies rests primarily on a conceptual issue: the meaning of 'crisis impact'. Warr interprets this to mean a comparison of actual post-crisis with actual pre-crisis levels of poverty incidence. Kakwani interprets it to mean a comparison of actual post-crisis poverty incidence with *counterfactual* post-crisis poverty incidence – an estimate of what poverty would have been without the crisis.

The above discussion illustrates two different approaches to analysing the effects of an event like the 1997 crisis. The first method (as in Warr) is to compare *before* and *after.* In this case, 'before' might mean 1996 and 'after' might mean, say, 1998 or later. The second method (as in Kakwani) is to compare *with* and *without.* In this case 'with' might mean the actual observed data for, say, 1998, and 'without' might mean a counterfactual estimate of what would have occurred at that same time (say, 1998) if the event had not occurred. The advantage of the before–after approach is that it is straightforward and easily implemented. Its disadvantage is that some of the differences between the before and after situations might not properly be attributable to the event of interest (the crisis), but to something else, which just happened to occur at the same time.

The with–without method has the conceptual advantage that it is, in principle, capable of isolating the effects of the event in which we are interested, but its validity, in practice, rests on the method used to estimate the counterfactual 'without' situation. It is important to emphasize that the 'without' situation is *not observed.* It is always hypothetical, an estimate of 'What would have happened if...?' Data alone can never answer such a question. A model of some kind must be employed to estimate this counterfactual, but the models that are used are always subject to criticism and debate. Different models can always be used and they will often produce different results. However, deciding between them is difficult, sometimes impossible. Consequently, applying the with–without method is far from straightforward.

For example, Kakwani's method of estimating what poverty incidence *would have been* in 1998 *without* the crisis is, first, to estimate the trend rate of decline of poverty incidence observed from 1988 to 1996 and, second, simply to project this trend to 1998. In other words, it assumes that if 'the crisis' had not occurred, the trend rate of decline of poverty incidence would have continued unchanged, at least until 1998. What this implicitly assumes is that the pre-crisis rate of decline was *sustainable.* If it was not, for example because the pre-crisis rate of economic growth was unsustainable, then Kakwani's estimates of the 1998 levels of poverty 'without' the crisis and the estimates of crisis impact based on it would be meaningless; they would refer to a hypothetical situation that could not have existed. A major problem with the with–without method is that, in practice, it often produces inconclusive debate about matters of this kind.

Less simplistic methods are available for estimating counterfactuals, but they are always partial and subject to dispute. To apply this method to estimating the effects that the crisis had on poverty incidence, what must be done is (i) to identify the economic variables influencing poverty incidence and which changed during the crisis; (ii) to estimate the amount by which they changed because of the crisis; (iii) to determine the quantitative relationship between changes in poverty incidence and these crisis-affected variables; and (iv) to use the above information to project the changes in poverty incidence that are attributable to these changes in the crisis-affected variables.

To apply the with–without method satisfactorily, it would be necessary to recognize that poverty incidence in Thailand depends on more than just the passage of time (Kakwani's approach) or the rate of economic growth (Warr's approach) but also other factors affecting income distribution and the situation of the poor. For example, poverty incidence in Thailand tends to be closely related with the performance of the agricultural sector. Bergemeier and Hoffman (1988) studied the principal characteristics of poverty concentration in 1981, pointing out that poverty incidence had a rural bias. Ahuja *et al.* (1997) analysed changes in poverty and inequality in East Asia, including Thailand. Based on 1975–92 data, the study concludes that there has been a tendency towards greater concentration of poverty among groups traditionally most vulnerable to it, especially farmers and uneducated persons.

The relationship between the prices of major crops and poverty incidence in Thailand is made clear by several earlier studies. Suganya and Somchai (1988) studied the worsening poverty incidence in 1985/86 and asserted that poverty incidence was lower in 1980/81 than in 1985/86, because of the effect of the extra high crop prices in the former year. Similarly, Medhi *et al.* (1991) showed that, in almost every region, there was a lower percentage of rural Thais in poverty in 1988 than in 1985/86. They argue that the 1988 situation was similar to that in 1980/81 and argue that the major determinant was crop prices, which were at a peak in 1980/81 and 1988.

In the presence of an event such as the 1997 crisis, increases in crop prices should therefore insulate the rural population from falling into poverty, compared with the situation that would otherwise occur. The negative impact of the crisis on the rural sector, where the majority of poor live, should be magnified by any decreases in crop prices or be reduced (and possibly even reversed) by any increases in crop prices. It is widely believed that, because of high agricultural prices following the crisis, farmers, and especially those in the Central, the North and the Northeast regions were indeed at least partly insulated from the crisis. Exchange rate depreciation and increases in world demand for major crops led to sharp increases in the prices of major crops between 1996 and 1998.

Based on data from the Ministry of Agriculture and Cooperatives, the prices of major crops in the year 1997/98 were higher than in the preceding 14 year period (Table 1 in Sawalak, 1999). An example is cassava, which is a major crop among poor farmers, especially in the poorest region, the Northeast. Its 1998 price was nearly twice the 1996/97 price, although the average annual rate of inflation over this period was only around 7 per cent. Similarly, the 1997/98 prices of sugar-cane, maize and rice were approximately 24 per cent, 12 per cent and 8 per cent above their 1996/97 prices, respectively. There was no significant drop in the production of these major crops, so farm income should have significantly increased. Rural poverty incidence should have decreased, compared with the situation where these price changes did not occur.

If we were to apply the with–without method to assess the impact of the crisis, a basic question would arise. To what extent were these price changes attributable to the crisis, and to what extent were they incidental? To the extent that depreciation of the Thai baht was a cause of the price increases, this may reasonably be attributed to the crisis. But international prices for these commodities also increased and this seems unlikely to be attributable to the crisis, although some effect of this kind is not impossible. Having identified the degree to which each of these price changes was attributable to the crisis, it is then necessary to estimate the changes in poverty incidence that they would have produced, recognizing that while increases in agricultural prices reduce rural poverty, they may increase urban poverty by raising the cost of food.

Similar problems arise in assessing events following 1998. In 1999, the appreciation of the Thai baht lowered rural prices, and drought created production problems for the rural sector. The exchange rate appreciation may be attributable to the after effects of the crisis (the effects of exchange rate over-shooting) but the drought was certainly not caused by it. Applying the with–without method would require separating the effects of these events. It is clear that a rigorous application of the with–without method of analysis to an event such as the 1997 crisis involves formidable conceptual and empirical problems. For this reason, the analysis in this chapter will apply the before–after method. In doing so, the potential pitfall of this method must be kept in mind – not all changes that followed the crisis are necessarily a consequence of the crisis itself.

Poverty measurement

The measurement of poverty involves the use of a poverty line. This is a level of household income per household member (as in Thailand) or household expenditure per household member (in some other countries, such as Indonesia) below which all members of the household concerned are deemed to be poor. The magnitude of this poverty line is adjusted over time with movements in consumer prices. Table 4.1 compares the official data on average consumer price levels (collected and analysed by the Ministry of Commerce) and those of the official (NESDB) poverty line. From 1990 to 1994, the average official poverty line moved more or less in line with changes in the aggregate price level – the official inflation rate. But it did not do so in 1996 and 1998.

Using 1990 as a base period (1990 prices set equal to 100), the average price levels in 1996 and 1998 were 133.8 and 152.7, respectively. The official poverty line in those years was (again setting 1990 at 100) 141.2 and 168.2, respectively. While the annual inflation rate over the 1996–98

Table 4.1 Comparison between official poverty line, official consumer price index and old poverty line, 1990 to 2000

Year	Official consumer price index (1990 = 100)	Official poverty line		Old poverty line	
		Level (baht per person per month)	Index (1990 = 100)	Level (baht per person per month)	Index (1990 = 100)
1990	100.0	522	100.0	481	100.0
1992	110.0	600	114.9	527	109.6
1994	119.5	636	121.8	581	120.8
1996	133.8	737	141.2	649	134.9
1998	152.7	878	168.2	742	154.3
2000	155.6	882	169.0	758	157.6

Source: Consumer price index from Ministry of Commerce. Official poverty line from NESDB. 'Old poverty line' from Oey (1979), updated by consumer price index for urban and rural areas from the Ministry of Commerce, aggregated by urban and rural population shares of each year, population data from National Statistical Office.

period was around 6.8 per cent, the official poverty line increased over the same period at an annual rate of approximately 9.1 per cent. The fact that measured poverty incidence is positively dependent on the magnitude of the poverty line is well known. For example, by changing the poverty line from $1 to $2 per day, Ahuja et al. (1997) demonstrated that measured poverty incidence is very sensitive to the magnitude of the poverty line.

Kakwani (1999) states that adjustments over time to the official (NESDB) poverty line are due to many factors, including increases in food and non-food prices, and the population structure. There has been no evidence that the population structure changed significantly during this period, so the large divergence between the official poverty line data and the official price level data must be due to differences in the composition of the commodity baskets used to adjust the two series. By construction, the official price level data are based on the actual consumption basket of Thai households and better reflect the actual purchasing power of households' incomes.

Because the official poverty line increased much more rapidly after the crisis than actual consumer prices, there is a danger that the use of this poverty line may have overstated the degree to which poverty really increased. This study will therefore recalculate poverty incidence using a poverty line that moves in line with consumer prices. For the purposes of the present study, our base level poverty lines are based on the estimates of Oey (1979), because their use allows comparisons of changes in poverty incidence with past poverty reports, as mentioned above. The value of these poverty lines is then adjusted over time in line with changes in the consumer price index. The resulting urban and rural poverty lines are weighted and aggregated by the population shares of both areas. The national aggregated poverty lines are shown in Table 4.1, where they are labelled 'Old poverty line'.

The analysis reported in this chapter uses these poverty lines in combination with the raw data from the Socio-economic Surveys assembled by the National Statistical Office for the years 1990 to 2000. These data are used to analyse the changes in poverty incidence which occurred over this period. The changes in poverty incidence are decomposed by region, rural–urban location, farm and non-farm employment, and gender of the household head. The findings are reported in Tables 4.2, 4.4, 4.6, 4.8 and 4.10, and the results are explained below.

Overall change in poverty incidence

Table 4.2 shows that average nominal per capita household incomes increased continuously over the entire 1990 to 2000 period. However, real per capita incomes show a different pattern. Between 1990 and 1996, their annual rates of increase were between 5 and 10 per cent. Following the onset of the crisis, they declined slightly, at annual rates less than 0.5 per cent. But how were these incomes distributed? While real per capita household income was rising, the Gini index of inequality first increased from 0.513 in 1990 to 0.531 in 1992 and then declined continuously to 0.518 in 1994 and 0.511 in 1996. The decline continued in the early post-crisis period, to 0.508 in 1998. The trend was reversed in 2000 and the inequality index rose significantly, to 0.524, a level slightly higher than in 1994.

The decline in the average real per capita household income and the improvement in income distribution from 1996 to 1998 indicate that the immediate impact of the crisis was mainly on people in the upper income classes. The subsequent decrease in real per capita incomes and the worsening income distribution from 1998 to 2000 indicate that, finally, people in lower income classes incurred the burden of the economic crisis. The results on poverty incidence reported in Table 4.2 reflect these trends.

The crisis interrupted the pre-crisis trend of rapid poverty reduction. However, contrary to many earlier reports, its effect was not strong enough to increase the proportion of poor in the population in 1998 from the 1996 level. Immediately after the onset of the crisis, although real per capita household incomes declined slightly, the decline was concentrated in upper income classes and poverty incidence declined slightly, from 6.35 per cent in 1996 to 6.1 per cent in 1998. However, by the time the impact of the crisis was fully realized, in 2000, poverty incidence had risen to 8.45 per cent, which was significantly higher than the 1996 level.

Now suppose that, as in Kakwani (1999), we project the trend of

Table 4.2 Poverty and income distribution, 1990 to 2000

Index	1990	1992	1994	1996	1998	2000
Mean per capita income, current prices	1330.27	1780.97	2165.77	2890.47	3282.81	3313.03
Consumer price index (1990 = 100)	100.00	110.00	119.50	133.80	152.70	155.60
Real per capita income	1330.27	1619.06	1812.36	2160.29	2149.84	2129.20
Annual growth rate of real per capita income over preceding two years (%)	–	10.15	5.96	9.18	–0.24	–0.48
Gini coefficient	0.5126	0.5313	0.5179	0.5114	0.5076	0.5240
Poverty incidence (%)	20.09	14.54	11.47	6.35	6.10	8.45

Source: Author's calculations based on Socio-economic Survey data from the National Statistical Office, Bangkok.

Notes:
1 Based on the 1990 poverty lines of 7,646 baht/person/year in urban areas and 5,115 baht/person/year in rural areas. Municipal areas and Sanitary districts are defined as urban. Villages are defined as rural.
2 These estimates of poverty incidence are slightly different from our past estimates due to the discrepancies in consumer price index.
– Not available.

poverty reduction that would have occurred in the post-crisis period, based on the pre-crisis rate of poverty reduction. Based on poverty incidence between 1990 and 1996, a simple non-linear relationship was estimated between the percentage of poor in the total number of population, or head count ratio (HCR) and a time variable. Based on this estimated equation,[3] if the crisis did not occur, the incidence of poverty would be around 3.04 per cent in 1998. Compared with the actual 1998 figure of 6.1 per cent (as estimated in the present study and reported in Table 4.2), a projection of this kind would indicate that the crisis added 3.06 per cent of the total population to the total number of the poor, or around 1.8 million people. Of course, comparisons of this 'with–without' kind are subject to the qualifications noted above. If the pre-crisis rate of decline was unsustainable, it could not reasonably be said that an external event ('the crisis') was responsible for this large increase in poverty.

The following sections apply the before–after approach to analyse the spatial, sectoral and gender dimensions of the changes in poverty that occurred following the crisis.

Poverty incidence by region

Prior to the crisis, the regional distribution of population was quite stable (Table 4.3). The share of the Northeast was 35.8 per cent in 1990 and decreased slightly to 35.4 per cent in 1996. The share of Bangkok followed the same trend as that of the Northeast. The share of the North decreased somewhat between 1990 and 1996, from 20.2 per cent to 19.2 per cent. Over the same period, the share of Bangkok Vicinity (outer Bangkok) in the total population increased by half of one per cent of the total population. Migration from the regions to the capital was primarily to Bangkok Vicinity, rather than to Bangkok proper. Following

Table 4.3 Population share by region, 1990 to 2000

Region	Population share					
	1990	1992	1994	1996	1998	2000
Bangkok	10.13	9.54	9.35	9.83	10.58	10.96
Central	17.18	18.55	19.00	18.65	18.24	18.32
North	20.22	19.62	19.41	19.16	18.53	18.64
Northeast	35.82	35.46	34.47	35.33	35.41	34.89
South	13.78	13.59	14.19	13.68	13.87	13.97
Bangkok Vicinity	2.86	3.24	3.58	3.35	3.37	3.22
Whole Kingdom	100.00	100.00	100.00	100.00	100.00	100.00

Source: Author's calculations based on Socio-economic Survey data from the National Statistical Office, Bangkok.

the onset of the crisis, the population shares of Bangkok and the South increased. These increases were at the expense of the Central, the Northeast and the Bangkok Vicinity. The changes indicate an out-migration from the latter three regions, especially to Bangkok, but not Bangkok Vicinity. Despite the slowdown in economic activity, higher income in the capital city was evidently still a factor pulling migrants from other regions.

The results on poverty incidence at the regional level are summarized in Table 4.4. The results indicate that the impact of the crisis was not uniform across regions. Between 1990 and 1996, poverty incidence declined continuously, almost everywhere.[4] From the onset of the crisis until 1998, poverty incidence decreased in the Northeast and the North, the two poorest regions, and in the Bangkok Vicinity, but increased in the South, Bangkok and the Central region. Poverty incidence in the South increased significantly from 6.9 per cent in 1996 to more than 8 per cent in 1998. Thus, the immediate impact of the crisis was mainly on low income people in these regions.

The situation was almost the opposite during the 1998–2000 period. While poverty decreased in the South, Bangkok and the Central region, it increased dramatically in the two poorest regions, and increased slightly in the Bangkok Vicinity. This indicates that the negative impact of the crisis took some time to trickle down to people in the poorer regions, while poor people in Bangkok, the Central and the South were better protected.

Table 4.4 Poverty incidence by region, 1990 to 2000

Region	Percentage of population in poverty					
	1990	1992	1994	1996	1998	2000
Bangkok	1.98	1.07	0.56	0.06	0.35	0.13
Central	13.87	6.66	5.86	3.10	3.39	2.71
North	17.77	14.76	10.90	5.83	5.51	8.42
Northeast	30.93	24.09	18.15	10.41	9.23	15.11
South	20.04	12.57	13.35	6.89	8.24	7.71
Bangkok Vicinity	2.71	1.66	0.96	1.00	0.45	0.46
Whole Kingdom	20.09	14.54	11.47	6.35	6.10	8.45

Source: Author's calculations based on Socio-economic Survey data from the National Statistical Office, Bangkok.

Notes:
1 Poverty incidence is measured by the head count ratio, based on the poverty lines reported in Oey (1979), updated by consumer price index published by Ministry of Commerce, Bangkok. See Table 4.1 for these poverty lines.
2 Poverty incidence in sanitary districts is based on the urban poverty line.

Poverty incidence by rural–urban location

The trend of rural-to-urban migration has not been uniform (Table 4.5).[5] However, the rural population share, which was around 74 per cent in the early 1990s, declined to 72 per cent in 1996 and to 71 per cent in 2000. Immediately following the crisis, poverty reduction tended to decline in both rural and urban areas, but the decline was significant only in rural areas (Table 4.6). This significant decline in rural poverty could be the result of the increases in major crop prices. The situation changed significantly between 1998 and 2000 when rural poverty rose from less than 7 per cent to more than 10 per cent in 2000 and urban poverty increased from 3.9 per cent to 4.5 per cent of the total rural and urban populations, respectively.

Poverty incidence by farm and non-farm employment

The share of the population living in non-farm households increased continuously from less than 50 per cent in 1990 to around 63 per cent in 1996. Shortly after the onset of the crisis in 1997, this movement of

Table 4.5 Population share by rural–urban location, 1990 to 2000

Location	Population share (%)					
	1990	1992	1994	1996	1998	2000
Rural	74.13	74.82	71.65	72.24	71.74	71.00
Urban	25.87	25.18	28.35	27.76	28.26	29.00
Total	100.00	100.00	100.00	100.00	100.00	100.00

Source: Author's calculations based on Socio-economic Survey data from the National Statistical Office, Bangkok.

Table 4.6 Poverty incidence by rural–urban location, 1990 to 2000

Location	Percentage of population in poverty					
	1990	1992	1994	1996	1998	2000
Rural	22.95	16.88	13.14	7.26	6.97	10.07
Urban	11.92	7.59	7.22	3.99	3.89	4.47
Whole Kingdom	20.09	14.54	11.47	6.35	6.10	8.45

Source: Author's calculations based on Socio-economic Survey data from the National Statistical Office, Bangkok.

Note:
As in Table 4.4.

population between farm and non-farm households reversed slightly (Table 4.7), but then jumped to more than 65 per cent in 2000. Concerning land ownership, the population shares of people living in farm households mainly owning land decreased continuously over the 1990–98 period and this trend continued between 1998 and 2000. At the same time, the share of farm households in other categories, including those renting land, which had decreased over the pre-crisis period, increased significantly after the onset of the crisis. It rose from 10 per cent in 1996 to 11 per cent in 1998 and 12 per cent in 2000. This suggests that the destination of reverse migrants caused by the crisis was mainly to farm households renting land, rather than those owning land. It may also reflect an increase in landlessness following the crisis.

Before the onset of the crisis, the percentage of the population living in poverty decreased continuously for each of the above categories (Table 4.8). For non-farm households, the incidence of poverty decreased from around 10 per cent in 1990 to about 3 per cent in 1996, respectively. For the two categories of farm households, the incidence went down from 29 and 33 per cent in 1990 to 12 and 14 per cent in 1996, respectively.

The crisis had different effects on farm and non-farm households. Here again it is essential to distinguish the immediate effects of the crisis, as reflected in the data for 1998 and the longer term effects, as revealed by the data to 2000. For non-farm households, poverty incidence appeared to increase marginally from 2.8 per cent in 1996 to 3 per cent in 1998. There was a further moderate increase to 3.64 per cent in 2000. Overall, these changes in poverty incidence for non-farm households were very small.

For farm households, the story was entirely different. For those owning land, poverty fell quite significantly from 1996 to 1998 and then, between 1998 and 2000, it rose to well above the 1996 level. The effects of the increase in agricultural prices shortly after the crisis, followed by price declines and drought thereafter, as described above, are quite evident in these data. For households primarily renting land and farm workers, the

Table 4.7 Population share by farm and non-farm employment, 1990 to 2000

Sector	Population share (%)					
	1990	1992	1994	1996	1998	2000
Non-farm	49.82	52.98	62.01	63.48	62.75	65.15
Farm, owning land	38.10	35.60	27.17	26.49	26.21	22.69
Farm, not owning land	12.08	11.42	10.82	10.03	11.04	12.16
Total	100.00	100.00	100.00	100.00	100.00	100.00

Source: Author's calculations based on Socio-economic Survey data from the National Statistical Office, Bangkok.

Table 4.8 Poverty incidence by farm and non-farm employment, 1990 to 2000

Sector	Percentage of population in poverty					
	1990	1992	1994	1996	1998	2000
Non-farm	9.92	6.31	6.11	2.79	3.00	3.64
Farm, owning land	29.29	23.79	19.94	12.13	9.87	15.95
Farm, not owning land	33.06	23.90	20.89	13.61	14.79	20.19
Whole Kingdom	20.09	14.54	11.47	6.35	6.10	8.45

Source: Author's calculations based on Socio-economic Survey data from the National Statistical Office, Bangkok.

Note:
As in Table 4.4.

incidence of poverty increased from 13.6 per cent in 1996 to 14.8 per cent in 1998 and then rose further, and dramatically, to 20.2 per cent in 2000. Although farming households comprise only about a third of all households, most of the significant changes in poverty incidence which followed the crisis occurred within this group. Farm households not owning land were negatively affected throughout the crisis period. But for land-owning households, these negative effects occurred only *after* 1998.

Poverty incidence by gender of household head

The share of the population living in households headed by males has decreased over time, from around 83 per cent in 1990 to 78 per cent in 2000. These trends are detailed in Table 4.9. It is not widely realized that female-headed households have consistently exhibited lower levels of poverty incidence than male-headed households (Table 4.10). While the percentage of the poor who lived in both male-headed households and female-headed households was around 20 per cent in 1990, the figure decreased to 6.33 per cent for male-headed households and 5.28 per cent for female-headed households in 1998. Although both categories of households were adversely affected by the crisis, this effect was evident only *after* 1998. The magnitude of the impact was not the same in these two groups of households. Between 1998 and 2000, poverty incidence increased by about 1.5 per cent among female-headed households and by 2.5 per cent among male-headed households.

Consequences for economic welfare

The effects that an event like the 1997 economic crisis has on poverty incidence are of obvious interest, but as an indicator of overall changes in

Table 4.9 Population share by gender of household head, 1990 to 2000

Gender	Population share (%)					
	1990	1992	1994	1996	1998	2000
Male	82.97	83.47	79.92	79.13	78.27	78.02
Female	17.03	16.53	20.08	20.87	21.73	21.98
Total	100.00	100.00	100.00	100.00	100.00	100.00

Source: Author's calculations based on Socio-economic Survey data from the National Statistical Office, Bangkok.

Table 4.10 Poverty incidence by gender of household head, 1990 to 2000

Gender	Percentage of population in poverty					
	1990	1992	1994	1996	1998	2000
Male	20.12	14.66	11.54	6.61	6.33	8.91
Female	19.99	13.94	11.18	5.38	5.28	6.81
Whole Kingdom	20.09	14.54	11.47	6.35	6.1	8.45

Source: Author's calculations based on Socio-economic Survey data from the National Statistical Office, Bangkok.
Note:
As in Table 4.4.

economic welfare, poverty analysis has serious limitations. A change in poverty incidence mainly reflects an increase or a decrease in the economic welfare of households with incomes close to the poverty line. The impact on other income brackets is ignored, unless their incomes happen to rise above or fall below the poverty line.

Based on compensated demand functions for 20 consumer goods among ten types of households, Isra Sarntisart (1999) estimates the economic welfare impact of the crisis on each of these household groups. The impact was measured as the amount of money that must be given to consumers in the post-crisis situation in order to make them as well off as in the pre-crisis situation. This measure is known as *compensating variation*. The comparison period is the first half of 1996 compared with the first half of 1998. It should be emphasized that changes that occurred over this period should be interpreted as a more immediate impact than changes that occurred between the whole 1996 period and the whole 1998 period. In addition, effects occurring after mid-1998 are not covered. The following are some of the findings.

Overall welfare impact

Although the depreciation of the exchange rate raised some domestic prices and unemployment was also reported, the average living standard of Thai households actually improved between 1996 and 1998. At the national level, the economic welfare of the average household was estimated to increase by approximately 900 baht per month. Thus, the results of this study support a central conclusion of the poverty analysis presented above. The immediate consequence of the crisis (that is, up to 1998) was a small *reduction* in poverty and a small *increase* in average economic welfare.

Across the country, the average change in household economic welfare tended to move in line with the degree of urbanization. The increase was higher for an average household in municipal areas (around 1,490 baht per month).[6] This was approximately twice that of an average household in sanitary districts (around 550 baht per month) and rural areas (around 780 baht per month). By region, the average change was highest in Bangkok (an increase of approximately 1,830 baht per month), followed by the South (1,340 baht), the North (820 baht), the Central (710 baht), the Northeast (600 baht), and Bangkok Vicinity (520 baht).

Better-off and worse-off households: two sides of the coin

While the economic welfare of households increased on average, some enjoyed improved standards of living and others were hard hit. Following the onset of the crisis, approximately 60 per cent of households, or 9.7 million households, experienced an improvement in economic welfare. The average improvement was equivalent to 3,648 baht per month. At the same time, 40 per cent of households – that is, 6.6 million households – suffered a decline in economic welfare, averaging approximately 3,108 baht per month. These results are summarized in Table 4.11.

The immediate impact of the crisis was focused around Bangkok and Bangkok Vicinity. Approximately 55 per cent of households in central Bangkok experienced a welfare decline. This is equivalent to nearly 4

Table 4.11 Estimated changes in household economic welfare, 1996 to 1998

	Per cent of households experiencing gains and losses		Average change in economic welfare (baht per household per month)	
	Worse off	Better off	Worse off	Better off
Whole Kingdom	41	59	−3,108	3,648
Urban	52	48	−3,736	6,397
Rural	36	64	−2,698	2,712

Source: Isra Sarntisart (1999).

million people. In the outer vicinity of Bangkok, 53 per cent of households, or slightly over 1 million people, suffered a decline in welfare. In other regions, the percentage of worse-off households in the total number of households was between 37 and 40 per cent. It was more likely for households in urban areas than those in rural areas to be worse off immediately following the crisis. Approximately 53 and 49 per cent of these households in municipal areas and sanitary districts were found to experience a decline in economic welfare, respectively. For villages, nearly 36 per cent of households suffered an economic welfare decline.

By dividing urban households into five equal population classes, arranged by expenditures, it was found that the percentage of worse-off households was higher for upper expenditure classes. In ascending order of per capita household expenditure, approximately 39 per cent, 49 per cent, 56 per cent, 59 per cent, and 51 per cent of urban households in the five classes were worse off following the crisis. In rural areas, the percentage of worse-off households in the four lower expenditure classes was only around 30–35 per cent compared with more than 45 per cent for the top rural class.

Estimates of the changes in economic welfare point to the uneven distributional impact of the crisis across regions. Better-off households in the capital city had their economic welfare increase most, by nearly 8,800 baht per month while worse-off households experienced an average decline in welfare of around 3,900 baht per month. Average increases in welfare of better-off households in the vicinity of Bangkok and the South were estimated to be around 5,700 and 4,100 baht per month. Average decreases in welfare of worse-off households in the two regions were 4,100 and 3,300 baht per month, respectively. In other regions, the average increases in economic welfare of households were around 2,600–3,000 baht per month while the average decreases were around 2,100–3,300 baht per month.

Consequences for employment

Changes in employment are important for understanding the factors behind the poverty and welfare consequences of the crisis. Four recent studies discuss the employment impact of the crisis. These are Kakwani (1998), Sawalak (1999), the Brooker Group (1999), and World Bank (1999). Their analyses of the employment effects of the crisis did not extend beyond 1998. These four studies reached consensus on the point that the crisis adversely affected employment. The impact was said to be more severe on less well-educated persons and the non-agricultural sectors, especially on construction workers. Their main findings were as follows.

Kakwani concludes that the employment impact of the crisis was more or less uniform across the various regions of the country. It pointed to a shift in employment from wage and salary to farm work and argued that this led to an increase in underemployment in the agricultural sector. This helps explain the finding that the crisis did not have a significant impact on farm income despite the fact that farm employment increased. It is concluded that the rate of unemployment could be as high as 10 per cent. People with secondary education suffered the most severe unemployment impact from the crisis and the unemployment rate among people with a secondary educational background significantly increased.

The World Bank report states that the impact of the crisis on employment was significant. Based on the February 1998 round of the Labour Force Survey, unemployment at February 1998 was at 1.48 million. The World Bank study adds that the increase in underemployment between February 1997 and February 1998 reached nearly one million. On a regional basis, Sawalak points out that the statistics support reverse migration of unemployed former workers from Bangkok to other regions. Employment in the construction sector dropped sharply by almost 1 million. However, although the informal sector was expected to absorb the unemployed workers, the number of self-employed did not increase substantially. Based on a sectoral comparison of the unemployed former workers, the study also states that 400,000 were from the agricultural, and 500,000 were from construction and manufacturing sectors.

The Brooker Group study also reports a substantial fall in employment in 1998: around 853,000 persons in the dry season and 1,024,000 persons in the wet season. By region, the Northeast rural areas were hardest hit, contradicting Kakwani's conclusion that the impact was uniform across the country. Reverse mobility in rural areas from non-farm activities to farm activities was also reported. The same study also states that the crisis severely hit employed persons under 30 years old and those whose education had not gone beyond the primary level. However, for those with secondary and higher education, the number of employed persons increased by approximately one million in August 1998. The construction sector was found to account for the greatest loss of employment, by 942,000 in the dry season of 1998, while, on the other hand, the services sector generated employment of approximately 242,000. By gender, women were said to suffer greater employment declines.

The report of reverse migration seems to be in conflict with the regional population share analysis presented earlier in this chapter, pointing to an increase in the population share of Bangkok and decreases in population shares of the Central and North. An explanation for this point could be that the unemployed former workers migrated back to the Northeast while new migrants from the Central and North still came to Bangkok. It should be noted that most of the reverse migrants were from the construction industry while the new migrants, especially from the North, joined the service sectors.

In 2000, the impact of the crisis was more fully realized. Although unemployment seemed to abate, labour market conditions deteriorated in other respects. Widespread exploitation of the labour force was reported in terms of working overtime without compensation.

Consequences for incomes from wages and salaries

The crisis affected household economic welfare not only through price rises and effects on employment but also through effects on wages and salaries. Following the crisis, average income from wages and salaries was found to increase in nominal terms but to decrease in real terms. Kakwani finds that the crisis contributed to a decline in real income in all areas, but that the reduction was higher in urban areas, especially in municipal areas, than in rural areas. This apparently occurred because the average real income in the agricultural sector did not decline significantly, owing to sharp increases in agricultural prices. Further, the crisis led to a significant reduction in real income among almost all levels of education. Those with a university education suffered the largest decline in real income.

The evidence of declining wages is also supported by two other studies. The World Bank report states that, between February 1996 and February 1998, average money wages fell in real terms by approximately 6 per cent across all worker categories identified by the Labour Force Survey. The Brooker Group study points out that the total nominal wage bill in the private sector fell back to near the 1996 level. Thus, since consumer prices increased, real wages fell. The loss of real income per earner reached 17 per cent in the dry season and 21 per cent in the wet season.

This seems to support Table 4.2, which reports a decrease in real per capita household income between 1996 and 1998. It should also be noted that labour earnings is only one source of income. Its share in total household income differs across household groups. On average, the share was approximately 41 per cent in 1988 and almost a half of total income in 1992 (Isra Sarntisart 1997). Other important income sources are farm and non-farm profit, comprising nearly 40 per cent of total income, and transfer income.

Moreover, an analysis of the causes of unemployment suggested that a significant proportion of unemployed workers may have other employment alternatives. Sawalak points to wage reduction as an important reason for unemployment. Nearly one-quarter of the unemployed during 1997–98 cited dissatisfaction with rates of payment as causes for their unemployment. More than one-quarter were laid-off or lost their jobs after the closing down of businesses, and nearly half attributed their unemployment state to factors such as waiting for new jobs, illness, or injury.

Consequences for education

The crisis affected education in several different ways. The declining real incomes of households negatively affected by the crisis became a factor reducing parents' ability to support the education of their children. A series of budget cuts, especially on education, and delayed disbursement of the approved budget after the onset of the crisis, adversely affected the quality of public education.

Following the crisis, the number of children attending school apparently declined. Kakwani reports that many children were taken out of school. The crisis caused a significant reduction in the average working hours of young workers, accompanied by a decline in average income. For partial child labour, children who go to school and who are also in the workforce, the study states that the incidence of this form of employment did not change significantly but that their real earnings declined. The Brooker Group also states that a large number of primary school age children were not in school.

On the other side, public education could be congested and the quality of education could fall. Sawalak argues that falling private investment in facilities such as schools will push more people to use limited supplies of public services. However, social services programmes were greatly affected by budget cuts during the crisis. The same study also points to a report by the Ministry of Education stating that, following the crisis, school dropout rates increased from previous years. According to the Brooker Group, budget cuts and delays plagued many schools, while non-governmental supplementary funds dropped in the wake of the crisis. Moreover, the number of school leavers at the secondary level increased.

The above studies point to a negative impact of the crisis on children and on the provision of education, which could have long-term consequences for the development of human capital. These effects will have a negative impact on the distribution of income. Isra argues that education expansions, especially at the university level, have contributed to increases in inequality in labour earnings. He recommends that Thailand should concentrate on educational expansion at lower levels, especially the secondary and vocational levels, rather than the university level. Hyeok Jeong (1998) also argues that, among factors contributing to inequality, the pattern of human capital accumulation explains a significant proportion of the increase in inequality.

Conclusions

This chapter reviews the socio-economic consequences of the 1997 crisis. The findings suggest that earlier studies, based on the official poverty data, may have overestimated the negative consequences that the crisis had on poverty incidence. Contrary to the widely-held belief, from the onset of the crisis to 1998, the percentage of the poor in the total population may not have increased at all from the 1996 level, in either urban or rural areas. It was not until 2000 that actual poverty increased and it did so in both rural and urban areas. However, the increase was larger in rural areas. By region, the immediate adverse impact of the crisis on poverty in the North and the Northeast was not very severe. However, the opposite was the case between 1998 and 2000. While poverty incidence in other regions decreased or increased very slightly, it rose dramatically in the two poorest regions of the country.

The consequences of the crisis tended to be most severe among people living in farm households but not owning land. These people generally rent land or are farm workers. Poverty among these households increased continuously between 1996 and 2000. However, farm households primarily owning land were found to be well insulated from the immediate adverse impact of the crisis. This outcome is attributed to an increase in farm prices caused by the exchange rate depreciation of late 1997 and 1998. Poverty did not increase among these households until after 1998, when exchange rate appreciation reduced farm prices and drought reduced output.

The review of the welfare impact of the crisis also points to similar conclusions. On average, the 1997 crisis negatively affected the urban rich. Urban households, especially those in the top income quintiles, were more likely than rural households to be worse-off following the crisis. The impact on worse-off households in Bangkok and Bangkok Vicinity was also found to be stronger than that on worse-off households in other regions.

A significant increase in unemployment followed the crisis. The impact was severe on uneducated persons, especially construction workers. The ability of the agricultural sector to insulate rural sectors from the crisis was confirmed, but this insulating effect was short-lived.

Education was also severely hit by the crisis. Increased dropout rates, increases in the number of children not attending school and a lack of funds, both public and private, point to long-term negative consequences for the development of human capital at the primary and secondary school levels. These outcomes threaten further increases in income inequality.

Appendix: data sources and definitions

The data set used in examining the socio-economic consequences of the 1997 economic crisis on population structure, incomes, income distribution, education, and employment is the socio-economic surveys (SES) produced by the National Statistical Office. Six SES datasets are used in this study: those for 1990, 1992, 1994, 1996, 1998 and 2000. The SES provides detailed information of households' income, expenditure, savings, and various socio-economic variables, with a weight attached to each observation drawn from a stratified two-stage sampling technique. Groups of provinces in each region and the greater Bangkok area constitute strata. Each stratum is divided into three parts: municipal areas, sanitary districts, and villages.

The analysis in this study is carried out for four sets of household characteristics. These are region, rural/urban location, farm and non-farm employment and gender of the household head. These characteristics are defined as follows:

The six geographic regions are: (1) Bangkok; (2) Vicinities of Bangkok, including three provinces surrounding Bangkok (Nonthaburi, Pathum Thani, and Samut Prakarn); (3) the Central; (4) the Northeast; (5) the North and (6) the South. Rural/urban location is based on a local administrative definition: municipal areas and sanitary districts are urban areas, and villages are rural areas. Socio-economic classes are used to define the sectors of households. Generally, this is the occupation (of a member or members of households) that provides most of the household income. Households are defined as 'farm households, mainly owning land' if their socio-economic classes are farm operators (primarily owning land). They are defined as 'other farm' if their socio-economic classes are farm operators (primarily renting land) or fishermen or forestry or farm workers. Otherwise, they are defined as 'non-farm households'. Gender refers to the sex of the household head.

Notes

1 The Gini index can range from 0 to 1, with higher values indicating greater inequality.
2 Official data for 1998 did not appear until 2000. Fortunately, this delay in the release of the official data has recently been reduced.
3 $HCR = 4,426 - 2.214*year$, $R^2 = 0.995$.
4 The minor exception is the Bangkok Vicinity, where poverty incidence increased very marginally between 1994 and 1996.
5 It should be noted that these data could be affected by changes in definition, because some areas that were counted as rural in a particular year could have been counted as urban in following years.
6 Municipal areas are inner urban and sanitary districts are generally outer urban. Villages are rural.

References

Ahuja, V., Bidani, D., Ferreira, F. and Walton, M. (1997) Everyone's miracle? Revisiting poverty and inequality in East Asia, *Directions in Development*, Washington, DC: World Bank.

Bergemeier, David and Hoffman, Richard (1988) *Economic Survey of Thailand*, Manila: Asian Development Bank.

Brooker Group Ltd, Chulalongkorn Economic Research Centre, and Development Assistance, Inc (1999) Socioeconomic challenges of the crisis in Thailand. Research report submitted to the National Economic and Social Development Board under the Asian Development Bank T.A. No. 2920 Social Impact Analysis of the Crisis, Bangkok.

Foster, J., Greer, J. and Thorbecke, E. (1984) A class of decomposable poverty measures, *Econometrica*, 52: 761–6.

Hyeok Jeong (1998) *Decomposition of Growth and Inequality in Thailand*, Mimeo.

Isra Sarntisart (1995) An estimation of consumer demand, adult equivalence scale, and income distribution in Thailand: 1988, 1990 and 1992. Research report submitted to the Ratchadapisek Sompote Fund, Bangkok: Chulalongkorn University [in Thai].

Isra Sarntisart (1997) Educational expansions and labour earnings inequality: the case of Thailand between 1988 and 1992, *Chulalongkorn Journal of Economics*, 9: 127–74.

Isra Sarntisart (1999) Impact of the crisis on household welfare, in Brooker Group Ltd. *et al.*, Socioeconomic challenges of the crisis in Thailand. Research report submitted to the National Economic and Social Development Board under the Asian Development T.A. No. 2920 Social Impact Analysis of the Crisis, Bangkok.

Kakwani, N.K. (1998) *Impact of the Economic Crisis on Employment, Unemployment and Real Income*, Bangkok: National Economic and Social Development Board.

Kakwani, N.K. (1999) Poverty and inequality during the economic crisis in Thailand, *Indicators of Well-Being and Policy Analysis*, National Economic and Social Development Board, volume 3.

Lerman, R. and Yitzhaki, S. (1994) Effect of marginal changes in income sources on U.S. income inequality, *public finance quarterly*, 22: 403–17.

Medhi Krongkaew, Pranee Tinnakorn and Suphat Suphachalasai (1991) Priority issues and policy measures to alleviate rural poverty: the case of Thailand. Research report submitted to the Asian Development Bank.

Oey Meesook (1979) Income, consumption, and poverty in Thailand, 1962/63 to 1975/76, Staff Working Papers, No. 364, World Bank, Washington.

Sawalak Kittiprapas (1999) Social impact of Thai economic crisis: a background paper for the case of Thailand. Paper prepared for the Study on Impacts of Asian Economic Crisis Funded by Ford Foundation, TDRI, Bangkok, November.

Suganya Hutaserani and Somchai Jitsuchon (1988) Thailand income and poverty profile, and their current situations. Paper presented to the 1988 TDRI Year-End Conference on Income Distribution and Long Term Development, Thailand Development Research Institute Foundation, Bangkok, December.

Warr, P.G. (1998) Growth, crisis and poverty incidence in Southeast Asia. Paper presented to the American Committee on East Asian Economic Studies, Chulalongkorn University, Bangkok, 16–18 December. Revised version published in J. Behrman *et al.* (eds.) (2001) *Restructuring Asian Economies for the New Millennium*, Amsterdam: North-Holland/Elsevier.

World Bank (1999) *Thailand Social Monitor 1999: Challenge for Social Reform*, Bangkok: World Bank.

Chapter 5

Developing social alternatives

Walking backwards into a khlong[1]

Pasuk Phongpaichit

Being a tiger is not important. What is important is to have enough to eat and to live; and to have an economy which provides enough to eat and live. Having enough to eat and to live means supporting oneself to have enough for oneself...

I used to say that this sufficiency doesn't mean that each household has to produce its own food, weave its own cloth. That is too much. But within a village or district, there must be a certain amount of self-sufficiency. Anything which can be produced beyond local needs can be sold, but maybe not sold too far away, to minimise transport costs...

If we can change back to a self-sufficient economy, not completely, even not as much as half, perhaps just a quarter, we can survive...

But people who like the modern economy may not agree. It's like walking backwards into a *khlong*. We have to live carefully and we have to go back to do things which are not complicated and which do not use elaborate, expensive equipment. We need to move backwards in order to move forwards. If we don't do like this, the solution to this crisis will be difficult.

H.M. King Bhumibol Adulyadej
4 December 1997

Since the early 1980s, ideas about the importance of locality and community have been proposed in opposition to the emphasis on growth and urbanization. This 'localism discourse' has largely been ignored by mainstream economists and social scientists. If it is addressed at all, it is seen in the context of Luddism, allotment movements, Amish communities, Ranters and Shakers – futile attempts to obstruct history's march to modernism in the name of backward-looking rural utopianism.

Yet this discourse, and in particular some of its keywords – locality (*thongthin*), community (*chumchon*), self-reliance (*pheung ton eng*), self-sufficiency (*pho yu pho kin*) – have achieved considerable prominence in the context of the crisis. A number of intellectuals and social commentators associated with this discourse have been very vocal. Moreover, the spread of the discourse has not been limited to academics and public intellectuals.

The King's birthday speech in December 1997 gave the discourse new legitimacy. The speech was delivered (on television) at an especially bewildering stage of the crisis – the sort of time when the King has traditionally provided public guidance. The speech linked the crisis, the principle of self-sufficiency, and the idea of returning to a simpler economy. The importance of this message was immediately recognized. The press recounted the key sections of the speech at much greater length than normal. Key extracts were constantly rerun as inter-programme fillers on television and radio. Quotations appeared on billboards outside government offices. While the speech had ranged over many topics, these replays focused on the relatively short passage in the speech about self-sufficiency (see above). The whole speech was quickly printed and distributed – the manual for the Great Leap Backwards.

Even more striking was the reception, especially in rural Thailand. Anyone visiting villages in early 1998 could not avoid being struck by the frequency with which key words and phrases from the speech would appear in conversations with farmers – particularly *pho yu pho kin* (enough to eat and live – self-sufficiency) and *tissadi mai* or 'new theory', which quickly became the shorthand reference to the King's ideas. Partly, of course, this reflects the great respect for the King and the success of the official effort at dissemination. But not every phrase uttered by the King is so readily adopted. Clearly the King's words had struck a chord. Or, to put it another way, the speech reflects the King's sensitivity to ideas and sentiments circulating in rural society. Moreover, this rural response cannot be attributed simply to the crisis. At this stage, farmers were relatively insulated from the crisis as the 1997 harvest had been good, and the baht price of rice had soared to record levels. The impact of disemployment, back-migration, rising input prices, and the collapse of ancillary industries would not be felt until mid-year. The rural interest in self-sufficiency and self-reliance had emerged during the preceding boom, which had increased social dislocation and social division.

Taking its lead from the King, the Ministry of Interior adopted the principle of self-sufficiency and self-reliance. In early 1998, the Ministry launched a major programme to educate its own personnel on the meaning of the principle and its application. A large slice of the Ministry's budget was ear-marked for programmes to promote self-sufficiency and self-reliance to counter the impact of the economic crisis. The team assembled to work on this project was intriguing. Alongside the Ministry officials were some veterans of the coup-making Young Turk military group and some former student radicals who had spent time in the jungle with the Communist Party of Thailand.

The Royal Thai Army also adopted the policy, and allocated plots of land within military establishments for growing crops for military consumption. To publicize this project, the army commander appeared on television throwing rice seed into a flooded paddy field (he wore Wellington boots).

Other organizations fell in with the trend. The Democrat Party, now at the head of the ruling Cabinet coalition, officially committed itself to the policy – although not without assuring everyone that it would continue to pursue export-led growth in the 'upper economy' while promoting self-sufficiency in the 'lower economy' (*Bangkok Post*, 19 April 1998). Other parties, including New Aspiration, began to promote rural projects based on the self-reliance ideal as part of their campaign to build rural support. At least three television programmes appeared devoted to propagating the idea and showcasing successful examples of local self-reliance. Several leading monks publicly espoused the principle. The attempt to domesticate and propagate the idea of 'good governance', promoted by the World Bank, was transformed into a restatement of the ideas of locality, community and self-reliance.

The 'localism discourse' had emerged from the late 1970s and, a decade later, was running under the title *watthanatham chumchon* or 'community culture'. The two words were significant. The discourse made the *community* central, both as a source of value and as a political construct. The discourse made *culture* (rather than economics, politics or whatever) the area of contestation between the community and outside forces (state, capitalism). Two quotations from Chatthip Nartuspha's (1991) review of the discourse, give the main flavour. In the first, he is summarizing Bamrung Bunpanya, and in the second, Prawase Wasi.

The village culture is independent of the middle-class and upper-class culture. It is related to a way of life which is in close touch with nature, and relies on the use of physical labour; a community of kinship and a village community. It is 'the oldest form of society'. No matter what outside circumstances have been and how they have changed, the essence of a village or a community, its economic, social and cultural independence has remained for hundreds of years. The village community thus has its own independent belief systems and way of development. However this line of economic development that Thailand follows is an imported idea, which is linked to internal state power. This is, namely, the capitalist way of development geared to supply the needs of Westerners. We are at a disadvantage in this kind of development. The more development there is, the poorer we are. Those who get rich, of whom there are few, apart from the Westerners, are those who serve the Westerners. . . The direction of development should be changed so that the villagers rely on themselves as they had done in the past. They must begin by being independent minded and conscious of their own identity.

(Chatthip Nartsupha 1991: 121)

The rural communities must be strengthened [through] a subsistence mode of production of integrated agriculture; economic self-reliance and the eradication of external dependence; communal life, the institutions of family and *wat*, and a common culture of mutual aid. This rural community will develop its knowledge and expertise from original knowledge which is called 'popular wisdom' . . . and combine it with international knowledge . . . without a moral and ethical base, there can be no real development for the people, because human beings will promote themselves, be selfish, have *kilesa* (vices) and *tanha* (desires), which will overshadow wisdom and other virtues.

(Chatthip Nartsupha 1991: 124–5)

The global–local theme has not been limited to Thailand but has become an international debate.[2] This chapter examines how some of the main propositions of this 'localism discourse' have developed in Thailand in the context of the economic crisis. The chapter is divided into sections examining specific themes within the debate, namely: the role of Buddhist values relating to economic issues; the ethical values summarized in the concept of community; the importance of agriculture; and the political role of culture. At the end, I look briefly at the main objections raised against the discourse and consider some possible impact on Thailand beyond the crisis.

Buddhist economics

In truth, if we look from another angle, maybe its lucky that this failure and this crisis make us take a good look at ourselves.

(P.A. Payutto, 19 December 1997)

The idea that the Buddhist conception of moderation could serve as a counter to the principle of acquisitiveness at the heart of market economics has been around for a long time. However, the idea gained greater popularity and precision against the background of rapid growth and associated social change from the mid-1980s onwards.

In 1988, the leading Buddhist scholar, P.A. Payutto (Phrathammapitok) published a small book on *Buddhist Economics*, and over the next few years lectured several times on the topic. Payutto made the whole concept of Buddhist economics more precise in three important ways. First, he related the major propositions (about moderation, wealth, work, acquisition and the role of government) back to scriptural references. Second, he positioned his Buddhist economics as a direct criticism of market economics. He contended that modern economics had become divorced from any social theory or ethical base: 'economics has become a narrow and rarefied discipline; an isolated, almost stunted, body of knowledge, having little to do with other disciplines or human activities'

(Phrathammapitok 1992: 15–16). He argued that, from a Buddhist view, economics could not be separated from an ethical stance, a view of nature, and a concept of society. By using the concept of 'well-being', he adjusted what he saw as the central motor of market economics: 'in contrast to the classical economic equation of maximum consumption leading to maximum satisfaction, we have moderate, or wise consumption, leading to well-being' (Phrathammapitok 1992: 69).

Payutto himself used this basis to criticize the rapid growth of materialism and a consumer society in the boom-and-bubble economy. However, others were more interested in the implications for environment and agriculture. Around this same period, several university professors incorporated Buddhist economics as a part of courses on development, environment and agricultural economics – particularly Aphichai Phuntasen at Thammasat, and Preecha Piempongsarn in Chulalongkorn. For a broader public, Prawase Wasi had already become an important popularizer of Buddhist concepts applied to everyday life. In the early 1990s, he brought together two ideas: first, the importance of reviving agriculture as it remained the economic base of the majority of people (on which more below); and second, the importance of Buddhism and especially the Buddhist concept of moderation for constraining materialism. Out of this came *Phuttha-kasetakam*, or Buddhist agriculture. As Aphichai explained Prawase's idea: 'Briefly and simply, it means agriculture for self-reliance, meeting the basic human needs through a way of production and a way of life which match together, production which is related to nature and religious principle' (Aphichai 1996: 362).

In sum, in the few years prior to the crisis, the growing interest on the relationship between Buddhism and economics had two important consequences. First, it provided a base for criticism of the destructive impact of economic growth, particularly on the environment and on local communities. Second, it helped to popularize two concepts – self-sufficiency (*pho yu pho kin*) and self-reliance (*pheung ton eng*). Self-sufficiency simply summarized the Buddhist concept of moderation as an antidote to acquisitiveness. Self-reliance conveyed both an idea of insurance against the dangers of market exposure, and also an idea of personal freedom. As Aphichai related in reference to the idea of Buddhist agriculture: 'Among the principles of Buddhist agriculture, self-reliance is the very heart, because it is an important principle which helps farmers to determine their own way of life' (Aphichai 1996: 364).

Is this just academic debate? Talking to northeastern farmers in mid-1998, I was surprised how often they themselves referred to the concepts of self-sufficiency and self-reliance without any prompting. Their thinking was very practical. Many were aware that, in recent years, their usage of cash had significantly increased. During the boom, their cash income had grown with proceeds from migrant labour and ancillary industries. In parallel, cash outlays had grown on both inputs and consumer goods. With the crisis now rapidly squeezing their cash position – through the decline in migrant labour opportunities, and the rise of input prices – they were aware of the need to reduce cash outlays. Several mentioned, in particular, the electricity bill, which had not existed before the coming of an electricity connection, but which was now a regular monthly event. Plans to increase local self-reliance, either at the household or community level, were appealing.

In the crisis, however, the meaning of self-reliance was set for expansion beyond its application to the household or community. In a talk delivered just a week after the King's speech, and hence in the same context of bewilderment, P.A. Payutto reflected on the crisis:

When we study the reasons which made us fail ... did it arise from misguidedly developing the country in a way which relied too much on the outside? We did not try to stand on our own. We were rich because we borrowed money to use, happy because we borrowed others' property to enjoy...

This is the lesson. We should not lose our way again. Don't get lost playing around in the world on a stage set by others... Don't get lost in free trade, the globalized financial system, and false freedom. In the end we get pulled into the whirlpool of freedom. But deep down it means becoming a slave. Because we misdeveloped the country towards consumerism, we ended up slaves of the countries which produce, slaves of the countries which have more financial strength, because the principle is that big money sucks up little money.

(Phrathammapitok 1998: 3–4)

The journal *Withithat*[3] extracted the word 'slave' as a theme for a special issue on the crisis and its impact on the locality (Pithaya 1998a). In various different ways, the contributors to that volume – and to many other forums – attributed the crisis to the *nation*'s overreliance on things from outside – capital, consumer goods, ideas, technology.

Through early 1998, Prawase Wasi expounded this theme in a series of speeches and seminar presentations that attracted the interest of a press sensitive to the popular need for guidance. One of Prawase's major themes was that the Buddhist search for moderation was threatened by mental subjection to the materialism learnt from the west. The pursuit of self-sufficiency and self-reliance were thus important at a personal level, community level and national level.

Community as base

> We were like the Royal Plaza Hotel [which collapsed in Korat] which was heavy at the top and shaky at the bottom.
>
> (Prawase Wasi, March 1998)

The idea of strengthening local communities as a counterweight to globalization is not confined to Thailand. Rather it is a worldwide trend that arose in counterpoint to the enthusiasm for globalization from the early 1980s onwards. Just three points can be noted about the development of this idea in Thailand before the crisis. First, the discourse on the importance of community culture became a rallying point for NGO and local activists in the late 1980s and early 1990s. Second, the main proposition was that, to resist the destructive forces of globalization and outward-oriented development, communities needed to look inwards and strengthen their own foundations of resources and culture. Third, the discourse was criticized from many angles, but particularly for imagining and idealizing a community that had possibly never existed, or had been much less benign, or had been superseded by the modernizations of the last half-century.

In the context of the crisis, the idea of the community was developed most subtly and most effectively by Saneh Chamarik. His authority to speak on the issue was enhanced by the fact that he had retired from Academe to a northeastern village, where he had founded a school and project to put the discourse into practice.

In the context of the crisis, Saneh expanded the community discourse in several important ways. First, he broadened and emphasized the importance of looking inwards for a basis to resist the destructive forces of globalization. The real crisis, he argued, was not the short-term financial bust but the longer-term commitment to a western-oriented, export-oriented growth, which placed the Thai economy ever more at the mercy of the world's great economic powers. The financial crisis was just a stage, a result of this longer-term misdirection. The costs of this national strategy were evident in the destruction of the environment, neglect of agriculture, increasing social division, and growing human problems. Moreover, he went on, 'the problem today of world society, not just of Thai society, is the problem that mankind, human values and social values are falling under the destructive dominance of economics' (Saneh 1999: 28). Moreover, economics, which, up until Keynes had still been concerned with social values, had more recently become focused wholly on concepts of efficiency and business profit to the exclusion of any social dimension.

Second, the idea of community thus became the basis for restating ideas of human and social need in opposition to the dehumanization of economics. In this sense, community was much more a *moral* idea than a physical idea. It was not, he made clear, the same concept as the government's definition of a community or village. Saneh argued that 'to escape from the world economic order which destructively threatens mankind, human values and society, we must look to the community in this light – as a target or answer for building a new order of society' (Saneh 1999: 35). In other words, it did not matter whether the community had never existed or never been as good as imagined. It was still necessary to *invent* or reinvent the community as a principle. The ultimate aim would be to 'create a new social order in which the economy serves society, rather than society serves the economy' (Saneh 1999: 37).

Third, this reinvented community was not seen as a means of escape from globalization and modernity – a rat-hole down which people could hide away from destructive forces. Rather, the community strategy would offer a long-term way to integrate everyone into the national and international economy *from the bottom up*, in opposition to the processes of peripheralization and exclusion within globalization. Communities must build from their own wisdom and resources, but not statically and not in isolation. Local wisdom should be developed by adoption from modern ideas and technology. While the primary aim of the community economy should be self-reliance and security, the next step should be the development of a surplus, the evolution of ever more sophisticated local economic institutions, including banks and industries, the gradual broadening of external economic networks, with the ultimate goal of full integration with the national and international economy on a basis of strength (Saneh 1998; Pithaya 1998b: 78–81). This of course would be a long process: 'I don't want to call it a 10-year plan or a 20-year plan. But I think we must look at the development strategy, not just plans of this sort' (Saneh 1999: 37).

Saneh's ideas around this time amounted to a mobilization of the idea of community, which had been a rather passive element in the earlier construction of *watthanatham chumchon*. A similar theme ran through Prawase's series of speeches and writings over the first year of the crisis. More importantly, this more assertive attitude to the role of community shaped the adaptation of 'good governance' into the Thai context.

In early 1998, the student leader of 1973 turned 'social critic', Thirayuth Boonmee, proposed that the idea of 'good governance' could serve as the focus for a wholesale social reform to move beyond the crisis. He offered a (later controversial) Thai translation for the phrase 'good governance' (*thammarat*) and an interpretation intended to be relevant to Thailand. He began from the international interpretation of the phrase – transparency, honesty, accountability, efficiency – but reinterpreted with 'a Thai soul and international heart', and elaborated as a 'national project' involving government, private sector and local communities (Thirayuth 1998). This initiative was warmly welcomed by the pro-globalizer and hero of technocratic modernism, Anand Panyarachun, who had been promoting 'good governance' for some time. For a time this looked like an interesting alliance across barriers of class, generation and ideology.

But not for long. Thirayuth's involvement attracted the interest of radicals and social reformers. But they were highly critical of his espousal of a concept that was widely seen as part of the plot to make Thailand a safe place for foreign capital. Saneh called the Thirayuth–Anand version elitist. He argued that good governance in the Thai context should be reinterpreted to mean grassroots participation. Prawase Wasi redefined *thammarat* as a self-sufficient, community-based economy and society. Quickly the Anand–Thirayuth axis pulled apart. Anand headed up a taskforce to draw up plans for good governance along the lines of the international agenda. Thirayuth headed up meetings of NGOs, activists and local community groups which totally reinterpreted good governance to follow the localist community agenda.

At a meeting in July 1998, Thirayuth opened by proposing that *thammarat* meant that each person is the owner of the nation, that in the past government had been too powerful and too centralized, and that the task was to shift the balance between individual and state. He offered several models for this change including a liberal model, a citizenship model, and a community-based model. The meeting, however, ignored all except the latter. The debate concentrated wholly on shifting the power balance between local community and state. The ideal was defined as *chumchonaphiwat*, community rule. Thirayuth later summarized the concept along these drastically modified lines:

> National good governance is a movement based on the power of local organizations, community civil society, to understand the problems, be self-reliant, self-help, self-reform; and at the same time to build the strength to truly examine what is bad and ugly ... Mainstream thinking on development has created problems over environment, society, disease, and the problems from this crisis. As a result, the development strategy based on self-sufficiency is growing ever stronger day by day side by side with mainstream development.
>
> (Thirayuth 1998: 16, 31)

The revival of agriculture

> Since our economy now completely depends upon foreign capital, it is time for the government to go beyond and select a way of relying on the country's original potential to become independent.
>
> (Saneh Chamarik, November 1998)

The crisis revived interest in agriculture and rural society. The contrasting impact of the crisis on Thailand and Indonesia emphasized the importance of national self-sufficiency in food. As currency values dropped precipitately, the cost of imported food in Indonesia soared, resulting in food riots and widespread distress. In Thailand, the price of food – virtually all locally produced – stayed steady. Moreover, the fall in currency value initially boosted the baht earnings from crop exports and helped to cushion the rural economy against the impact of the crisis.

Further, as some two million were disemployed in the urban economy, the village was expected to serve as the social safety net. This had worked in the past. The early 1980s' urban crisis saw a large rise in the number of rural poor, but no serious social and political disorder. There was some fear that this social safety net would not be so efficient this time round. The crisis was more violent. And the foregoing boom had transferred more people to the city on a more permanent basis, which would make it more difficult for them to return.

These facts re-emphasized the *social* and *political* importance of the rural economy. They also highlighted how much the rural sector had been neglected in the previous two decades. As long as the urban economy was growing rapidly, it was fashionable to assume that the rural sector would simply decline into insignificance, as in other industrialized nations. Growth could be achieved more easily by transferring people out of agriculture to the urban sector, rather than by improving the productivity or efficiency of farming. The crisis restated the economic importance of the rural sector, but even more, its social and political importance.

While localist advocates such as Saneh Chamarik welcomed this revived interest, they argued strongly against viewing the rural sector simply as a shock-absorber for the urban economy's volatility. Rather, Saneh pointed out that the rural economy had significance for itself, and that this significance would increase on a global scale in the near future:

> Why do I attribute such importance to the countryside? Because the Thai countryside is not like that of England, Europe and cold countries. The Thai countryside is part of the hot zone of the world which is rich in resources and biodiversity ... The hot zone covers just 7 per cent of the surface area of the world but has 60–70 per cent of the biodiversity, and is important to major industries of significance for mankind, namely the food industry and many others ... 70–80 per cent of the pharmaceuticals made from bioresources from the hot zone have been taken by foreign scientists from the local wisdom of villagers. This statistic is very revealing. It indicates the potential. And this potential can develop the Thai economy, society and politics in the future.

> (Saneh 1999: 35–6)

In parallel, Chatthip Nartsupha, who had earlier helped define the community culture approach, recognized that one major failure of the approach had been its lack of any economics. He began by restating that the strength of the approach was its peasant's eye view of the world and its emphasis on survival:

> The community culture approach starts from the concept of survival. The peasants' rights in production stem from their moral right to survival. The organization of economy and society is designed to ensure survival ... The approach attempts to explain peasant society as one form of society which exists on a basis of equality with other societies outside the peasant's world. It focuses study on four main aspects of the peasantry: community culture; the peasants' world-view; mixed farming; and self-reliance.
>
> (Chatthip *et al.* 1998)[4]

However, the local/community approach, Chatthip continued, had concentrated too much on culture, and too little on economics. This had effectively allowed agricultural economics to be conducted with the tools and perspectives of urban economics:

> Agricultural economics has tended to analyse the farm as a capitalist enterprise. It has concentrated on the market and the pricing of different agricultural products, rather than studying the organization of family production which is at the heart of the Thai peasant economy. Also there has been almost no study of peasant economic networks, and of the relations between the peasant community economy and other economic sectors in the national economy.
>
> (Chatthip *et al.* 1998)

Chatthip's group proposed that what was needed was 'a theory of production organization of the peasant family' perhaps using the perspective and methodology of the Chayanovian school, but adjusted to the political and economic realities of contemporary Thailand. That would have to begin with village-level research.

Moreover, as with Saneh's approach, the aim was not to portray or promote a view of the village economy as autarchic, isolated and deliberately backward. Rather, 'study should also be made of the relations between the local economies and the national economy, with the ultimate objective of a national prosperity founded on the flourishing of local community economies'. Strengthening agriculture should lead the way to community involvements in agri-processing, more sophisticated forms of financial and corporate organization, and non-agrarian forms of enterprise. As with Saneh, the overriding vision was to increase the productive capacity of the rural economy – not just its agrarian component – and find appropriate institutional ways to integrate it with the national and international economy on more equitable terms.

The journal *Withithat*, which appeared on the eve of the crisis, had rapidly become a focus for debate on the origins, meaning and implications of the economic crisis. The issues through 1998 concentrated on the structure of globalization and Thailand's vulnerability. In searching for solutions and responses to the crisis, the journal's editors and regular contributors were drawn, bit by bit, to concentrate on the importance of the community as the basis of the society, and on agriculture as the basis of the social economy. In late 1998, the journal published the works by Saneh and the Chatthip group cited above. In February 1999, it issued a volume on the *Sustainable Economy*, which gave space to some long-standing advocates of village self-reliance (Banthon Ondam, Seri Phongphit), expounded Gandhi's ideas on community economics, and advocated a transnational peasant response to the crisis. In the editor's introduction, Pithaya Wongkun argued that Thailand could survive this and previous economic crises, such as the 1930s depression, because of the self-reliance and sustainability of the peasant economy, which still supported the majority of the population:

> For this reason [the loss of sovereignty to the IMF], the national spirit of developing the community and Thai society should be the main direction in the future. The national economic and social development plans and the government's economic strategies should focus on developing the structure and the diversity of the community economy, and on building communities as centres of diversity across the country. Then development will harmonize with the social foundations, natural foundations, cultural foundations, and the thinking of present-day community leaders. And Thailand will have a civil society which is civilized, secure and sustainable.
>
> (Pithaya 1999: 10)

Culture and coping with globalization

> Today Thailand faces a catastrophe in the economy, in politics and in culture. Each day more people realize that this crisis is more violent than any instance in all our previous history.
>
> (Yuk Sri-ariya 1997)

In the early 1990s, the political scientist Chai-Anan Samudavanija had been one of the most enthusiastic exponents of globalization. On the eve of the crisis (1997), he published a book, *Watthanatham ku thun* [Culture as Capital], which marked a significant re-think.

Chai-Anan began by taking issue with Samuel Huntington's 'clash of civilizations' argument, which not only posited cultural warfare replacing politico-economic warfare in the post-Cold-War world, but appeared to give little room for non-major cultures such as those of Thailand. Chai-Anan proposed instead a 'splash of civilizations', an efflorescence of local cultures rather than a homogenization within a major model.

Chai-Anan went on to endorse the idea, first proposed by Rangsan Thanapornphan (1996), that culture represents a form of capital. He noted that the crisis emphasized that Thailand had little of its own stock of other forms of capital, particularly financial capital and technology; that Thailand had tried to develop by borrowing these from the advanced world; and that the crisis had arisen because these loans could be easily withdrawn and transferred elsewhere. By contrast, Thailand had a large stock of cultural capital. This was evident from surveys that showed tourists chose Thailand as a destination because of monuments, cultural performances, food, and service attitude – all products that embody a high element of cultural capital. Similarly they rated Thailand low for products that embody technology (for example, hotels, communications) and public capital (infrastructure, traffic).

Chai-Anan further pointed out that the inheritance of cultural capital also extended to social values – such as mutual sympathy, respect for elders, compassion – which would not only help Thailand to survive the crisis, but would provide the basis for the construction of a superior social model over the long term.

Chai-Anan pointed out that this stock of cultural capital had been built up through investment in the past, and needed to be maintained by constant reinvestment. He summed up:

> ... when we appreciate culture as a form of capital, we can have a culture strategy which can serve as a tool for the Thai state in the context of globalization ... Even though Thai society has little economic capital, low economic production capacity, low savings, low labour skills, yet we still have people who smile easily, a long-standing heritage of cultural capital, values that remain strong and do not need to be rebuilt. This is different from many western societies which need to rebuild a foundation of values and principles – such as gratitude to parents, family warmth, respect for elders.
>
> (Chai-Anan 1997: 85–6)

Suvinai Pornvalai has put out a prodigious volume of writing, combining economics, aspects of eastern cultures, and sophisticated versions of 'how to' literature – the manuals for success in anything, but especially business, which have become the largest segment of Thai publishing. In early 1998 he published *Sethakit fong sabu: botrian lae tang rot* (*The Bubble Economy*

– *Lessons and Survival*), introduced as a book to help non-economists understand the crisis.

Suvinai explained the economic crisis through two parallel processes at work within international capitalism. The first is the gradual increase of financial capital in comparison to industrial capital. Speculative financial investment now far exceeds productive investment as an activity of the international system, resulting in the series of overinvestment bubbles that have afflicted Europe, the US, Japan and now Southeast Asia in the past two decades. The second is the advance of consumerism, through which Thailand has become ensnared in this trail of bursting bubbles.

According to Suvinai (1998: 31–2), capitalism grows by continually expanding the limits of consumption. From the 14th to the 19th century, this was achieved by overcoming boundaries of space through exploration and colonialism. In the early 20th century, this phase reached a dead end with the advent of world wars, socialist revolutions, and anti-colonialist struggles. In a second phase, from around 1930 to around 1980, expansion was sustained by increasing the levels of consumption within the heartland countries of international capital, by reshaping and redirecting 'wants' to focus on 'products'. Since 1980, this same process has been extended across the world:

> Globalization is the last manifestation of capitalism which uses communications technology and builds a high image for the modern lifestyle to stimulate people's wants and expand the borders of people's wants with a success that the socialist countries could not match.
>
> (Suvinai 1998: 33)

In the advanced stages of this phase, consumption becomes an end in itself. For countries such as Thailand, absorbed into the fringes of the spread of consumerism, patterns of consumption become separated from the local heritage of culture and ways of life. Borne up by the illusions of the overinvestment bubble, consumption focuses on goods whose whole purpose is to display the fact of consumption itself.

Until ten years ago, Suvinai continued, Thais' consumption patterns reflected the restraints and limitation of wants common to a peasant-based society. But in the bubble, and under the influence of consumerism, the middle class has pioneered a change and expansion of consumption culture that has affected the whole society. Suvinai concluded:

> The first thing everyone must do to pull the country out of this economic disaster is to change from the consumption habits which come with the bubble and the ideology of consumerism . . . the real route to

survival will begin, not from any political change which is far from certain, but from change by the Thai middle class itself.

(Suvinai 1998: 84–5)

In a similar vein, Pithaya Wongkun argued that a society that blindly follows an outside model, fails to see its own value, and fails to understand its own cultural roots, will suffer a gradual change in its own culture and way-of-life, such that 'in the end that society will gradually change to a slave society, modern-style' (Pithaya 1998d). The spread of a western model across the world has created an 'imperialism of the mind', which is reproduced across economics, politics and cultures. The free-market ideology provides cover for speculative capital to invade weaker countries, collapse their economies, and buy up the wreckage cheap. The command of weaponry and international organizations enables the USA and Europe to dominate world politics.

The spread of western images through advertising and film, Pithaya continued, has led to gradual adoption of a western lifestyle. 'Cultural slavery has already spread through Thai society ... Now that the knowledge, mentality, way-of-thinking and way-of-life of most people is Westernized, in what way will we still be a Thai society? This kind of society is a modern-style slave society, under a mental imperialism which is spreading throughout the world' (Pithaya 1998d).

In 1994–95, Prawase Wasi spoke and wrote extensively on the issue of development, largely in connection with the effort to make the Eighth Plan a very different document from its predecessors. He used a concept of culture to criticize the imbalance in Thailand's previous development. He defined culture as a society's accumulated knowledge and practice. Implicitly, culture is a more powerful concept than people, nation or state. Past development has been marked by 'compartmentalized thinking', which focuses on a few parts rather than the whole. In particular, it focuses on developing wealth rather than humanity, business profits rather than society. In 1997–98, Prawase extended this line of thinking against the background of the crisis. The result of this compartmentalized approach to development is not only lop-sided and unsustainable, but represents a deep form of threat to Thailand *as a culture.*

If Thailand focuses only on developing business, Thai culture will disappear from this country called Thailand. When you lose culture, it's equal to losing nation.

(Prawase 1998: 13)

Prawase pointed out that the bubble burst in the 'upper economy', in the ranks of finance and large-scale business. By contrast, the 'lower economy' of agriculture and small business was less affected. 'This is because the upper economy is fake but the lower economy is real' (*Bangkok Post*, 28 December 1997). On a broader basis, the old path of development was at odds with the cultural base, and particularly with the economy of local communities. This badness-of-fit had resulted in the neglect of agriculture, a widening gap between rich and poor, destruction of the environment, and loss of ethics. The solution lay in redefining development on a community base.

Prawase's thinking went beyond a simply economistic interpretation of self-reliance. Speaking at the height of the crisis, he depicted self-sufficiency as a 'moral economy' in contrast to 'the economy that presses for money and that destroys everything including the culture' (*Bangkok Post*, 2 February 1998). The route to recovery lay not in the finance industry and the macroeconomy, but in the school, *wat*, family, and local community. A few months later, he called for a 'war of national salvation' in which the National Culture Commission would be wheeled out as one of the battalions (*Bangkok Post*, 21 July 1998).

In sum, from a variety of perspectives, intellectuals have looked to a concept of 'culture' as defence against globalization. The participants define 'culture' very broadly – as way-of-life, the society's accumulated learning from the past, or simply as 'knowledge'. While there is an implicit us/them theme present, this is not the driving force of these arguments. The call is not so much to 'defend Thai culture', but to draw on Thai culture and local community cultures to rescue the society from disaster. The call then is to look inward, have less faith in globalization, and leverage benefits from the society's inheritance rather than relying on borrowed money and technology.

Running away from the *khlong*

One measure of the importance of this discourse of locality against globalization lies in the fierceness of the opposition it provoked. In the period before the crisis, the idea of community culture was challenged from the angle of liberal modernism, most notably by Anek Laothamatas (1995; Anek *et al.* 1995). In the context of the crisis and the heightened profile of the self-reliance idea, this challenge was restated in fiercer and more emotional terms by Kamchai Laisamit (1998). Besides attacking assumptions and logical inconsistencies in the localism discourse, these challenges make four main points.

First, the idea of the local community as a source of moral values is a hopeless idealization. The local community in this form probably never existed. It has certainly been transformed by the ever-closer relations with urban capitalism over the last century. And it could never be invented or reinvented in real physical form within the contemporary context.

Second, the dominant reality of rural society is not egalitarian and cooperative communities but the patronage system (*rabop uppatham*) characterized by inequality, economic exploitation, and political domination. This patronage system constrains the development of the rural economy and undermines Thailand's progress towards democracy. Provincial bosses with an electoral base in rural society dominate parliament and other representative bodies and pervert their operation. As elsewhere in the world, democracy cannot flourish in the context of a backward peasant society.

Third, for Thailand to progress both economically and politically, the village should not be conserved but transformed. Farmers should not try to revive local wisdom but should try to become better capitalists so they can compete more efficiently. Farmers should not try to preserve local communities, but should escape from them into free individualism so that they can recombine in the free associations which are the basis of civil society and democracy (Anek: 1995, 82–92).

Fourth, the localism discourse is a conservative force, promoted by utopians and conservative nationalists, which threatens the march of progress and may even damage what urban modernism has achieved. Kamchai (1998: 79) argued:

> Why should we think of going back to recall the community culture as a direction to fight the economic crisis at the national level, when this community culture is weaker than capitalism and has already collapsed once in the past? This time it will not only be the community which will be in a mess. It will lead the city, which is the most progressive element in the country, to total collapse along with it.

Diverting the *khlong*

At the outset of the crisis, many mainstream thinkers and public leaders made similar statements reaffirming their faith in urban-led progress. Anand Panyarachun, for instance, argued that the crisis should not be blamed on globalization but on Thailand's failure to manage it. He insisted Thailand should not react by turning away from the world. However, the length and depth of the crisis eventually sparked a broader interest in the localism discourse. The aggression shown by foreign interests, the extent of the damage to the Thai urban economy, and the prospects for social distress and disorder, persuaded even some ardent globalizers to think again. Even Anand's faith seemed to waver. In December 1999, the Thailand Development Research Institute – the leading technocratic think-tank and spiritual home of mainstream economics – devoted its flagship year-end conference to the theme of the 'Sufficiency Economy' laid out in the King's 1997 speech.[5] Anand was chairman of the

Institute. Aphichai Puntasen opened the event with a discourse on Buddhist economics.

The conference statement of definition presented the concept of a sufficiency economy as 'moderation and due consideration in all modes of conduct, as well as the need for sufficient protection from internal and external shocks'. This moderation was needed in order 'to cope appropriately with critical challenges arising from extensive and rapid socioeconomic, environmental, and cultural changes occurring as a result of globalization'. In the hands of TDRI, the principle of sufficiency had been transformed into a technique for negotiating a more conditional accommodation with globalization: 'The philosophy points the way for recovery that will lead to a more resilient and sustainable economy better able to meet the challenges from globalisation and other changes'. Anand closed the conference by describing the sufficiency economy as a tool for adjusting mainstream development economics to become more self-reliant, balanced, and sustainable, and for containing globalization's tendency towards social division:

> We can summarise that the approach of the sufficiency economy does not conflict with mainstream economics which emphasises optimality. It's an approach which offers an 'optimum' strategy for all aspects of development. For the sake of the Thai way-of-life, it is necessary to lay a new theoretical foundation in the future which does not rely on others, stands on its own feet, is self-critical, takes the middle path, and adopts a development process which is continually adjusted … Besides, the sufficiency economy accords with the unique character of Thai society with its mutual consideration, mutual assistance, goodwill and good intention towards others, resulting in pursuit of the common benefit more than personal benefit.
>
> (Thailand Development Research Institute 1999)

Not everyone welcomed this broader interest in the localism discourse, which snowballed over the crisis. Those who see the discourse as an attempt to shift the balance of power between state and locality resented the Ministry of the Interior's official adoption and promotion of self-reliance, which they felt was opportunistic and damaging to the power of the discourse in the long run. Similarly, some opposed the business sponsorship of community projects, such as Suphon Suphaphong's Bangchak schemes and Mechai Viravaidya's TBird – as distorting the concept of self-reliance for political and business gain. Some felt that the attempts by Anand and others to yoke the sufficiency principle with mainstream economics was an attempt to pre-empt and neutralize a powerful radical message (Kasian 2000).

Conclusions: beyond community culture

The discourse on *watthanatham chumchon*, which gelled in the late 1980s and early 1990s, has been substantially changed against the background of the economic crisis. The earlier version focused on community *as a culture*, encompassing knowledge, local practices, and social relations. It asserted the importance of this culture as a counter to centralized political domination, top-down development planning, and urban-triumphalist cultural segregation. It amounted to an assertion of the importance of the rural locality. However, as a concept it remained somewhat passive. It attracted a rather confused debate over whether the 'community' was supposed to be a description of historical fact, or an idealized image guiding the way to the future.

The King's speech on self-sufficiency broadened interest in the discourse. Many of the official actions which stemmed from this initiative – particularly those of the Democrat Party and the Ministry of the Interior – were conceived as forms of short-term disaster management. However, at the same time, the discourse also advanced in ways that may be important over the longer term.

Saneh clarified that 'community' is important as an ethical construct needed to reassert human and moral values in the face of the dehumanizing narratives of modern economics and in the face of the propensity to social catastrophe built into the international economic system. As such, 'community' has much the same status in the discourse as the idea of a 'state of nature' had in the evolution of modern western liberal theories. It is a philosophic statement about the human condition and human needs, which serves as the starting point for building social and political theories.

Religious scholars such as P.A. Payutto and academics such as Aphichai Puntasen gave the ideas of self-reliance and self-sufficiency a grounding in Buddhist philosophy, and sparked interest in 'Buddhist economics' as a counter-discourse to modern economics.

A very broad range of intellectuals, including Rangsan, Chai-Anan, Suvinai, Prawase, and Pithaya, drew attention to *culture* as a social, economic, and political asset. As with other assets, culture needs to be protected from losing its value, and constantly renewed by reinvestment. Also as with other assets, culture can deliver profits in the form of social strengths and economic revenues whose value becomes evident when a crisis leads to the rapid destruction of other forms of asset.

These clarifications and extensions of some key concepts within the discourse of community culture served as the basis for a more activist and assertive version of community or locality based theorization. In the thinking of Saneh and of Chatthip's group, the restatement of the community as a moral necessity became the basis for a rescripting of rural economics based on the existing natural and human resource endowment, rather than as an adjunct of theories of urban economic expansion. NGO and community groups adopting and adapting *thammarat* called for a more aggressive approach to decentralization and 'community rule'. In the thinking of Buddhist scholars such as Payutto and lay popularizers such as Prawase Wasi, self-reliance became a national project, not only a personal or community strategy. Similarly, the idea of 'culture' was adopted much more widely than the idea of 'community culture' to provoke debate on visions of a Thai future that need not follow the pattern or the urging of the West. The severity of the crisis induced some ardent globalizers to look at the community discourse as a framework for adding some conditions to global integration and rampant development.

Critics of the localism discourse reflect a different vision of the Thai future – a vision of urbanism, capitalism, and democracy triumphant. While delivered in the name of liberalism and progress, this critique is sometimes surprisingly alarmist, attacking exaggerated versions of what the localists actually propose. For example, some critics interpret 'self-reliance' as meaning a complete withdrawal from the market economy, while others depict the call for a rural focus as a denial of the right of the city to exist and prosper.

The rise of the localism discourse has been a function of the social division and environmental damage which are features of the development of urban capitalism all through history and all round the world. The localists argue that the liberal-modernists have no arguments, no social philosophy to manage these destructive consequences. The liberal modernists reply that this is simply a stage that has to be traversed, and costs that have to be borne – resisting the flow of history will ultimately be more costly. The localists reply that the modernists' vision of capitalism and democracy is losing adherents even in its western heartland. Besides, the trend of the world economy is to freeze more and more areas, more and more segments of the population, as peripheral and excluded, rather than fully integrated into the benefits of capitalism. Localism is a form of guerrilla resistance to this peripheralization.

In nineteenth-century Europe, against the background of the rise of industrial society, arguments in favour of free trade were locked in combat with arguments that the excesses of the free market were a threat to human values, social values, and the growth of democracy. Critics pointed out that the free market not only generated massive economic inequality but also cultivated utilitarian ways of thinking, which threatened the European inheritance of humanist values. These critical arguments often looked backwards to a 'golden age' or 'state of nature' to build philosophical foundations for their critique, and simultaneously looked forward to visions of utopia or improvement. There were many strands in this critique which variously led towards romanticism, nationalism and socialism. As a whole, they were eventually successful in bringing about state-led and society-led initiatives to moderate free market liberalism.

This comparison is not meant to suggest that Thailand will follow the same path. The era is different, and Thailand's intellectual inheritance is different. The comparison is merely meant to indicate that the mobilization of ideas about community, locality and Buddhist values to oppose the neoliberal agenda, follows a known historical pattern. Societies under pressure discover that social and cultural values that do not figure in market economics are important to the society's survival and well-being. The increased salience of these localist ideas, and their intellectual development during the crisis, offer some hope.

Notes

1 *Khlong* means canal. The phrase 'walking backwards into a *khlong*' means being conservative or backward.
2 See for example Campferns (1997); Kaufman and Haroldo-Dilla (1997).
3 This journal, which began on the eve of the crisis, published two issues in pocket-book form every quarter, containing articles mid-way between academic analysis and journalistic comment.
4 See especially the final chapter. All the quotes used here are taken from the English-language summary of the project, prepared for the Thailand Research Fund.
5 This mainstream reinterpretation liked to take the 'self' away from the 'sufficiency' in order to downplay the element of withdrawal from the wider economy. This linguistic nicety, of course, only meant anything to those sophisticated enough to know English.

References

Anek Laothamatas (1995) *Song nakara prachathipathai: naew thang patirup kan muang sethakit peu prachathipathai* [A tale of two cities of democracy: directions for reform in politics and economy for democracy], Bangkok: Matichon [in Thai].

Anek Laothamatas, Seksan Prasertkun, Anan Kanchanaphan and Direk Pathamasiriwat (1995) *Wiphak sangkhom thai* [Critique of Thai society], Bangkok: Amarin [in Thai].

Aphichai Phantasen (1996) *Khwam wung thang ook lae thang leuk mai* [Hopes, exits, and new options] Bangkok: Munnithi phumipanya [in Thai].

Campferns, Hubert (ed.) (1997) *Community Around the World: Practice, Theory, Research and Training*, Toronto and London: University of London Press.

Chai-Anan Saumudavanija (1997) *Watthanatham ku thun* [Culture as capital], Bangkok [in Thai].

Chatthip Nartsupha (1991) The 'community culture' school of thought, in: Manas Chitkasem and Andrew Turton (eds) *Thai Constructions of Knowledge*, London: School of Oriental and African Studies.

Chatthip Nartsupha, Chinasak Suwan-Achariya, Aphichat Thongyou, Voravidh Charoenloet and Maniemai Thongyou (1998) *Tissadi lae naewkit sethakit chumchon chaona* [Theories and approaches to the economics of the peasant community], Bangkok: Viththat Local Wisdom Series 7 [in Thai].

Kamchai Laisamit (1998) *Wichan neung nak setthasat* [One vision of an economist], Bangkok [in Thai].

Kasian Tejapira (2000) Setthakit pho phiang thuan krasae a-rai? [What approach does the sufficiency economy oppose?], *Nation Sutsapda*, 8: 21–7 [in Thai].

Kaufman, Michael and Haroldo-Dilla, Alfonso (eds) (1997) *Community Power and Grassroots Democracy*, London and New Jersey: Zed Books.

Narong Petprasoet (ed.) (1999) *1999: jut plian haeng yuk samai* [*1999: Turning Point of the Era*], Bangkok: Sethasat kan muang (peu chumchon) 8 [in Thai].

Phrathammapitok (P.A. Payutto) (1992) *Buddhist Economics: A Middle Way for the Market Place*, trans. Dhammavijaya and Bruce Evans, Bangkok: Buddhadhamma Foundation.

Phrathammapitok (P.A. Payutto) (1998) Khwam romyen nai vikrit thai: phutthwithi nai kan kae panha vikrit khong chat [Shelter in the Thai crisis: a Buddhist way to solve the problem of the national crisis], in: Pithaya Wongkun (ed.) *Thammarat: jut plian prathet thai?* [Good governance: a turning point for Thailand?], Bangkok: Viththat Globalisation Series 7 [in Thai].

Pithaya Wongkun (ed.) (1998a) *Thammarat: jut plian prathet thai?* [Good governance: a turning point for Thailand?], Bangkok: Viththat globalisation series 7 [in Thai].

Pithaya Wongkun (ed.) (1998b) Than chumchon prachasangkhom thammarat lae chumchon atipathai: thang rot nai yuk vikrit sethakit sangkhom thai [Community base, civil society, good governance and community rule: survival routes in the crisis of Thai economy and society], in: Pithaya Wongkun (ed.) *Thammarat: jut plian prathet thai?* [Good governance: a turning point for Thailand?], Bangkok: Viththat Globalisation Series 7 [in Thai].

Pithaya Wongkun (ed.) (1998c) *Thai yuk watthanatham that* [Thai in the Age of Slave], Bangkok: Viththat Globalisation Series 4 [in Thai].

Pithaya Wongkun (ed.) (1998d) Kamnam: phumibanya that sang watthanatham that [Preface: slave wisdom creates slave culture], in: *Thai yuk watthanatham that* [Thai in the Age of Slave], Bangkok: Viththat Globalisation Series 4 [in Thai].

Pithaya Wongkun (ed.) (1999) *Rap wikhrit sethakit lok pi 2000: sethakit yang yeun* [*Withstanding the World Economic Crisis of Year 2000: the Sustainable Economy*], Bangkok: Viththat Globalisation Series 10 [in Thai].

Prawase Wasi (1998) Watthanatham kan phatthana [The culture of development], in: *Thai yuk watthanatham that* [Thai in the Age of Slave], Bangkok: Viththat Globalisation Series 4 [in Thai].

Rangsan Thanapornphan (1996) Thun watthanatham. Unpublished paper [in Thai].

Saneh Chamarik (1998) *Than kit su thang leuk mai khong sankhom thai* [*Foundations of Thought for New Options for Thai Society*], Bangkok: Viththat Local Wisdom Series 3 [in Thai].

Saneh Chamarik (1999) 1999 jut plian haeng yuk samai: chak lokaphiwat su chumchon [1999: turning point of the era: from globalisation to community], in:

Narong Petprasoet (ed.) *1999: jut plian haeng yuk samai* [*1999: Turning Point of the Era*], Bangkok: Sethasat kan muang (peu chumchon) 8 [in Thai].

Suvinai Pornvalai (1998) *Sethakit fong sabu: botriean lae tang rot* [The bubble economy – lessons and survival], Bangkok: Thammasat University [in Thai].

Thailand Development Research Institute (1999) *Ekkasan prakop kan sammana wichakan pracham pi 2542 setthakit pho phiang*. Papers from the 1999 annual seminar on the sufficiency economy, Ambassador City, Jomthien, 18–19 December [in Thai].

Thirayuth Boonmee (1998) *Thammarat haeng chat: yutthasat ku hayana prathet thai* [*National Governance: Strategy to Save Thailand*], Bangkok: Saithan [in Thai].

Part III

The new environment for economic policy making

Chapter 6

Public sector reform
A post-crisis opportunity

Stefan G. Koeberle[1]

Weak governance – spanning legal, corporate and public sector dimensions – was arguably one of the fundamental causes of Thailand's economic crisis of 1997. The ongoing debate concerning the appropriate strategy for economic recovery has emphasized weaknesses in the outcomes of public sector performance: macroeconomic policy, financial sector management, competitiveness and poorly targeted service delivery. However, to date, less attention has been given to the fundamental weaknesses in public sector governance that emerged during the crisis and which impede the restoration and sustainability of economic development. These matters are the focus of this chapter.

Thailand received considerable praise for managing its aggregate fiscal accounts during the decade preceding the 1997 economic crisis. But international comparisons suggest weaknesses in the performance of public institutions, which came to the fore during the crisis. The current administrative reality is of a highly centralized, albeit fragmented, public sector, which runs on principles of automaticity, seniority and hierarchy. The sustainability of future growth will depend on a better-functioning public sector. To lay the foundation for a new decade of sustainable growth, Thailand needs to confront the challenges of efficiency, sustainability, equity, and transparency in its management of public resource mobilization and expenditures.

Greater *efficiency* in the use of public resources will require a serious review of the role of the state in future development, better evaluation of the outcomes and outputs of expenditure decisions and more effective budget management. Medium-term *sustainability* in the context of careful macroeconomic demand management has been the traditional hallmark of Thailand's fiscal policy approach. Its continuation will require cautious management of public sector debt. Achieving greater *equity* will require improved targeting of public expenditures to reach the poor and disadvantaged and increased progressivity and coverage of taxation. Improved *transparency* will require a disclosure of the fiscal risks posed by contingent liabilities, improved budget coverage and effective counter-corruption measures.

Thailand's economic crisis demonstrated the need for broad-based governance reforms. But even without the crisis, the weaknesses of its public sector would have limited the ability to achieve sustainable and equitable development. Its public institutions must thus provide effective leadership to guide the economy towards recovery and to deliver better services to the poor. This means overcoming wasteful spending, corruption, interagency fragmentation, weak management, non-transparent finances, unclear laws and excessive reliance on public sector provision.

Several interrelated challenges can be identified:

- improving government services in terms of access, timeliness and quality;
- curtailing corruption and increasing the confidence of the Thai people in their government;
- containing the continually rising administrative costs of government services;
- improving the targeting of public service delivery to the poor and disabled;
- enhancing citizen participation through provision of better information and decentralization;
- reforming state-owned enterprises to allow competitive private provision of infrastructure services;
- improving public sector governance, including better quality of public services, greater efficiency in the management of public resources and more transparency; and
- ensuring that government financial management supports the objective of returning to high economic growth.

Several factors favour public sector reform in the post-crisis setting. One is a democratic opening provided by the implementation of the 1997 Constitution, which allows a greater voice for citizens, more responsive political and administrative institutions, and increased pressure from press and interest groups for cleaner government and better service. Another is the financial crisis, which has focused national attention on value for money and equity in government expenditures. A third factor is the diffusion of global ideas about government re-invention that encourages Thais to modernize their public administration in the image of developed country models. Finally, with the current *Thai Rak Thai* government of Thaksin Shinawatra, there is the historic opportunity of a government with a comfortable parliamentary majority, which should give it a more solid base for pushing through reforms than its multi-party coalition predecessors.

There are other factors working against reform, including: the possible closing of the window of opportunity for reform when the crisis fully abates; the lack of high-level leadership within the government for a concerted reform push, despite the initiatives of some government actors to move forward on a reform agenda; the deeply entrenched values of hierarchy and individualism that impede efforts towards coordination and improved performance; and the still evolving nature of political (particularly electoral) accountability and the degree to which citizen-based reform pressure becomes organized into voting blocs that affect politicians' survival.

The economic crisis drew attention to these public sector weaknesses, but it has also provided an opportunity and a renewed resolve for broad-based governance reforms. This chapter develops the case for better governance through reform of key public sector institutions. The next section examines the weaknesses in Thailand's fiscal policy performance, with an emphasis on public expenditures. It is followed by an overview of options for improving public expenditure management and a review of the reform efforts undertaken so far. The final section concludes.

Weaknesses in public expenditure management

Public expenditure management in Thailand has traditionally been poorly prioritized, pays minimal attention to the results of spending, and lacks accountability for the quality of services provided. Linkages among planning, budgeting and sectoral policy are weak. The fiscal planning process has an annual focus and lacks a medium-term approach. It is based on cash flows of the central government and does not cover non-budgetary fiscal operations such as contingent liabilities and quasi-fiscal operations. Fiscal accounts are not fully transparent and do not meet the minimum standards of generally accepted international practice. Expenditures and subsidies to reduce poverty are often ineffective due to poor targeting and limited evaluation.

Despite the above limitations, most of the key elements needed to construct a modern performance-based budget management system already exist in some form. The strengths of the current process have enabled the government to perform well on some key dimensions of budget performance, notably aggregate fiscal discipline. The government consistently ran surpluses in the years prior to the onset of the economic crisis and these surpluses were positively correlated with the rate of growth (Figure 6.1).[2] However, the highly centralized, control-oriented process has created disincentives for using the budget process to empower line agencies and local governments to find policy solutions to increase the efficiency, effectiveness and equity of expenditure programmes.

Overview of fiscal institutions

On issues of fiscal planning, four central agencies interact to control the level of spending and thus the deficit: the National Economic and Social

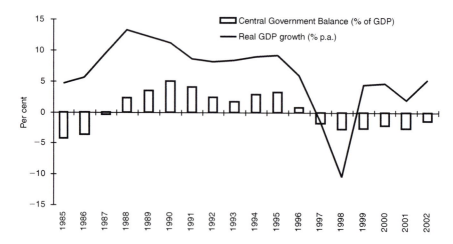

Figure 6.1 Economic growth and fiscal balance, 1985 to 2002 (source: Bank of Thailand).

Development Board (NESDB), the Ministry of Finance (MOF), the Bank of Thailand (BOT), and the Bureau of the Budget (BOB) in the Prime Minister's Office. This 'gang of four' provides the macroeconomic framework from which aggregate expenditure ceilings are determined. The roles of these central agencies in fiscal decision-making are highly fragmented.

- The BOB is primarily responsible for preparing the recurrent budget, whereas the NESDB is responsible for long-range planning and the development (investment) budget.
- The MOF exercises general budget control.
- The Fiscal Policy Office (FPO) processes externally financed projects and also external borrowing.
- The Comptroller General's Department (CGD) controls government accounts, cash flow projections and domestic borrowing.
- Debt is managed by a committee that includes the FPO, the Revenue Department, BOB, and the BOT.
- The macroeconomic outlook is projected by NESDB.
- Revenues are projected among a consortium of agencies, with the MOF determining the final forecasts.
- The NESDB approves multi-year projects that are proposed by line agencies.
- The BOB formulates annual allocations for these multi-year projects.

Despite the use of committees and subcommittees to coordinate tasks, the above fragmentation weakens the overall effectiveness of fiscal planning and management, and diminishes accountability and transparency. This fragmentation was a significant obstacle to generating the necessary analysis to take decisions quickly during the economic crisis. A realignment of responsibilities will be necessary if these agencies are to modernize expenditure management and develop better strategic planning.

Fiscal planning[3]

The NESDB is the major public planning and inter-sectoral coordination agency in the Thai government. However, its role and influence in setting the policy agenda appears to have diminished in recent years. While its five-year plans and annual development plans are intended to set the overall direction of government, they seem to have little direct effect on specific policies. In particular, line ministry plans are not coordinated with the national plan and national budget allocations are determined independently of the plan. However, the five-year plans have had an effect on some structural changes within the government. For example, the eighth plan, covering the years 1997–2001, which focused on democratizing policy, was a driving force in enacting the new Constitution. The ninth plan, covering the years 2002–06, sets out a strategy for making public expenditures more equitable. The plans have also highlighted areas where regulatory changes and policy frameworks must be developed.

Within the 'gang of four' committee, NESDB provides the economic growth forecasts, but it has little influence on allocations within the budget. While the national plans are supposed to provide guidance for budgetary allocations, the plans often do not prioritize policy objectives nor provide strategies that are detailed enough to achieve those objectives. A major problem with the effectiveness of planning is that there is no formal organizational role for the plans in the decision-making process. Once the plans are drafted, no incentives exist for other governmental units to pay attention to them. For example, while the BOB solicits NESDB comment on its budgetary allocations, BOB is free to ignore the NESDB's input.

NESDB's ability to influence budgets and evaluate proposed projects funded by external debt is hindered by flaws in the Thai budgetary process. The government allocates the national budget across programmes separately from the allocation of projects funded through external debt. There is no integrated budget or master plan for setting the total amount spent in each area. Nor are these data reported comprehensively. As a result, NESDB's project appraisals are conducted outside the context of a comprehensive budget expenditure plan. Project appraisal consumes a substantial amount of NESDB resources, but given the problems with the non-integrated budget process, the appraisals themselves are of limited value from a planning point of view. However, NESDB's role in appraising sectoral investment plans is important and could replace specific project appraisal.

Institutional arrangements for expenditure management

The performance of a country's institutions for formulating and executing fiscal policy depends on the incentives governing the size, allocation and use of budgetary resources. Institutional arrangements shape the quality of outcomes on four broad levels: (i) aggregate fiscal discipline; (ii) resource allocation and use based on strategic priorities (allocative efficiency); (iii) efficiency and effectiveness of programmes and service delivery (technical or operational efficiency); and (iv) fiscal transparency. The following section documents the strengths and weaknesses of Thailand's institutional arrangements for expenditure management in these four areas.

Aggregate fiscal discipline

Thailand meets several key requirements for the use of budget planning processes as a tool of effective macroeconomic management. Two predominate. First, countries with weak aggregate fiscal discipline generally have a relatively weak Ministry of Finance (or the equivalent body responsible for budgeting) and spending pressures drive the budget planning process rather than being subordinated to the requirements of macro fiscal management. The dominant role of BOB in budget preparation ensures that expenditure proposals are consistent with macro fiscal policy planning. This control extends through to budget execution, where the allotment system ensures that spending does not run ahead of revenues.

Second, a frequent cause of weak macro fiscal control is the propensity of governments to amend the budget during the course of budget execution in response to newly recognized political pressures. Even countries with relatively refined budgeting systems are subject to this form of loss of budget discipline. In Thailand's case, in addition to strong bureaucratic management of the budget process, there is also a clear political commitment to enforce the agreed budget ceiling rather than adding additional spending during the course of the budget year. However, the allotment system and associated delays in the receipt of funds lead to frequent underspending of budget allocations by agencies. While this contributes to aggregate fiscal control, it compromises the allocative and technical efficiency of the budget.

Perhaps the key question relating to the effectiveness of macro fiscal management is not the ability to enforce fiscal targets, but the process of target setting itself. This requires adequate and timely national income accounting data together with forward indicators capable of picking up turning points in the economy. It further requires a national accounting consistency framework for modelling national savings and investment.

A final issue relating to macroeconomic planning is the current reliance on *annual budgeting* rather than budgeting within a medium term expenditure framework. In this annual budget framework, government agencies have little assurances about resource availability beyond one year. This creates uncertainty about resources and impedes planning. Moreover, it complicates the consideration and funding of new projects: would resources be available to fund them (especially if they are multi-year) and have the operation and maintenance funding implications of such projects (and ongoing projects which are also being implemented) been allowed for?

Budget planning does not take place within a formal medium-term framework. Forward estimates of *development* expenditures are published in the budget documents. However, they are of variable quality and, for BOB analysis and planning purposes, they are not regarded as robust forward estimates. Forward estimates for other components of expenditure are not available.

More realistic budgetary planning requires that plans for spending carryovers from past budgets be included in budget plans and that expenditure plans be tailored more carefully to the actual implementation capacity of government agencies. Two important benefits are to be gained from more accurate tax and expenditure plans. First, the budget would provide a clearer picture to market participants in the real and financial sectors (both domestic and international) of the government's actual spending intentions and fiscal stance, which would enhance the credibility of government policy. Second, the budget would provide a firmer basis for planning and managing government expenditures, both in the aggregate and for individual sectors.

Allocative efficiency

Allocative efficiency relates particularly to the appropriateness of the size of the capital budget relative to the recurrent budget, and the composition of activities in each of these categories. Actual allocations reflect the effectiveness of the underlying budget processes. In this context, planning for overall budget allocations among sectors seems to suffer from a similar problem to that of macroeconomic control. While sound budget processes are in place, the information systems required to make them work effectively have weaknesses. The key shortcoming is a lack of performance information feeding back into budget planning. This reflects a general orientation of the budget process to one of considering inputs, rather than outputs and performance management.

Thai budget processes are strongly centralized by the standards of well-performing countries. For each work plan and project, separate budget ceilings are provided for up to seven different categories of operating costs. Since there are normally numerous work plans and/or projects in a single programme, the number of separate budget ceilings for different cost components within a single programme is often very high. This input focus compromises the allocative effectiveness of the budgeting process in several respects:

- limited flexibility of programme managers to direct budget funds to those uses that will generate the highest returns for their programmes;
- inadequate justification for new project proposals and project selection;
- limited project monitoring, other than through a cash allotment process; and
- lack of systematic re-prioritizing between the baseline recurrent budget and new policy proposals.

Resistance to change is reinforced by the conundrum pointed out by Dixon (2002): extensive centralized control undermines agency management – but it persists because of weak agency management. Without incentives to use the budget process as an essential management tool, policy solutions to increase the efficiency, effectiveness and equity of programmes are unlikely to be considered. In addition, the capital budget is more easily postponed than work plans, owing to the finite duration of investment projects. This may lead to a postponement of productive investments and a continuation of unproductive recurrent programmes.

Programme budgeting, introduced in the early 1980s, was intended to provide performance feedback. While the budget is set up by programme areas such as education and transportation, performance budgets are not used for planning purposes, for setting strategic priorities or for evaluating progress towards objectives. While these programmes are linked by common themes, they are not cost centres; they are implemented by many different agencies and often across several ministries; and they have no manager accountable for programme outcomes. In this instance, budget structure is essentially used for line item budgeting, which fosters micromanagement and control over details, but which offers little assurance about whether progress towards government objectives is being achieved. From a management perspective, budgeting based on cost centres rather than programmes has the advantage of more clearly pinpointing responsibility for performance than under programme budgeting, while still providing information on the outcomes achieved by individual cost centres. The reforms envision introducing cost allocation methods and cost centres to the line ministries so that the linkages between performance and costs are defined more clearly and can be monitored more effectively. Another shortcoming in the link between budget planning and allocative efficiency relates to *budget coverage*. Comprehensive planning of sector allocations requires comprehensive budget coverage. At present, it is not possible to get a clear picture of the overall impact of government spending on economic activities, nor is it possible to know the full range of government activities in most sectors because the central government budget provides only a partial picture of public-sector activities. Local government, state enterprise and extra-budgetary funds are all omitted, along with encumbrance expenditures and expenditures financed by foreign aid or foreign borrowing. The capital budget excludes donor contributions to projects, which limits the ability to plan budget spending on the basis of overall investment in different sectors. This limited budget coverage is likely to become more acute in the future as local government and social insurance funds assume a larger role in providing and financing public services.

Operational efficiency

The operational efficiency of government can be measured across two dimensions: (i) the ability of government agencies to reflect Cabinet priorities in their strategic plans and (ii) their ability to deliver promised results. In each step in the budget cycle – planning, preparation, execution, monitoring and evaluation, and audit – it is possible to identify weaknesses, and some fundamental deficiencies, that inhibit the operation of a system designed to deliver outputs, with agencies accountable for the quality of delivery. While the concept of performance measurement is not unfamiliar in Thailand, and the budget coding structure would support programme budgeting, programme and performance budgeting has not been implemented extensively.

Significant weaknesses also exist in the translation of sectoral policies and priorities into effective results. The sector policies that exist are often narrowly conceived, inconsistent and driven by special interest groups. The capacity for policy making still suffers from the fragmentation that hampered its performance prior to the economic crisis. These weaknesses in sector policy making affect the budget process, especially in the weak linkages among planning, budgeting and sector policy making. During budget preparation, the NESDB and the BOB generally deal directly with departments, avoiding the sector ministries and limiting Cabinet discussion, and potentially undermining ministerial responsibility for sector policy making. This problem is an obstacle to devolving budgetary decision-making to ministries and to moving towards a performance-oriented budgeting system.

Fiscal transparency

Fiscal transparency in Thailand falls short of international good practice. The government does not have a clear medium-term fiscal strategy. Fiscal planning is based on cash flows of a narrowly defined central government, and the existence of off-budget operations dilutes fiscal responsibility and accountability. Currently, the central government's financial statements do not include the operations of extra-budgetary funds and revolving funds, and do not reflect the commitments and assets of the government. Fiscal risks arising from the government's contingent liabilities are not considered properly. In addition, since the central government's accounts are not consolidated with the other parts of the public sector, the financial statements fail to reflect the financial position of the government as a whole. The areas that are not covered by the financial statements lack transparency. The lack of ministry and department level financial reporting hides the true cost of their policies and services.

Also absent in the budget reporting system are activities conducted by the central bank and state enterprises – often called quasi-fiscal activities – such as subsidized lending and business rescue operations, as well as tax expenditures. Tax expenditures estimate the foregone revenues associated with all forms of tax reductions, such as tax incentives for economic development, tax credits for new businesses, and local government relief of local property taxes.

Projects funded by external sources also bypass the normal budget process. Projects funded by foreign loans – either fully or partially – do not go through the BOB normal budget process. This means that counterpart funding for these projects bypasses the prioritizing scheme used by BOB for other projects, which tends to distort prioritization within the budget process.

The budget process

Budget preparation

The current budget structure is used primarily for line item budgeting, micro-management and control of details. The structure is based on a conventional coding system used by several countries. The coding system allows budget information to be consistently reported at all levels. However, the use of this coding system inhibits programme analysis and performance measurement.

Programme activities are not systematically reviewed. Projects and work plans have generally been incrementally funded, and have rarely been subjected to systematic and periodic evaluation and review. As such, their usage for budgeting purposes, their performance, their historical funding trends, their service delivery capabilities, and the quality and usefulness of their services are undocumented. Moreover, due to the lack of clear definition, these two budget entities, instead of being vehicles for budgeting, in some cases have gradually become an accounting convenience for storage of specific or miscellaneous accounting information. Introducing block granting within a performance framework should vitiate this concern.

Budget adoption

For oversight purposes, Parliament requires good and timely information on the economic and fiscal impact of the budget policies. The provision of line-item information in budget documents provided by the BOB invites micro-management questions from the Parliament. However, the information needed for this purpose is generally not available or not delivered in a timely fashion during the parliamentary deliberation of the budget. As a result, the parliamentary budget review is largely passive.

The Parliament depends totally on the executive branch for information and staffing during the budget adoption process. Information is provided by either central or line agencies. During the session, the Budget Scrutiny Committee is staffed by the executive branch. The Minister of Finance serves as the Chairman, the BOB Director as secretary, and BOB budget analysts as fiscal staff. In addition, the parliamentary process is limited to the central budget only. Projects involving external loans or foreign assistance, such as infrastructure building or social adjustment loans, do not go through normal legislative process. These projects are approved by the Cabinet before they are handed to BOB for processing and inserting into budget documents. These projects come to the Parliament as a fait accompli.

Budget execution

The budget execution process is fragmented, to the extent that the *allotment process* is, in many ways, a commitment authorization, preceding the contract or commitment stage and ultimate payment against an account payable. The allotment process also appears to be a second attempt at budget preparation, to review more thoroughly expenditure proposals that have already been approved or budgeted, but which were not adequately developed at the time of budget preparation. In this approach, the BOB is able to go over the detail again, which by this time may have been better developed, to confirm the expenditure requirement. The CGD's practice of replenishing department accounts on a transaction-by-transaction basis is not only antiquated, but it abdicates responsibility for setting financial management standards suitable for the more devolved decision making that is inherent in the BOB reforms.

The complex and apparently time-consuming transfer system appears to have been generated to make allowance for the detailed appropriation structure. In essence, there is little flexibility within the appropriation structure for managers to re-deploy funds to accommodate changing circumstances, without the application of formal rules to ensure that legal requirements and associated record keeping is correct. Block granting should substantially enhance flexibility in managing resources.

In the Thai budget process, budget documents include physical output levels for each work plan as well as the associated financial allocations. These physical output levels are *not* used as a control device in budget execution, because the BOB does not measure outputs. Since this physical and financial information is not linked to activity costing, it is impossible to ensure that budget funds are used effectively.

The *carryover process* for small amounts of expenditure, where invoices have been received, is consistent with a modified accrual accounting approach. However, when the process is applied to larger amounts related to projects or capital contracts, it means that expenditure in any one year is set against both the budget of that year and of previous years. The ability to carry over appropriated funds in this way also represents another opportunity to correct deficiencies in the earlier budget analysis stages.

The above approach tends to make budget priority setting fragmented. The budget preparation process is setting priorities for the budget year at the same time that Cabinet is setting priorities for carryover into the budget year by a separate mechanism. It is also not clear how the carryover system will be sustained in circumstances where budget expenditures increase above the customary 80 per cent level, collected revenues fall short of estimates, and the government budgets for a deficit. In these circumstances, the disbursement process will become another venue for priority setting as various projects, work plans and recurrent expenditures compete for the limited cash available.

Monitoring, evaluation and audit

Although an evaluation system is in place in the Evaluation Office of the BOB, it focuses on compliance issues rather than examining the cost effectiveness of programme outputs and outcomes. In addition, the links between the Evaluation Office and the Analysts' Offices responsible for individual ministries are very weak.

Monitoring, evaluation and audit should be integrated to provide a coherent framework for analysis and evaluation of government activities, to ensure both accountability for resources consumed, and for determining the effectiveness of programmes in meeting government priorities. The outputs from the various processes should be readily available for use in the budget process to ensure that lessons learnt during implementation of programmes are reflected in future financial allocations. To ensure that this happens, some elements of the process should be internal to the government, such as internal audit being responsive to the agency head, and the evaluation process should be designed to guide resource allocation. On the other hand, external audit activities should be reported separately to the legislature as a means of insuring the accountability of the government.

With this framework in mind, the Thai process displays some shortcomings. First, the Office of Auditor General reporting structure is inappropriate. Its procedure of reporting to the Prime Minister (in effect, to the government) is not consistent with best practice for external audit conducted by a Supreme Audit Institution. The revised Audit Act addresses this issue. Second, the audit of individual agencies is incomplete. The process of auditing receipts and expenditures of individual agencies does not address the fundamental requirement to audit the performance of an economic entity in the carrying out of its business. This is due in large measure to the incomplete financial reporting requirements specified for agencies.

An internal audit performs a mixed role. Its activities are directed to providing audit facilities and reports to external agencies for accountability purposes. This is inconsistent with an internal audit function, which is designed to advise and assist management in meeting its compliance obligations, and to perform more efficiently. In this sense, there is a conflict of roles assigned to the internal auditor. *Ex post* evaluation is limited to capital projects. The evaluation process, while addressing project performance issues, does not cover ongoing or recurrent budget activities. To this extent, a large component of government expenditure is not systematically evaluated for effectiveness, efficiency or indeed to confirm continuing relevance.

Reforming expenditure management

Thailand has launched a comprehensive modernization programme intended to address many of the shortcomings identified above. A 1999 Cabinet resolution on Public Sector Reform outlined the key objectives of expenditure management reform over the medium term: (i) improving the capability of strategic planning of sector ministries; (ii) introducing performance-based budgeting for line ministries; (iii) strengthening the capability of central agencies to review and evaluate sector policies and performance; (iv) improving fiscal transparency; and (v) establishing a medium-term fiscal strategy. Provided there is sufficient political will, reforms can be implemented to achieve these objectives. The following sections describe the rationale and the reform actions that are underway in each of these reform areas.

Improve the capability for strategic planning

A key to promoting better allocation of resources is the establishment of what have been called strategic results areas and key results areas for each sector ministry. A ministry must have a clear vision of its role and this depends in part on the government's overall vision for the public sector. Strategic results areas are medium-term objectives for the public sector that contribute significantly to the government's longer-term policy goals and objectives. Key results areas define the critical areas that each ministry focuses on in the medium term in contributing to the government's strategic results areas. Establishing a corporate plan, which includes the vision and mission statements along with key results areas and performance indicators will enable ministries to specify clear strategies for moving towards a results-oriented public service.

Implement performance-based budgeting

Some trade-off between effective control of the overall budget deficit and allocative and operational efficiency of line agency programmes is inevitable. Modernizing the Thai budget processes will significantly reduce this trade-off. Under the BOB's budget modernization proposals, this high level of budget detail will be reduced. Spending agencies will be given freedom to allocate funds more flexibly. Increased flexibility to direct funds to their most effective uses within a programme will thereby increase the cost effectiveness of budget execution.

The concept of performance measurement is understood in Thailand and the budget coding structure would support programme budgeting, but programme and performance budgeting has not been implemented extensively. The proposed reforms provide the foundation for a new budget formulation process that focuses not on inputs but on outcomes and outputs. Central agencies would gradually devolve detailed line item controls to line ministries, monitor their performance and hold them accountable for results. Management reforms within the line ministries would shift the management culture from 'compliance' to 'managing for results'.

The expected outcomes of these reforms include: improved performance accountability and transparency in key ministries, linking policy objectives with organizational objectives at the ministry and agency level, directing the budget formulation process towards achieving results; allocating public resources to strategic priorities of ministries; giving managers more flexible resource use and holding them accountable for probity and performance.

The reforms begin by identifying strategic priorities across the government: key ministries, departments and public organizations will be required to produce strategic plans showing their objectives and desired outcomes, outputs, performance standards, management plans and resource requirements. These plans will be published and disseminated widely. Central agencies will review these strategic plans as part of the budget formulation process with an emphasis on whether they reflect the government-wide priorities and whether they are well prepared. After this review, resource agreements will be formed between the central agencies and line ministries where, for a given level of resource allocation and flexibility, the expected performance of a line ministry will be clearly defined and agreed.

Improving the management of outputs and outcomes rather than input controls relies primarily on a shift towards *performance*. The task of the central agencies – particularly the Bureau of the Budget – is to define the new 'flexibility and accountability' framework for sector ministries and then to enable the sector ministries to implement the framework. Since 1999, the Bureau of the Budget has been developing a framework for this delegation in the context of performance-based budgeting. This involves three changes to current budgeting arrangements.

- The Bureau of the Budget (BOB) has been 'broad-banding' existing, highly detailed, line items in the budget (work plans and objects of expenditure) to grant line ministries greater freedom in spending the funds they are allocated.
- In this more devolved environment, line ministries are to develop greater responsibility for pro-actively improving their programme outcomes. This responsibility stems from developing their capability for review and re-prioritization rather than simply perpetuating past spending patterns. However, broad-banding line items in the budget does not itself ensure that line ministries will actually re-prioritize their actions. On the contrary, performance focus within line ministries is expected to develop only slowly after financial decontrol, increasing rather than reducing the possibility of waste and misuse of budget funds in the de-controlled environment.
- Financial decontrol for individual spending agencies is therefore intended to take place only when 'threshold' financial control and performance reporting systems are in place in the agency, providing a 'hurdle' approach to financial decontrol. The hurdle approach provides both an incentive to line agencies to improve their management, in order to win the benefits of financial decontrol by BOB, and a safeguard against misuse of the new freedoms.

Under this performance-based budgeting framework, agency management is strengthened before rather than after central controls are eased. The means include:

- clear rules for sector ministries to allocate resources to service delivery organizations;
- principles, standards and guidelines issued by central agencies to implement sound financial management systems at the service delivery level – altogether seven hurdle standards covering budget planning, output costing, procurement, budget and funds control, financial and performance reporting, asset management, and internal audit;
- performance reporting requirements for service delivery units include objectives, success factors, performance indicators and service standards; and
- capacity building activities in BOB to improve its capability to monitor, review and evaluate performance and analyse policy.

Within this framework, increased financial autonomy provides clear incentives for agencies when they improve their management. In 1999, the BOB identified six agencies where this framework would be pioneered, involving pilot departments in the Ministries of Public Health, Education, University Affairs, Commerce and Foreign Affairs. The BOB signed a Memorandum of Understanding (MoU) with each of the responsible Ministries indicating the steps for increasing flexibility by broad-banding budget line items in pilot departments. These MoUs specified future requirements and identified the terms of reference for gap analysis and gap filling in core areas. They also specified the dates and actions for reaching a 'Resource Agreement' between the BOB and the Ministry. By 2001, the BOB eased some central controls on the six pioneer agencies by moving towards block grants through partially reduced line item details in their budget allocations.

At the same time, the Comptroller General's Department (CGD) identified the financial reporting requirements for ministries and departments, improving the government's accounting policies, and developing an integrated financial management system that would define government-wide standards for the 'financial management' issues listed above. Ministries and departments were also required to report their off-budget fiscal operations (revolving funds, extra-budgetary funds, foreign finance projects and quasi-fiscal operations) as part of their financial statements.

With continuous review and refinement by the BOB and CGD, this performance-based budgeting framework was to be extended progressively to other ministries and departments and eventually to all budget-funded entities. Reviewing the experience with Thailand's hurdle approach, Dixon (2002) found slow progress and much confusion in pioneer agencies. This reflected overly ambitious standards and was aggravated by limited technical assistance for budget reform, although improvements in financial management largely followed, rather than preceded, the move towards block grants. Only in 2002 did the number of pioneer agencies increase beyond the original six. The budget reform process was given renewed impetus with the Prime Minister's request to present the fiscal 2003 budget on an output basis. This requires all agencies to achieve the hurdle of output costing, replaces the envisaged resource agreements with public service agreements and extends block grants to agencies that base budget allocations on output contracts.

Dixon draws three key lessons: political reform is needed for budget reform to overcome inertia and resistance; the original hurdle approach with seven hurdles was too complex and should have simply involved the dual demands of a sound, computer-based accounting system and identification and costing of agency outputs; and finally, technical assistance should have been better integrated with budget reforms by focusing on basic management systems.

Strengthen the capability of central agencies to evaluate policies and performance

In the new performance framework, as central agencies relinquish line-item control, they focus more on reviewing and evaluating the performance of ministries and departments and on analysing whether their polices are consistent with the government's strategic priorities. Hence, another element of the 'performance-based budgeting framework' is improving the capability of the BOB and NESDB to review and evaluate performance and policy.

The BOB's assessment of the geographical distribution of major government programmes in the health and education sectors documented that the current distribution does not reflect the government's equity and poverty alleviation policies. Given Thailand's extreme regional disparities, the government can play an important role in reducing regional inequalities by geographically targeting its spending progressively towards poorer regions, since overall public spending is not pro-poor. A general symptom is the pro-rich geographic targeting of public expenditures at the sectoral level. For example, partial estimates based on outlays incurred at the regional government level indicate that the Northeastern region receives the lowest per capita outlays in agriculture, education, health and social services. Thus, the pattern of regional government expenditures is not pro-poor but instead reinforces the underlying income disparities.

The two main objectives for change are to strengthen the information base for regular monitoring of distributional incidence of government expenditures, and to institutionalize the routine use of distributional criteria in making *ex ante* expenditure decisions for improving the progressivity of subsidies. Key policy actions to implement these objectives focus on monitoring distributional incidence, including multipurpose household surveys on the utilization of public services in health and education, and resource agreements with programme managers based on outputs they produce for poverty alleviation programmes.

Coordinated evaluation and policy analysis between BOB and NESDB is uncommon. Their combined effort would have greater synergy and policy impact. The BOB and NESDB have agreed to prepare a joint evaluation work programme with the Ministries of Health and Education and to submit it to the Cabinet. This work programme will serve as a vehicle to coordinate their actions with the sector ministries at the Cabinet level. If these reforms are carried out systematically, coordinated efforts between NESDB and BOB in reviewing and evaluating performance and analysing policy would eventually make a significant contribution to a variety of results:

- transparent and effective government programmes in key sectors such as health and education;
- improved policy analysis and prioritization in these key sectors;
- improved poverty alleviation focus to resource allocation process; and
- effective evaluation that provides feedback to decision-making.

Improve fiscal transparency

Over the medium term, improving the transparency of the budget process would require a number of changes:

- improvement in budget coverage to include donor-funded activities;
- improved whole-of-government reporting formats by publishing comprehensive Government Financial Statements;
- clearer standards for reporting off-budget fiscal operations as part of budget documents and financial statements; and
- an eventual move to accrual budgeting, which would permit a clearer accounting of contingent liabilities.

Financial reporting requirements for governments have been established by the International Federation of Accountants, which is also preparing public-sector accounting standards. The new Government Finance System that is being prepared by the IMF supports these requirements. Compliance with these requirements and international best practices will improve both transparency and credibility in international financial markets. Preparing these reports comprehensively for the government as a whole, and in accordance with internationally accepted accounting standards, will improve fiscal planning; preparing them at ministerial and agency levels can make the public sector more results-oriented and enhance accountability for performance.

While there is no single government policy to improve fiscal transparency, the BOB and CGD are working to develop a policy to improve 'financial transparency'. The CGD has begun reviewing the guidelines published by the International Federation of Accountants (IFAC) and the International Organization of Supreme Audit Institutions (INTOSAI) on government financial reporting requirements in order to improve government financial reporting, accounting, policies and standards along these guidelines. IFAC guidelines show the desirable form and contents of financial statements at the whole of government and department level and address accounting policies to produce these statements. INTOSAI provides implementation guidelines. The new Government Financial Statistics (GFS) framework developed by the IMF shows how to link these financial statements with the government's fiscal statements.

The BOB and CGD have also agreed to develop standards for reporting off-budget fiscal operations at the department, ministry and whole-of-government level as part of budget documents and financial statements. BOB has begun compiling information on off-budget fiscal operations, such as revolving funds, extra-budgetary funds, foreign financed activities, quasi-fiscal operations and contingent liabilities.[4] A Public Debt Management Office has been established to analyse and manage the government's liabilities. Its functions include debt service forecasting, debt management, cash management, risk management project finance related transactions, and tracking of contingent liabilities.[5]

Another key issue of fiscal transparency is that Thailand does not yet have an independent Supreme Audit Institution (SAI) that audits the executive branch and reports to the Parliament. The Constitution requires its establishment. The Auditor General currently reports to the Prime Minister. A law has been prepared that establishes a collegiate Supreme Audit Institution, named the State Audit Commission, which will audit the government and report to the Parliament. Once established, it is expected to promote fiscal transparency, to adapt the Generally Accepted Audit Principles declared by the International Organization of Supreme Audit Institutions to the Thai government, and to develop a code of conduct for Thai public auditors.

Establish a medium-term fiscal strategy

The lack of a medium-term framework in Thailand's existing budget planning system may reduce operational efficiency in at least two respects. First, the absence of a medium-term fiscal strategy and the current annual focus of the budget process means that provision for operation and maintenance of completed projects is not treated on a systematic basis in budget planning. Given high levels of investment before the economic crisis (and implied high levels of subsequent recurrent expenditure) this could be cause for concern. Second, the absence of a medium-term fiscal strategy reduces the certainty of funding for ministries and departments over the medium term, which restricts their ability to plan spending on work plans and projects over a multi-year horizon.

A key means to provide flexibility in fiscal adjustment is to prepare a medium-term fiscal strategy within which the government estimates its resources and calculates the costs of its current policies and contingent liabilities. Since the aggregate cost of policies is expected to be higher than incoming resources, policies must be adjusted to fit available resources. This information will enable the government to make strategic choices on how to cut expenditures while protecting its priority pro- grammes – thereby improving the quality of fiscal adjustment. Further- more, this framework encourages more predictable resource flows to sector ministries and programme managers, and eliminates resource con- straints being used as a justification for low performance. Conservatively defining the medium-term aggregate resource base will also help to change the psychology of budgeting from a 'needs' to an 'availability' mentality.

The introduction of a medium-term fiscal strategy will facilitate the link between policy, planning and budgeting. Under this strategy, the financial decontrol offered to the pilot agency is reinforced by a set of firm esti- mates of budget funding which BOB will make available to the agency over the subsequent three years. This has the further advantage of focus- ing budget preparation on policy changes as they relate to the next few years, which in turn assists in closing the loop between the development of performance information at the department level and the budget prepara- tion process.

The medium-term fiscal strategy provides the agency with a surer medium-term environment within which to plan its future programme allocations in the decontrolled environment. It also enables new spending decisions to be made by the government with full knowledge of their medium-term implications for the budget deficit, and cuts in particular activities that are difficult to achieve in a single budget can be pro- grammed over a period of three years subsequent to the budget.

It is notable in the Thai budget reforms that a more comprehensive Medium Term Expenditure Framework is not being introduced across the board. Rather, it is offered on an agency basis through Resource Agree- ments with the pilot agencies (and along with block granting) in return for improved financial and performance improvement standards. Eventu- ally, the forward estimates for each pilot agency will be underpinned by activity costing that will calibrate the estimates with physical output assumptions. This will be implemented through the Resource Agreements drafted between each pilot agency and the BOB.

Conclusions

Thai public organizations exhibit low levels of financial and performance accountability. The rule-driven budget system of detailed central control has helped contain the risk of overspending. But this strong fiscal control has also limited the government's efforts to achieve the best value for money, and provides agencies with little incentive to improve their performance.

Thailand has taken the first path-breaking steps with its ongoing reforms of the budget formulation processes. Although it is still too early to return a verdict, these efforts offer the promise of providing performance incentives by granting greater budgetary flexibility to public organizations in return for improving their performance and financial management systems. Similar reform efforts are still critical for public reporting frameworks to improve the fiscal and financial transparency at all levels of government, and to analyse and mitigate the fiscal risks arising from outstanding public debt obligations and contingent liabilities.

Thailand's history of short-lived coalition governments has traditionally allowed senior bureaucrats to enjoy a more powerful position vis-à-vis the executive than in most other countries, and this has provided limited incentives for changing the status quo. The present political situation is quite different. However, generating and maintaining the momentum for public sector reform will still require the combined political pressure of government leadership and civil society demands for better public services.

Notes

1 The author is particularly indebted to Alex Mutebi, Geoff Dixon, Serif Sayin, Dana Weist, Lars Sondergaard and Steen Byskov who made major contributions to the World Bank's Thailand Public Sector Reform Project and the Public Finance Review on which this chapter draws.
2 For a discussion of Thailand's fiscal performance since the crisis, including expenditure management, tax policy and its strategy for decentralization, see World Bank (2000).
3 This discussion draws on Gertler (1999) and World Bank (2000).
4 As a credible step in this direction, the BOB required pilot departments as part of the performance-based budgeting initiative to produce financial statements that include off-budget operations.
5 For a discussion of the tasks and capacity building required for this office, see World Bank (2000).

References

Dixon, Geoff (2002) *Thailand's Hurdle Approach to Budget Reform*, PREM Notes No. 73, Washington, DC: World Bank.
Gertler, Paul (1999) A diagnostic assessment of the NESDB. Report prepared for the NESDB, Bangkok, August.
World Bank (2000) *Thailand: Public Finance in Transition*, Report No. 20656-TH, Washington, DC: World Bank.

Chapter 7

Dealing with debt

NPLs and debt restructuring

Pakorn Vichyanond

Non-performing loans (NPLs) represent both causes and consequences of the economic crisis that has plagued Thailand since 1997. All concerned parties, including government agencies, have therefore tried numerous means of resolving NPL problems by restructuring debts and adjusting financial institutions' credit extension. Such efforts are important because, without successful debt restructuring and prudent credit extension, the economy may remain trapped in a vicious circle. The reason is that, in branch-banking economies like Thailand, credits from financial institutions, especially commercial banks, are an indispensable lubricant for economic activities. This chapter thus discusses the primary causes of NPLs, measures taken after the meltdown of 1997, and possible means of resolving NPLs, including debt restructuring, corporate transformation, and the establishment of the Thai Asset Management Corporation (TAMC).

Background

The financial sector in Thailand has been dominated – in most respects such as asset size, geographical coverage, saving mobilization, and credit extension – by private commercial banks. Second to commercial banks were finance companies. Between 1990 and 1997, commercial banks and finance companies captured 85 per cent of household savings in all financial institutions (Table 7.1). Meanwhile, credits extended by these institutions added up to 89 per cent of the total offered by all financial institutions (Table 7.2). This demonstrates the minor role played by other types of private financial institutions (life insurance companies, agricultural cooperatives, savings cooperatives, pawnshops, credit financier companies, and mutual fund management companies), as well as units established by the government to serve particular purposes (Government Savings Bank, Bank for Agriculture and Agricultural Cooperatives, Industrial Finance Corporation of Thailand, Government Housing Bank, Small Industry Finance Corporation, Export-Import Bank of Thailand).

Table 7.1 Household savings at financial institutions, 1990 to 2002 (outstanding at year-end) (percentage share) (billions of baht)

	1990	1991	1992	1993	1994	1995	1996	1997	1998	1999	2000	2001	2002
1 Commercial banks	1,149 (77.3)	1,332 (76.6)	1,552 (74.7)	1,775 (73.4)	1,995 (71.7)	2,372 (71.5)	2,643 (70.5)	3,061 (80.6)	3,338 (79.0)	3,321 (79.3)	3,529 (78.2)	3,720 (77.1)	3,770 (76.2)
2 Finance companies	149 (10.1)	202 (11.6)	294 (14.1)	374 (15.5)	477 (17.2)	572 (17.2)	661 (17.6)	183 (4.8)	182 (4.3)	126 (3.0)	127 (2.8)	142 (2.9)	128 (2.6)
3 Life insurance companies	34 (2.3)	45 (2.6)	56 (2.7)	67 (2.8)	83 (3.0)	99 (3.0)	117 (3.1)	140 (3.7)	154 (3.6)	166 (4.0)	197 (4.4)	234 (4.8)	277 (5.6)
4 Credit financier companies	2 (0.1)	2 (0.1)	4 (0.2)	5 (0.2)	5 (0.2)	5 (0.2)	6 (0.2)	5 (0.1)	3 (0.1)	3 (0.1)	3 (0.1)	4 (0.1)	4 (0.1)
5 Government Savings Bank	112 (7.6)	119 (6.9)	130 (6.3)	142 (5.9)	156 (5.6)	179 (5.4)	205 (5.5)	235 (6.2)	325 (7.7)	349 (8.3)	392 (8.7)	454 (9.4)	493 (10.0)
6 BAAC[1]	14 (0.9)	15 (0.9)	18 (0.8)	23 (0.9)	31 (1.1)	45 (1.4)	57 (1.5)	65 (1.7)	86 (2.0)	93 (2.2)	112 (2.5)	128 (2.7)	153 (3.1)
7 IFCT[2]	–	–	–	–	–	–	–	–	–	–	–	–	–
8 Government Housing Bank	25 (1.7)	23 (1.3)	25 (1.2)	32 (1.3)	36 (1.3)	47 (1.4)	59 (1.6)	110 (2.9)	134 (3.2)	128 (3.1)	152 (3.4)	142 (2.9)	122 (2.5)
9 Small Industry Finance Corp.	–	–	–	–	–	–	–	–	–	–	–	–	–
10 EXIM Bank	–	–	–	–	–	–	–	–	–	–	–	–	–
Grand total	1,486 (100)	1,739 (100)	2,078 (100)	2,417 (100)	2,783 (100)	3,320 (100)	3,749 (100)	3,800 (100)	4,222 (100)	4,187 (100)	4,512 (100)	4,823 (100)	4,946 (100)

Source: Bank of Thailand.

Note:
1 BAAC = Bank for Agriculture and Agricultural Cooperatives.
2 IFCT = Industrial Finance Corporation of Thailand.

Table 7.2 Credits extended by financial institutions, 1990 to 2002 (outstanding at year-end) (percentage share) (billions of baht)

	1990	1991	1992	1993	1994	1995	1996	1997	1998	1999	2000	2001	2002
1 Commercial banks	1,482 (77.3)	1,789 (75.8)	2,162 (74.3)	2,669 (72.9)	3,431 (71.8)	4,231 (70.8)	4,825 (69.8)	6,037 (73.9)	5,372 (73.0)	5,119 (79.0)	4,586 (76.9)	4,299 (75.6)	4,603 (78.1)
2 Finance companies	315 (16.4)	416 (17.6)	548 (18.8)	733 (20.0)	1,008 (21.1)	1,301 (21.8)	1,488 (21.5)	1,284 (15.7)	1,120 (15.2)	498 (7.7)	450 (7.5)	360 (6.3)	178 (3.0)
3 Life insurance companies	17 (0.9)	19 (0.8)	21 (0.7)	21 (0.6)	21 (0.4)	24 (0.4)	30 (0.4)	36 (0.4)	41 (0.6)	42 (0.6)	40 (0.7)	38 (0.7)	39 (0.7)
4 Credit financier companies	3 (0.2)	4 (0.2)	5 (0.2)	6 (0.2)	6 (0.1)	7 (0.1)	7 (0.1)	6 (0.1)	6 (0.1)	4 (0.1)	3 (0.1)	4 (0.1)	5 (0.1)
5 Government Savings Bank	11 (0.6)	15 (0.6)	18 (0.6)	31 (0.9)	33 (0.7)	39 (0.7)	56 (0.8)	118 (1.4)	145 (2.0)	130 (2.0)	149 (2.5)	229 (4.0)	261 (4.4)
6 BAAC[1]	39 (2.0)	52 (2.2)	65 (2.2)	81 (2.2)	101 (2.1)	130 (2.2)	170 (2.5)	197 (2.4)	207 (2.8)	222 (3.4)	257 (4.3)	277 (4.9)	289 (4.9)
7 IFCT[2]	21 (1.1)	26 (1.1)	36 (1.2)	47 (1.3)	59 (1.2)	78 (1.3)	104 (1.5)	156 (1.9)	132 (1.8)	136 (2.1)	148 (2.5)	156 (2.7)	156 (2.6)
8 Government Housing Bank	30 (1.5)	40 (1.7)	54 (1.8)	72 (2.0)	101 (2.1)	142 (2.4)	199 (2.9)	279 (3.4)	296 (4.0)	284 (4.4)	278 (4.7)	278 (4.9)	309 (5.2)
9 Small Industry Finance Corp.	–	–	–	–	–	1	1	1	2	2	3	5 (0.1)	11 (0.2)
10 EXIM Bank	–	–	–	–	15 (0.3)	27 (0.4)	33 (0.5)	58 (0.7)	40 (0.5)	42 (0.7)	48 (0.8)	42 (0.7)	43 (0.7)
Grand total	1,918 (100)	2,360 (100)	2,909 (100)	3,661 (100)	4,775 (100)	5,979 (100)	6,912 (100)	8,171 (100)	7,360 (100)	6,479 (100)	5,962 (100)	5,687 (100)	5,894 (100)

Source: Bank of Thailand.

Note:
1 BAAC = Bank for Agriculture and Agricultural Cooperatives.
2 IFCT = Industrial Finance Corporation of Thailand.

Thailand's acceptance of the International Monetary Fund (IMF) Article VIII in May 1990, which lifted foreign exchange controls on current account transactions, marked the beginning of a series of financial liberalization measures. On the exchange control front, the second round of liberalization abandoned most restrictions on capital account transactions in April 1991. The third round, in February 1994, gave more freedom to outward direct investment, travel expenditures, and provided additional channels of cross-border payments. In March 1993, the Bangkok International Banking Facilities (BIBF) were established as a means to develop an international financial centre. To enable the BIBF to compete with other centres, BIBF transactions were granted some tax privileges (for example, reduction of corporate income tax, exemption from special business tax and withholding tax on interest income). Furthermore, in January 1995, the government decided to allow the BIBF to open branches in up-country provinces.

In terms of interest rates, the authorities gradually removed interest rate ceilings in order to encourage savings mobilization and make the financial system more dynamic. Interest rate ceilings on long-term time deposits were abolished in June 1989, on savings and short-term time deposits in January 1992, and on loan rates in June 1992. In addition, the central bank in 1992–93 gave commercial banks more flexibility by relaxing the requirement of government bond holding as a prerequisite for opening up new branches. The commercial banks' obligations to extend credits to rural borrowers or those in the vicinity were relaxed to cover more related occupations and wider geographical areas. Furthermore, the definition of 'liquid reserves' was broadened to include Bank of Thailand and state enterprise bonds, as well as debt instruments issued by financial institutions or government agencies approved by the Central Bank.

Commercial banks were permitted to undertake new businesses, such as debt underwriting and dealing, acting as securities registrars and custodians, selling public sector debt instruments, mutual fund management, financial consulting, and feasibility studies. Finance and securities companies were also allowed to extend the scope of their operations. New activities included leasing, management of provident/private/mutual funds, custodial services, and foreign exchange businesses.

Meanwhile, a number of new frameworks or organizations were formulated. For example, the Securities and Exchange Act was passed in May 1992, giving a limited number of companies access to direct finance by issuing common stocks and debt instruments. The Act established the Securities and Exchange Commission as an independent agency responsible for supervising capital market activities related to equities, bonds, and derivatives. In 1993, the government spearheaded the formation of a credit rating agency, Thai Rating and Information Services, and in 1994 private parties organized a bond dealers' club to function as a secondary debt market, adding more liquidity to debt instruments. Regarding payment systems, the central bank improved the clearing and settlement processes, lowering transaction costs and facilitating business expansion. The BAHTNET and THAICLEAR networks were put into effect to serve customers' needs. The latest development on this front was electronic retail funds transfer through Media Clearing.

This process of financial liberalization was undertaken between 1988 and 1996 in order to strengthen competition in the domestic financial system, foster more resilience in financial institutions, prepare for world-wide liberalization of trade and services, and expand the role of Thailand as a regional financial centre.

It should be noted that, although more freedom was given to capital flows across borders, Thailand's exchange rate peg to a currency basket, adopted in 1984, remained in effect. Given the predominant weight of the US dollar (85 per cent) in the basket, the baht did not move much against the US dollar, and its movement did not correlate at all with the volume or direction of transactions in the Thai foreign exchange market. Instead, the central bank determined the daily value of the baht relative to the US dollar in consonance with fluctuations of the basket currencies' exchange rates in the world markets. Therefore, interest rate differentials between local and foreign currencies were not offset by exchange risks. Many private corporations and financial institutions took advantage of these differentials by borrowing abroad at low interest rates without purchasing any forward cover.

After a series of financial liberalizations, superfluous capital inflows flooded the Thai market between 1990 and 1996, fuelling investment spending, speculation, and current account deficits. Meanwhile, excessive and imprudent credit extensions engendered risk taking and asset quality deteriorated. Net capital inflows averaged between 10 per cent of Gross Domestic Product (GDP) each year, expanding the external debt from US$29 billion in 1990 to US$94 billion in 1997, or from 34 per cent of GDP to 59 per cent of GDP, respectively. Speculative and imprudent lending by financial institutions created several bubble sectors, not just real estate. For example, the automotive industry, private hospitals, steel, and petrochemical industries were all inflated.

Declining asset quality was not a surprise. What was a surprise, however, was its speed and extent. Distressed by possible financial panic or bank runs, the central bank could not resist extending financial aid to ailing commercial banks and finance companies, but this aid aggravated macro-economic imbalances. For instance, current account deficits climbed from 5 per cent of GDP in 1993 to 8 per cent of GDP in 1995–96. Meanwhile, Thailand's excess inflation over the United States' surged from 0.3 per cent in 1993 to 3.0 per cent in 1995–96. As a result, by mid 1997, investor confidence was critically shaken. Massive capital outflows, prompted by fears of currency devaluation and widespread bankruptcies, necessitated the floating of the baht, which triggered a series of financial crises throughout the region.

Thailand's economic meltdown in mid-1997, which sparked the East Asian financial crisis, was largely due to

- liberalization of foreign capital flows while keeping the exchange rate rigid;
- premature liberalization of financial institutions; and
- failure to supervise financial institutions in a prudent manner.

These errors demonstrated the importance of policy consistency. If foreign exchange funds are allowed to move freely across borders, their prices or exchange rates ought to be liberalized as well so as to reflect market conditions. Otherwise, excess inflows or outflows could easily materialize, depending upon market expectations. The liberalization of financial institutions is an equally controversial issue. Given that domestic financial institutions were not adequately prepared or experienced, the question is whether they should have been liberalized, since liberalization could increase risks. However, once those immature entities were granted more freedom, it is unquestionable that the central authority should have closely monitored and carefully supervised them throughout the liberalization process.

Following the exchange rate float, the exchange rate depreciated dramatically. The central bank recognized the importance of limited foreign exchange reserves and did not aim for any exchange rate target. It sought only to smooth exchange rate variations in order to avert a depreciation-inflation spiral. It also resorted to credit and interest rate policies, rather than direct foreign exchange interventions, as a means of restoring exchange rate stability, because it had limited foreign exchange reserves. In other words, exchange rate policy was reversed from having an exchange rate target defended by reserves to having stable reserves defended by the exchange rate.

Several parties called for the creation of a currency board, in which the money supply in circulation would be entirely backed by foreign exchange reserves. Such a scheme, however, would lead to a substantial loss of sovereignty over monetary policy, which is extremely precarious, especially in a situation of financial havoc and highly mobile capital flows. The continuing banking crisis, the need for legal and institutional changes, and gathering political uncertainties all argued against a currency board.

Fortunately, the government emphasized correction of underlying weaknesses in economic fundamentals, since investor confidence and the country's credibility did not hinge solely on interest rates. According to a recent survey, the seven main factors, in order of priority, which influence investor confidence are

- political stability,
- competence of the economic management team,
- external accounts, including trade balance, current account, and balance of payments,
- efficiency and stability of the financial system,
- foreign exchange reserves,
- asset quality of financial institutions,
- policy consistency or rigidity.

The government's efforts to reduce distortions in fundamentals were successful to some extent, as confirmed by the rising value of the baht, its growing stability (Figure 7.1), and improvements in the current account (Figure 7.2), even though interest rates declined substantially. These results demonstrated some of the government's achievements in restoring investor confidence. The crisis was, however, a consequence of accumulated structural weaknesses rather than macroeconomic maladjustment. Lasting recovery will depend on comprehensive structural reform. Attempting to stabilize without introducing explicit structural reforms, especially in the financial and corporate sectors, would be a costly exercise in treating the symptoms without addressing the causes of the disease.

Exacerbated by the sharp currency depreciation, falling asset prices, and a strong downturn in economic activity, financial institutions' nonperforming loans (NPLs) jumped from 8 per cent of credit outstanding in mid-1997 to 20 per cent in December 1997 and to 45 per cent in December 1998. By the end of 1998, NPLs totalled 2.7 trillion baht or 59 per cent of GDP. Worse yet, a moral hazard emerged in the form of fake or strategic NPLs. In spite of their strong debt servicing capacity, numerous debtors were induced to suspend their regular debt servicing. Fake NPLs were estimated to amount to one-third of reported NPLs.

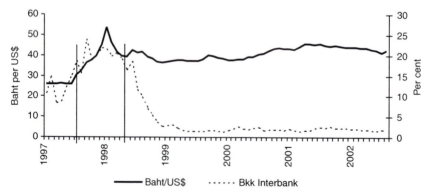

Figure 7.1 Thailand's Exchange Rate and Interbank Interest Rate, 1997 to 2002 (source: Bank of Thailand).

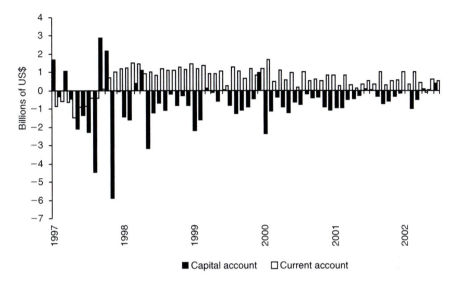

Figure 7.2 Thailand's current account and capital account balance, 1997 to 2002 (source: Bank of Thailand).

Primary causes of NPLs

The surge of NPLs between 1997 and 1999 was largely the outcome of a combination of several negative factors that unfortunately coincided. First, Thai commercial banks were technically weak and immature in handling tapped funds. As bank owners had many joint interests in many ventures, insider lending was rife and Thai bankers paid little attention to credit risk assessment. Instead, they demanded collateral or personal guarantees as prerequisites for loans. Unsurprisingly, extended credits tended to be linked with affiliated businesses or shareholders or directors regardless of the borrowing projects' viability. Even for collateral, which was excessively resorted to by Thai financial institutions, unrealistic prices were often adopted since there was no standard for pricing.

Second, a similar financial structure and culture was applicable to typical non-bank businesses. As most of them were family-run and wanted to retain control, they preferred debt to equity in financing. Besides, such preference was fiscally motivated, since tax allowances were given to debt servicing but not dividend payments. Thai corporations tended to be short-sighted and unscrupulous in terms of their funding. They therefore selected short-term credits even for long-term projects, as maturity mismatching was not deemed threatening to them. Worse yet, some entities, which hinged upon external funds, either utilized those funds in wholly baht businesses or left their net foreign exchange positions uncovered. This practice was in sharp contrast to foreign firms and their affiliates.

Third, financial institutions often had a weakness in monitoring/revising/controlling the progress of their credits after extension and disbursement. Likewise, the central authorities lagged behind in supervising and examining financial institutions. Nevertheless, they decided to liberalize the Thai financial markets in various respects (interest rates, credit extension, range of activities) in order to encourage more market competition and efficiency. Thailand's capital account was also opened up between 1990 and 1994. However, the exchange rate of the baht currency was continually pegged, mainly to the US dollar.

Fourth, during the country's economic bubble of 1990 to 1995, its real GDP growth rose to 8.2–11.2 per cent p.a. while that of advanced countries stayed in the range of 2–4 per cent p.a. Considerably lower foreign interest rates (3.25–6.5 per cent from 1994 to 1996) in comparison with domestic ones (11.75 to 13.75 per cent) induced private net capital inflows to jump from 2–8 per cent of GDP p.a. in 1987–89 to 8–12 per cent of GDP p.a. in 1990–96, leading to intense competition in lending and extravagant risk-taking. The resulting over-investment, especially in manufacturing and property, sharply raised the average debt/equity ratio of Thai businesses from 8 per cent in 1993 to 155 per cent in 1996, the highest in Asia, including Indonesia (92 per cent), Malaysia (62 per cent), Singapore (58 per cent), and Hong Kong (39 per cent). Seemingly attractive industries then were steel, cement, paper, concrete, furniture, automobiles, and electronics. But after heavy investments for supply expansion were pursued, actual demand for final products did not rise, and production capacity was thus considerably underutilized (45 per cent).

Fifth, regarding the exchange rate, another unfortunate event emerged when the value of the US dollar climbed significantly between April 1995 and June 1997. During this period the US currency appreciated 38 per cent against the yen and 27 per cent against the deutschmark. The baht value rose in tandem because it was tightly pegged to a currency basket that was heavily dominated by the US dollar. This appreciation of the baht definitely worked against Thailand's deteriorating current account deficits. Substantial capital outflows in the first half of 1997 thus came as a result of widespread speculation of baht devaluation. The volume of flows involved was so large that the floating of the exchange rate became inevitable. Thailand had to request financial assistance from the IMF and a very tough monetary policy was demanded. Domestic interest rates increased dramatically. The steep depreciation of the baht and the jump in local interest rates had a catastrophic impact on the cash flow of most private firms, especially those with large and unhedged foreign debt exposure.

Because of all the above factors, NPLs in the Thai financial system grew frighteningly from 20 per cent at the end of 1997 to peak at 48 per cent in May 1999, which was also higher than the peaks of other countries in the East Asian region, such as Malaysia (21 per cent in November 1998), the Philippines (17 per cent in November 1998), South Korea (8 per cent in December 1999), and China (28 per cent in May 2001).

Overall, the NPL problems in Thailand emerged primarily because of the lack of good governance on the part of debtors as well as that of creditors. Debtors did not pay adequate attention to the risks they faced. Creditors extended credits without conducting rigorous and in-depth credit risk evaluations beforehand. Neither did lending financial institutions closely examine and monitor the viability or progress of borrowers' business activities. Instead, they were stimulated to lend by the heavy influx of foreign capital and financial liberalization measures amid a rigid or stable exchange rate regime. In short, despite the central importance of borrowers' genuine debt servicing capacity (which involves project viability, likely returns, and pertinent or technical factors, not just collateral or guarantees or connections), this variable was frequently neglected. Otherwise, NPLs would not have climbed as high as they did and become a stumbling block to Thailand's economic growth path.

Measures after the meltdown

By the second half of 1996, it became clear that many finance companies were in serious trouble, mostly through their exposure to property loans. The government therefore tackled the problem by several means, e.g. offering civil servants and other reliable groups a soft-loan scheme to purchase property, setting up a Secondary Mortgage Corporation, establishing a Property Loan Management Organization to purchase impaired property loans. These measures failed due to a liquidity crunch and the circumstances deteriorated as the baht was severely attacked and finally floated. So, by August 1997, the authorities suspended 58 finance companies.

In December 1997, the authorities decided to close down 56 suspended finance companies and transferred their assets to a newly formed Financial Sector Restructuring Authority (FRA) to be disposed of within one year. The FRA proceeded to do this by auctioning them with the assistance of a parallel new agency, the Asset Management Corporation (AMC), which participated in the bids almost like an underwriter. The FRA auctions yielded a disappointingly low recovery rate of only a quarter of the face value. The main problem lay with the timing of sales, economic downturn, and sluggish pace of legal proceedings.

On 31 March 1998 the Bank of Thailand tightened regulations on loan classification, provisioning, and reporting standards, aiming to upgrade local financial institutions to international levels by the year 2000. New loan classification hinges upon clients' debt servicing capacity, cash flow management, valuation of back-up assets, and ageing of overdue debts. Effective 1 July 1998, the definition of non-performing assets was changed to cover loans three or more months in arrears, instead of the previous six (or 12) months. Two new loan categories, pass and special mention, require 1 per cent and 2 per cent provisioning, respectively. Meanwhile, commercial banks as well as finance companies have to increase provisions for substandard loans from 15 per cent to 20 per cent (Table 7.3). Doubtful loans require a 50 per cent provision rather than the previous 100 per cent, but loss loans continue to necessitate 100 per cent coverage. These new standards forced local banks and finance companies to increase their capital substantially.

The system adopted since March 1998 also calls for quarterly, instead of annual, audits and credit reports to be submitted to the central bank. Loan portfolio reviews have to cover at least 70 per cent of credit outstanding, including the top 100 clients and credits or commitments to related parties. The measures also demand that financial institutions tighten their lending practices and credit analysis procedures, focusing more on borrowers' cash flow and debt servicing ability, rather than on loan collateral. Debt restructuring or renegotiations must be subject to realistic assessment of the financial viability of clients or their projects.

As for the status of commercial banks, the government made a major announcement on 14 August 1998, which was intended to support private banks' recapitalization. If financial institutions committed themselves to comply with new loan loss provisioning earlier than the targeted year of 2000, they would be entitled to enlarge their first-tier capital by issuing preferred shares to the government in exchange for tradable government bonds. Furthermore, as a means to motivate debt restructuring or reconciliation with problem clients, the government proposed an option to financial institutions to increase their second-tier capital by exchanging non-tradable bonds with banks' newly issued debentures, equalling the losses suffered by financial institutions in their debt restructuring. What

Table 7.3 Loan-loss provisioning requirements for commercial banks

Loan classification	Months overdue	Previous provisions (%)	1998 system of provisioning (%)
Pass	<1 month	–	1
Special mention	0–3 months	–	2
Substandard	up to 6 months	15	20
Doubtful	up to 1 year	100	50
Loss	>1 year	100	100

Source: Bank of Thailand.

should be noted is that the 14 August capital augmentation measure was voluntary, depending on the discretion of financial institutions.

Few banks resorted to the capital enlargement opportunities offered by the government, particularly the tier-1 option. This indicates that banks were reluctant to write down their capital in return for public money and accept the dilution of ownership that would ensue. Instead, they raised capital by themselves through the issuance of preferred stocks linked with subordinate debentures.

Before examining the debt restructuring, it is worth noticing some major differences between the four types of financial institutions in Thailand: private Thai banks, state-owned banks, foreign banks, and surviving finance companies. Table 7.4 shows that, with respect to credit outstanding, private Thai banks commanded the largest share (51 per cent in 1998), while finance companies had the smallest (8 per cent). However, with regard to asset quality, the picture was almost the opposite, as finance companies' NPL share was the highest at 70 per cent in 1998, while private Thai banks' NPL share was 40 per cent. The high NPL share of state-owned banks (62 per cent) should not be misinterpreted. The primary reason for this is that the government took over six ailing private commercial banks after the crisis, so their NPLs raised the average of state-owned banks. Foreign banks were at the other extreme, holding the lowest NPL share (10 per cent), essentially because of their efficient and systematic management of credit risks and monitoring.

In light of the above discussion, it could be said that efforts at financial reforms in Thailand were made more successful because of increased foreign ownership and recapitalization. Foreign financial institutions acquired substantial shareholdings in small Thai banks and thereby enlarged their capital base. Some ailing banks were integrated with state banks. Meanwhile, large Thai banks were able to attract strong interest

Table 7.4 NPLs of different categories of financial institutions, 1998 to 2002 (per cent, by value)

	1998		1999	2000	2001	2002
	Share in total credit outstanding	NPLs Dec.	NPLs Dec.	NPLs Dec.	NPLs Dec.	NPLs Nov.
Private Thai banks	51	40	31	18	14	14
State-owned banks	28	62	63	22	6	5
Foreign banks	13	10	10	7	3	4
All banks	92	43	39	18	11	10
Finance companies	8	70	49	24	9	8
Grand total	100	45	39	18	10	10

Source: Bank of Thailand.

from general investors by issuing a new hybrid between preferred shares and subordinate debentures.

Even though the government tightened the rule after the crisis by making the definition of NPL stricter (three months of unpaid debt service, instead of six or 12 months as earlier), all types of financial institutions seem to have upgraded their asset quality, as their NPL shares declined steadily between 1998 and 2001. However, those statistics are somewhat misleading because not all of the decreases in NPLs represent conversion to performing loans. Parts of them are transfers to commercial banks' asset management companies (totalling 14 AMCs in 2000), debt restructuring, bad debt write-off, and others (e.g. partial principal repayments, write-off from losing right of claim and selling of debt, etc). And after those changes, the remaining NPLs seem to have stayed put. Since the end of 2001, no further progress has been attained. In other words, decreases in NPLs due to debt restructuring and others were matched with new and re-entry NPLs due to economic downturn and corporate mismanagement.

Table 7.5 disaggregates NPLs into 13 business categories. These records show that manufacturing, real estate, and wholesale plus retail trade represented the first (26 per cent), second (17 per cent), and third (15 per cent) troublesome sectors, respectively, to financial institutions. The majority of NPLs in manufacturing and wholesale plus retail trade belonged to private Thai banks, while state-owned banks were primarily

Table 7.5 Classification of NPLs by business sectors, 1999 to 2002 (per cent, by value)

	1999 Dec.	2000 Dec.	2001 Dec.	2002 Nov.
1 Agriculture, fishing and forestry	2.29	3.17	4.40	4.26
2 Mining and quarrying	0.44	0.73	0.61	0.56
3 Manufacturing	26.36	24.01	17.14	22.59
4 Construction	5.45	6.52	7.19	6.86
5 Wholesale and retail trade	15.72	15.70	19.91	18.72
6 Imports	4.60	3.05	2.58	1.74
7 Exports	2.82	2.25	1.90	1.32
8 Banking and finance	3.40	2.82	1.31	0.92
9 Real estate	17.58	15.09	11.13	10.95
10 Public utilities	1.64	1.27	1.47	1.75
11 Services	10.15	10.26	9.81	8.43
12 Personal consumptions	9.55	15.13	22.54	21.91
13 Hire-purchase	–	–	–	–
Grand total	100.00	100.00	100.00	100.00

Source: Bank of Thailand.

Note:
Data include NPLs of private Thai banks, state-owned banks, foreign banks, and finance companies.

responsible for NPLs in real estate. The status of the manufacturing and real estate sectors improved from 1999 to 2001. The sectors whose shares of NPLs moved in the opposite direction (i.e. increasing) were construction and personal consumption.

As regards the types of debtors, in the middle of 1999 when NPLs peaked, ordinary persons totalled 88 per cent of all NPL *cases* at Thai commercial banks. However, their suspended debt service amounted to only 24 per cent of all NPL *value*. The rest belonged to separate legal entities.

Debt restructuring

In June 1998, the government set up a Corporate Debt Restructuring Advisory Committee (CDRAC) to coordinate negotiations among debtors, their potential new partners, bankers, and finance company managers in mapping out debt restructuring measures. Frameworks of corporate debt workouts are based on the 'London Approach', under which creditors work together, share information about debtors, recognize the seniority of claims, seek out-of-court solutions, and agree to keep credit facilities in place. Normally, the debt restructuring cases that CDRAC helps expedite are the multi-creditor ones in which debtors voluntarily draft up the restructuring plans. (The single-creditor cases are mostly handled by the sole creditors or their AMCs.) Then CDRAC will process the plan for debtor–creditor agreement and inter-creditor agreement.

Examples of resolutions are interest rate reductions, grace periods, maturity stretching, partial write-offs, and debt–equity conversions. However, debt negotiation is not an easy task. It involves not only strong pressure from several parties (e.g. debtors, their potential new partners, local and foreign creditors, central bankers, internal revenue officers) but also legal and regulatory constraints. In this context, the government tried to help by amending bankruptcy and foreclosure laws. Meanwhile, the government removed tax disincentives in order to encourage debt renegotiations. Nevertheless, corporate debt restructuring remains a lengthy and difficult process.

One clear-cut example of the difficulties is the difference between Thai and foreign banks. As foreign banks typically extended credits on an unsecured basis (no collateral or guarantees), they were more willing than Thai banks to renegotiate with debtors after the crisis. Thai banks, on the other hand, hesitated to pursue a rescue package for ailing debtors. The collateral and/or guarantees that they commanded tempted them to try to foreclose the concerned assets or sue guarantors instead of petitioning for rescues. Worse yet, even though the bankruptcy law was amended in June 1998 with the addition of the possibilities of rehabilitation or rescue packages (like Chapter 11 of the US law), the rescue option requires consensus among creditors (or at least 75 per cent of creditors' voting rights covering at least 50 per cent of outstanding debts). This makes the banks' hesitation to renegotiate debts more influential. It is thus unsurprising that 90 per cent of the debt restructuring cases that experienced serious problems involved commercial banks.

In many cases, creditors tried to foreclose collateral. However, in Thailand, the foreclosure procedure is very tedious. Although the final outcomes of legal prosecution are likely to be favourable to creditors, the procedure is time-consuming and costly due to income foregone from the NPLs. On the other hand, debt restructuring, in a genuine sense, may yield quicker results and help avert NPL-related difficulties. However, creditors have to be assured of debtors' sincerity first because relaxing the terms of loan contracts means a reduction of creditors' income. Given that Thai banks typically command collateral and/or guarantees, they prefer extending repayment schedules to accepting any loss. In other words, Thai banks are rather tough as they often insist that debtors repay 100 per cent of the principal together with interest, which is drastically different from debt concessions abroad where only 50–70 per cent in returns is deemed excellent.

Debtors also face a series of dilemmas. Because of their excessive borrowing in the past and excessive capacity at present, they are overwhelmed by heavy debt burdens. Long acquaintance and good relations with particular creditors often tempt debtors to favour some creditors over others in the debt restructuring process. However, without consistent inter-creditor agreements, such bias can hardly be accepted. Inter-creditor agreements are often difficult to reach since different creditors have different conditions or back-up securities (guarantees or collateral), depending upon their loan contracts. On top of that, some debtors carry burdens from trade or supplier credits as well. If debtors resort to new partners to share debt servicing, the new partners have to be ones whose creditworthiness is acceptable to creditors. Meanwhile, new partners are tempted to demand several conditions or methods of protection before making capital investments or sharing debt obligations. Without new partners, either debtors could go bankrupt when sued by unsecured (foreign) creditors, or debtors' assets could be lost to foreclosure when sued by secured (Thai) creditors.

Financial advisors (FA) or independent accountants (IA) are typically called upon when creditors start to doubt debtors' sincerity or reliability and their confidence in debtors begins to weaken. The function of FA/IA is to facilitate the whole process of debt restructuring, including examination and appraisal of debtors' financial status (or the so-called due diligence), cash and performance monitoring, evaluation of project viability, financial projections, exploring restructuring options, negotiation and documentation. In conducting these duties, FA/IA encounter numerous problems. For instance, employees of some debtors view actions of FA/IA as unnecessary scrutiny. They are afraid of fault-finding and are thus unwilling to cooperate or provide management information even though FA/IA usually do not have technical expertise in debtors' businesses. In some cases, debtors belong to an intricate network of affiliated corporations. In other cases, FA/IA detect defects of debtors' operations, but cannot fully disclose them since the FA/IA are hired by debtors. The most difficult dilemma for the FA/IA is to maintain neutrality and suggest proper channels that will benefit both debtors and creditors.

One resolution for debt restructuring is swapping debts for equities or shares in debtors' companies. However, some debtors are reluctant to do this as they would like to retain the family-run nature of their companies. The unwillingness of others to adopt debt-to-equity conversion as a means to rehabilitate their businesses arises because this route would require disclosure of relevant information, some of which is deemed confidential in their family circle. In some cases (e.g. hospitals), the main shareholders (medical doctors) are from the same business circuit and want to avoid diversifying their ownership or management. In other cases, debtors (e.g. SMEs in up-country provinces) hesitate because they are ashamed of releasing their faltering financial status.

Creditors also pay little attention to the debt-to-equity conversion, even if a repurchase option for debtors is attached, since creditors lack expertise in debtors' businesses. For the same reason, few cases of successful debt restructuring principally count upon adjustment of debtors' internal production or management structure. Typically, the creditors pay more attention to debtors' cash-flow positions and adjustment of debt terms. Another resolution is partial or total write-off, or the so-called 'hair cut'. Some creditors offer these partial reductions of debt service as a stimulus to debtors only if they can repay the rest of their obligations as soon as possible. Nevertheless, creditors find it very difficult to choose among these options, e.g. to sue if holding collateral/guarantees, to write off (which may conflict with headquarters' guidelines and may necessitate increases of capital funds), to relax terms of remaining debts, to reschedule or stretch maturity of repayments.

It should also be noted that whether any channels of debt restructuring will work successfully or not also depends upon the economic environment later on. If the economy recovers appreciably, domestic consumption will be healthy and automobile or hospital markets can easily recuperate. Otherwise, re-entry NPLs may emerge, especially when rescheduling is selected as a method of debt restructuring.

Ordinarily, commercial banks have to pay taxes on accrued interest and principal even though they have yet to collect them. In the midst of debt restructuring efforts, banks thus request tax credits or refunds on the non-recoverable portion of accumulated debt service. But the tax law demands official prosecution if the money involved exceeds 500,000 baht. As for debtors, forgiven debts are treated as income subject to the 30 per cent business tax. This requirement decreases the incentives for debtors to restructure their debts. Moreover, since the Revenue Department has priority over other creditors when claiming debtors' income or assets, such priority makes creditors less willing to write off parts or all of their overdue loans.

However, creditors' hesitation to restructure debts could also be costly because they have to pay taxes on overdue debts and the longer the debts are overdue means larger provisions or capital supports become necessary. Abiding by such a rule is very painful, as financial institutions often find tapping scarce capital funds a formidable task.

Another vicious circle of NPLs occurs when commercial banks are reluctant to extend credits to, or rollover maturing debts of, even good clients. A precarious economic environment drives banks to retrieve most credits as soon as possible. This reluctance creates pressure upon banks' clients, and they could consequently become new NPLs, necessitating additions to the banks' capital funds. Commercial banks are aware of this vicious circle, and are thus often caught in a quandary.

The central authorities were also trapped in a dilemma on the issue of whether domestic interest rates should be reduced. Lowering interest rates will certainly help speed up the resolution of bad debts and easier credits will facilitate economic recovery. However, this channel cannot be resorted to frequently because, in the midst of financial liberalization, relatively low domestic interest rates could easily induce net capital outflows or repayments of foreign debts. Such outflows will lessen precious foreign exchange reserves of the country and/or depress the value of the local currency, which will have far-reaching repercussions. Although the government has made some encouraging moves on bankruptcy and foreclosure, it has not motivated mergers and acquisitions as a means to restructure debts.

In short, the problems engendered by the various parties in the debt restructuring process may be summarized as follows:

Creditors
- Lacking thorough understanding of debtors' businesses.
- Inefficient cooperation or conflicts among themselves in multi-creditor cases.
- Too stubborn when collateral or guarantees are held.
- Different status of creditors allow different concessions to debtors (e.g. rescheduling versus write-off).
- Unwilling to extend or roll over credit lines to debtors.

Debtors
- Lacking good governance.
- Conflicts among shareholders.
- Inefficient business operations.

- Unwilling to cooperate with negotiators or creditors and disclose relevant information.
- Having no previous experience in debt restructuring.
- Demanding strong debt concessions and retention of ownership.

Independent specialists (financial consultants, accountants, legal consultants, independent engineers, negotiators, judges).

- Charging high fees.
- Having no expertise in debtors' businesses, thus lacking relevant information.

Besides the above, all parties tend to be self-centred and try to defend their own rights or preserve their possessions rather than searching for mutual benefits.

Despite numerous difficulties involved in the debt restructuring process as described above, the government's Corporate Debt Restructuring Advisory Committee (CDRAC) contributed appreciably to the reduction of NPL in October 1999–July 2001. Roughly a third, or 37 per cent, of the NPL reduction was the result of debt restructuring, while 28 per cent was due to transfers to AMCs and 14 per cent due to hair cuts. The largest proportion of completed restructuring *cases* belonged to the personal consumption sector (43 per cent), followed by the wholesale-retail sector (21 per cent) and the agricultural/fishery/forestry sector (15 per cent). However, with respect to the *value* of successful debt restructuring, the manufacturing sector ranked first at 30 per cent, followed by wholesale-retail trade (14 per cent) and services (14 per cent). The most prevalent restructuring methods were extension of loan maturity (41 per cent), grace periods (21 per cent), and interest rate reductions (20 per cent).

Stretching loan maturity was preferred by both creditors and debtors, as this method was viewed as entailing minimal costs to creditors while they still had faith in debtors' survival. This channel allowed continuation of debtors' businesses while preserving their ownership plus executive power. However, all debt restructuring methods, as adopted, did not resolve the fundamental problems in production, pricing, marketing and corporate structure of debtors' undertakings. Thus, there is no assurance that NPL problems will disappear or that debtors will achieve better capacity in coping with market competition.

Thai Asset Management Corporation

Given that a sizeable portion of NPLs belonged to state-owned banks and their officers were hesitant about making decisions on debt concessions, the government believed that having a central agency to handle NPLs may be helpful. Moreover, such a central agency would help resolve problems from multi-creditor conflicts and assist private banks in eliminating their NPLs as well. The government therefore issued an executive decree in June 2001 to set up the Thai Asset Management Corporation (TAMC). It was intended to purchase 1.37 trillion baht (US$35 billion) of bad assets from local banks. Within this total amount, the majority (80 per cent) or 1.12 trillion baht was from state-owned banks, while the rest, or 0.25 trillion baht, was expected from private banks. Transferred assets must involve debt over 5 million baht belonging to at least two creditors. Loan assets would be purchased by 10-year bonds to be issued by the TAMC and losses incurred afterward would be split under a loss-sharing formula. By May 2002, the TAMC had already bought 357 cases of overdue debts worth 158 billion baht.

The dual objectives of TAMC are: (a) to enable debtors to repay their outstanding debts and efficiently continue their businesses; and (b) to help financial institutions avert losses that could endanger stability of the system. As regards pricing, the TAMC board approved the use of central bank valuation, instead of that set by the Land Department, for assets pledged as collateral for bad loans to be transferred to the TAMC. This decision, which favours commercial banks in selling NPLs, is based on the view that existing values used at the Land Department are outdated and reappraisal by that organization will be costly and time-consuming.

An Asset Management Corporation can bring about both positive and negative consequences. The experience of other countries includes Fobaproa (Mexico), APT (Philippines), DGF (Spain), RTC (USA), Arsenal (Finland), Npart (Ghana), Securum (Sweden), Darnaharta (Malaysia), KAMCO (Korea), and IBRA (Indonesia). Many factors come into play, such as asset quality, valuation of NPLs and their collateral, experience of concerned staff in debt collection, acquaintance with troubled debtors, independence of decision-making, and legal authority.

In the case of Thailand, where most of the NPLs targeted to be transferred to the TAMC belong to state-owned banks, the underlying rationales of TAMC are the following.

a   The asset quality of those state-owned banks' NPLs is extremely low because those assets originally belonged to private banks which have already collapsed. Chances are therefore slim that state-owned banks can sell those to any other AMCs or new partners. Those extremely bad NPLs need special treatment by the TAMC.

b   Worse yet, executives of state-owned banks tend to hesitate to decide how to handle those NPLs (restructuring or write-off), because the chances of success are very low and decision-makers are susceptible to legal penalties as those banks and their bad assets belong to the government.

c Uniting creditors into the TAMC is expected to help reduce the problems arising from conflicts among creditors along the debt restructuring process. Such uniting should also lead to more negotiating power.
   In other words, once the TAMC becomes the sole creditor, final
   decisions on debt restructuring can be reached more rapidly.
d After the NPLs of commercial banks are moved to the TAMC, banks'
   risk exposure will fall and they will be able to extend more credits,
   which would facilitate quicker economic recovery.

Even though unifying creditors into the TAMC may sound promising in
expediting the task of clearing up financial institutions' balance sheets, in
practice the TAMC could easily encounter or engender many problems.

a The lack of familiarity with bank clients means that the TAMC is likely
   to face some difficulties in collecting overdue debts. Any efforts to
   compensate for such deficiency will certainly add costs to the TAMC.
b Some private creditor banks may be reluctant to sell NPLs to the
   TAMC because prices are too low or attached conditions are too stringent (e.g. the first 20 per cent of loss wholly borne by banks, the next
   20 per cent equally shared with the TAMC).
c The TAMC could easily be trapped by fake NPLs (which in the past
   amounted to a third of total NPLs). It may also generate moral hazard
   on the part of both financial institutions (in exerting less caution in
   credit extension) and capable debtors (in breaching debt contracts),
   as they feel that they can resort to assistance from the TAMC.
d A centralized AMC like TAMC will be susceptible to political influences and interference or biases in its decisions, such as whether to
   purchase an NPL, from which bank, in which sector, at what price,
   and how to retrieve overdue debt obligations.
e Gigantic costs of the TAMC will add financial burden to the government, as NPLs will be purchased by issuance of government bonds.
   These bonds will exacerbate heavy existing public debt obligations
   (2.8 trillion baht or 56 per cent of GDP in mid-2001) accumulated
   since the eruption of the financial crisis. Worse yet, private banks that
   sell NPLs will be tempted to prolong the debt collection period since
   they will definitely receive interest payments from the government in
   the meantime.

Overall, the TAMC could help in retrieving debt payments from the NPLs
of state-owned banks. However, such gains come with costs. Private banks
should not be expected to participate to a large extent, primarily because
commercial banks are not lacking capital funds and market liquidity is
plentiful. They are typically reluctant to take losses or risks. In short, the
TAMC may help in rectifying some intrinsic drawbacks of the Thai

financial system. But its costs should not be overlooked, neither should one ignore the possibility of its adverse repercussions or side effects.

Corporate restructuring

The above analysis shows that even though, in the past few years, the Bank of Thailand has succeeded in improving the culture of prudence and good governance in the financial sector, reforms in the real sector moved at a much slower pace. Corporate culture and the operational structure of local Thai corporations prove hard to bend. Their overriding concern is to maintain the family-owned and family-run feature. This can be firmly supported by evidence or data in every sector, even in the Thai financial circuit. For instance, when the government offered commercial banks up to 300 billion baht in public funds for recapitalization in return for corporate restructuring and new business lending, only one-fifth of this amount was used because the controlling shareholders of remaining private banks were unwilling to dilute their ownership or to risk loss of control.

Nevertheless, it remains unquestionable that the typical corporate culture needs to be reformed in the direction of better corporate governance. Otherwise, any economic recovery would not be long lasting and financial crises could revisit, as chances are that the government's assistance cannot persist on a continual basis. Local corporations, especially the small- and medium-sized enterprises, have to adapt or improve their financial discipline, as financial institutions at present have paid less attention to collateral but more to cash-flow management, experience, vision and viability. Other facets of prudent financial discipline are avoidance of over-leverage, excessive intra-affiliate lending, and over-investment, especially of a speculative kind.

Along with the attempt to improve corporate governance, the government is capable of providing assistance or motivation. For instance, it could amend weaknesses or loopholes in the current regulations on accounting standards, taxes, bankruptcy, foreclosure, and forbearance. In addition, the government's expansionary policies (such as credit lines offered by the Government Savings Bank to SMEs, village funds) should impose certain conditions upon the recipients or beneficiaries in order to achieve prudential and orderly corporate governance. This policy direction will not only accelerate the rehabilitation process but also upgrade the corporate culture of local enterprises.

Alternative viewpoint

Table 7.6 summarizes the movements of NPLs since 1999. It can be seen that NPL statistics are highly volatile. Their increases could come from either new NPLs or re-entry NPLs. Meanwhile, NPLs could fall because of debt restructuring or transfers to an AMC. Statistics on NPLs may not reflect the overall health condition of financial institutions or the financial system because, other than retail lending, another function of financial institutions is to undertake large-scale investment in either securities or factories directly. Financial institutions also obtain income from various kinds of services offered to their clients. Because of these shortcomings of NPL data, an international comparison of NPLs becomes meaningless. An overall rate of return will be more indicative than NPL statistics in demonstrating the efficiency of financial institutions' business management. A series of those rates of returns or their steadiness would show the degree of associated risks.

In the case of debt restructuring, more attention should be focused upon the fundamentals of debtors' operations, the productivity of their businesses, instead of debt burden scheduling. The underlying reason is that productivity has a direct impact on the debt servicing capability of debtors. Factors that affect productivity are capital allocation, the organization and mechanism of the production process, and technological advancement. External variables such as government regulations and foreign competition also play prominent roles. Competitive forces induce all players to improve productivity to survive in the domestic market, and productivity is also a crucial element of competitiveness in the world market. A study by McKinsey & Company (2002) measures productivity and makes comparisons across countries in 2000/2001. Its results are alarming in suggesting that

Table 7.6 Movements of financial institutions' NPLs, 1999 to 2002

	1999[a]	*2000*	*2001*	*2002*[b]
Total new NPLs	170,093	490,771	406,124	305,019
New NPLs	137,432	281,064	170,352	108,227
Re-entry NPLs	32,661	209,707	235,772	196,792
NPL reductions	606,443	1,727,855	789,474	312,341
Restructured debts	258,263	607,662	287,678	152,419
Accrued interest payments	70,375	113,929	76,030	41,726
Transferred to asset management companies	139,598	443,536	297,729	29,041
Write-off	69,534	298,251	63,234	3,466
Others	68,298	264,476	64,802	85,689
Net change	−436,350	−1,237,084	−383,350	−7,322
Total NPLs	2,094,425	857,341	473,991	466,668
(% of credit outstanding)	39	18	10	10

Source: Bank of Thailand.

Note:
a Oct–Dec.
b Jan–Nov.

production inefficiency must have been a significant factor underlying Thailand's difficulties in achieving economic recovery.

Conclusions

In the five years following the 1997 Asian financial crisis, almost every part of the Thai economy suffered. The financial sector suffered in particular, since it had close interaction with real sectors. Thus far, the government has been moderately successful in handling the problems of ailing financial intermediaries. Rising foreign ownership together with satisfactory performance served as a good example. However, more attention should be devoted to the fundamental problems of NPLs and debt restructuring, if corrective actions are to have favourable and sustainable effects.

On the part of debtors, financial restructuring represents only one component of complete debt resolution. Two other vital ingredients are often neglected: operation restructuring and corporate restructuring. The former refers to adjustment of their operating mechanisms, aiming at greater efficiency, while the latter is meant to disentangle excessively intricate cross holding of shares among affiliated firms so that more effective management is achieved and ongoing projects become more viable.

On the part of financial institutions, improvement is needed on the calibre of staff, management tactics, and ethics. Otherwise, imprudent credit extension or restriction, further NPLs, and another financial crisis may recur. More accountability may be required from bank executives or operators, since their actions or decisions have a strong bearing on their banks' performance. These executives should be held liable to criminal charges, or they should be required to put up some of their own stake as contingent liabilities in the case of poor performance of their institutions. This will help motivate bank executives or operators to exert more caution on the efficiency and asset quality of their banks.

On the part of central authorities, regulations upon financial institutions should be classified or spelled out by functions, not types of institutions. Otherwise, they can become ineffective because of leakage as a result of financial liberalization. Before any further liberalization is adopted, the authorities should be confident about the readiness of the involved financial institutions and supervisors, given the prevailing economic atmosphere. Both examiners and supervisors should focus their attention on forward-looking analysis or indicators instead of just monitoring past accounts.

Finally, capital market development should be continually pursued in order to complement bank loans, as bank loans are intrinsically volatile. In this regard, special emphasis should be placed on small- and medium-sized enterprises (SMEs), since the number of these SMEs is enormous and they have strong implications for economic development, income distribution, and social welfare. Besides, upgrading debtors' transparency as well as corporate governance will ultimately help reduce both NPLs and the need for debt restructuring.

References

Ammar Siamwalla (2001) Picking up the pieces: bank and corporate restructuring in post-1997 Thailand. Paper presented at the Sub-regional Seminar on Financial and Corporate Sectors Restructuring in East and South-East Asia, Seoul, Korea, 30 May–1 June.

Bank of Thailand (1996) Analysing Thailand's short-term debt, *Bank of Thailand Focus*, 1.

Bank of Thailand (2000) Supervision report 2000. Report, Bank of Thailand, Bangkok.

McKinsey & Company (2002) Thai productivity report, prosperity through productivity. Report, Bangkok.

Nopporn Ruangsakul (1989) *Nayobai Kae Panha Wikrit nai Thanakarn Panit Thai [Policies to Resolve Banking Crises in Thailand]*, in Thai with English summary, Bangkok: Thailand Development Research Institute.

Pakorn Vichyanond (1994) Thailand's financial system: structure and liberalization, Thailand Development Research Institute Research Monograph No. 11, Bangkok.

Pakorn Vichyanond (2000) *Financial Reforms in Thailand*, BMl, Bangkok: Thailand Development Research Institute.

Pakorn Vichyanond (2001) Complicated difficulties behind financial resolution: the case of Thailand. Paper presented at the Sixth Shizuoka Asia-Pacific Forum, Shizuoka, Japan, 1–2 December.

Thailand Development Research Institute (1991) Karn Kaekai Panha Staban Karn Ngoen lae Botbat khong Staban Prakan Ngoen Faak [Resolution of Financial Institution Problems and the Role of Deposit Insurance Institute]. Working paper, Thailand Development Research Institute, Bangkok.

The Economist (2001) A survey of corporate finance, 27 January–2 February: 19.

Tumnong Dasri (ed.) (2001) Corporate debt restructuring: lessons from the aftermath of Thai economic crisis [in Thai with English summary], report, Bank of Thailand, Bangkok.

Yos Vajragupta and Pakorn Vichyanond (2001) Thailand's financial evolution and the 1997 crisis, in: D.G. Dickinson, J.L. Ford, M.J. Fry, A.W. Mullineux and S. Sen (eds) *Finance, Governance and Economic Performance in Pacific and South East Asia*, Cheltenham, UK: Edward Elgar.

Chapter 8

The implications of a flexible exchange rate

Bhanupong Nidhiprabha

The exchange rate float of July 1997 significantly altered several aspects of Thailand's economic policy environment. The change occurred at a unique time. Never before had the Thai economy simultaneously encountered large foreign exchange risks, asset price deflation, income and wage reductions, recession, widespread bankruptcies and financial instability. As Warr (1999) remarks, Thailand's crisis can be thought of as the collapse of a boom. To some extent, the exchange rate played an important role in this collapse.

The exchange rate can be viewed as an asset price. As such, it is affected by expectations of its future purchasing power and it can be as volatile as these expectations. Both fundamentals and psychological factors can have an important impact on currency value. Thailand entered the flexible exchange rate system when both fundamentals and market sentiments were in disarray.

A flexible regime has a clear advantage over the fixed exchange rate system with regard to the controllability of the money supply. With no intervention in foreign exchange markets the central bank can adjust the level of the monetary base and can also induce foreign exchange rates to move endogenously according to policy goals, thus enhancing the effectiveness of monetary policy. On the other hand, the stabilizing role of fiscal policy is also potentially important as a source of aggregate demand management, and many argue that fiscal policy could lose its strength under a flexible exchange rate system.

This chapter examines the implications of Thailand's adoption of a flexible exchange rate system. First, it discusses the fluctuations of the baht–dollar exchange rate by reviewing overshooting exchange rate theories. Then it addresses the questions of whether the exchange rate should be stabilized and whether Thailand can regain its former competitiveness. A discussion of capital flight and an argument in favour of prudential capital controls follow. Then, the adjustment problem is discussed, together with the roles of monetary and fiscal policies under a flexible exchange rate regime.

Excess volatility

Erratic fluctuations in the exchange rate are viewed as a serious drawback of a flexible regime. During the first seven months after the float, Thailand suffered continuous exchange rate depreciation, with each day bringing another drop in the value of the baht. This deterioration led to a general pessimism about the future of the Thai economy. At the end of 1997, Thailand's total external debts stood at US$106 billion, with 36 per cent of these in short-term debts. For every one-baht rise in the price of the dollar, total foreign debts rose by more than one billion baht. If expectations were backward looking, one would expect a further depreciation of the baht. As a result, exporters were unwilling to submit dollar receivables, while domestic firms hoarded dollars. Because of lack of experience of a flexible rate, economic agents tend to form their exchange rate expectations without reference to fundamental macroeconomic variables.

Gruen *et al.* (1998) argue that such a lack of experience tends to cause foreign exchange markets to overreact. Thus, the Australian dollar fell to a record low in 1995 after the float in December 1993, despite a substantial lapse between the abandoning of the fixed rate and the adoption of the flexible exchange rate. If this hypothesis is correct, the baht–dollar exchange rate should fluctuate less when market participants have formed realistic expectations.

On the other hand, it could also be argued, along the lines of Dornbusch (1976), that the overshooting of the baht was caused by a rapid expansion of the money supply. Between 1991 and mid-1997, when the bubble burst, Thailand's monetary base and the volume of bank credit grew at average rates of 16 and 22 per cent, respectively. There is also evidence that the wholesale price index (WPI) in Thailand adjusts faster than the consumer price index (CPI) (Bank of Thailand 1996). This finding indicates a certain degree of stickiness in the price of non-traded goods, which would place the burden of adjustment on a free variable, the exchange rate. The depreciation of the baht should be faster than the growth of the money supply so it can compensate for the slow adjustment of goods and services prices.

Another plausible explanation for the overshooting is offered by Frankel and Froot (1990) in their theory of 'speculative bubbles' in exchange rates. Chartists, who forecast economic variables by extrapolating trends, were close to being correct during the six-month period of upheaval which followed the float. Portfolio managers seemingly paid more attention to chartists than to fundamentalists, who forecast exchange rates on the basis of fundamentals such as Purchasing Power Parity (PPP). Chartists' forecasts were self-realizing and roughly correct, at least for the six months after the July float, until the exchange rate fell completely out of line with the fundamentals. It was then, as the exchange rate appreciated to a more realistic level, that portfolio managers turned to fundamentalists for advice.

The International Monetary Fund (IMF) prescribed a tight monetary policy for Thailand. This was justified by the necessity of maintaining high interest rates to prevent speculation against the baht. As long as depositors can earn high interest rates from holding baht, the severity of overshooting can be lessened somewhat. Signs of an increasing trend in the short-term interest rate (the inter-bank rate) became apparent in May 1997, when the inter-bank rate was 12.1 per cent. The inter-bank rate rose to 18.6 per cent in July and remained at a double-digit level until August 1998. Since then, the short-term interest rate has declined sharply. There are several reasons for this decline. First, the Federal Funds rate was cut three times and fell from 5.5 per cent in September 1998 to 4.75 per cent in November 1998. Second, the appreciation of the baht in February 1998 suggests that the Bank of Thailand was able to adopt a low interest rate policy. Third, an economic slump tends to lead to decreased money lending and borrowing, thereby raising liquidity levels. If the interest rate parity condition holds, a narrowing interest rate differential indicates a lower degree of anticipated depreciation of the baht.

In early April 1999, the inter-bank rate in Thailand was lower than the Federal Funds rate. The Interest Rate Parity Theorem suggests that the baht should appreciate further, turning the forward premium into a forward discount. Once exchange rate overshooting has ceased, the interest rate can return to a normal level.

In addition to other Asian currencies' competitive depreciations in early 1998, the rise of the dollar against the yen also contributed to the weakening of the baht. In February 1998, however, the baht regained strength, while the dollar continued to appreciate against the yen until July 1998 (Figure 8.1). Thus, the strength of the dollar against the yen cannot fully explain the fall in the value of the baht. Before the float, the strength of the dollar against the yen implied that the baht would appreciate against the yen, since the dollar had the highest weight in the basket value of the baht. But the baht's appreciation against the yen cannot be entirely attributed to the fall in exports from Thailand to Japan, which can be explained by the slowdown in economic activity in Japan. In other words, the Japanese income effect on Thailand's exports was stronger than the substitution effect.

After the float, the baht–yen exchange rate was permitted to rise rather than fall, so that the strength of the dollar would not hurt Thailand's exports to Japan. After February 1998, when the baht regained its strength relative to the dollar, the baht also appreciated against the yen (Figure 8.1). When the dollar reached its peak against the yen in June 1998 and then fell to close to 115 yen/dollar, the baht weakened against the yen.

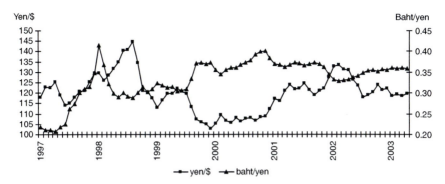

Figure 8.1 Exchange rate overshooting, monthly, 1997 to 2003 (source: Monthly data from Bank of Thailand).

Thus, exchange rate instability was caused by fluctuations in the yen–dollar exchange rate as well as other internal factors, such as domestic monetary shocks and political uncertainties. A flexible exchange rate system does not fully shield Thailand from foreign exchange volatility.

Should the exchange rate be stabilized?

When the exchange rate fluctuates dramatically, both exporters and importers incur heavy losses. Bilson (1985) has established a model to show a theoretical link between currency risk premiums and the variability of exchange rates and interest rates. Since interest rate fluctuations are a causal factor in the business cycle, as currency risk premiums increase, interest rates must also increase to compensate for the added risk. Thus, the combination of real interest rate instability and real exchange rate instability must have an adverse effect. Foreign exchange rate instability can therefore be said to have caused a painful transfer of wealth between debtors and creditors, both domestically and internationally. Mikesell (2001) has proposed that a country facing a financial crisis should temporarily adopt a dual exchange rate system to protect the current account exchange rate from substantial depreciation caused by sudden capital outflow. Mikesell argues that, to achieve this, the foreign exchange market should be divided between capital transactions and current account transactions.

Foreign exchange volatility also increases the risk involved in international trade and investment. If this risk is diversifiable, however, exporters and importers can rely on forward contracts. The volume of these contracts was expected to increase after the adoption of the flexible exchange rate regime. Krugman (1989) argued that the gains from international trade would decrease, since exchange rate instability blurs the price signals supposed to regulate international markets. When future exchange rates are uncertain, firms tend to be more cautious and to delay investment, even with increased demand for their exports. They will lose if the currency appreciates, and sacrifice some profits but still be able to invest later if it depreciates. Firms choose to err on the side of caution. This creates a case for central bank intervention in foreign exchange markets.

As Milton Friedman pointed out, as long as market participants act rationally, speculations are likely to have a stabilizing affect. As long as markets operate efficiently, there is no room for destabilizing speculation. The efficiency of foreign exchange markets can be detected from deviations from the forward parity relationship. If the risk is not too large, we would expect the forward premium on a currency to be an unbiased predictor of the currency's actual depreciation rate in the future. Krugman stresses that there is no positive evidence of efficient asset markets. In the case of Thailand between 1998 and 2002, we also observe deviance from the uncovered parity line. Figure 8.2 presents observations pertaining to both the northeast and the southwest quadrants of the diagram. It can be seen that speculation might actually have a destabilizing affect, with negative externality justifying government intervention.

The Bank of Thailand cannot change the movement of the baht, since to a certain degree it is determined by the yen–dollar exchange rate. The Bank can only intervene temporarily to prevent abrupt changes in the value of the baht. In the long run, it cannot significantly influence the exchange rate, whose movements are dictated by market conditions. In

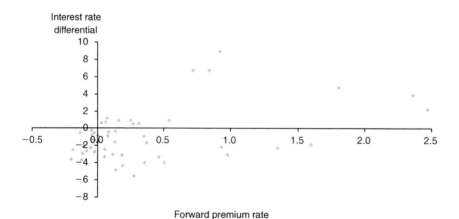

Figure 8.2 The interest rate parity relationship, 1998 to 2002 (source: Monthly data from Bank of Thailand and International Monetary Fund, *International Financial Statistics*, various issues).

June 2001, in an effort to shore up the value of the baht, the Bank of Thailand raised the repurchase market rate by 100 basis points from 2 to 2.5 per cent. Because Federal Funds rates had been cut 11 times in 2001, in January 2002 the Bank of Thailand had to reverse its policy stance by reducing the key policy interest rate to 2 per cent.

Can a central bank engineer a change in the exchange rate? Dominguez and Frankel (1993) argue that foreign exchange intervention can work if properly conceived and executed, and challenge the view that intervention can affect the exchange rate if and only if it changes the money supply. The important point in their argument is that if foreign exchange traders react to intervention by revising their forecasts of future exchange rates, they will change current exchange rates. But this is unconvincing, particularly in relation to Thailand since the crisis, where policy credibility is not high. It is exceedingly difficult to alter market perceptions when asset prices are determined mainly by mass psychology and herd behaviour. It is also possible for central bankers and interventionists to send the wrong signals to foreign exchange markets and thus elicit a completely unanticipated reaction from speculators.

Substantial departures from PPP, even in a world of flexible exchange rates, can exist in the short run and even over decades (Obstfeld and Rogoff 1995). With considerable differentials between productivity growth rates in tradable and non-tradable goods sectors, a country can experience rises in the relative price of non-tradable goods and appreciation of the real exchange rate based on the CPI. It is therefore impossible to pinpoint the exact equilibrium value of the exchange rate from deviations from PPP. Nor can the current account deficit be used as a measure of the overvaluation of the exchange rate. Investment–saving relationships and public deficit levels also influence the current account. Indeed, intervening in foreign exchange markets in order to obtain an appropriate exchange rate value is exceedingly difficult, considering the complications that can arise from the impact of exchange rate changes on internal balance.

If a central bank needs to intervene in foreign exchange markets to create orderly movement in exchange rates, its total international reserves should not be less than the amount of funds required in the fixed exchange rate system. The IMF conditionality for Thailand stipulates a minimum of US$23 billion in international reserves to be held by the Bank of Thailand.[1] This is to prevent the Bank of Thailand from intervening in foreign exchange markets in order to prop up the value of the baht to such a level that it might cause another serious misalignment. It is possible that the Bank of Thailand will not intervene in the foreign exchange markets, in the realization that it may not be effective as long as the IMF conditionality holds. In addition, issues of income distribution are always involved in decisions about foreign exchange market intervention.

Thailand has long regulated public borrowing by stipulating the maximum foreign debt the government is allowed to incur each year. When the IMF's conditionality no longer holds, the same principle can be applied to stipulate the floor level of foreign international reserves and thus guard against future attempts to prop up the value of the baht. Many countries, however, seem to be happy with large amounts of international reserves. It is understandable for China and Hong Kong to maintain large amounts of international reserves (US$247 billion and US$112 billion, respectively, in 2002), because they are under the dollar-peg regime. But other countries that engage in a soft dollar peg prefer large holdings of dollar reserves as precautionary ammunition for future fights against speculative attack. South Korea and Taiwan are in the same league as Hong Kong, both countries having more than US$115 billion in reserves.

Export competitiveness

The notion that currency depreciation enhances competitiveness is seemingly a myth. A country cannot export its way out of recession simply by devaluating its currency. A country's international competitiveness depends on its productive labour force, its savings and its technological progress. It is possible for a strong currency to be associated with a country's export competitiveness. A country with a high rate of saving and rapid productivity growth will experience real exchange rate appreciation, while commanding a considerable degree of international competitiveness. It has been suggested that Thailand needs a weaker baht for its exporters to increase their competitiveness. During harvesting seasons, the argument goes, the baht should remain weak, so that exporters will have a strong incentive to buy crops at high (baht) prices, knowing that they will receive high (baht) prices when the commodities are exported. In turn, poor farmers can indirectly stimulate the economy by increasing their consumption as their incomes increase with baht depreciation.

It should be noted that changes in the prices of foreign currencies have a profound effect on all commodity prices. One has to look carefully into the impact of changes in foreign exchange rates on the rest of the economy before making hasty exchange rate policy recommendations. The flexible exchange rate has brought into the open the issue of distributive income between exporters and importers, tradable and non-tradable sectors, and creditors and debtors of foreign currencies.

Figure 8.3 shows both nominal and real depreciation of the baht, calculated on a year-on-year basis. In January 1998, the baht depreciated by 50 per cent in nominal terms. It is clear that the real depreciation rate was lower than the nominal depreciation rate, because Thailand's inflation rate was higher than the United States'. Nonetheless, the gap between nominal and real depreciation narrowed because of a declining trend in

Thailand's inflation rate. After October 1998, the baht rebounded and depreciation turned into appreciation, eroding the competitiveness gained during the early period of the float. Nominal and real exchange rate movements converged as inflation differentials between Thailand and the United States became smaller. During the long boom period in the 1990s, increased competition and technological advances enabled the US economy to grow without lifting the inflation rate, while the price of oil declined and deflationary pressure in Thailand caused inflation there to drop sharply relative to inflation in the United States.

According to the Open Fisher condition, expected inflation differentials reflect interest rate differentials. Interest rates in Thailand tended to fall as the Thai economy moved from overheating to sluggishness. When the baht–dollar exchange rate had remained stable for some months, an expected depreciation turned into an expected appreciation. When the interest rate in Thailand fell below that in the United States, the baht appreciated rapidly (Figure 8.3), by more than 40 per cent from January 1998, suggesting a return to the level dictated by fundamentals. By the second quarter of 2002, the baht had begun to depreciate. During this period, real exchange rate volatility lessened. Hau (2002) uses evidence from OECD countries to show that real exchange rate volatility is negatively related to economic openness, since non-tradables increase aggregate price rigidity, unlike tradables, which facilitate relative price level adjustment under exchange rate pass-through. Because the openness of the Thai economy has tended to increase since the crisis, the lesser real exchange rate volatility can be partially attributed to Thailand's commitment to trade openness and market-oriented policy.

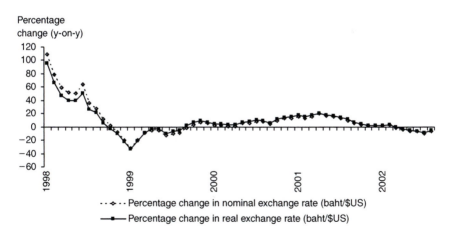

Figure 8.3 Exchange rate depreciation, 1998 to 2002 (source: Monthly data from Bank of Thailand and International Monetary Fund, *International Financial Statistics*, various issues).

Government intervention has been kept to a minimum in the product and labour markets. The 1997 float brought about a real depreciation of the baht. Inflation peaked at 10.6 per cent in June 1998 before falling to 2.5 per cent in March 1999. The nominal wage rate did not rise, and real wage rates thus declined in both manufacturing and services sectors. As Table 8.1 shows, nominal wage rates in both sectors increased by about 6 per cent in August 1997, when the contractionary effect of devaluation was not apparent. Six months after the float, however, the nominal wage rate actually declined, with the most severe adjustment occurring in the service sector, which experienced a 10 per cent drop in the nominal wage rate. National Statistical Office (NSO) statistics indicate that, by August 1998, workers were trying to maintain their wage losses, pushing up the nominal wage rate to compensate for their loss in purchasing power. Nonetheless, the real wage rates in both sectors declined after the float.

Wage flexibility does indeed exist, and it can explain Thailand's successful maintenance of the fixed exchange rate for so many years. According to Obstfeld (1998), before the crash in 1997 Thailand had been a puzzle, since it was very rare for countries to maintain a fixed exchange rate for more than five years. Wage and price flexibility made it possible to adjust real wages during periods of macroeconomic imbalance without the necessity of a flexible exchange rate. Furthermore, conservative fiscal policies helped absorb large capital inflows through budget surpluses, while open capital accounts prevented the monetary base growth from becoming explosive and thus threatening price stability. Nonetheless, this insulating mechanism broke down when the monetary authorities attempted to bail out certain financial institutions to prevent system-wide financial instability. With so many new policy objectives, the fixed exchange rate system, previously so effective as a domestic anchor, had to be sacrificed.

One conclusion to emerge from Thailand's experience of flexible exchange rates so far is that flexible rates are not necessarily inflationary. An inherent inflationary bias might arise if depreciation raises the prices

Table 8.1 Flexibility in nominal and real wage rates (percentage change from previous six months)

	Manufacturing		Services	
	Nominal	Real	Nominal	Real
August 1997	6.5	1.7	5.8	1.04
February 1998	−0.03	−6.9	−5.4	−9.12
August 1998	6.83	3.28	10	6.34

Source: Calculated from National Statistical Office, *Labour Force Survey*, various issues.

of traded goods while appreciation does not reduce the prices, creating a ratchet effect. The situation in Thailand shows that this is not the case as long as there is flexibility in the labour market. In addition, inflation can occur with both fixed and flexible exchange rates because of excessive monetary expansion.

Since January 1997, Thailand has experienced declining terms of trade. The decline accelerated greatly after July 1997. Both export and import prices declined in dollar terms, the latter falling somewhat less rapidly than the former (Figure 8.4). Consequently, Thailand suffered from a sharp deterioration in its terms of trade – by 10 per cent between July 1997 and April 1998. If devaluation causes the terms of trade to deteriorate, a country can suffer from income loss due to reduced domestic absorption (Laursen and Metzler 1950). The proponents of baht devaluation prior to July 1997 did not anticipate competitive devaluation and abundant excess capacity in other Asian countries, which exerted downward pressure on export prices in dollar terms. As a result, Thailand's export revenue in dollar terms did not rise as anticipated. Imports in dollar terms, however, fell more sharply than exports.

This contraction of imports in dollar terms occurred less because of the rise in import prices in baht terms and more because of output contraction. Since a large part of Thailand's output, especially its exports, requires imported raw materials, it is not surprising that imports fell together with exports. Economic recovery must produce a rise in imports of raw materials. Indeed, a current account surplus is a sign of a weakening economy. Not surprisingly, in 2002, as the Thai economy recovered from the low growth rate of 1.8 per cent in 2001, the current account surplus dwindled.

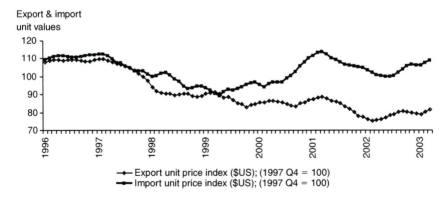

Figure 8.4 Declining terms of trade, 1996 to 2003 (source: Monthly data from Bank of Thailand).

Capital flight and capital controls

A lesson Thailand learned from the crisis is that a fixed exchange rate system and an open capital market are incompatible. In the past, the fixed exchange rate worked as long as a certain degree of capital control ensured monetary autonomy. In 1993, however, capital controls were relaxed with increasing liberalization. As Bhagwati (1998) points out, there is a difference between trade liberalization and capital convertibility. Thailand has come a long way in financial liberalization, flexible exchange rates and capital convertibility.

As Figure 8.5 indicates, private capital inflows began to slow down in the third quarter of 1996, as expectation of currency depreciation gradually grew. Capital flight occurred throughout 1998, after the Bank of Thailand was forced (in the third quarter of 1997) to disclose the true level of its international reserves. As long as expectations of devaluation remained, Thailand would suffer from capital flight, despite the Bank of Thailand's efforts to raise the interest rate. When the solvency of financial institutions became questionable, capital flight intensified. In turn, the impact of capital flight on exchange rate depreciation threatened the stability of the entire banking system, since major borrowers from banks, like the commercial banks themselves, had engaged in unhedged foreign borrowing. As the baht depreciated further, the current account deficit turned into a surplus. No evidence of the J-curve effect appeared, since both imports and exports adjusted rapidly to changes in prices and output. Nevertheless, the current account surpluses that were recorded reflected the weakness, not the strength, of the Thai economy of the time.

The exchange rate itself is determined by trade flows and capital flows, in addition to external factors and exchange rate expectations. Exchange rate movements can be thought of as an indicator of country risks. Politicians must therefore take care lest their actions cause loss of confidence and capital flight, a sharp plunge in the value of the baht indicating

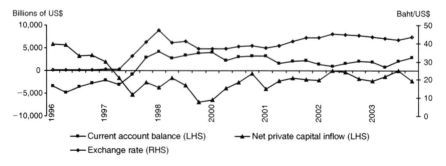

Figure 8.5 Capital flight and exchange rate depreciation, 1996 to 2003 (source: Quarterly data from Bank of Thailand).

government mismanagement. The sharp deterioration of the external value of the baht in the last quarter of 1997, to some extent, reflected the government's loss of credibility during this period of turmoil.

Since capital controls are costly to enforce and can reduce the welfare benefits arising from efficient adjustment of inter-temporal consumption, total capital control is out of the question. Nevertheless, to the extent that excessive short-term capital flows also increase the possibility of financial crisis, such hot money flows should be limited through the establishment of prudential regulations on private sector foreign borrowing.

The flexible exchange rate system also sends a signal to the private sector that borrowers of foreign capital must internalize some of the costs of failing to hedge against unanticipated movements of exchange rates. If the government continues to intervene in the foreign exchange market in order to stabilize the exchange rate, the private sector could become complacent and might never learn to hedge itself against currency risk. Flexibility in foreign exchange rates guarantees that no serious misalignment of the exchange rate occurs, thus reducing the likelihood of capital flight, provided that both good economic fundamentals and political stability prevail.

The recent increasing trend in foreign equity ownership in Thai financial institutions implies that Thai commercial banks are aware, more than ever, of foreign exchange risks. As the incidence of capital flight subsides, the need for strict capital controls is reduced. Prudential capital controls continue to ensure the soundness of financial institutions. As Tobin (2000) suggests, what is needed is a combination of a floating exchange rate, slower foreign capital inflows and greater policy independence. We now turn to discuss the role of stabilizing policies under the flexible exchange rate system.

The adjustment problem

A fixed exchange rate system cannot cope with a constantly changing environment. Shocks can arise from goods markets (through investment and export instability) and money markets (through foreign exchange volatility). Adjustments to external imbalances within a fixed exchange rate system are made through price inflation and deflation. The advantage of the flexible exchange rate in this respect is that it makes it possible to change exchange rates so as to affect prices and wages indirectly rather than having to undergo the pain of booms and busts. A flexible exchange rate system facilitates changes in real exchange rates over time, as required by structural changes.

As in William Poole's analysis of interest rate versus monetary targets, Obstfeld (1985) builds a model to illustrate that if shocks originate from goods markets, that is, the *IS* curve, then output fluctuations will be smaller under the flexible exchange rate regime than under the fixed exchange rate system. On the other hand, if the shocks stem from money markets, that is, the *LM* curve, fixed exchange rates will be more stabilizing than flexible rates.[2] Unless the money markets are unstable, flexible exchange rates provide a better adjustment mechanism against various shocks in the form of external disturbances in the terms of trade, shrinking world trade volume, investment shocks, and so on.

Within a few years of experience under a flexible exchange rate system, it should be apparent whether flexible exchange rates can provide an adequate insulating mechanism. But there is a complication. When a country claims to be floating, it may not actually be doing so, because the central bank is intervening in currency markets. Thailand's international reserves have been climbing back to their pre-crisis level, meaning that the Bank of Thailand has prevented the baht from appreciating. As Calvo and Reinhart (2002) observe, the 'fear of floating' seems to have become epidemic.

What is important now is the ability to deal with shocks originating from money markets. Financial instability, currency speculations and financial innovation can lead to instability in money markets. An extra instrument is needed to deal with *LM* shocks, if flexible exchange rates are to be employed to deal with *IS* shocks such as investment fluctuations and export instability. This is where capital controls can play a role. We cannot expect flexible exchange rates to stabilize both internal and external balances. Monetary and fiscal policies must also be deployed to this end, and their respective strengths must be exploited in order to stabilize the economy under new conditions of capital mobility and exchange rate flexibility.

Monetary policy

If the exchange rate is allowed to adjust to conditions in the balance of payments, and if trade volumes respond to changes in the exchange rate, then monetary policy can play a vital role in stabilizing the economy. During a monetary expansionary, the baht would depreciate, stimulating net exports, which in turn would trigger capital outflows. On the other hand, during a monetary contraction, the baht would appreciate, curbing rising aggregate demand, and this in turn would raise domestic interest rates and induce capital inflows. The resulting balance of payments surplus would appreciate the baht and reduce net exports.

After the abandonment of the fixed rate system, the monetary authorities desperately needed a clear domestic anchor. A large number of countries with flexible exchange rates, for example the United Kingdom, Australia and New Zealand, now employ inflation targets. The case for inflation targeting becomes stronger when the relationship between monetary aggregates and goal variables becomes unstable and inconsistent.

The experience of these countries indicates fluctuations in both the velocity of circulation of broad money and the money multipier of M2. Employing M2 as an intermediate target, given an acceptable level of control error, can lead to prediction error and complicate monetary stabilization programmes.

According to Robert Lucas's critique, the shift to a flexible exchange rate system will lead to changes in private sector behaviour. Some of the close and consistent relationships established under the fixed exchange rate system between monetary aggregates and policy goal variables would be altered. Because of long and variable lags, discretionary monetary policy may prove exceedingly difficult, which is why discretionary monetary policy should be combined with rules to produce an informational approach to monetary policy strategies. Monetary authorities would have to monitor exchange rate movements – not as a monetary target, but as an information variable used in adjusting monetary policy instruments. Thus, the reaction function of monetary policy instruments must include inflation targets, deviations of actual output from potential levels, and exchange rate movements.

To establish an inflation target, the central bank must operate independently (Grenville 1997). An independent central bank can enhance the credibility of an inflation target and thus lower inflationary expectations. The Bank of Thailand adopted inflation targets in 2001, although Parliament had not yet approved the New Central Bank Act that would establish the bank's independence. Bernake (1999) argues that inflation targeting is no panacea, since a trade-off between low inflation and output loss still occurs. In addition, adoption of an inflation target does not bring about instantaneous credibility. The central bank must earn credibility through showing the ability and the will to contain inflation. During this period of debt deflation in the wake of the crisis, inflation targeting is not being put to a stringent test, since inflation is not an issue under conditions of economic downturn and low energy prices.

Fiscal policy

Bond-financing of budget deficits will be ineffective if the crowding-out effect is so strong that it induces capital inflows and currency appreciation. On the other hand, budget deficit spending financed through foreign borrowings and printing money can effectively stimulate the economy during an economic recession. How would fiscal policy effectiveness change under a flexible exchange rate system? According to the Mundell–Fleming model, fiscal policy becomes less effective under a flexible exchange rate system, while monetary policy becomes more powerful. This conclusion is based on the assumption that a country will experience a balance of payments surplus after it implements expansionary fiscal policy and a balance of payments deficit after implementing a monetary easing. The exchange rate appreciation *mitigates* the expansionary effect of the fiscal policy, while depreciation of the exchange rate *enhances* the expansionary effect of the monetary policy.

Despite the Mundell–Fleming argument, under certain circumstances fiscal policy can, in fact, be effective under a flexible exchange rate system. It is not unusual, if the income elasticity of demand for imports is very high, for expansionary fiscal policy to lead to a deficit in the balance of payments; meanwhile, because of high transaction costs, risk premiums and capital controls, the responsiveness of capital flows to interest rate differentials is very low. Exchange rate adjustment after fiscal expansion brings about currency depreciation instead of appreciation, intensifying the multiplier effect of fiscal policy through increased net exports.

During fiscal contraction, output reduction leads to reduced imports, while falling interest rates do not induce the capital outflows needed to offset the reduction in imports. The resulting balance of payments surplus would imply currency appreciation and magnify the output contraction effect of fiscal austerity through reducing net exports. According to this analysis, fiscal policy may not be completely ineffective in Thailand, where the income elasticity of demand for imports is high and capital flows are not very sensitive to changes in interest rate differentials. Viewed in this light, prudential capital control can enhance the effectiveness of fiscal policy, since it can make the exchange rate move according to fiscal policy goals.

Conclusions

Some instability in foreign exchange rates is a natural consequence of the adoption of a flexible exchange rate regime. When Thailand floated the baht from its previous untenable fixed level, the baht–dollar exchange rate experienced overshooting. Various factors contributed to this phenomenon, including speculative bubbles, price stickiness, the rapid strengthening of the dollar against the yen, political instability, and lack of policy credibility. In addition, market participants lacked experience in the new exchange rate system.

Volatility in exchange rates creates risks and uncertainties in trade and investment. There may be compelling reasons for Thailand to intervene in foreign exchange markets, but this may not be politically feasible, since the government must satisfy IMF conditionality by maintaining a minimum level of international reserves. Furthermore, since the exchange rate is an asset price, it tends to change with changing expectations. It is exceedingly difficult to determine appropriate exchange rates using fundamental factors such as PPP or the current account balance. This chapter has argued that the cost of intervention in foreign exchange markets could be too high to warrant it. Intervention should not be employed in order to change the direction of exchange rate movements. There is, however, some room for the creation of an orderly and gradual movement of the exchange rate to reduce the amplitude of swings. But Thailand cannot lean against the wind of volatile changes in the yen–dollar rate.

Flexible exchange rates, just like the fixed exchange rate, can impose discipline on the government. Exchange rate movements trace the anticipated successes or failures of the government's economic management. After the baht float, currency depreciation did stimulate exports as expected. The sudden deterioration of the terms of trade reduced the benefits of baht depreciation. The transformation of the current account deficit into a surplus was the result of import compression caused by output contraction.

Prudential capital controls are required to prevent further financial instability. This is not to deny the benefits of long-term capital inflows, but capital flight can be eliminated only with the establishment of sound macroeconomic fundamentals. A certain degree of capital control is needed to prevent instantaneous and perfect capital mobility and thus enhance the effectiveness of fiscal policy. Under certain circumstances, when imports are highly responsive to changes in absorption and when capital flows do not respond significantly to changes in interest rate differentials, both fiscal and monetary policies can be expected to play an important stabilizing role. In addition, the flexible exchange rate system is expected to insulate the economy from shocks originating in the goods market. But it is asking too much to expect it to cushion instability originating from money markets hit by crises of confidence in the financial system.

Thailand's adoption of the flexible exchange rate system makes it necessary for the monetary authorities to establish a new monetary strategy to deal with the constantly changing behaviour of the private sector. Inflation targeting, a move independent central bank, adoption of an informational variable approach to monetary strategy, and implementation of prudential capital controls, are preconditions for the success of stabilizing policies adopted in response to a rapidly changing international environment.

Notes

1 By October 2002, total international reserves had risen to $37 billion – $2 billion short of the July 1997 pre-crisis level (excluding forward liabilities).
2 For a textbook exposition of the use of IS and LM curves in macroeconomic analysis, see, for example, Ethier (1995: 516–20).

References

Bank of Thailand (1996) Thailand's inflation: developments and issues, *The Bank of Thailand Economic Focus*, 1, pp. 1–22.

Bernake, Ben S. (1999) *Inflation Targeting*, New Jersey: Princeton University Press.

Bhagwati, Jagdish (1998) The capital myth, *Foreign Affairs*, 77, pp. 7–12.

Bilson, John (1985) Macroeconomic stability and flexible exchange rates, *American Economic Review*, 79, pp. 62–7.

Calvo, Guillermo A. and Reinhart, Carmen M. (2002) Fear of floating, *The Quarterly Journal of Economics*, May, pp. 379–408.

Dornbusch, Rudiger (1976) Expectations and exchange rate dynamics, *Journal of Political Economy*, 84, pp. 1161–76.

Dominguez, Kathryn M. and Frankel, Jeffrey A. (1993) *Does Foreign Exchange Intervention Work*, Washington, DC: Institute for International Economics.

Ethier, W.J. (1995) *Modern International Economics*, 3rd edn, New York: W.W. Norton & Co.

Frankel, Jeffrey and Froot, Kenneth (1990) Chartists, fundamentalists, and the demand for dollars, in: A.S. Courakis and M.P. Taylor (eds) *Private Behavior and Government Policy in Interdependent Economies*, Oxford: Clarendon Press.

Grenville, Stephen (1997) The evolution of monetary policy: from money targets to inflation targets, in: Reserve Bank of Australia, *Monetary Policy and Inflation Targeting*, Canberra: Reserve Bank of Australia.

Gruen, David, Gray, Brian and Stevens, Glenn (1998) A tale of two crises: Australia's experience in the 1980s and 1990s, in: R. Garnaut and R. McLeod (eds) *East Asia in Crisis*, London: Routledge.

Hau, Harald (2002) Real exchange rate volatility and economic openness: theory and evidence, *Journal of Money, Credit and Banking*, 34, pp. 611–30.

Krugman, Paul (1929) The case for stabilizing exchange rates, *Oxford Review of Economic Policy*, 5, pp. 61–72.

Laursen, Sven and Metzler, Lloyd A. (1950) Flexible exchange rates and the theory of employment, *Review of Economics and Statistics*, November, pp. 281–99.

Mikesell, Raymond (2001) Dual exchange markets for countries facing financial crises, *World Development*, 29, pp. 1035–41.

Obstfeld, Maurice (1985) Floating exchange rates: experience and prospects, *Brooking Papers on Economic Activity*, 2, pp. 369–450.

Obstfeld, Maurice (1998) The global capital market: benefactor or menace?, *Journal of Economic Perspectives*, 12, pp. 9–30.

Obstfeld, Maurice and Rogoff, Kenneth (1995) The mirage of fixed exchange rates, *Journal of Economic Perspectives*, 9, pp. 73–96.

Tobin, James (2000) Financial globalization, *World Development*, 28, pp. 1101–4.

Warr, Peter G. (1999) What happened to Thailand?, *The World Economy*, 22, pp. 631–50.

Part IV

The long term: human capital, urbanization and the environment

Chapter 9

Education
The key to long-term recovery?

Sirilaksana Khoman

The crisis of 1997 resulted in a series of emergency measures, restructuring plans and stimulus packages, combined with sectoral reform proposals aimed at redressing past inefficiencies. In the education sector, the reform movement is the most comprehensive and far-reaching in Thailand's recent history. Problems relating to equity, quality and financing had long been recognized as plaguing the education system. Until recently, however, policy proposals had been confined to specific issues, and reform had been perfunctory at best. The ambitious National Education Bill, drafted at the height of the economic boom, embodied much of what reformers had in mind for decades. It exemplified a shift in philosophical underpinning that could translate into a major overhaul of the education system.

The Bill became law in 1999, when the country was hardest hit by the crisis, and managing resources in the midst of austerity was an unforeseen challenge. The lingering economic crisis compounds the urgency of reform, and indeed, an overhaul of the education system may be vital for long-term recovery. But uncertainties abound and many obstacles loom ahead, with the potential to obstruct and deflect the reform movement into wrong directions.

This chapter examines the education sector as a potential key to long-term recovery. The main problems in the education sector are discussed in the following section and the impact of the crisis is then briefly reviewed. The next section outlines the salient features of the reform movement embodied in the National Education Act. Potential pitfalls are discussed and conclusions are presented in the final section.

Main problems in the education sector

Even before the crisis, the pursuit of growth over the preceding three decades had raised questions about the ability of the economy to sustain past performance, to distribute the gains of development more equitably, to reverse environmental degradation, and to enhance overall social well-being. Pockets of poverty remained in spite of double-digit growth. The decrepit political system made it clear that a well-working system of representative government would require the kind of well-informed voting public that is difficult to create out of a high-growth, but economically polarized, society.

Within the education sector itself, four interrelated concerns can be identified: low secondary enrolment; inadequate quality of education; lack of equity in access to education and inappropriate subsidy.

Low secondary enrolment

International comparisons of enrolment ratios, educational attainments, and sectoral employment show that Thailand's situation is incongruous with the pattern seen in other countries. More than 60 per cent of the Thai labour force is still in the agricultural sector, as opposed to 40 per cent in the Philippines and 55 per cent for the Republic of Korea as early as 1965. Even though educational opportunities have increased, the overall structure of educational attainment has not changed significantly. Out of the total labour force, as many as 70 per cent still have primary education or less, compared with 49 and 44 per cent for the Republic of Korea and Taiwan even ten years earlier (Table 9.1). Current trends also indicate that about 65 per cent of the total labour force will still not be educated beyond the primary level in the next five years.

Even in the mid-1990s, almost half of the children who completed primary school did not go on to receive secondary education. Thailand's secondary enrolment ratio was one of the lowest of all the ASEAN countries, and far below that of the Republic of Korea (Table 9.2).

The problematic low rate of continuation to the secondary level has

Table 9.1 Proportion of workforce with primary education or less: selected countries

	Per cent of workforce
Thailand (1991, 1998)	73.9, 72.0
Republic of Korea (1980)	49.1
Taiwan (1980)	44.0
Singapore (1980)	62.7
China (1982)	71.3
Malaysia (1980)	58.4
Philippines (1980)	56.5

Sources: For Thailand, National Statistical Office, Labour Force Survey, 1991 and 1998, and National Economic and Social Development Board (1996). For other countries, Psacharapoulos and Arriagada (1986), cited in Pernia (1990).

Note:
Earlier data are cited for comparative purposes.

Table 9.2 Gross enrolment ratios: selected Asian countries

	Primary	Secondary	Tertiary
Thailand (1996)	86.9	56.4	22.1
Republic of Korea (1996)	94.0	102.0	60.4
Singapore (1996)	94.3	74.1	38.5
Hong Kong (1995)	94.0	73.0	21.8
Indonesia (1996)	112.7	55.7	11.3
Malaysia (1995)	103.4	58.7	11.7
Philippines (1995)	114.1	77.5	29.0
Vietnam (1996)	115.0	52.0	6.9
Brunei (1995)	108.0	80.2	6.6

Source: UNESCO (1999).

long been seen as one of the most important impediments to economic and social development (Sirilaksana 1993). Because of education's lagged effects, past enrolment numbers are significant. The enrolment ratios for lower and upper secondary education in 1986 were estimated by the National Education Council[1] to be as low as 41 per cent of those aged 14–16 and 28 per cent of those aged 17–18. This ratio was the lowest among all comparable middle-income countries, and shows that more than half of Thai children in the age group 14–18 were out of school. In addition, while the percentage of students continuing to the next grade has always been fairly high (85–98 per cent) in the primary grades, the percentage of those continuing on to secondary school after completion of the final primary grade dropped dramatically to not more than 40–50 per cent, during the last two decades.

Nevertheless, there are some signs of improvement. At least prior to the crisis, the lower secondary enrolment ratio had shown a steady increase, and registered close to 72 per cent in 1996. Estimates for 2001 show that this number has risen to more than 82 per cent (Table 9.3)

In addition, the crude transition rates for continuing to the next grade, presented in Table 9.4, show that significant improvements had been made. Even within a period of one year, transition rates from primary to the first secondary grade increased from 62 to 68 per cent between 1995 and 1996, the most dramatic increases occurring in public schools.[2] Thus was the situation before the crisis.

The improvement in the transition rate can be attributed to various measures undertaken to reduce the cost of school attendance, particularly in the provincial areas. These measures included free schooling, school lunches, free uniforms and textbooks, and the addition of secondary grades to several existing rural primary schools with excess classroom and teacher capacity, thus increasing the geographic accessibility of secondary schools to the rural population.

Table 9.3 Gross enrolment ratios by level of education, 1994, 1996 and 2001

Level of education	Age group	1994		1996		2001[a]
		(a)	(b)	(a)	(b)	
Pre-primary	3–5	64.60		78.36		96.00
Primary	6–11	98.97	94.03	95.14	90.01	103.70
Secondary	12–17	75.50	48.53	89.44	56.88	70.90
Lower secondary	12–14	101.90	63.45	110.90	71.50	82.80
Upper secondary	15–17	49.30	33.77	68.31	42.51	59.20
Academic	15–17	33.79	18.25	49.18	23.40	38.70
Vocational	15–17	15.51	15.51	19.13	19.10	20.50
Tertiary	18–21	24.95	13.24	29.29	16.79	25.00
Total	3–21	78.73	57.49	88.88	61.57	74.40

Sources: Population statistics from National Economic and Social Development Board, quoted in Office of National Education Commission (1997, Table 2); student population figures from the same source, Table 1.

Notes:
Student numbers in (b) exclude the following at the relevant level: non-formal education, monks, students in open universities, and graduate students.
a Estimates recalculated from Amornvich (2002: 21).

Table 9.4 Crude transition rates of students continuing to next grade in general education, by type of school and level of education, 1995 and 1996

Level of education	1995			1996		
	Total	Public	Private	Total	Public	Private
Primary						
Primary 1	—	—	—	—	—	—
Primary 2	89.6	90.5	83.1	86.7	86.8	85.4
Primary 3	98.6	98.7	98.0	92.3	91.6	98.6
Primary 4	99.3	99.3	99.2	92.2	91.4	99.6
Primary 5	99.0	99.1	98.1	93.9	92.9	98.2
Primary 6	97.0	96.8	98.8	90.1	89.2	99.0
Lower secondary						
Secondary 1	61.6	62.3	54.9	68.0	69.4	54.2
Secondary 2	97.1	97.2	96.1	97.0	97.0	97.7
Secondary 3	97.4	97.3	98.0	97.4	97.3	98.3
Upper secondary						
Secondary 4	44.7	47.6	23.3	46.7	49.6	23.6
Secondary 5	90.4	90.6	87.4	91.2	91.4	88.3
Secondary 6	90.0	90.6	81.9	90.3	90.8	83.1

Source: Office of the National Education Commission, Education Statistics, 1996.

Higher incomes during the boom years also played a role. Continuation rates had always been found to be lower among children from socially and economically disadvantaged backgrounds. In 1988, about 88 per cent of the youths aged 12–14 were still in school in the urban areas, whereas the corresponding figure for rural youths in the same age group was a mere 68 per cent (National Statistical Office 1988). Economic growth helped raise the corresponding figures to 92 per cent and 75 per cent respectively by 1991 (National Statistical Office 1993).

However, some of this improvement is more apparent than real, and part of it was due to the changing demographic situation. Low secondary enrolment is common where there is rapid expansion of primary enrolment, and transition rates tend to increase at lower levels first, as schooling becomes more universal. With the expansion of primary education diminishing due to successful family planning in the 1980s, the pressure on places in secondary schools had been eased. Moreover, the crude transition ratio merely reflects the ratio of the number of students in the next grade, compared with the students in the preceding grade, and thus may reflect the changing demographics and/or new recruits from those who had previously left school, and not continuation from the preceding grade.

Table 9.5 presents what is called the crude completion (or survival) rate. This compares the number of students completing a given level with the number that entered that level, and is an estimate of a cohort rate. There are mixed signals. At the primary level, a completion rate of around 70 per cent can be considered low. This is particularly alarming when comparison is made with the 1993 rate of more than 81 per cent. It is also

Table 9.5 Crude completion (survival) and continuation rates, by level, 1993 and 1996 to 1998

Level	Academic year			
	1993	1996	1997	1998
Primary (P.6/P1)	81.40	69.40	72.50	73.20
Secondary (P6/S1)	41.00	90.06[a]	91.22[a]	88.30[a]
Lower secondary (S.3/S.1)	94.60	93.28	92.62	91.85
Upper secondary	n.a.	81.21	80.92	79.84
Academic (S.6/S.4)	81.70	81.35	82.67	83.09
Vocational (V.3/V.1)	n.a.	81.04	78.82	75.94

Sources: 1996–98 data from ONEC (2003), tables 15, 17, and 18; 1993 data from Ministry of Education (MOE), Education Statistics.
a From Office of the National Education Commission (2003, Table 13).

Note:
Primary grades run from Primary 1 (P.1) to Primary 6 (P.6);
lower secondary runs from Secondary 1 (S.1) to Secondary 3 (S.3);
upper secondary (academic) runs from S.4 to S.6;
upper secondary (vocational) runs from V.1 to V.3.

puzzling, since the drop occurred even before the crisis. Data problems may be at work here.

The secondary completion rate appears to be better, and a vast improvement over the 1993 rate.[3] The continuation rate from Primary 6 to Secondary 1 is also presented in Table 9.5. This had improved dramatically, from around 40 per cent in 1993 to over 90 per cent in 1996 and 1997, but fell off to 88 per cent when the crunch of the crisis was felt in 1998.

Table 9.6 provides a more dismal insight into the path taken by school entrants. It shows the crude survival rate for the cohort starting school in 1990. It can be seen that only about 42 per cent managed to survive and complete upper secondary education in 2001.

The problem of attrition and survival translates into low educational attainment among Thailand's youth. In the years leading up to the crisis, the Children and Youth Survey (National Statistical Office 1993) showed the consistent pattern that, among children and youth aged 6–24 not attending school, the majority (64 per cent) had primary education or less. Among the 15–19 year-olds not in school, as many as 79 per cent did not go beyond primary school, and 58 per cent of the 20–24 year-olds were in the same educational category. Among the 12–14 year-olds, a staggering 86 per cent of those out of school left school after completing primary education (Table 9.7). An overwhelming number of children and

Table 9.6 Crude survival rates, estimate of cohort of 1990 completing upper secondary in the year 2001

Grade	Year	Number of students	Survival rate
Primary			
P.1	1990	1,228,403	100.00
P.2	1991	1,131,096	92.08
P.3	1992	1,127,796	91.81
P.4	1993	1,083,823	88.23
P.5	1994	1,056,486	86.00
P.6	1995	982,818	80.01
Lower secondary			
S.1	1996	853,135	69.45
S.2	1997	818,178	66.61
S.3	1998	783,878	63.81
Upper secondary/vocational			
S.4/V.1	1999	634,261	51.63
S.5/V.2	2000	563,815	45.90
S.6/V.3	2001	526,420	42.85

Source: Office of the National Education Commission (2003: Table 5).

Note:
See notes to Table 9.5.

Table 9.7 Distribution of children and youth aged 6–24 not in school, by educational attainment, age, and residence, 1992

Age group	Total	No education	Less than primary	Primary	Lower secondary	Upper secondary	Upper secondary: vocational	Tertiary	Other and unknown
6–11	100.0 (773.5)	88.5	10.8	0.2	–	–	–	–	0.5
12–14	100.0 (696.5)	5.0	8.2	86.1	0.4	–	–	–	0.3
15–19	100.0 (4,075.8)	2.0	8.1	79.1	9.0	1.1	0.5	0.1	0.1
20–4	100.0 (5,636.1)	2.2	15.1	58.2	10.9	6.2	3.4	3.5	0.5
Urban	100.0 (1,310.2)	6.5	9.0	42.5	19.4	7.6	7.0	7.8	0.2
Rural	100.0 (1,310.2)	8.6	12.2	66.3	7.4	3.0	1.2	1.0	0.3
Whole Kingdom	100.0 (11,182.1)	8.3	11.8	63.6	8.8	3.5	1.9	1.8	0.3

Source: National Statistical Office, Children and Youth Survey (1993).

Note:
Numbers in parentheses are numbers of children and youths, in thousands.

Table 9.8 Distribution of the labour force by level and type of education, 2001

Level	Round 1		Round 2		Round 3	
	Urban	Rural	Urban	Rural	Urban	Rural
None	2.2	4.3	2.1	4.2	2.1	4.1
<Primary	27.4	46.5	27.4	45.7	27.6	46.4
Primary	17.1	24.6	17.5	24.7	17.0	25.1
Lower sec.	15.9	10.9	15.3	11.6	15.1	11.6
Upper sec.	14.4	7.3	14.8	7.7	14.5	7.1
Academic	8.5	5.2	8.7	5.6	8.2	5.2
Vocational	5.8	2.0	6.0	2.1	6.1	1.8
Education	0.1	0.1	0.1	0.0	0.1	0.1
Tertiary	22.8	6.3	22.4	5.9	23.2	5.6
Academic	12.7	2.1	12.5	1.9	13.0	1.9
Vocational	6.3	2.3	6.2	2.2	6.3	2.2
Education	3.8	1.9	3.7	1.8	3.9	1.6
Other	0.1	0.0	0.1	0.0	0.1	0.0
Unknown	0.3	0.0	0.6	0.1	0.6	0.1
All levels	100.0	100.0	100.0	100.0	100.0	100.0

Source: National Statistical Office, Labour Force Survey, 2001.

Note:
Urban = municipal areas, rural = non-municipal areas.

youth can still be expected to attain only primary education, so that even though transition rates are now improving, the impact on the overall educational attainment of the population will be not be felt until way into the future.

The *Labour Force Surveys* of 2001 still indicated that, in the rural areas, around 75 per cent of the labour force still have primary education or less. The corresponding figure is 46 per cent in the municipal areas (Table 9.8). Increased secondary enrolment will have a perceptible effect on the economy only after a long lag. For example, even if 100 per cent continuation had been achieved in 1996, the proportion of the workforce with primary education or less would still have been no greater than 70 per cent by 2010.

Quality of education

In spite of three decades of rapid expansion of education, quality remains a key concern. Even though innovative methods of learning, such as distance learning, student-centred rather than teacher-centred learning, as well as work apprenticeships, have been experimented with, and mass education through satellite relays initiated, these are exceptions rather than the rule. In addition, these are mere techniques that may not translate into inspired curricula or learning processes. Rote learning is pervasive even in the best schools, and innovative forms of learning are confined only to small segments. Vocational schools lack equipment and teachers lack motivation. Moreover, the improper targeting of beneficiaries has led to problems of regional disparity, inequality of access, and inefficient resource use.

The initial path of import substitution required little upgrading of the skills and capabilities of the general workforce. Industrial promotion favoured the use of imported capital, and the indigenous labour utilized was mainly unskilled. The reversal of policy in the 1970s towards export promotion further depended on the country's vast supply of low-cost labour, largely with low education.

The need to equip the workforce with upgraded skills as well as capability in science and technology had hitherto not been felt. It was not on the political agenda because, for that to occur, a plaintiff is required; unlike unemployment or inflation, where people are directly affected and votes can be linked to policy success, problems with the quality of education produces no obvious victims.

Today, as Thailand struggles to recover, the ability of the labour force to adapt to rapidly changing skill requirements has become ever more crucial as technologically sophisticated sectors become more prominent. As production technology becomes more complex and as employment shifts increasingly out of agriculture and into industry, emphasis on quality education is crucial.

The alternative path of greater self-reliance also requires a re-education and re-discovery of indigenous potential and traditional knowledge, again an uncharted path with unknown probabilities of success. The link between traditional knowledge and augmented welfare and efficiency is unclear. Moreover, the educational institutions are, in general, ill-equipped to deal with the nation's manpower needs, whether along the traditional path, or the mainstream course. Constraints are felt both in terms of resources to deal with the immediate problems of reviving the economy, and to keep up with advances in knowledge and maintenance of facilities and retaining quality staff. In terms of immediate manpower requirements, the education infrastructure is inadequate to deal with the demands that restructuring and reform impose.

In terms of long-run educational infrastructure, the high cost of operating and keeping up with new technologies (new equipment, materials, and so on) and the much higher salaries for selected personnel in private industry that attracted away qualified staff in the past decade, added to the difficulty of educational institutions in producing adequate manpower supplies, especially in science and technology. Inadequate research and development activity limits the nation's access to discoveries, technology and innovations developed elsewhere in the world. This constrains the country's ability to adapt technologies, to draw upon and assimilate the world's scientific and technological resources, to support new productive activities, upgrade existing techniques, and accumulate the kind of knowledge that leads to sustained increases in productivity and international competitiveness. Such capability is essential for the process of drawing upon indigenous skills and knowledge and using local materials, processes, and know-how.

The questionable quality of education and the low continuation to secondary school are a major hindrance of the first step towards production of a skilled and adaptable labour force, not to mention the creation of scientific, engineering and technical manpower to enhance technological capability. In addition, strategies for *human* development through education will be ineffective unless society itself rewards creativity, social responsibility, and ethical behaviour. These may be difficult to define, but clear examples abound in every society. In a society where unethical behaviour is tolerated, or even condoned and rewarded, no amount of drilling in schools will convince young people to behave otherwise, except by chance.

The aftermath of the crisis clearly brings out five underlying weaknesses that contribute to 'bad governance': (i) the lack of a clear division between public and private matters, such that the tendency to use public resources for private gain is not counteracted; (ii) the failure to set up a clear legal framework whereby government action can be predicted to prevent arbitrary behaviour; (iii) regulatory frameworks that make rent-seeking behaviour pervasive; (iv) priorities in development that encourage inefficiency in resource use; (v) non-transparent decision-making processes. These weaknesses point to the fact that the quality of human resources and social institutions to deal with transmitted disturbances from the world economy has been inadequate.

Access to education

Inequity of access to education is clearly evident. The various *Surveys of Children and Youth* conducted by the National Statistical Office have invariably found that students in urban areas tend to leave school at a higher age than rural students. In 1993, in rural areas, the majority of children not in school (71 per cent) left at age 12–14, whereas in urban areas only 43 per cent left school at that age (National Statistical Office 1993).[4]

Financial difficulties are usually cited as the major reason for leaving. Indeed, the cost of education imposes a disproportionate burden on the poor relative to their incomes. The total time and money cost to a village household of sending a child to a public lower secondary school in town can amount to an increase of almost four times the cost of his/her primary education. If the child fails to get admitted into a public school, which normally selects students by means of a competitive entrance examination, the cost of going to a private school would amount to more than half of their total annual income. Because of the sequential nature of the curriculum, if it is perceived that only completion of the higher level would make the lower level worthwhile, there would be no incentive to go to the lower level if the total financial burden of completing the curriculum up to the highest level is prohibitive. Thus, low participation rates are mainly confined to the most disadvantaged groups: low income, rural households. And the problem is transmitted vertically along the education ladder, since several screening examinations have to be passed.

Table 9.7 above also shows that among urban youth not in school, 42 per cent had attained secondary education and above. The corresponding figure for rural youth was only 14 per cent. This of course reflects the urban–rural differential in terms of availability of jobs requiring different qualifications, but also indicates the disadvantages of the rural population.

The question of quality can be seen as a question of equity and access as well. Large divergences in quality exist between schools in terms of input measures such as availability of textbooks, instructional materials, laboratory equipment, computer usage and teacher qualifications. Access to better-quality schools tends to be based on region of residence and socio-economic status. The marked differences in quality penalize the children in rural schools, unless these families incur substantial additional costs to attend the better-quality urban schools right from the primary level.

Among the reasons why the least-advantaged groups invest less in the education of their children are market conditions, which work against the poor, and perhaps also the limitations on employment opportunities imposed by societal stratification and entrenched networks of information and contacts. Only in the formal labour market, particularly in the public sector and the larger private firms, are there clear returns to education. Thus, if the prospect of gaining employment in the formal sector is believed to be low, many of the poor rural families would opt for no schooling beyond the primary level because of the high cost and low perceived returns.

This situation compounds the problem of inequity since low education begets low incomes. The inter-generational perpetuation of inequality is likely to accelerate as production technology becomes increasingly more complex. In the process, the demand for educated workers would increase and their wages would be driven upward relative to those with less education. The crisis may have reversed this trend somewhat, according to Jaroenjit (1999).

Various studies also show that having a large number of siblings also depresses the chances of a child continuing on to secondary school. This finding brings out the link between fertility and the demand for education.

High fertility tends to be associated with low-income rural households, and the link to low educational attainment can thus be seen as a segment of the well-known vicious circle.

In addition, even when remaining in school and when educational opportunities are present, children from poor families do not perform as well as other children. High birth-order has been found to have an independent negative effect on school performance and, possibly, the ability to learn. Sirilaksana (1986) found that the main causes of drop-out and repetition of grades were poverty, malnutrition, illness and absenteeism. This situation exacerbates the problems of unequal access, low continuation rates, and low income among rural households.

On the supply side, the uneven geographic distribution of schools has been one of the main causes of non-continuation and thus low secondary enrolment among the disadvantaged groups. Out of the total number of private secondary schools in the country, almost half were located in Bangkok, and none in the villages (Ministry of Education 2000). In the case of municipal schools, enrolment in Bangkok alone was almost equal to total enrolment for the rest of the country. All public kindergarten schools are located in urban areas, not to mention the heavy urban concentration of private kindergartens and schools. Plans to remedy the situation have been made, and distance learning should ease the problem in the future. Education and technology need to go hand in hand; where shortages of qualified teachers occur, distance-education through satellite relays can now be used.

The overall pattern of employment indicates that workers with mere primary education are more than proportionately found in segments of the economy that are less prosperous and less progressive. In particular, agriculture has been, and still is, the main employer of those with primary education and it is the sector with by far the lowest value added per head. The large differential between the share of employment in agriculture and the share of agriculture in GDP indicates a high degree of income inequality between agriculture and non-agriculture. To the extent that income determines the accessibility of education, especially beyond the primary level, this would lead to lower enrolment at the secondary level among agricultural households. In fact, analysis of the 1994 and 1996 Socio-economic Survey data reveals that this is the case. Income gaps between agricultural households and non-agricultural households have been widening since the mid-1970s. Thus, the income gap between those with primary education and those with more education has also been widening.

Because the relative position of those with primary education is deteriorating vis-à-vis the better-educated groups, differential participation in the educational system is an important cause of income inequality and of its perpetuation over time.

Inappropriate subsidy

The direct cost of many kinds of public education is borne almost entirely by the government. Fees charged, as a percentage of costs, range from 2 to 22 per cent for secondary schools, from 4 to 37 per cent in vocational education, from 30 to 42 per cent in teacher training, and from 7–14 per cent in public closed universities (Sirilaksana 1997). Consequently, calculations of the rate of return on investment in education invariably show private rates of return exceeding social rates at all levels.

Until the early 1990s, tuition fees at the tertiary level amounted, on average, to only 3.5 per cent of the annual family income of university students (National Education Council 1991). In addition, it appears that higher levels of subsidy tended to be received by higher-income students (Thailand Development Research Institute 1998). University students in general come from higher-income families, whose average income is more than 70 per cent higher than for primary and 15 per cent higher than lower secondary.

Pricing is intimately linked to how services are financed and thereby involves broader concerns regarding the total quantity of resources devoted to education, the amount that should be spent by the government, and how much burden non-government sources should bear. Low-cost recovery means that the burden is passed on to non-users through reliance on general tax revenues. Stark differentials between costs and fees also lead to misleading signals to both provider and user. Low fees lead to excess demand, and non-price methods are usually resorted to as an allocative device instead of the price mechanism. Users begin to seek preferential access to services through personal connections, position and clout, leading to greater inequity. In addition, the quality of the services tends to be driven down due to the lack of resources.

Low fees and charges are supposed to help the disadvantaged groups. However, as we have seen, the clearly disadvantaged groups are most likely to be unable to gain access even to secondary education. On the other hand, low fees in the (heavily subsidized) public schools and the control on fees of private schools prevents both school expansion and quality improvements, as well as quality-enhancing competition. The highest fees charged by the public schools have been less than 20 per cent of the maximum fees allowable at the corresponding levels in the private schools. Such controls have limited the ability of the private sector to expand. Thus, the easing of controls on private initiative and the infusion of private-sector discipline into public schools and universities that has already begun should not only enhance quality, but should serve equity and efficiency goals as well.

Table 9.9 also shows that the per capita expenditure for primary education is over 10 per cent higher than for secondary education. A comparison with a country such as Malaysia shows that the expenditure on secondary

Table 9.9 Education expenditure per capita by level, 1996 (baht per year)

Education level	Expenditure per capita
Pre-primary	7,024
Primary	9,057
Secondary	8,086
Tertiary	
Diploma	29,752
Degree	47,152

Source: Office of the National Education Commission (1997), *Finance Study: Education in Thailand*, Bangkok.

education per pupil in Malaysia is about 1.6 times that for primary education (Cresswell 1999). The per capita expenditure for degree-level education in Thailand is almost six times that for secondary education. Even though tertiary education is more costly and joint products such as research and other academic outputs are produced, this pattern still contrasts with what is found in other countries.

Ratios for selected developed countries in Table 9.10 show a markedly different pattern, per capita expenditure on higher education being less than three times the expenditure on secondary education. For Malaysia, the ratio of higher education to secondary education expenditures per head was approximately 2.5 to 1 in 1995 (Cresswell 1999). The huge expenditures on higher education in Thailand may reflect a catching-up phenomenon, but the point is the low contribution of fees to total cost and the extent of subsidy that is received by higher-income groups.

Table 9.10 Ratio of higher-to-secondary-education expenditures per pupil, OECD countries, 1998

	Annual expenditure per student (US$)			
	Primary	Secondary	Higher	Ratio of higher to secondary
Australia	3,981	5,830	11,539	1.98
Japan	5,075	5,890	9,871	1.68
Korea	2,838	3,544	6,356	1.79
New Zealand	2,570	4,290	8,020	1.87
United Kingdom	3,329	5,230	9,699	1.85
United States	6,043	7,764	19,802	2.55
Mean	3,973	5,425	10,881	2.55

Source: OECD, *Education at a Glance-OECD Indicators*, 2001.

Note:
Data for New Zealand are for 1997.

In terms of the benefits received from government expenditure, the Thailand Development Research Institute (1998) estimates that the opportunity to benefit from government expenditure on education varies significantly with respect to income, occupation, region and the poverty status of households. Table 9.11 shows that higher-income households

Table 9.11 Distribution of benefits from government expenditure on education, 1994

Household groups	Distribution of benefits (millions of baht)	Per cent distribution
By income		
Poorest 10%	8,912.6	7.6
Next 10%	9,209.8	7.9
Next 10%	9,346.2	8.0
Next 10%	8,937.8	7.7
Next 10%	8,925.2	7.7
Next 10%	9,566.7	8.2
Next 10%	10,223.0	8.8
Next 10%	12,235.8	10.5
Next 10%	16,514.6	14.2
Richest 10%	22,838.4	19.6
Total	116,710.1	100.0
By occupation		
Farmers	32,456.2	27.8
Landholding <10 rai	5,626.2	4.8
Landholding 10+ rai	17,864.8	15.3
Tenants	3,845.1	3.3
Hired workers	5,120.1	4.4
Employer	11,415.0	9.8
Self-employed	23,491.0	20.1
Private professional	10,863.0	9.3
Private employee	8,048.3	6.9
Government professional	14,612.4	12.5
Government employee	1,195.3	1.0
Unemployed/retired	14,628.9	12.5
Total	116,710.1	100.0
By region		
North	18,185.9	15.6
Northeast	33,991.7	29.1
Central	19,703.1	16.9
South	16,403.0	14.1
Bangkok	28,426.5	24.4
Total	116,710.1	100.0
By poverty index		
Below poverty line	16,121.3	13.8
Above poverty line	100,588.8	86.2
Total	116,710.1	100.0

Source: Thailand Development Research Institute (1998: Table 12.9).

stand to benefit from government expenditure more than medium-to-low income households. This is basically because of the differences in opportunity to gain access to the educational services, particularly at the higher education level, which receives the largest per capita outlay.

In terms of occupational breakdown, Table 9.11 shows that farmers and agricultural households receive greater benefits from government expenditure than households in other occupations. This is mainly because of the larger number of school-aged children present in the households engaged in agricultural activities. The regional breakdown in Table 9.11 also shows that households in the Northeast are the largest beneficiaries of government educational expenditures, but Bangkok households closely follow. Moreover, when the poverty line is used to classify households into those above and below this line, actual expenditures that are likely to benefit the poor fall well below the expenditures that are likely to benefit the non-poor.

Crisis impacts and responses

The economic crisis had a threefold impact on the education sector: (i) it placed strains on government resources, reducing the amount available for direct support of education; (ii) it impacted individual and household incomes, reducing the ability to bear the costs of education; and, consequently, (iii) it affected school finances, resulting in shifts in enrolment. The effect on the government budget and on the household is examined here.

Government budget for education

Government expenditure on education comprises about one-fifth of the national budget, which is larger than other major sectors of activity by a substantial margin. This budget has also increased as a percentage of GDP, as Table 9.12 illustrates. Budgetary allocations made possible the rapid increases in school enrolments at all levels in the past. In the first decade of planned development (1960–70), enrolments doubled at the lower secondary level and tripled at the upper secondary level, with secondary enrolment as a whole growing at an annual rate of 12 per cent. Pre-crisis enrolment in compulsory education (nine years) reached 98 per cent in 1996 (National Economic and Social Development Board 1996).

In 1993, enrolment in public institutions as a proportion of total enrolment was 84 per cent. More recently, however, attempts have been made to accommodate greater private sector participation, especially in areas where external benefits are not perceived to be significant. In pre-primary education, the government share is currently only about 58 per cent, and

Table 9.12 Government expenditure on education, as a percentage of the government budget, and as a percentage of GDP, 1989 to 2001

Year	Education budget as percentage of government budget	Education budget as percentage of GDP
1989	16.6	2.6
1990	17.9	2.7
1991	19.3	3.0
1992	18.6	3.0
1993	19.3	3.4
1994	19.5	3.5
1995	19.2	3.4
1996	20.3	3.7
1997	21.9	3.9
1998	24.9	3.9
1999	25.3	4.0
2000	25.7	4.5
2001	25.5	4.4

Sources: Office of Prime Minister, *Government Budget*, various years, GDP figures from Bank of Thailand.

at the undergraduate level its share, excluding the open universities, has dropped from 75 to 69 per cent during the last decade. Private participation in vocational training, in particular, had increased so significantly that the public sector share dropped from 90 per cent in 1979 to only 53 per cent in 1993.

With respect to non-formal education, the government operates a wide spectrum of programmes, ranging from functional literacy groups, mobile technical-training units, seminars, radio programmes, correspondence courses, and reading corners. These services are likely to have contributed to the advances in literacy achieved over the years, catering to those missing out on formal opportunities of learning. Consequently, literacy rates in Thailand are among the highest in the region, particularly for females.

In the post-crisis environment, the government is attempting to maintain, and even augment, budget allocations for education, as Table 9.12 demonstrates. Appropriations for education increased, in the midst of the crisis, to 24.93 and 25.29 per cent of the budget in 1998 and 1999, respectively, and have since been sustained at these levels. Key education programmes were largely unaffected.

Immediately following the crisis, the reductions in some areas, such as personnel development and education standards, were very large while other areas remained virtually intact (Table 9.13). There was an effort to protect core programmes and maintain direct school services (noticeably

Table 9.13 Response to crisis: adjustments to education budget, 1998

Project/department	Reduction (%)
1 School lunch programme	2.7
2 General administration	15.7
3 Pre-compulsory education	7.0
4 Primary education	7.7
5 Equal opportunity in education	9.6
6 Supervision and monitoring	0.9
7 Education evaluation	11.8
8 Education standards	27.0
9 School health	1.6
10 Education research and development	20.8
11 Personnel development	66.7
12 Teaching development	22.0
13 Pre-compulsory education (Bangkok Metropolitan Area, BMA)	0.9
14 Primary education (BMA)	1.8
15 Equal opportunity (BMA)	25.1
16 Primary education, Central office	6.0
17 Compulsory education (Local Administration, LA)	0.6
18 Primary administration (LA)	0.9
19 Equal opportunity in education (LA)	22.3
20 Teaching training and seminar (LA)	20.7
21 Child development (Dept. of Community Development)	10.6
Total basic education budget reduction	7.8

Source: Bureau of the budget.

the school lunch, school health and primary education programmes), at the expense of indirect or more discretionary areas, in order to minimize the impact on basic services and operations. However, this may not be an effective strategy for longer-term viability, since the costs of catching up in terms of maintenance and staff and programme development can rise exponentially when deferred, and crucial staff upgrading forgone will impact on future quality improvements.

Differential impact by educational attainment

The crisis affected persons and households in many ways. Incomes were adversely affected due to increased unemployment, underemployment, and reduced productivity and wage rates. These effects were related to the level of educational attainment. In addition, the ability to bear the costs of education may have been reduced due to the costs of movement where there is geographical displacement, and higher prices for some goods and services.

Impact on employment and incomes

Because three quarters of the labour force still possess only primary education or less, the breakdown of unemployment by educational attainment largely mirrored the unemployment rate of the total labour force in 1996. However, as the crisis struck in 1997 and deepened in 1998, a clear divergence could be seen between the fate of those with primary education or less, and the rest of the workforce.

Figure 9.1 shows that unemployment rates soared following 1996, in each round of the Labour Force Survey, and that those with primary education were more adversely affected than those with more education. Even the seasonally inactive labour force, where those with primary education dominate, showed signs of becoming larger among those with low education.

As in other countries, educational attainment is a major determinant of income. The average income of a university graduate is almost seven times that of the person with less than primary education. This gap had been narrowing somewhat, but with the onset of the crisis, this trend was reversed. NESDB's 'crisis indices', which basically reflect percentage divergences of observed outcomes from expected (estimated) long-term trends (Jaroenjit 1999), as shown in Figures 9.2 and 9.3, indicate that persons with primary education or below suffered the greatest effects on both employment and real income. It is clear that the economic crisis adversely impacted the unskilled labour force most severely.

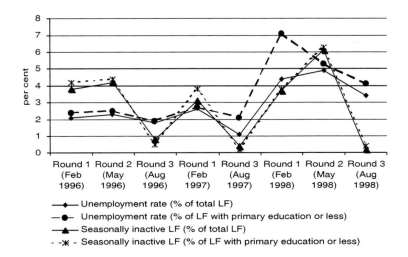

Figure 9.1 Unemployment rates, 1996 to 1998 (source: NSO, Labour Force Surveys (various years and rounds)).

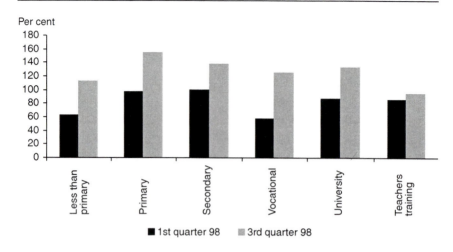

Figure 9.2 Impact of economic crisis on unemployment rate by education (source: NESDB, 1998).

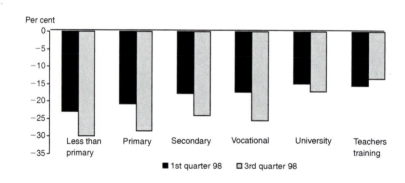

Figure 9.3 Impact of economic crisis on income (source: NESDB, 1998).

Impact on spending on education

Estimates of private household contributions to total expenditures on education in Thailand (Sirilaksana 1999) show that, in 1996, while the government allocated 169,561 million baht for education, household expenditures totalled 88,650 million baht, representing more than 50 per cent of government expenditure on education.

To estimate the effect of income reductions on education expenditure, the nationwide household Socio-economic Survey data are used. Even though the information is for the pre-crisis years, the results nevertheless represent the minimal response that can be expected. It can be seen from

Table 9.14 Factors affecting the size of household monthly expenditure on education: regression results, 1994 and 1996

Independent variables	1994		1996	
	Regression coefficient	t-statistic	Regression coefficient	t-statistic
Number of household members	132.974	34.238**	167.876	49.364**
Educational attainment of household head	22.353	11.277**	33.981	23.917**
Household income	0.008595	20.371**	0.005362	18.863**
Northeastern region	−495.12	−21.057**	−580.375	−28.980**
Urban residence	81.735	5.606**	74.179	5.964**
Farming occupation	−93.831	−5.532**	−34.338	−2.101*
Southern region	−393.807	−15.546**	−467.954	−21.117**
Northern region	−405.335	−16.793**	−447.002	−21.232**
Central region	−378.933	−15.872**	−445.262	−21.235**
Male household head	−62.342	−3.935**	−94.033	−7.074**
Non-farm, non-professional occupation	–	–	38.789	2.689**
Professional occupation	−12.732	−0.386	–	–
Unemployed	−80.093	−4.131**	–	–
Constant	91.724	2.943	46.028	1.698
R-squared	0.111		0.171	
Adjusted R-squared	0.11		0.17	

Source: Estimated from unpublished data from National Statistical Office, Socio-economic Survey household data for each year indicated.

Notes:
** Statistically significant at the 99 per cent level.
* Statistically significant at the 95 per cent level.
For a fuller discussion of the regressions, see Sirilaksana (1999).

Table 9.14 that household expenditure on education is significantly influenced by a number of factors, and the pattern is consistent through time. Household income can be seen to exert a strong influence on the amount allocated to education, so that income loss can be expected to affect household educational expenditures significantly.

The educational attainment of the household head also has a significant influence on the amount of household spending on education. An increase of one year of schooling raised educational expenditures by 22 baht and 33 baht in these two years. Household income and urban residence also had the predictable positive effect on the amount spent on education. The results also bring out the magnitude of the effect of household location in the various regions of the country, in comparison with households located in the Bangkok Metropolitan Region (BMR). Northeastern households consistently spent less than BMR households by about 580 baht per month.

The negative influence of 'professional occupation' on spending on education may seem surprising. The results in Table 9.14 show that households headed by professionals, as opposed to farmers and non-professionals, tend to spend less on education. However, the size of the influence is not statistically significant, and if we bear in mind that the influences of income, educational attainment of household head, and other factors are already taken into account, the result simply shows that the positive relationship that we might expect is already taken care of through income, the education of the household head, and other variables, so that being a 'professional' in itself, does not influence expenditure on education.

Another, possibly unfamiliar, result is that, given the same level of income, education, and other characteristics, male household heads tend to spend less on household education than females. This confirms the results from numerous studies on nutrition, child health, and child education in developing countries that have found that child quality is greatly affected by the presence of the mother as the economic decision-maker in the household. The negative effect on education expenditures of the male household head is consistent here in both years under analysis, other things being equal. The significance of this finding for policy measures aimed at improving education and targeting cannot be overemphasized.

When expenditures on education are calculated as a proportion of household income, the expected Engel pattern is seen. Table 9.15 divides households in each region into income quintiles, and shows that the proportion of household income spent on education varies inversely with the level of income. Even though high income families spend more on education in absolute terms, these expenditures remain a smaller proportion of their income than in the case of poorer families. This can be taken to indicate the 'burden' of educational expenditures, that falls disproportionately on the lower income groups.

The patterns revealed by these results re-affirm the need to target subsidies in favour of low-income groups. Identifying individuals or households that are 'poor' may be intractable, given the data requirements, the prevalence of subsistence activities, under-reported incomes, and the tendency for some groups to pass themselves off as 'poor'. But other targeting methods may be used, including (i) geographical demarcation, whereby poor areas are defined for coverage, (ii) self-targeting, using variations in the cost and quality of services to induce self-selection, and (iii) targeting based on socio-demographic characteristics, such as age, gender, occupation and ethnicity if financial vulnerability is believed to be based on these characteristics.

For example, as noted above, it is clear from the regression analyses that, for the same level of income and other characteristics, a female household head tends to spend more on the household's education than a male house-

Table 9.15 Average expenditure on education as a percentage of average income, 1994 and 1996

	Bottom quintile		Next quintile		Next quintile		Next quintile		Top quintile	
	1994	1996	1994	1996	1994	1996	1994	1996	1994	1996
BMR	6.77	4.11	4.36	5.74	3.72	4.32	5.17	5.24	5.2	4.73
Central	6.09	5.77	5.12	5.11	4.67	4.82	4.26	4.09	2.73	2.72
North	5.72	5.1	5.1	5.29	4.51	4.59	3.98	4.42	2.64	2.72
Northeast	5.43	6.61	4.92	5.07	3.94	4.19	3.86	3.4	2.42	2.2
South	8.09	7.99	6.02	6.8	5.55	5.39	5.07	4.08	2.86	2.52
Whole Kingdom	6.01	6.21	5.16	5.43	4.52	4.67	4.42	4.18	3.35	3.05

Source: Calculated from National Statistical Office, Socio-economic Surveys, 1994 and 1996.

hold head. Thus, families in poor geographical areas with females at the head of the household would be more suitable for subsidy. The first step would therefore be to ensure that an up-to-date information system exists.

Drop-out rates

The expected effect that the crisis would have on education would be reductions in enrolments due to inability to pay tuition and fees, or late payment, increased student loan demand and default rates, or shifts in enrolments from higher cost to lower cost schools where available. Indeed, the number of students owing fees soared in the first two years of crisis (Cresswell 1999).

However, there is much debate about the number of drop-outs due to the economic crisis. On the one hand, National Economic and Social Development Board (1998) stated that

empirical data do not provide any evidence of drop-outs during the crisis period. As a matter of fact there has been an improvement in the percentage of children not attending ... school in all age groups. For instance, the expected percentage of children not attending the school is 31.3 per cent in the 15–17 years age group whereas the actual value is only 25.3 per cent which implies that the crisis has led to an improvement in drop-out rates by about 6 per cent points.

The NESDB figures are reproduced in Table 9.16.

Table 9.16 Percentage of children not attending school, 1988 to 1998 (NESDB)

Period	0 to 4 years	5 to 11 years	12 to 14 years	15 to 17 years	18 to 24 years
1988	95.8	18.9	32.4	69.1	89.1
1990	94.8	17.7	29.0	67.6	88.6
1992	94.3	14.7	21.1	56.6	85.8
1994	90.8	11.4	12.0	42.7	83.2
1996	87.8	7.8	7.0	32.7	80.4
1998	83.0	4.1	6.1	25.3	72.7
Percentage change					
1988 to 1990	−1.1	−6.6	−10.5	−2.3	−0.6
1990 to 1992	−0.5	−17.1	−27.1	−16.3	−3.2
1992 to 1994	−3.7	−22.2	−43.2	−24.6	−3.0
1994 to 1996	−3.4	−31.9	−41.6	−23.4	−3.4
1996 to 1998	−5.5	−46.7	−13.5	−22.5	−9.6
Crisis index	−4.9	−44.0	−6.3	−19.1	−9.0
Expected value	87.3	7.4	6.5	31.3	79.9

Source: National Statistical Office, Socio-economic Surveys. Processed by Development. Evaluation Division, National Economic and Social Development Board.

The Office of the National Education Commission (1999), on the other hand, countered that the proportion of the population not in school was much greater than the NESDB estimates. The ONEC figures are presented in Table 9.17. For the crucial 12–14 age group, the ONEC shows an increase in the number of children not in school from 9.5 per cent in 1996 to almost 20 per cent in 1997 and 1998, significantly different in terms of both direction and magnitude from the NESDB estimate of a decrease from 7 to 6.1 per cent.

In calculating the crisis index, the NESDB study takes into account an estimated 'normal attrition rate'. More detailed figures of student numbers from schools and survey drop-out rates by ONEC (whose numbers have been adjusted for obvious errors in Table 9.17) shed some light on changes in enrolment, but do not offer any insight into the dynamics of the problem, or the discrepancies between the two agencies. There is no clear picture of where those leaving school go, and whether there are other causes involved, such as illness, accidents, or temporary movement. Further analysis is required.

Features of the reform movement

The current thrust of educational reform includes steps towards decentralization of decision-making and curriculum diversification, greater participation of stakeholders, empowerment of those groups of stakeholders traditionally omitted from the decision-making process, and rationalization of financing to effect appropriate empowerment, responsibility (including financial responsibility) and accountability. Such de-control is envisaged as leading to the kind of flexibility that would be required to enhance quality and respond properly to the education needs of the country.

The 1999 National Education Act (hereafter referred to as the Act) contains important changes in financial, administrative, and pedagogical policies. The main substance of these reforms is discussed here.

Free basic education

One of the most important and far-reaching initiatives in the Act is the stipulation that 'all individuals shall have the right to receive basic education of quality, free of charge, for the duration of 12 years' (§10, Ch. 2). The Act does not make upper secondary education compulsory, but it does expand the range of 'basic education' through the secondary level, and requires 12 years of education to be free. This is a major policy change, and the budgetary implications are expected to be formidable. In addition, this provision may conflict with the principle of benefit pricing if not carefully administered.

Table 9.17 Proportion of population not in school, 1996 to 1998 (ONEC)

Age group	1996			1997			1998		
	Population	Not in school	Per cent	Population	Not in school	Per cent	Population	Not in school	Per cent
3–5	3,203,000	1,675,276	52.0	3,202,000	952,866	29.8	3,192,000	1,067,893	33.5
6–11	6,592,000	460,198	7.0	6,539,000	890,134	13.6	6,497,000	877,792	13.5
12–14	3,422,000	325,977	9.5	3,395,000	670,908	19.8	3,364,000	664,790	19.8
15–17	3,481,000	1,961,360	56.0	3,464,000	1,490,830	43.0	3,440,000	1,431,049	41.6
18–24	8,102,000	7,262,680	90.0	8,120,000	6,838,059	84.2	8,125,000	6,829,864	84.1

Sources: Population estimates from NESDB. Distribution by age group calculated by ONEC. Student numbers from ONEC (total of 49,754 schools and educational institutional nationwide).

Moreover, granting this right implies open access, and the main policy body, the National Education Commission (ONEC), has gone beyond the language of the Act and stated that

> secondary education has become basic education for all in the period of the Eighth National Education Development Plan (1997–2001). This implied that by the year 2001 there would be no entrance examination to secondary schools and admission would be based on the consideration of those living in the school service zone.
>
> (ONEC 1997, p. 81)

The implementation of this policy has been delayed, due to disagreements over the 'school service zone' and the demarcation of the 'local education area'. In October 2002, the number of the latter appeared to have been settled at 175 (Ministry of Education 2003a).

Demand-side financing and budgetary process reform

There is a major shift in the process for allocating subsidies towards providing lump sum amounts based on some form of student count. This may be implemented through the use of vouchers to the students for use at public or private institutions. In the language of the Act:

> The State shall be responsible for ... the distribution of general subsidies for per head expenditure commensurate with the needs of those receiving compulsory and basic education.
>
> (§60, Ch. 8)

This new allocation system changes the process of budget allocation and expands opportunities for attending both government and private schools. The intention is to inject competition into the provision of education and to end government monopoly. Where private alternatives exist, this allocation system would force public facilities to improve performance and ensure consumer satisfaction.

However, if these grants are not sufficient to induce private-sector initiatives, the goal of fostering competition may not be achieved. The new system has the potential to shift attendance patterns among schools, by providing some additional opportunity for choice. Students could seek places in the more desirable government schools or private schools, which might otherwise be unaffordable. However, the opportunity for choice may be illusory if no actual alternatives are available within reasonable distance, due to lack of places or the absence of alternatives.

The voucher system can, of course, be a mere accounting procedure, with the government transferring to each school an amount determined by multiplying the number of students enrolled by the appropriate per-head amount for each level. In fact, under the existing system, much of the allocation is actually based on, or strongly influenced by, the school's enrolment. For example, the number of teachers to which a government school is entitled is based largely on enrolment and class-size standards, as is the size of budget for many routine expenses and lunch programmes. Subsidies for private schools are allocated on a per capita basis as well. Funds for special programmes, quality improvement and capital invest-ment are allocated more on a case-by-case basis, but these make up a relat-ively small proportion of the budget. In fact the largest variation in current budget allocation per head is caused by the composition of the teaching staff in terms of qualifications and length of service, since the single most important cost category in education is currently salaries. The problem here is how to determine the appropriate 'per head subsidy' and define the package that constitutes 'basic education' that is to be subsi-dized. There is much wrangling and conflict here.

Decentralization

The reform efforts include a number of decentralization initiatives, with provisions for increasing budgetary and administrative autonomy in schools and particularly higher education institutions.

A budget allocation method based on unit cost principles, as proposed, would have important implications for teaching-staff management as well, since the concept implies that the allocation to schools would be a lump sum, rather than the existing mix of in-kind and category-based alloca-tions. Eventually, it is envisaged that staff would no longer be allocated to schools from a central authority, as is currently the case, but would be hired at the local level, using local budgets that would combine contribu-tions from the central government as well as funds raised in the commun-ity. This would alter the entire personnel management system and shift the control of local financial decision-making from the centre to the local level.

The involvement of stakeholder interests in decision-making has long been advocated. It is clear that the institutions themselves are in closer touch with the needs of the 'clients', namely students (and parents) and employees, than centralized government agencies. But educational institu-tions with greater financial and administrative autonomy must also be accountable. Many schools may not be ready for autonomy, and interim measures need to be devised. Perhaps school networks could be formed or encouraged through fiscal incentives, whereby high quality schools can help less advantaged schools in the network. Such financial and adminis-trative reform should improve access and quality, as well as resource use.

Decentralization is intended to achieve administrative reform and quality improvement, and is widely welcomed and supported by disinterested parties. However, decentralization by itself is no panacea. Several important considerations need to be borne in mind. Decentralization is not a valuable public policy simply because existing public systems are inadequate. Decentralization of services, management, and service delivery incentives may be desirable, but what is difficult is the translation of ideas into workable solutions. Decentralization should accomplish improvement in the delivery of services, efficiency, better performance of personnel through improved incentives, and elimination of waste and inefficiency through too highly structured administrative systems in the centre.

However, it is unclear what should be decentralized and how the process of decentralization should work. For example, should everything from personnel and procurement to budgetary decisions be devolved from the centre? Are there any activities that would be better done in a centralized fashion, that is, that have demonstrable economies of scale? How can success or failure be measured? These are questions that require careful study.

There are obstacles to overcome, such as resistance to the redistribution of political power and empowerment of disadvantaged groups. Strong resistance also comes from the teaching staff who face important challenges. Decentralization implies added responsibility for unfamiliar tasks such as bookkeeping and management. Decentralization also requires quality assurance and licensing, and preparations are just beginning in this area. Per head subsidies could also lead to shortfalls of funds for salaries and other expenses. This problem can be avoided if staff are redeployed, but again, this is an unpopular avenue. In addition, a complete and timely information system would be an essential ingredient, and perhaps this is what the central authority should do. If decentralization is to be beneficial, training in management would also be crucial. This underlies the difference between a 'local education service area' which was the norm in the past, and a 'local education administration area' which has greater autonomy and responsibility.

De-institutionalizing education

The Act contains a new philosophical shift in stipulating that 'alternative avenues of learning' will have the same status as formal schools. That is, parents have the right to arrange for their children's education, in the form of 'home school', with the state acting only as standards regulator, with performance evaluation and achievement tests introduced to ensure quality, and allow transferability between different avenues (§12, Ch. 2; §15, Ch. 3). Specifically, families, religious groups, community groups, private enterprises, and other social institutions are given the right to provide education, with linkage and transferability between formal, non-formal, and informal education, including individual learning.

The objective is to break down education's formal rigidity, to allow students to learn at their own pace and to de-institutionalize education, allowing greater diversity. The concept of apprenticeship is also being revived, to allow young people to divide their time between school and training, with provision for adult education to allow workers to retrain for new jobs, keep up with developments in fast-moving fields and learn new skills. However, the need to develop improved monitoring capacity, performance-based management systems, and acceptable evaluation criteria in line with budgetary and administrative autonomy of formal schools and the right to run 'home schools' will be onerous, and may prove intractable.

In addition, even if the Act allows greater freedom of curricula, once certain paths are institutionally established and ingrained in custom and routine, it is easier to walk in the paths that have been beaten than it is to work out what is practically involved in providing a more stimulating environment of learning. And there is no guarantee that quality improvements will be achieved.

In terms of curriculum reform, Dewey (1938) expounded decades ago that a coherent theory is needed: 'affording positive direction to selection and organization of appropriate educational methods and materials, is required by the attempt to give new direction to the work of the schools'. This process is slow and arduous.

Equity

Equity considerations figure prominently in the policy and reform initiatives. The Act lays down requirements for equity in resource allocation in many places, and stipulates that 'persons with physical, intellectual, emotional, social, communication and learning deficiencies, those with physical disabilities, or those who are destitute or disadvantaged, shall have the right and opportunity to receive basic education specially provided' (§10, Ch. 2). It is also envisaged that there would be 'equalizing grants' to take into account greater need, which may be due to location, learners' disability, or outstanding ability. 'Education for the specially gifted shall be provided in appropriate forms in accord with their competencies' (§10, Ch. 2).

It is envisaged that the central government would provide an entitlement for basic education support for all, and additional funds for special needs or circumstances. The Act does not go into detail about how these additional amounts are to be decided or allocated, and indeed, specifics were removed from earlier Drafts. To achieve this, the strain on the government budget would be considerable, particularly in times of crisis. Noble ideals indeed may be practically unworkable, but such goals indeed need to be stated.

Resource mobilization and stakeholder involvement

A major feature of the current educational policy initiative is the mobilization of greater local and private support for education. The Act contains provision for mobilizing resources from the government, local administration and organizations, and the private sector. But if these initiatives are attempts to reduce the burden on the central government, this is not likely to happen, since the 12-year free education is widely publicized and generally misunderstood to mean that are schools will now be free. The keyword is *basic* education that would be free, much like healthcare where such items as elective surgery are usually not considered a basic need.

The mobilization of local and community resources, if it does occur, is aimed more at increasing the perception of ownership and involvement in education. The common perception is that education is the government's responsibility. Thus, these initiatives are designed to involve local authorities and parents more directly in the financing of the schools, thus increasing their overall involvement and commitment to education, which should in turn lead to overall quality improvements. The danger here is the free-rider problem. Anyone involved with parent action or advisory groups knows too well that mobilizing stakeholder participation can be a Sisyphean task.

The financing of education should be based on the fundamental requirement that social benefits[5] and costs are closely aligned. In principle, this would mean a whole package of differential fee structures to reflect social costs and benefits, deregulation, and student loans, taking the place of government control and direct provision. The current policy direction is towards a direct subsidy to the student rather than the school, and student loan programmes have begun. However, tackling the problem calls for three types of public finance reform: redirecting spending towards activities in which government participation is most critical, increasing reliance on user and other benefit-related charges to finance such spending, and decentralizing some public responsibilities to those in closer touch with local needs and conditions. Thus, the whole spectrum of measures needs to be considered as a package programme: selected user charges, student loans, scholarships for the truly needy, and/or bonding (which, in effect, is a subtler kind of loan).

Conclusions

Much of the reform effort has been carefully thought out and is in line with efficiency and equity considerations. These efforts, if implemented appropriately, could do much to address the key concerns in financing, administration, equity, and the quality of education. However, there are inconsistencies in the reform efforts, particularly the stipulation that basic education of 12 years will be free of charge.

It has to be recognized that, in some cases, efficiency considerations favour a greater burden of the cost of education to be placed on certain households. Equity considerations suggest that those households should primarily be the non-poor. Charging cost-based user fees for services that have large private benefits, such as training, which mainly benefits the individual, results in efficiency in both production and consumption. In addition, it also mobilizes resources to finance the expansion of priority services, many of which are used primarily by the poor. Subsidizing mobile rural services, for example, is one way to give the poor access to services, with at least part of the cost borne by others. Such fees lead to gains on all fronts: the supply of publicly-provided goods and services is allocated more efficiently, the reliance on fees avoids the need for distortionary taxes, and at the same time equity goals are served. But these general principles are only partly adhered to in the language of the Act, and this is where the danger lies.

Reform of the budgetary process should be accompanied by de-control of fees with cost-related fees in government-owned schools as well. But because the 12-year free education policy is now much publicized, such a move would be practically impossible.

In principle, non-critical services should not be subsidized, but be charged to those receiving the service, unless there are special considerations. The charges can then be earmarked to finance the expansion of priority services, while increasing rather than decreasing efficiency. Publicly-provided goods and services will be used efficiently if they are priced to reflect the cost of production as well as externalities and other market imperfections. In contrast, subsidized (or underpriced) services result in excessive consumption and excess demand, and the taxes needed to pay for such subsidies often create distortions elsewhere in the economy. User charges lead to a double efficiency gain: they allocate the supply of public goods and services efficiently, and their use avoids the need for distortionary taxes. However, the inclusion of 12 years of free education may work against these principles.

While this policy initiative of expanding the scope of free basic education to 12 years can help ameliorate crisis impacts, this policy has long-term financial and efficiency implications. The dilemma is to balance short-term crisis management with long-term efficiency and equity goals.

Public provision, the nature and type of financing schemes, the level of fees, all affect the behaviour of producers and consumers and influence the distribution of wealth and income. If the beneficiaries are not the truly needy, then public provision can be distortionary. Whether a disproportionately heavy burden is placed on the poor depends on how spending is allocated and revenue raised. If wealth taxes such as property taxes, capital gains taxes, and inheritance taxes are low or non-existent, then public provision of education services could have regressive elements.

The reform movement currently under way may or may not prove to be the key to long-term recovery, but it is certain that without reform, a long-term recovery would be beyond reach.

Notes

1 The name of the National Education Council was changed to Office of National Education Commission in the late 1990s.
2 Transition rates are similar for boys and girls, so gender breakdown is not shown.
3 The upper secondary completion rate needs to be interpreted with care. In the past, large numbers of students took the school leaving equivalence examination that allows them to apply for tertiary education without completing the final grades in school. A newly revised university entrance policy, requiring inclusion of school grades in entrance scores, is designed to reverse this trend.
4 The Survey of Children and Youth has been conducted every 4 to 5 years.
5 Social benefits here include equity considerations that yield benefit to society as a whole.

References

Amornwich Nakorntap (2002) The current state of education in Thailand: the reform knot, Bangkok: Office of the National Education Commission. Available at http://www.onec.go.th/publication/re_amon/amon.pdf [in Thai].

Cresswell, Anthony (1999) Educational finance in Thailand: a review and recommendation for improving allocative efficiency. Paper submitted to UNESCO under the ADB Technical Assistance Project: TA 2996 – Education Management and Financing Study.

Dewey, John (1938) Experience and education, in: Mortimer J. Adler (ed.) *Great Books of the Western World: Philosophy and Religion*, Chicago: Encyclopaedia Britannica.

Jaroenjit Pothong (1999) Impact of economic crisis on the standard of living in Thailand, *Indicators of Well-being and Policy Analysis Newsletter*, Development Evaluation Division, National Economic and Social Development Board, Bangkok, January.

Ministry of Education, *Education Statistics*, Bangkok, various issues.

Ministry of Education (2000) *Education Statistics*, Online. Available at http://www.moe.go.th/main2/stat-thai/school_AMP43.xls.

Ministry of Education (2003a) *Education Statistics*, Online. Available at http://www.moe.go.th/main2/www02.htm.

Ministry of Education (2003b) 175 local education areas (30 October 2002), Bangkok, Online. Available at http://www.moe.go.th/new_stru/175.xls.

Ministry of Science, Technology and Environment (1996) *Science and Technology Development Plan by Field*, Bangkok.

National Economic and Social Development Board (1996) *Eighth National Education Plan*, Bangkok.

National Economic and Social Development Board (1998) Indicators of well-being and policy analysis, *Newsletter*, 2, p. 4.

National Education Council (1991) Costs and contribution of higher education: a case of Thailand, Educational Research Division, Bangkok [in Thai].

National Education Council (1992a) *Costs of Higher Education*, Bangkok.

National Education Council (1992b) *School Finance Study*, Bangkok.

National Education Council (1995) Evaluation of educational management and performance of the seventh national educational development plan, Bangkok [in Thai].

National Statistical Office (1977, 1983, 1987, 1988 and 1993), *Survey of Children and Youth*, Bangkok.

National Statistical Office (various years and rounds) *Labour Force Survey*, Bangkok: NSO.

National Statistical Office, *Survey of Population Change, 1987–88*, Bangkok.

Office of the National Education Commission (1997) *National Education Data, Academic Years 1994–1996*, Bangkok.

Office of the National Education Commission, *Education Statistics and Indicators, 1996, 1997, 1998*, Bangkok.

Office of the National Education Commission (2003) *Education Statistics*, Online. Available at http://www.onec.go.th/publication/data2544/data2544.pdf.

Office of the National Education Commission (1999) ONEC stands by its drop-out figures, press release, Bangkok.

Office of the Prime Minister (various years) *Government Budget*, various years, Bangkok.

Pernia, Ernesto (1990) Introduction and perspective, in: *Human Resource Policy and Economic Development: Selected Country Studies*, Asian Development Bank, Manila.

Sirilaksana Khoman (1986) Malnourished children: an economic approach to the causes and consequences in rural Thailand, East-west Population Institute Paper Series, No. 102, East-West Center, Honolulu.

Sirilaksana Khoman (1993) Mechanisms of socio-economic change in rural areas: the case of education and health in Thailand, *Review of Marketing and Agricultural Economics*, 61, p. 2.

Sirilaksana Khoman (1997) Thailand's economic crisis and the challenges in education. Paper presented at the conference *Thailand: At the Crossroads?*, organized by the National Thai Studies Centre, Australian National University, in Melbourne, September.

Sirilaksana Khoman (1999) Demand-side analysis and the financing of education. Paper submitted to UNESCO in fulfilment of the contract under the ADB Technical Assistance Project: TA 2996 – Education Management and Financing Study.

Thailand Development Research Institute (1998) Draft report on the distribution of burden and benefits of taxation in Thailand. Submitted to the Ministry of Finance, TDRI, Bangkok.

UNESCO (1999) *Statistical Tables*, CD-ROM.

Chapter 10

Urbanization

New drivers, new outcomes

Douglas Webster

The outsider's image of urban Thailand has invariably been Bangkok – an eclectic, cosmopolitan, third-world mega-city. But the reality of urban Thailand is much more than this and it is changing rapidly, driven by strong internal and external forces. These drivers include the aftermath of the financial crisis of 1997, the rise of China as the factory of the world, and an atypical demographic structure for a developing country.

Bangkok, with over 17 million people living in the extended region, retains its economic, and to a lesser extent demographic, dominance. At the same time, however, middle-sized cities, peri-urban areas, and new multi-nodal spread cities have appeared, based on the rapid rise (and decline) of differing economic activities, especially tourism, and they are beginning to play increasingly important, although specialized, roles in the country's development. At the same time, the extended Bangkok region's economy is also changing, chasing new competitive niches, such as advertising and film making, international health care, and advanced business services, to compensate for loss of increasingly vulnerable old functions, such as manufacturing based on low-cost labour.

This chapter looks into the future, speculating on the roles that Thai urban areas will play, identifying likely new patterns of urbanization, and discussing the implications that rapidly changing urban dynamics will have for Thailand, its citizens and economy. The current and emerging characteristics of Thai urbanization are discussed in the following section. Consistent with the theme of this book, the impact of the 1997 financial crisis on the Thai urban system, and particularly Bangkok, which was impacted most, is discussed next. Emerging drivers likely to influence urbanization, many associated with the 1997 crisis, are discussed in the following section. Based on assessment of the impacts of key drivers on the emerging urban system, expected urbanization outcomes are identified in the final section.

Much is at stake. Urban regions account for over 80 per cent of the country's output and will be the home of the majority of the population by 2015. In an increasingly open world, Bangkok looks outward, mediating relationships, economic, political, and cultural, with the rest of the world. Bangkok represents Thailand to the outside. This contrasts with pre-1980s Thailand, when Bangkok largely looked inward to its hinterland, when rice, wood, and other agricultural products dominated exports rather than the manufactured products of multinational corporations that dominate now. At the same time, Bangkok, as the centre of the economy, political life, and society, articulates Thai society in areas such as culture, fashion and lifestyle. The regional centres act as conduits of national culture but are also centres of regional culture, such as Nakorn Ratchasima for the Northeastern (Isan) region and Chiang Mai for the Northern (Lanna) region.

Characteristics of urbanization in Thailand

Levels and rates of urbanization

The rate of urbanization has been relatively slow since the 1997 financial crisis. It is estimated that Thailand was about 37 per cent urbanized in 1995, at the peak of the economic boom before the financial crisis (NESDB/Norconsult 1997: 34). In 2003, the real level of urbanization is probably about 40 per cent.[1] Thus, the urbanization level has increased by only around 3 percentage points over the last 8 years. Further analysis indicates that at least 1.1 million fewer people live in urban regions than would have been the case if the financial crisis had not occurred (NESDB/ADB 2000: 106–7). Given extremely low fertility rates, but improving economic performance (opposing drivers in terms of the rate of urbanization), the urbanization level is forecast to be 42 per cent at the end of the Ninth Plan period, 2006.[2] What is of major concern is not the rural–urban transition itself, which is inevitable, but the developmental implications of the process.

Urban areas are prosperous compared with rural areas, and this is true even in the poorest regions such as the Northeast.[3] Geographic income disparity is mainly rural–urban, rather than inter-regional. To a significant extent, lower average incomes in regions such as the Northeast can be explained by lower levels of urbanization. Mean household incomes in Bangkok are about 3.4 times those of the nation as a whole, and eight times incomes in rural areas in the poorest provinces of the Northeast. Furthermore, urban areas have relatively low levels of poverty incidence, at least as measured using official poverty lines. A recent study by Warr and Isra (2002), which took account of the existence of peri-urban areas, found that 15.2 per cent of Thailand's poor live in urban areas, properly defined. The same study indicated that 38 per cent of Thailand's people live in urban areas, implying that an urban resident is less than half as likely to be poor as a rural resident.

At face value, it would appear that urban regions are effective poverty-fighting machines, both for those living in cities, and those who might migrate to them. The large rural–urban disparities can be viewed as signals to people (and to capital) that they should move to urban areas to enjoy higher standards of living. Of course, this does not mean that urban slums are non-existent. Approximately 1.3 million of Bangkok's people live in substandard housing, and approximately 2 million urban residents nationwide, reflecting pronounced income disparities and the relatively low wages earned by many workers in the informal sector. However, the geography of urban poverty is changing rapidly. While the number of slums, and the number of people living in them, is declining in core urban areas, new slums are emerging in peripheral areas, particularly in industrial areas to the north and east of Bangkok. Slums are also arising around the edges of major regional centres such as Nakhon Ratchasima and Udon Thani.

The rural–urban geographic disparities noted above are not particularly surprising. Rural–urban disparity ratios for several other developing East Asian countries, such as China, are similar. What is surprising is the *level* of urbanization – very low, considering the level of economic development. For example, urbanization levels in much poorer East Asian nations such as the Philippines or Indonesia are higher: 42.1 per cent in Indonesia in 2001; 59.4 per cent in the Philippines (United Nations 2002). The second surprise is the very slow *rate* of urbanization in Thailand. It is unusual to find a Thai urban region growing faster than 2 per cent; most are growing in the neighbourhood of 1.5 per cent to 2 per cent, not strikingly faster than the nation's overall demographic growth rate of about 1.2 per cent.

Core Bangkok, the area covered by the Bangkok Metropolitan Administration (BMA), is growing extremely slowly (under 0.5 per cent annually), well below the national demographic growth rate. This is a product of very low fertility rates and migration from core Bangkok to outer Bangkok. In Bangkok, the mean number of children born to women aged 15–49 (the international measure) was 1.51 in 2000[4] and continues to fall. Around 2.1 children per woman are needed to sustain a population in the long term. Suburban Bangkok (The Bangkok Metropolitan Region [BMR] minus BMA) and the peri-urban Eastern Seaboard (ESB), stretching along Thailand's Eastern coastline with the Gulf of Thailand, are growing considerably faster at about 2 per cent annually.[5]

Even these rates of population growth are very low for developing East Asian urban centres. For example, the real rate of urbanization in Indonesia is currently approximately 4.4 per cent per year, while China is now urbanizing at about 3.5 per cent per year.[6] However, real population growth is higher than these data indicate in all three areas of the Extended Bangkok Region (EBR), which includes inner and outer

Bangkok, and especially in the peri-urban area, because the population enumeration system significantly undercounts in-migrants to urban areas.[7] The National Economic and Social Development Board (NESDB) estimates that 51 per cent of incremental population growth in the EBR will occur outside BMA over the next 20 years (NESDB/Norconsult 1997). However, as will be argued below, this may be an overestimate because of economic re-structuring that will favour the urban core and emerging centres outside the EBR.

Slow population growth in the EBR belies the image of third-world cities growing at phenomenal rates, creating hopelessness among both the people and urban policy makers. This image may be true of places such as Manila, but not Bangkok, nor urban Thailand as a whole. This means that Thai decision-makers have the option of significantly improving the quality of Thai cities. They are not bogged down with a huge backlog of unmet needs, nor are there overwhelming demands for capital investment in schools, health facilities, and so forth. In fact, in much of urban Thailand, elementary schools are being closed for lack of students.

Of course, the foregoing picture hides considerable differences in growth rates within the urban system. In addition to over 2 per cent growth in peri-urban areas, key tourism centres, particularly in the South, such as Phuket, are also growing relatively fast. On the other hand, in the North, where deaths exceed births in much of the region, limiting the pool of migrants and natural growth in cities,[8] urban regions such as Chiang Mai and Chiang Rai could experience population decline over the coming two decades. This would be a new challenge for urban stakeholders and policy makers.

Drawing a sharp line between rural and urban Thailand may be artificial. First, as noted, the fastest growth in urban areas has been in low density peri-urban areas on the edge of existing settlements, such as the Hua Hin–Cha Am west coast amenity area, and the Ayutthaya and Eastern Seaboard industrial areas. These transitional areas are characterized by patchwork landscapes of rural and urban land use, punctuated by employment nodes (industrial estates or clusters of hotels), making it difficult to characterize them as either rural or urban. Second, 70 per cent of Thais live within 75 km of a city of at least 50,000 population, meaning they can easily access sizeable urban areas, even work in them on a daily basis. Rural–urban public transportation is relatively good, be it on the virtually ubiquitous motorcycles operating as taxis or the modified pickup trucks that charge less than US$0.50 per trip.

Third, even in areas that appear obviously rural, most income is derived from non-farm sources. For example, 62.6 per cent of *farm* household income in the North is earned off-farm, 80.6 per cent in the Northeast, 53.7 per cent in the Central Region, and 51.3 per cent in the South (Webster and Nopanant 2002). Most of the non-farm income is from urban-type jobs such as drivers, government workers, agri-processing factory workers, and shopkeepers, or from remittances from the cities or from abroad. These factors encourage urban patterns of consumption. When combined with the fact of high rural population densities in areas of high agricultural capability, such as the Central Plains, where population densities approximate those in a North American suburb, a case can be made that Thailand is already highly urbanized. Telecommunications technologies, such as cell phones and the internet, are further blurring the distinction between urban and rural areas.

Bangkok's dominance

Bangkok is a classic primate city. It dominates its country and the urban system to an extent matched by few other cities in the world, similar to Santiago, Chile. It is one of the world's most cosmopolitan cities, a magnet for both Thais and foreigners. The extended urban region of 17 million people, half of whom live in the core city, is home to over 800,000 expatriates and receives close to 10 million tourists a year. It is a 24 hour city; traffic jams occur at midnight and later as people move between entertainment venues.

Bangkok was at the centre of a severe recession in the early 1980s, peaking in 1984, which forced the national government to reorient its closed, import-substitution development strategy to one of openness and export-oriented manufacturing. Yet, by the late 1980s and early 1990s, Bangkok was one of the fastest growing urban economies in the world, with output growing at an annualized rate of 17.2 per cent between 1990 and 1996, a rate surpassed during that period only by coastal Chinese cities.[9] The EBR became the engine of the post-1984 boom, based on manufacturing and driven to a considerable extent by foreign direct investment (FDI). But Bangkok was 'ground zero' in the Asian economic crisis that started in July 1997. By 1999, Bangkok's economy had returned to positive growth, but at a much lower rate – approximately 3 to 5 per cent per year from 1999 to 2000 (World Bank 2002: 3). However, by the first half of 2003, Bangkok's economy was again growing at an annual rate in excess of 6 per cent.

The Bangkok Metropolitan Administration area contains about 8 million people (2001). The five adjacent provinces, which together with the BMA constitute the Bangkok Metropolitan Region,[10] are home to about 3.5 million more people, yielding a total of 11.5 million people in the BMR.[11] Areas of the extended Bangkok region (EBR) outside the BMR, where major peri-urban industrial clusters are located, contain about 6 million additional people, about half of whom can be described as urban. In sum, a total of 17.5 million people live in the broadly defined EBR. Since Thailand's current population is 62 million, about 13 per cent of Thais live in core Bangkok (BMA), 19 per cent in the BMR, and 29 per cent in the EBR.

There is a considerable variation within the EBR in terms of economic structure and built form. The core city has been propelled by service activity since the early 1990s, including producer, personal, retailing, aviation, tourism, hospitality, international governance, media and health services. In 1999, the service sector accounted for 62 per cent of core Bangkok's output (Gross Regional Domestic Product), compared with only 20 per cent in the peri-urban ESB. Conversely, manufacturing accounts for 57 per cent of economic output in the ESB, versus 32 per cent in the core city. The economic dominance of manufacturing in peri-urban (and suburban) Bangkok is among the highest in the world.

Bangkok's inner core is composed of tourist, hospitality and retail zones, financial districts, the government area (Rattanakosin), and Chinatown, in an overall environment of mixed land uses. At a finer scale, areas of functional specialization can readily be identified, such as the jewellery district.[12] Modern and post-modernist constructions are everywhere: condominiums, hotels, office and retailing complexes, served by a 23 km elevated rail mass transit system (BTS), which is connected by a system of pedestrian skypaths to most important venues along its route. Various ethnic areas are readily identifiable in the city, including Japanese, European, Indian, Moslem and African.

There are two dominant images of Bangkok's suburbs, both grounded in reality. One is residential – of suburban villages, varying from 'no frills' row housing to luxurious gated communities containing golf courses, swimming pools and country clubs. The more expensive of these villages are similar to gated communities in suburban Manila and 'new towns' near Jakarta.[13] The other image is of non-competitive, increasingly closed or closing, labour intensive or heavy industry factories in suburban provinces, particularly Pathum Thani and Samut Prakarn. Interspersed are slum communities, particularly in low-lying areas, along canals and rail lines, and near factories.

Peri-urban, in the Bangkok context, refers to areas beyond suburbia where industrialization is occurring rapidly, yet where agriculture and other rural activities coexist with this modern economy. Large-scale peri-urbanization, which took off in the mid- to late 1980s, is found in the Eastern Seaboard (ESB), and in the Ayutthaya area, to the north of the BMR.[14] By 1997, the peri-urban arc beyond the eastern and northern suburbs, anchored at one end by the ESB and at the other by Ayutthaya, was known as the Industrial Heartland. This appellation is not a misnomer. By the mid-1990s, it was the most important industrial area in Southeast Asia. Most firms are located in industrial parks. The Rojana Industrial Park in Ayutthaya is typical, employing 40,000 people, and containing major multinational manufacturers, including Honda.

The Eastern Seaboard is a public-sector-led regional development initiative planned in the 1970s and largely implemented in the 1980s and 1990s. It is well known internationally because of its scale and relative success. The government, in effect, through its guidance and catalytic investment, created a multi-nodal spread city of three million people. Government decisions to develop two large ports in the ESB – Map Ta Phut and Laem Chabang – and to invest heavily in other infrastructure such as expressways, supported rapid peri-urbanization. Much of the infrastructure development has been financed by international borrowing, particularly from the Japanese government's 'soft loan' Overseas Economic Cooperation Fund (OECF).[15] Approved OECF lending for infrastructure spending in the ESB area totals 179 billion yen. Cumulative lending by OECF in the EBR totals 328 billion yen, the highest for any city in the world, followed in East Asia by Jakarta (259 billion yen) and Manila (146 billion yen) (OECF 1997, Figure 1-4-1).

Urbanization policies

To what extent are the low levels and rates of urbanization the result of government policies, versus demographic dynamics and cultural preferences? This question may be unanswerable, but it is clear that Thai national governments since the Second World War have been suspicious of cities, viewing them as agents of spatial inequality. Some critics of urbanization argue that cities contribute to rural underdevelopment, despite the fact that rural areas would almost certainly be poorer were it not for the existence of strong urban economies.

The rural bias comes through strongly in all nine five-year plans produced by the NESDB to date, in policies and programmes administered by the Ministry of Interior, in rural development programming that stresses self-sufficiency, and so forth. The majority of fiscal revenues are collected in Bangkok (BMA) but most public spending is outside Bangkok. The current decentralization plan, if implemented, will have the net effect of accelerating this redistribution of fiscal resources from urban areas to rural ones (Webster 2002b).

Thailand is clearly on the rural bias side of the policy continuum in East Asia. In contrast, China introduced, in its 2001 tenth national development plan, a high profile policy of *accelerated* urbanization to speed its development process (New Star Publishers 2001). Vietnam is considering the same (Douglass 2002). This is not to say the Thai policy of cautious urbanization is wrong. As noted above, in aggregate, demographic pressures are not significant. However, from a rural poverty and environmental pressures standpoint, the situation is serious.

The consensus estimate is that one-quarter of Thailand's rural population live in rural areas incapable of supporting families at an acceptable standard of living from agriculture. Ten to 12 million people have encroached onto marginal lands over the last two decades and are now rural squatters on untitled land in forest reserves (Pasuk and Baker 2000: 46–8). On the other hand, hyper-urbanization – the situation where growth in the population of working age exceeds employment creation – can be highly destabilizing. In essence, Thailand's urbanization policy reflects the Buddhist concept of the *middle way* (moderation), reflected in many national policies and most recently articulated in the Ninth Economic Social and Economic Development Plan (2001–06).

In terms of the spatial pattern of urbanization, the government has consistently been concerned about the primacy of Bangkok and has attempted to disperse secondary and tertiary activity. In particular, the national government, for at least the last 25 years, has tried to encourage the development of special economic zones, regional cities, and border towns. The special economic zone policy focused on development of the ESB, 190 km from core Bangkok at its eastern extreme in Rayong Province (Webster 2002b).

Efforts to promote regional cities are now showing results. Regional cities show the fastest labour force growth in the nation, often 10–20 years after investment in urban infrastructure. The lag time is not surprising. Cities are large and complex systems and change takes years, even with strategic intent. The border towns policy does not appear to have had much effect, partly because of economic weaknesses and political instability in bordering countries (Burma, Cambodia and Laos). Malaysia has been a solid economic performer but attempts to strengthen Hat Yai and other southern urban centres through development of a Penang–Hat Yai 'seamless development corridor' have not yet succeeded.

The current *Thai Rak Thai* government was elected in 2001 on a platform that stressed rural development. However, in power, it appears to recognize the developmental importance of urban areas, even more than previous governments. For example, it recently announced a programme to eradicate slums by supporting the construction of more than one million new housing units, most of which would be built in extended urban regions. The current government's attempts to support economic clusters where Thailand enjoys competitive advantage, not just supporting FDI investment in manufacturing in a 'cookie cutter' fashion, bodes well for core Bangkok and smaller centres.

The objective of strengthening the role of the provincial scale of governance could encourage rural–urban linkages at the regional scale, thereby reinforcing regional centres and smaller towns to which they are linked. Provinces are the lowest level of government that includes both rural and urban areas. Below that level, *municipalities* (urban) and *tambons* (rural) report separately upwards, working against development of strong rural–urban linkages. Furthermore, the current government has indicated its intention to support development of regional centres, particularly Chiang Mai and Phuket.

The *Thai Rak Thai* government advocates a two-track development strategy, which both supports rural self-sufficiency programming and recognizes the importance of selective global engagement in areas with competitive advantage. In the sense that the latter thrust is almost, by definition, urban-based, current national development policies seem to be moving towards giving urban development a higher profile in the nation's development.

In sum, national policies to date have largely treated cities, especially the BMA, with benign neglect relative to rural areas, letting market forces compensate. The exception has been heavy investment in the transportation infrastructure, particularly expressways, both within cities and between them. The policy has largely worked in competitiveness terms, in that Thai cities are not burdened with large, decaying public housing developments or high levels of taxation. However, their weakness, in terms of future international competitiveness, is human resource development and amenity, areas in which Thai cities score poorly compared with many of their East Asian competitors. Given the likely diminished importance of manufacturing in Thailand's economic future, these factors will become more important, and could prove major impediments to the restructuring of urban economies.

The impact of the 1997 financial crisis on the urban system

With the financial crisis of July 1997, Thai urban areas, and particularly Bangkok, experienced severe stress. The effects included increased unemployment, higher costs of many imported goods, and lower informal sector incomes.[16] Yet, to a significant extent, Bangkok's residents, whether living in the core or periphery, were able to adjust. Most of the forecasts regarding expected unemployment, growth in incidence of poverty, social disruption and unrest, issued at the beginning of the crisis, by agencies such as the World Bank, proved unduly alarmist. To a large extent, the adaptive capabilities of Bangkok residents and businesses were underestimated.

Crisis effects

Just as Bangkok had led the boom, it suffered most from the financial crisis. For example, the official unemployment rate in Bangkok (BMA) increased from 1.4 per cent in early 1997 to 5.1 per cent in 1999.[17] However, many of the negative effects were not the result of unemployment but income losses and sharp changes in the prices of essential imported goods. In terms of incomes, the informal sector was affected most. The impact was very significant, for example, on Bangkok's taxi drivers, numbering over 70,000. Although they did not become unemployed, their average net incomes dropped from approximately 700 baht per day to 200 baht or less, as a result of less business, increased petroleum prices and virtually no barriers to entry.[18] Similarly, informal food sellers were faced with growing competition as those laid off in the formal sector entered the informal sector; for example, selling sandwiches in office buildings. But a countervailing force was that many former middle class people consumed more of the lower cost food and other services sold in the informal sector as their incomes dropped.

Because of increases in the prices of imported goods, significant negative impacts were experienced by persons dependent on petroleum products, such as truckers, commuters, taxi drivers, and those dependent on imported (or licensed) medicines, such as the HIV-positive population. As in any urban economic crisis, the construction sector was hit hard. In core Bangkok (BMA), 103,000 jobs were lost and real wages fell 3.7 per cent for those who remained employed. But manufacturing in core Bangkok (BMA) was hit even harder: 120,000 jobs were lost, although the real wage decline was only 2.2 per cent in this sector. However, to concentrate only on the poor and working class would bias description of the crisis. Over 100,000 individuals were laid off in the financial sector,[19] many of them young professionals who had become middle class during the boom period.[20]

The economic crisis exposed both weaknesses and strengths in the EBR. The crisis sped up the ongoing process of deindustrialization in the core (BMA), weeding out uncompetitive firms. However, during the crisis, the peri-urban area gained 57,000 manufacturing jobs, indicating that the FDI-driven industrial structure, located in peri-urban areas, may have been more resilient than manufacturing in the core area.

At no time during the crisis did unemployment exceed 5.1 per cent in Bangkok; however, this was among the highest unemployment rates experienced anywhere in Thailand, exceeded only by the poor rural Northeast where unemployment, which is consistently high, peaked at 9 per cent. The economic crisis was centred in core Bangkok; regional cities (outer Thailand) did not develop high unemployment, nor did the peri-urban area.[21] Peri-urban unemployment peaked at 2.6 per cent, and unemployment in cities of the North at 2.6 per cent, the Northeast at 4.2 per cent, and the South at 3.8 per cent.

Based on official statistics, which undercount urban poverty, poverty remained low in Bangkok during the crisis, even though national poverty incidence increased from 11.4 per cent in 1996 to 15.9 per cent in 1999. In fact, the percentage of the population classified as poor in Bangkok (BMR) fell from 1.3 per cent in 1996 (pre-crisis) to 0.2 per cent in 1999.

The BMR contained 1.8 per cent of Thailand's poor people in 1996, but only 0.2 per cent in 1999 (World Bank 2000b, Table 1.1). It is difficult to explain these data, but it is clear that the urban area provided significant opportunities for people to adapt rapidly, earning incomes above the poverty line in the informal sector, although often accepting lower income, after being laid off from formal sector employment. Another factor at play was that many of the poor left Bangkok for their rural or small town roots, lowering poverty rates in the urban area, but increasing them in rural areas. The very low rate of growth of BMA's population since 1997 indicates that out-migration has been occurring since the onset of the financial crisis.

Predictions of social unrest in EBR proved to be completely unfounded. Why was Bangkok able to cope so well with a crisis that halved the value of the city's output (in $US terms) over a one year period? Why was there no massive social disruption? Why did Bangkok emerge a stronger player in the Southeast Asian system of cities? Evidently, households, workplace communities, and corporations in the EBR constitute an adaptable, flexible system, even though Thai governments were relatively slow in adapting.

Key adjustment mechanisms

The following mechanisms were important in easing the effects of the crisis.

i Thai families proved very resilient. Bangkok, like most East Asian cities, has seen the extended family, and even the nuclear family, weaken significantly over the last 20 years. Nevertheless, when the crisis occurred, the unemployed, and those who experienced dramatic declines in income, were supported by relatives either in Bangkok or in outer Thailand. Families or individuals were able to 'double up' in housing units and pool incomes. The World Bank estimates that transfers (including remittances), mainly private, resulted in national poverty incidence peaking at 15.9 per cent during the crisis, rather than at 18 per cent, which would have otherwise been the case. In other words, adaptation mechanisms, many of which were household or workplace based,[22] saved 2.1 per cent of Thailand's population from poverty during the crisis.

This does not deny that there were serious ramifications from the crisis. According to official BMA data, the slum population had been falling since the early 1990s and was 1,247,000 in 1996. It increased to 1,512,000 in 1998, an increase of 21 per cent over the two-year economic crisis period.[23] However, recent data suggests that the slum population has returned to close to pre-crisis levels, at approximately

1.3 million. Some of the poor may have left Bangkok after the economy failed to revive vigorously. Furthermore, the collapse of the Bangkok property market made housing more affordable than ever before in the modern era, enabling people to improve their housing conditions as the economy improved.

ii Multinational corporations in the EBR were, and are, dominantly Japanese owned. Traditional Japanese business culture prevailed and employees were not laid off. Instead, year-end bonuses were cut,[24] although this still led to some conflict. In addition, the dramatically lower value of the baht improved the performance of many export-oriented industries, sparing many jobs.

iii At the height of the boom, there were approximately 750,000 illegal Burmese immigrants in Thailand, many employed in construction. The construction sector was hard hit in the EBR, but it was possible to repatriate, or at least lay off, many Burmese workers without the social consequences being directly experienced in Bangkok.

iv Market dynamics created opportunities for the population of Bangkok, as well as suffering. For example, housing prices in Bangkok in 2002 were still only approximately half what they were in 1997. The speculators have been driven out of the market. Combined with lower interest rates (7 per cent instead of 15 per cent before the crisis), the result is greater housing affordability and a considerably higher home ownership rate than in 1997. New entrants to the housing market, particularly the young, have been net beneficiaries of the financial crisis in this regard. Housing prices fell much faster than wages, although in early 2003 they were starting to revive.

v Through short-term public works employment creation, rural areas received more assistance than the EBR, as would be expected given Thailand's rural policy bias. However, jobs were created in the Bangkok region, particularly in core Bangkok, resulting in new footpaths and landscaping, including the planting of hundreds of thousands of trees, organized by the BMA. In addition, individual citizens with time on their hands, or taking advantage of lower priced labour, undertook considerable renovation at the neighbourhood level. The result was that, in some respects, Bangkok became a more liveable city as a result of the crisis.

Changing drivers

Despite rapid, and impressive, adaptation to the financial crisis, the urban system will not return to its former state. Driving forces affecting the system have changed significantly. Below, some of the key changes in drivers are noted, setting the stage for the prognosis proposed in the following section.

Loss of share of FDI in manufacturing

Thailand's competitive advantage is increasingly in services such as producer and business services, design, fashion, tourism and hospitality, and agri-business, not in large-scale manufacturing. This stems from internal competitive and comparative advantages, the government's dual track development strategy, the rise of China as the factory of the world, and the decline of Japan as an East Asian manufacturing giant.

In 2002, China was the recipient of 70 per cent of FDI flowing to all developing countries. At the same time, there is an overall global decline in FDI, related to the growth in contract manufacturing by multinational corporations (MNCs).[25] Large-scale FDI flows to Thailand since the mid-1980s were the underlying driver of industrialization. Approximately 90 per cent of Thailand's FDI went to the EBR during the 1990s, much of it to peri-urban areas, where virtually all new foreign funded manufacturing facilities are located. Most of this FDI was Japanese in origin. However, Thailand's close links with Japan, which drove peri-urban manufacturing, have now, along with the rise of Chinese competition, turned into a weakness. In 1997, Japanese FDI to East Asia was US$11,094 million of which $1,867 million went to Thailand. By 2000, the respective figures were $5,713 and $931 million (Yusuf 2003, Table 1.4). It would appear wise for Thai urban regions to find new sources of economic and employment propulsion, not dependent on FDI, especially in the case of peri-urban areas.

In the early 1990s, FDI to Thailand was dominantly in manufacturing (48 per cent of FDI in 1990), trade (20 per cent), and real estate (12 per cent); however, by the latter part of the decade, the composition had shifted towards real estate and away from manufacturing.[26] This shift contributed to a property glut. Approximately 300,000 housing units in the BMR remained vacant in 2002.[27] Now, FDI flows to Thailand are moving in the direction of agri-processing and services, and away from large-scale manufacturing. For example, in 2001 FDI was 23.4 per cent in agri-related industries, 12.2 per cent in information technology, 9.5 per cent in automotives (the bright spot in terms of large-scale manufacturing), 4.7 per cent in services, and 1.8 per cent in fashion (Chatrudee 2002: 18–19).

This means that bottom-up production processes, which can more feasibly locate in smaller urban areas and rural areas, may become more important, along with business and producer services, that locate almost exclusively in *core* BMA. In spatial terms, the net losers from ongoing dynamics are likely to be peri-urban areas. As described above, their economic bases are overwhelmingly based on manufacturing, particularly FDI-driven manufacturing.

The economic rise of China

Not only is FDI increasingly flowing to China but Thailand is especially vulnerable in that its export mix closely resembles that of China. According to the World Bank, there is a 65.4 per cent overlap (2000 data) between Thailand's exports and those of China (Yusuf 2003, Table 1.6). This is a higher overlap than for any other East Asian country except Indonesia (82.8 per cent). In contrast, NICs such as Taiwan and Korea, and Singapore have overlaps less than 50 per cent. Given that Chinese wages for factory operatives are about one-third those prevailing in Thailand (Yusuf 2003, Table 1.6), this represents a serious challenge to Thailand's economy, and in spatial terms, to Thailand's peri-urban areas.

Implementation of the ASEAN Free Trade Area

It is not clear that the ASEAN Free Trade Area (AFTA) will develop meaningfully.[28] Rapid implementation of WTO measures may make AFTA largely redundant. Either way, it is probable that ASEAN will become more of a free trade zone. ASEAN's approximately 500 million population, with current mean per capita incomes about double those in China, make it a possible economic counterweight to China in terms of market scale, at least in the short run. A true free market in ASEAN would be to Thailand's advantage, leading to more specialization in manufacturing, with a few highly competitive, but larger industrial clusters, such as automobiles, propelling peri-urban areas.

Growth in the importance of tourism

Tourism accounts for over 6 per cent of Thailand's GDP according to the narrowest definition of the sector (hotels, tourist attractions), but as much as 20 per cent if a wider definition is used, which includes, on a pro-rated basis, aviation, domestic transportation, food and beverages and communications. The strength and importance of the tourism industry is nothing new. It has been flourishing since the first *Visit Thailand* year in 1989. However, its relative importance to the economy continues to grow. Thailand will attract over 10 million tourists in 2003; it is the nation's largest foreign currency earner.

Contrary to popular perception, tourism is primarily an urban economic activity. Most tourists spend their money in Bangkok and a few key regional centres such as Pattaya, Phuket, Hat Yai, Hua Hin–Cha Am, Koh Samui, Chiang Mai and Chiang Rai. Given excellent tourism marketing by the Tourism Authority of Thailand (TAT), its fine hotels, beaches, its role as the centre of youth culture, and Thailand's perceived safety in today's turbulent world (it is attractive to both Westerners and visitors from the

Middle East), the tourism sector is likely to grow in both absolute and relative terms. The one threat is terrorism. A major strike against a key Thai tourist destination could seriously wound the industry.

The Hua Hin–Cha Am new urban agglomeration typifies the importance of the tourist industry in driving urbanization. This urban area contains over 300,000 people, not including the tourists themselves, making it one of the larger urban agglomerations in Thailand. Yet it is not recognized as such because the more than 12 local governments making up the extended urban region are never aggregated. Like Phuket, virtually the whole urban system is driven by tourism and spin-off activities. The TAT indicates that the Hua Hin–Cha Am extended urban region (EUR) receives about 7 million tourists a year: 4 million Thais and 3 million foreigners. Its tourism-based economy creates special urban management challenges. The significant seasonal and weekly peaks require greater urban infrastructure capacities.

The south of Thailand (beach tourism) and Bangkok are the main destinations of foreign tourists; domestic tourists tend to visit the Northeast and the Central Plains, visiting relations. The increasing relative importance of the tourism industry is likely to benefit southern urban regions disproportionately.

Business, producer and international governance services

Turning to drivers affecting Bangkok's urban core, they too changed significantly during the latter stages of the boom period. The core developed a wider range of, and more sophisticated, financial and producer services, at the same time as its share of retailing was reduced by suburban competition. The financial function expanded as institutions developed to serve both producers and consumers benefiting from the boom. Bangkok became the financial centre of the 'baht Zone', which included Laos, Cambodia, and Burma. Other services grew rapidly, such as advertising, design and architecture,[29] fashion, media and journalism.

Such services were overlaid on a long tradition of international governance in Bangkok that predated the boom. Bangkok is the most important centre for international governance in Asia, hosting the headquarters of the United Nations' Economic and Social Commission for Asia and the Pacific (ESCAP), the International Air Transport Organization (IATO), regional offices of many UN agencies (including UNICEF and UNESCO) and the Asian Institute of Technology. In all, 66 international organizations are represented in Bangkok. Equally important, the diplomatic community is extensive in Bangkok (123 countries are currently represented), largely in response to the history of conflict in the immediate region, Bangkok's geo-strategic position, and the existence of a large number of international agencies. For example, the United States' Embassy in Bangkok is its second largest worldwide.

Bangkok's urban economy is increasingly based on delivery of high quality business services. For example, Bangkok is a leading Asian advertising and media centre, exporting television commercials and serving as a base for the production of movies.[30] Although most firms are MNCs, virtually all CEOs and Creative Directors are Thai, reflecting the high quality of Thai talent in design professions. Other business services are well represented in Bangkok's core, such as consulting companies (engineering, planning, computing), law firms, accounting firms and management consultants.

This agglomeration of high quality business and producer services in Bangkok, in turn, is increasing the productivity of firms operating in Thailand in other fields, such as manufacturing and agri-business, as well as making Bangkok more attractive for establishment of regional corporate headquarters. The value of the latter is recognized by the national government. The Board of Investment (BOI) has modified its industrial incentives programme specifically to target regional headquarters functions.

One trend appears to be consultants and high-end knowledge businesses basing themselves in Bangkok to serve the rapidly growing Chinese market. For example, Thai Airways has reoriented its network north and northeast to serve China, and away from Southeast Asia (in relative terms), facilitating this role, and reflecting Southeast Asia's diminishing role in terms of East Asia's real economy and real politik. The low cost of doing business, and living, in Bangkok continues to prove attractive to firms in the business and producer services sectors, as well as to headquarters of firms in especially cost-conscious businesses.

Bangkok competes directly with Kuala Lumpur for firms seeking lower costs, typified by aviation and retailing companies. Based on Economist Intelligence Unit data, of 25 major global urban regions monitored, Bangkok has the third lowest cost of living, while Kuala Lumpur has the fourth lowest. Bangkok and Kuala Lumpur have costs of living about 55 per cent of New York City while Singapore has a cost of living about the same as New York. For example, Air France and Makro (retailing) have established regional headquarters in Bangkok. Finally, business, producer and headquarters service activities, which are highly footloose because they are not capital intensive, are attracted to Bangkok because people like to live there, thereby assisting efforts to attract and retain human talent.

The spatial impacts of this driver are clear. High-end business services are increasingly being attracted to Bangkok, and its cosmopolitan core in particular. In fact, business and producer services are even more highly concentrated in the EBR than FDI (about 90 per cent) and manufacturing (about 80 per cent of value added). This is a concern, given attempts by the Thai government to disperse economic activity. However, there is virtually no way that such activities can be dispersed. The nature of these businesses virtually demands that they locate in cosmopolitan mega-city cores.

Amenity activities

Thailand has long been known for its design and fashion, and products with high cultural content, such as mudmee silk, cuisine, as well as its prowess in activities, such as health care, including alternative health care and spas, that require high levels of person-to-person contact. These industries, termed 'high touch' by Alvin Toffler (1971) are growing rapidly in Thailand.

Accordingly, urban areas associated with high amenity and high profile cultural products are likely to develop rapidly. An example is the Hua Hin–Cha Am area whose expanding economy is based on the quality of its food, beaches and spas. Again, Bangkok's core is benefiting from the rise in importance of these activities to the Thai economy. For example, Bumrungrad private hospital in Bangkok treats tens of thousands of foreigners annually, turning health care into an export activity. And certain types of fashion-oriented design and manufacturing, such as customized jewellery manufacturing, are likely to remain in Bangkok. Very importantly, creative/knowledge activities will demand high amenity locations.

Regionalization

Recent research indicates a surprising degree of regionalization, as measured by migration, telecommunication flows and vehicle flows.[31] For example, there is little migration from the most southerly provinces to Bangkok, but much to Hat Yai. Similarly, the Northeast region interacts intensively with Nakorn Ratchasima in terms of telecommunications and migration flows, and the Central Plains Region with Ayutthaya. Of course, all regions have strong ties with Bangkok, but regional linkages are surprisingly important. The spatial implications are clear, regional centres are likely to retain their importance as migration centres, regional business centres and cultural centres.

New migration patterns

In the past, rural–urban migration was largely to urban cores, particularly Bangkok. However, since the mid 1980s, these patterns have been changing. As noted, regional centres have become more attractive, but so have other new destinations. Most important have been peri-urban areas such as the ESB, which have attracted young, usually single, often female, migrants. These migrants have driven the establishment of new urban areas that do not look like traditional communities. The areas include linear settlements along expressways, or worker housing around industrial estates. Other new destinations for large numbers of migrants have been tourism centres. For example, tourism services in booming areas such as Koh Samui, Phuket, Hua Hin–Cha Am, have been significantly staffed by migrants from the Northeast, migrants who 25 years ago would probably have moved to core Bangkok in search of opportunity.

In summary, rural–urban migrant flows, although significantly dependent on the location of employment opportunities, are much more diverse in terms of destination than they were in the past. This is driving the creation of new communities, and in some cases, new types of communities. Some of these flows may slow in the future, including flows to peri-urban industrial areas, while others may increase, such as flows to amenity areas. Changes in migrant flows create significant new challenges in terms of delivery of social services and housing.

Little is known about how these changing migration patterns will affect social support systems, learning, family life and cyclical migration. Core Bangkok has been a very effective learning environment and urban staging area, supporting in-migrants in their efforts to take advantage of its diverse opportunities. Of particular concern is the lack of social capital in peri-urban areas. Unlike in core Bangkok, many new peri-urban communities lack generations of migrants from the same rural communities who can provide support and access to networks, particularly in 'settling in' and emergencies. Furthermore, although wages are relatively attractive, income in kind, such as family-owned housing and child care from relatives, found in the rural community or even core Bangkok, is often very limited in peri-urban Bangkok.

Changing government spatial policies

An important government agency directly shaping the urban system is the Board of Investment (BOI). Previously, its policies encouraged industry to locate at considerable distance from Bangkok, in Zone 3, favouring places such as Rayong that were as close to Bangkok as possible, while still qualifying for the most favourable Zone 3 incentives. However, these policies are being changed, with spatial criteria essentially eliminated. The effect should be to draw the peri-urban area in closer to Bangkok. This dynamic will be reinforced by the slowing of FDI in manufacturing, and loss of competitiveness in many manufacturing sectors.

Decentralization is another policy likely to affect the urban system, although its effects are difficult to predict. The government's original goal was to decentralize 35 per cent of public expenditure to local authorities by 2006. The government has now accepted that it will be impossible to meet this target. Nevertheless, further decentralization of public sector expenditure is likely to occur. The effect will be the emergence of new winners and losers in the urban system – as more responsibility is delegated to local governments they are likely to perform in an increasingly differentiated fashion.

Changing values and preferences

Obviously, this is a driver that can only be discussed in a cursory fashion. Thai society has changed enormously over the last 30 years, and considerably since 1997. Increasing individualism, and later marriage – or foregoing marriage completely by many educated women – the continued weakening of extended families, and small nuclear families means that people are more footloose, more able to chase employment opportunities or amenity.

The implications are that urban systems and labour markets are likely to become more efficient and productive as people fit themselves better to the most appropriate employment available. In addition, as people increasingly seek amenity, places that are attractive, such as hilly locales, beach areas, cities that are well planned and managed, are likely to attract and retain disproportionate numbers of people, especially talented people. An ever-increasing percentage of Thais with discretionary income will choose to retire in high amenity locations.

Transportation systems and motorization

Transportation infrastructure is the most important force shaping the internal structure of Thai urban regions. It is far more important than zoning or subdivision laws, which are often poorly enforced, particularly Department of Town and Country Planning land use maps. The development of the BTS system (23 km elevated heavy rail system linking the major business nodes) has transformed Bangkok, slowing centrifugal forces to a considerable degree. The BTS has enabled much higher inner-city densities in areas such as Silom, where development had been blocked by the lack of transportation capacity to move people in and out of the area at rush hour.

The opening of the Bangkok subway system in 2004 will further reinforce this dynamic. At the same time, the large number of expressways that have been built out to suburban and peri-urban areas enable the continued development of residences on the edge of the city, but with relatively easy access to the core. The EBR's transportation context has fundamentally changed since the early 1990s when gridlock at rush hour was the norm.

Equally important is large-scale construction of inter-city highways and expressways. These highways are increasingly drawing rural settlements to them as well as pulling the direction of new urban development, particularly commercial and business zones. For example, in Ayutthaya, the commercial centre is moving towards (and along) Highway 32 and along the main artery connecting Highway 32 to the historic core.

Rapid motorization reinforces the power of expressways in shaping the urban system. As the ratio of vehicles to population continues to increase, this will have dramatic affects on urban form, encouraging low-density spread settlement – new types of urban form outside city cores. Interestingly, in Bangkok, the ratio of motorcycles to automobiles continues to fall, indicating a movement to all-weather, more comfortable transport. This dynamic will filter down to the regional and smaller centres, encouraging longer commutes.

Rural depopulation

Rural depopulation is a reality in Thailand, and will accelerate. In fact, as a global leader in family planning, Thailand's population is likely to grow very slowly, or even stabilize, over the next three decades. This overall slow demographic growth, combined with the ongoing rural–urban transition, means that rural areas will necessarily continue to experience absolute population decline for the first half of this century. Of course, large-scale rural depopulation has already occurred in developed East Asian countries, most rapidly in South Korea and Japan, and before that in western countries.[32] Already in Thailand, many rural areas are experiencing absolute population loss, especially in the North Region.

However, because urbanization in Thailand is much slower than in most comparable East Asian (and world) developing countries, the slow growth in overall population will not translate into overly rapid rural depopulation. Rural depopulation will be orderly. In fact, Thai rural depopulation (−0.22 per cent per year over the next 30 years) will occur at a slower rate than Indonesia (−0.63 per cent), China (−0.51 per cent) and Japan (−1.34 per cent), but faster than Burma (−0.10 per cent) and the Philippines (−0.17 per cent) (United Nations 2001, Table V.3).

Nevertheless, within two decades, the pool of rural people will be reduced to the point where fluidity in the urban system is likely to decline. The ageing population is likely to stay in the cities where they live, while there will be fewer new migrants, second- and third-generation migrants will become more numerous. In others words, fluidity in the urban system will start to decrease dramatically in 15 to 20 years.

Movement from export to consumer-driven economy

Throughout East Asia, since the 1997 crisis, there has been a tendency, driven by governments, to reduce the role of exports in economic growth, and increase the role of consumer expenditure. For example, Thailand, as well as countries such as South Korea, has encouraged consumer credit through low interest rates and greater use of credit cards. The result is that consumer spending accounts for an increasing percentage of GDP. To be sustainable, consumer-driven growth will require higher wages and lower savings, but in the short run, loosening of credit is driving a consumer-driven urban economic upturn.

This fundamental shift in Thailand's economy has major implications for the urban system. Consumption, to a large degree, is an urban activity – larger centres, the site of retailing complexes with a greater range of goods and services, are likely to benefit relative to smaller settlements.

Expected outcomes: a year 2015 scenario

In 2015, more than 50 per cent of Thais will live in urban regions. What is Thailand's urban system likely to look like? Based on existing dynamics and the foregoing drivers, the following scenario seems likely.

To a significant extent, Thailand's new urban landscape will be less industrially dominated than now, and certainly less so than was forecast at the peak of the boom. This means that growth of industrial peri-urban areas will slow, if not stagnate. This will be especially true in the Eastern Seaboard (ESB), because it is outside of Bangkok's daily commuting radius, but less so in Ayutthaya because it also has a potentially strong tourism economy, and will increasingly act as a bedroom community for core Bangkok – a role it already plays. Other functions in the ESB, such as tourism in the Pattaya area, may take on more importance in driving urbanization. The slowing of industrial investment, combined with ever-slowing national demographic growth, means that the ESB will not become a contiguous part of Bangkok's urban fabric. In fact, it is likely to be spatially stranded, in a patchwork of rural and urban development. Accordingly, the ESB should not be viewed as being in transition to 'normal' Bangkok suburbia but as a separate unique type of settlement system.

Core Bangkok will be critical to Thailand's future success. Much of the niche high-end service sector activity that is emerging to replace slow growth in manufacturing is core centred, such as business and professional services, fashion and design, media and advertising, conventional and alternative health care and international governance. The core will increasingly function as a sophisticated creative economy, based on a fusion of Thai culture and global influences – a role that core Bangkok has already shown it can play well.

The developmental challenge will be to ensure access to this employment system by a broad spectrum of the Thai population, especially young graduates. The number of jobs that can be created in these activities, and access to them, are real issues. The relatively easy entry to blue-collar manufacturing jobs, provided one has middle school education or better, does not hold for much of this creative, knowledge sector. It demands creative thinking individuals who have more than just credentials. The Thai educational system will need to produce appropriately educated individuals to meet the demand.

As noted, BMA lost 120,000 manufacturing jobs during the financial crisis. However, most manufacturing firms still standing are appropriately located. Custom jewellery manufacturing, media production and fashion garments are manufacturing functions that require close access to highly specialized professionals and technicians. If first-world urban trajectories are a guide, these functions can flourish in core areas, operating in multistorey buildings. They do not require the one storey, long perimeter factories needed by large-scale just-in-time production manufacturers in peri-urban areas. A benefit of the financial crisis was the speeding up of the dispersion or closing of industry unfit to be located in the core, such as manufacturing requiring large land plots, heavy polluting firms, users of hazardous materials, or heavy truck traffic generators.

The existence of two heavy rail systems in Bangkok by 2004 will make it possible to increase the density of BMA even more in terms of employment and housing. Centrifugal forces are likely to slow, a process already underway with the opening of the BTS in 1999, meaning that properties in the core will rise in value faster than in suburbia and in the peri-urban areas. Accordingly, the risk of Bangkok's core 'hollowing out', as has occurred in cities such as Manila and Detroit, is quite low. Nevertheless, the bulk of new housing will be added in suburbia, with increasing numbers of people commuting by automobile. At some point, introduction of mechanisms such as High Occupancy Vehicle lanes may be needed to handle suburban–core flows, although at present, in most directions, there is expressway overcapacity.

Interestingly, given Bangkok's vibrant night-life, it is the only major city in the world where dominant flows are into the core city both during the morning and evening rush hours. Many people who work in the suburban and peri-urban areas come to Bangkok in the evening to eat, drink, and participate in social events, joining core workers who stay on after the end of the working day. Thus, inbound transportation to the core will remain critical.

Key tourism centres will continue to grow rapidly and new ones will emerge. Phuket, for example, has 'taken off', based on initial advantage in the tourist economy. Now, large-scale, high-amenity, residential developments are sprouting throughout the island catering to both the domestic and foreign market. Consultants and small knowledge companies are using the island as a base, as intended in the national government's strategy for Phuket. Essentially, the whole island has become an extended urban region. Because tourism demands the same services as the knowledge economy (good aviation, restaurants, telecommunications, English language and cosmopolitanism), a developmental synergy that extends beyond tourism is rapidly developing in key tourist areas such as Phuket, Pattaya and Chiang Mai. This dynamic will increasingly spin off small knowledge firms, and possibly knowledge clusters, from Bangkok. In many cases, it will be easier to attract talent to these high amenity urban areas, providing Thailand with competitive advantage over competing East Asian urban regions.

Aviation is closely associated with tourism. Bangkok is a prime aviation centre – one of the world's 15 leading international aviation centres. It is one of the most central places in the world in terms of the number of people who can be reached in 5 hours' flying time. The new airport (Suvarnabhumi), east of the city will result in at least 600,000 additional people living along the eastern developmental axis of the EBR (NESDB/Norconsult 1994). In relative terms, the northern corridor will be weakened. To some extent, the development of the new airport will compensate for the potential slowing of industrial activity in the ESB, to the east of the new airport.

Kasarda (2002) and others have argued that airport districts may become more important than Central Business Districts in leading world cities. Although this is unlikely to be the case in Bangkok, given the dynamism of Bangkok's core, the new airport will become the number two node in the EBR. The area will attract a host of airport-related functions, ranging from the obvious, such as courier companies, hotels, and logistics firms, to less obvious functions that will benefit from such a location, including convention centres, manufacturers of high value to bulk products and regional corporate headquarters. It is essential that the area be well planned. It will be a city of approximately 500,000 by 2015, or shortly thereafter.

Housing is another critical area. Over the last 20 years, the number of slums and slum dwellers in Thailand has stabilized or declined, except for the blip upwards immediately after the financial crisis. Taking into account population growth, the percentage of Thais living in substandard housing, not all of whom are poor, has declined. If, despite its difficulty, the current government succeeds in delivering one million new housing units for the poor, this would address most of the backlog nationwide. Market mechanisms are also working in favour of improved access to housing, and the percentage of Thais owning their own homes is likely to increase by 2015.

As the absolute number and percentage of the urban poor declines with economic growth, the location of the poor is likely to continue to change. In particular, as land in the urban core becomes more expensive, and as more jobs accessible to those with high school education or less continue to appear on the periphery of cities, slums are likely to be increasingly found in suburban and peri-urban areas. This has been the trend for the last 20 years.

The housing of service workers around fast growing 'new cities', such as in tourism areas, will be an issue. It remains to be seen whether extensive slums will develop in these new urban areas. They may not, given the record of the private sector in Thailand in providing affordable dormitory-type housing to workers. In Ayutthaya, private developers have literally built dormitory cities, such as Kan Ham, to house workers in reasonable comfort. Interestingly, Kan Ham *tambon* has a population of over 20,000 although it does not exist officially as an urban area – official data indicates a year 2000 registered population of 4,381. This disparity between the data and reality in fast growing new urban agglomerations is typical. Official data sets are based on an outdated conception of what is urban.

For the middle class, housing preferences will continue to focus on the suburban edge, where more space can be obtained for a given amount of money. This is essentially the trajectory seen in North America during the post-war period. However, high income individuals are being attracted to inner city condominiums to gain access to key decision-makers, as well as the cultural and entertainment attractions of the core city, and to reduce the loss of valuable time in commuting. This trend is likely to accelerate.

In outer Thailand, beyond the EBR, there will be greater variation in terms of performance among urban centres. As noted, areas associated with fast growing niche and specialized activities will grow quickly. For example, the Lampang area is becoming known worldwide for the quality of products produced in its ceramics cluster. Khon Kaen, Chiang Mai, Nakorn Ratchasima and Songkhla are growing, based on large-scale educational activity. Other communities may promote themselves as retirement centres to both domestic and international markets, the latter based on the availability of retirement visas.

However, centres that depend on more traditional economic bases may struggle, unless they can develop agro-processing functions. Poor urban management is likely to have more serious consequences than in the past. In other words, as the Thai economy becomes oriented to a series of fine-tuned niches, cities will vary widely in their performance, depending on whether they can adapt to produce products demanded by Thai and world consumers. Merely being able to make something will count for little, the ability to market products or services in demand is what will determine the fate of many smaller Thai urban settlements.

Other new spread urban agglomerations are arising around the nation and need to be identified and better understood, so that appropriate regional scale action can be taken to improve their functioning. To a significant extent, the shape of these new cities reflects increasing widespread automobile ownership. Automobiles make low density urbanization possible. The overall growth of these cities, their internal spread and extended spatial structures are closely associated with motorization. Tourists can easily drive to Hua Hin–Cha Am and workers can commute daily from Ayutthaya to Bangkok.

By 2015, demographic changes will have changed the human face of virtually every Thai city. There will be fewer children, and many more old people. Already, over 8 per cent of BMA's population is over 60 years of age. In the Ayutthaya EUR, it is 12 per cent. In some areas where fertility fell fast early, such as Chiang Mai, Chiang Rai and Ayutthaya, this change in demographics will be particularly pronounced over the next two decades. These urban demographic changes will put stresses on social service delivery systems catering to the elderly, disabled and unemployed, and relieve some pressures in terms of education, particularly at the elementary level, where enrolment rates already approach 100 per cent. Higher levels of education, such as tertiary technical education, will continue to flourish even with falling enrolment cohort populations because of higher enrolment rates, and the need for mid-career training.

Throughout the country, cities are likely to be more orderly, with traffic better managed, and streets cleaner, mimicking BMA's very successful anti-littering campaign, with more greenery and landscaping. These changes will be a continuation of trends evident over the last 15 years in most Thai urban regions. However, it will remain to be seen whether three critical urban environmental challenges of Thai cities can be solved.

Wastewater. Investment in wastewater treatment facilities, totalling billions of US$, has been extremely ineffective, with most facilities not operating, or operating far below capacity. The failure is mainly due to institutional factors, particularly related to cost recovery. Most built up urban areas are not served by sewerage systems.

Air Quality. Air quality is improving in Bangkok and most urban areas, but challenges remain related to construction dust, particulates from diesel fuel and tyres.

Solid and hazardous waste disposal. Garbage pickup functions well in most Thai cities, but disposal is a problem in many. The hazardous waste disposal problem is especially serious, with only a minority of hazardous wastes being properly treated/disposed.

Given the growth of new spread cities and regional cities, the development of a new aviation city east of Bangkok, and the ageing of BMA's population, BMA will continue to lose some of its demographic dominance in the urban system. However, in terms of power, innovation, and high-end economic activity, its dominance is likely to increase. Many of the services in which Thailand has a competitive advantage, such as business and producer services, design, quality health care and large-scale trade expositions, are strongly oriented to a big city location – even more so than manufacturing. Bangkok, as the only metropolis, will remain the place to be for most types of innovative, creative, and entrepreneurial activity. It is difficult to see how this outcome could be reversed without seriously damaging the country's overall economic performance.

Near urban areas, after controlling for other factors, agriculture tends to be more intensive, higher in value. This is true around large urban systems such as Bangkok, and around smaller regional centres such as Nakhon Ratchasima, Khon Kaen and Udon Thani in Northeast Thailand. In fact, losses of agricultural land through conversion to urban uses in extended urban regions are more than compensated, in economic terms, by increased value of production near cities. This is not only because of the effect of local urban markets, but also because urban areas provide intermediary services such as processing, packing, distribution and credit that facilitate intensified agricultural production. Furthermore, the higher price of land near urban areas may encourage farmers to invest in agricultural technologies to produce higher value products, such as specialized herbs and fruits, to justify the high cost of the land.

As agriculture is intensified near cities, which are usually located in areas of high agricultural capability, the blurring of what is rural and urban will increase. Over the last 20 years, about 15–20 per cent of urban population gain in Thai urban regions was the result of the envelopment of existing settlements including rural settlements, through outward movement of urban people, rather than through rural–urban migration or natural growth. Over the next 20 years, it is expected that envelopment will account for even more of Thailand's urban growth, as low-density urbanization moves out into the surrounding countryside and as agriculture increasingly shifts from marginal areas to high capability farmland nearer cities. This trend that will be accentuated by absolute declines in rural populations, that will make farming in truly marginal areas less necessary.

Conclusions

It is clear that a developmentally successful Thailand will be one that moves into activities with high cultural content, that require creativity in their design and production, that respond to market needs, and that are not easily commoditized.[33] The chief potential stumbling blocks to realizing these opportunities are likely to be lack of enough appropriately educated people and urban areas that lack sufficient amenity to attract and retain high-end technicians, tourists, capital and technology. Cities will need to specialize to fit the types of economies that will grow up in specific places in response to niche opportunities. Urban development, propelled by manufacturing of increasingly commoditized products, is increasingly under threat.

Urban areas have proven effective as economic growth mechanisms and as poverty fighting devices. Thus, a case could be made for acceptance of somewhat accelerated urbanization, if urban economic re-structuring is successful. Most of urban Thailand will not be an industrial landscape, but one of diversity, both within the extended Bangkok region, and among smaller places. Decentralization, which puts more responsibility on local officials and stakeholders, new economic forces, and changing social preferences, particularly for amenity, will alter the roles, shape, and importance of urban settlements.

Notes

1 Warr and Isra (2002) provide a detailed data analysis incorporating peri-urban areas, which indicates that, based on population density data, Thailand was 38 per cent urbanized in 2000, the latest year for which appropriate data were available.
2 For a technical description of this forecast, see NESDB/ADB (2000).
3 This is especially the case if lower costs of living in regional centres in the North and Northeast, relative to Bangkok, are taken into account. Analysis by NESDB/Norconsult (1997), for example, showed that real incomes in the leading Northeast urban centres (Nakhorn Ratchasima, Khon Kaen, Udon Thani) were 70 per cent of BMA's, once differences in the cost of living were taken into account.
4 National Statistical Office, *Population and Housing Census, 2000*, Bangkok.
5 These data relate to Thai urban area growth rates for the period 1997–2000.
6 For details on Chinese urban growth rates see Webster (2000) and for Indonesian urban growth see Webster (2003a, pp. 10–12).
7 The foregoing population growth rates are based on registration data from the Ministry of Interior. Since there is little incentive for individuals to re-register after moving, the system consistently undercounts urban populations, especially in rapidly growing areas such as the Eastern Seaboard.
8 This demographic situation in the North is the product of low fertility (family planning efforts were successfully introduced early in the North by the PDA and the Ministry of Health), as well as higher death rates (largely attributable to higher rates of HIV-AIDs infections in the North).
9 The economic growth data refer to the Bangkok Metropolitan Administration (BMA) area, and are based on Gross Regional Domestic Product (GRDP) data published by the National Economic and Social Development Board (NESDB).
10 The Bangkok Metropolitan Region consists of BMA plus five adjacent provinces: Nonthaburi, Samut Prakarn, Pathum Thani, Nakon Pathom and Samut Sakhon.
11 Population data have been rounded to the nearest 0.5 million to reflect the low degree of accuracy of urban demographic data in Thailand.
12 The jewellery industry employs over 100,000 people in Thailand, most working in the EBR.
13 For detail concerning Manila, see Connell (1999). For the Jakarta case, see Leaf (1996).

14 For more detail on Thailand's Eastern Seaboard, see Webster (2002a).

15 In October 1999, OECF and JEXIM (the Export-Import Bank of Japan) were merged to create JBIC (the Japan Bank for International Cooperation).

16 For indicators on sectoral, employment, and income impacts of the economic crisis in Thailand and Bangkok, see World Bank, (2000a) and 'How much did Thailand suffer?', *The Economist*, 22 January 2000, p. 41.

17 Based on third quarter labour surveys (1997 and 1999), Ministry of Labour, Royal Thai Government.

18 The number of taxis increased from 18,000 in 1992 to 70,000 in 2000. Most of this increase occurred after the onset of the economic crisis.

19 Using available statistics, it is difficult to track employment losses in financial, and other business/producer services occupations, because there were more than compensating gains in informal employment, which is also included in the service category. Overall, core Bangkok (BMA) gained 182,000 service jobs between 1997 and 1999.

20 For details on the employment and income impacts of the crisis, see Thailand Development Research Institute (1999).

21 Real wages in agriculture fell by 14.4 per cent between August 1997 and August 1999, the highest decline in any major sector. However, this can be explained more by physical conditions and world food markets, which were unfavourable during the latter part of the recession.

22 Similar dynamics occurred in workplace communities, where voluntary arrangements were made to share employment (less hours) or accept lower wages so that there would be no, or fewer, layoffs.

23 BMA, Statistical Profile of Bangkok 2001, 2000, 1999, 1998, 1994 (published annually), Bangkok: Department of Policy and Planning, BMA, 2001, 2000, 1999, 1998, 1994.

24 Japanese business culture is changing as a result of globalization pressures and this behaviour is unlikely to be the norm in the next severe Southeast Asian recession.

25 MNCs increasingly prefer to contract out to local (developing country) producers for supplies, rather than establishing production bases themselves. This is known as contract manufacturing. For an assessment of this trend, see Yusuf (2003, p. 27).

26 Comparable figures for 1995 are: manufacturing: 28 per cent; trade: 22 per cent; and real estate: 42 per cent.

27 For details on FDI and portfolio capital flows into the extended Bangkok region, see Uthis and Webster (1998).

28 The major stumbling block to the development of AFTA has been the provision that allows a country to protect one product. For example, Malaysia has been protecting its auto industry. The result has been a movement towards bilateral trade agreements between ASEAN countries and outside nations. For example, Singapore has signed bilateral trade agreements with New Zealand and the United States. Other ASEAN nations, particularly Thailand, are likely to follow.

29 For example, for a description of the growth and development of the architecture profession during this period, see Eckardt (1999).

30 For more detail on the increasing strength of Bangkok in terms of business and producer services, see Muller (2003a, 2003b).

31 For technical details, see Webster and Nopanant (2002).

32 The Korean case was the fastest the world has seen, in two generations (40 years) the rural population decreased from approximately 80 per cent of the

population to 18 per cent. Approximately a quarter of the rural population out-migrated in the 1970s, a further 35 per cent in the 1980s.

33 For a discussion on the threat from commoditization of manufacturing products to East Asian economies, see Yusuf (2003, pp. 27–8).

References

Chatrudee Theparat (2002) Competing for a shrinking pie, *Bangkok Post 2002 Year-End Economic Review*, 30 December, pp. 18–19.

Connell, J. (1999) Beyond Manila: walls, malls, and private spaces, *Environment and Planning A*, 31, pp. 417–39.

Douglass, M. (2002) *The Urban Transition in Vietnam*, Fukuoka: United Nations Centre for Human Settlements.

Eckardt, J. (1999) The Good, the Bad, and the Ugly: the architects, in: *Bangkok People*, Bangkok: Asia Books.

Kasarda, J.D. (2002) *Aerotropolis: Airport-Driven Urban Development*, Washington: Urban Land Institute.

Leaf, M. (1996) Building the road for the BMW: culture, vision, and the extended metropolitan region of Jakarta, *Environment and Planning A*, 28, pp. 1617–35.

Muller, L. (2003a) Advanced business services in Southeast Asia: an opportunity for localizing investment. Working paper on Services, Space, Society No. 9, Birmingham: Service Sector Research Unit, University of Birmingham.

Muller, L. (2003) Advanced business services in Southeast Asia: localization of international investment, PhD Dissertation, Department of City and Regional Planning, University of California at Berkeley.

NESDB (2002) *Thailand in Brief*, Bangkok.

NESDB/ADB (2000) *Assessment and Recommendations: NESDB's Ninth Plan Strategies*, Bangkok.

NESDB/Norconsult (1994) *Urban Impacts of the New Bangkok International Airport*, Bangkok.

NESDB/Norconsult (1997) Spatial aspects of Thailand's environment and natural resources, *Key Analysis: A Spatial Development Framework for Thailand*, Bangkok: NESDB/Norconsult.

New Star Publishers (2001) *The Tenth Five-Year Plan of China* (Summary), Beijing: New Star Publishers.

OECF (1997) Supporting urban infrastructure in developing countries, in: OECF, *OECF Annual Report 1997*, Tokyo, OECF.

Pasuk Phongpaichit and Baker, C. (2000) *Thailand's Crisis*, Chiang Mai: Silkworm Books.

Thailand Development Research Institute (1999) *Social Impacts of the Asian Economic Crisis in Thailand, Indonesia, Malaysia, and the Philippines*, Bangkok.

Toffler, A. (1971) *Future Shock*, New York: Bantam Books.

United Nations (2001) *World Population Monitoring 2001*, Department of Economic and Social Affairs, Population Division, United Nations, New York.

United Nations (2002) *World Urbanization Prospects: the 2001 Revision*, United Nations Population Division, United Nations, New York.

Uthis Kaothien and Webster, D. (1998) *Globalization and Urbanization: The Case of Thailand*. Input paper to World Development Report 2000, World Bank, Washington.

Warr, P. and Isra Sarntisart (2002) The role of urban regions in poverty reduction. Research paper, NESDB/ADB, Bangkok.

Webster, D. (2000) Shaping urban growth in China; policy considerations. Policy paper prepared for EASUR (East Asian Urban Unit), World Bank, Washington.

Webster, D. (2002a) *On the Edge: Shaping the Future of Peri-Urban Asia, The Urban Dynamics of East Asia Series*, Asia/Pacific Research Center, Stanford University.

Webster, D. (2002b) Implementing decentralization in Thailand: the road forward. Office of the Decentralization to Local Government Organization Committee/World Bank, Bangkok.

Webster, D. (2002c) Achieving sustainable urbanization in the Ayutthaya extended urban region: issues and possible strategic thrusts. Issues Paper, NESDB/ADB, Bangkok.

Webster, D. (2003) Achieving sustainable urbanization in a coastal amenity cluster: the Hua Hin–Cha Am coastal region. Issues Paper, NESDB/ADB, Bangkok.

Webster, D. (2003a) Urban dynamics and policy frameworks in developing East Asia. East Asia Urban Working Paper Series, World Bank, Washington.

Webster, D. and Nopanant Tapananont (2002) *Enhancing Rural-Urban Linkages in Thailand*, Bangkok: NESDB/ADB.

World Bank (2000a) *Thailand Country Dialogue Monitor*, Bangkok: World Bank, February.

World Bank (2000b) *Thailand Economic Monitor: December 2000*, Bangkok: World Bank.

World Bank (2002) *Thailand Economic Monitor 2001*, Bangkok: World Bank.

Yusuf, S. (2003) *Innovative East Asia: The Future of Growth*, Oxford: Oxford Press/World Bank.

Chapter 11

Natural resources and the environment

Mingsarn Kaosa-ard

In the history of Thailand, 1997 will be remembered as the end of an economic Golden Age. The decade of accelerated growth ending in 1997 was accompanied by an increase in educational opportunities, the communications infrastructure, and the information technology sector. Employment patterns, lifestyles, and consumption patterns all underwent substantial changes. Natural resources were severely degraded as unrestrained growth combined with ineffective institutional protection accelerated the extraction rate of natural resources and the creation of pollution. Thailand's natural resources and environment have paid the price for its phenomenal economic growth.

This chapter is organized as follows. The following section reviews the situation of natural resources over the past decade, during which Thailand was at the height of its economic boom. This discussion aims to reveal how the existing practice of open access to natural resources has come under stress as the result of rapid economic change. The next section describes mounting conflicts over the use and management of natural resources. The following section outlines sources of institutional stress, and the final section attempts to look to the future and to emphasize that the multiple-use conflicts found in environmental management need to be resolved by a variety of tools and not only the legal instruments that are currently in use.

Thailand's economic Golden Age was marked by several distinguishing features. First, the effects on the environment from the structural transition from an agrarian to an industrial economy became more readily apparent. Second, most of the development activity centred on Bangkok, which became an enormous mega-city attracting vast numbers of rural migrants. This has created serious problems of overcrowding and pollution, which require correspondingly expensive and complex solutions. Third, despite the enormous growth of the industrial sector, which constituted 30 per cent of national income in 1996, it only supported some 10 per cent of the population. This left the vast majority of Thais dependent on the service and agricultural sectors, with the majority (about two-thirds of the workforce) depending on agriculture in an increasingly degraded environment.

Fourth, the economic development spurred social changes that included the emergence of a middle class that called for democratic politics, and demanded public participation in making improvements to the quality of life and the securing of an environment of decent quality. Finally, real estate developments in that period led to explosive levels of speculation, including forest and rural land. Many acquisitions of certificates for land rights were marked by the abuse of power. These factors combined to create the context within which natural resources were depleted.

Natural resource depletion

Forest resources

Thailand was blessed with an abundance of forest resources. Only a century ago, 72 per cent of its territory was covered by forests, accounting for approximately 230 million *rai* of land.[1] Less than 40 years ago, in 1961, that number was still relatively high at 171 million *rai*, or 53 per cent of the country. Most recently, however, only about one-quarter (26 per cent), 81 million *rai*, of the country was under forest cover (Table 11.1 and Figure 11.1). From 1961–98 Thailand lost an average of 2.4 million *rai* of forest every year and has been transformed from an exporter of timber into a very significant importer.

Alarmed by the rapid rate of deforestation, in 1989 the government revoked all terrestrial forestry concessions by decree. Unfortunately, the logging ban has had little apparent effect on the rate of forest loss. The rate of loss in the seven years following the ban was 1.2 per cent annually, identical to the rate during the seven years that preceded the ban (Table 11.2 and Figure 11.2).

The replanting of forests has long been one of the main activities of the Royal Forest Department (RFD). From 1906–96 the RFD planted 5,436,999 *rai* of forests. This amount is insignificant when compared with the amount of forest that has been lost. Despite the importance which the government claims to place on the management of forest resources and reforestation, the budgets these have been allocated have been inadequate. Principally due to budget limitations, the RFD was only able to replant one-third of the target area to be reforested as set out in the two National Economic and Social Development Plans covering 1982 to1991.

The roles and values placed on forests have undergone drastic changes. Forests were originally valued mainly for timber and as land reserves for agriculture, military use or even for landfill sites. Today, they are valued not only as a source of land, timber, and other forest products but also for

Table 11.1 Forest area in Thailand by region, 1961 to 1998 (unit: *rai*)

	Region					Total
	North	Northeast	Central and west	South	East	
1961	72,671,875	44,315,000	22,287,812	18,516,250	13,226,875	171,017,812
	(68.54)	(41.99)	(52.91)	(41.89)	(57.98)	(53.33)
1973	70,996,875	31,669,375	14,981,250	11,521,875	9,397,500	138,566,875
	(66.96)	(30.01)	(35.56)	(26.07)	(41.19)	(43.21)
1976	63,954,375	25,933,750	13,641,250	12,586,875	7,894,375	124,010,625
	(60.32)	(24.57)	(32.38)	(28.86)	(34.60)	(38.67)
1978	59,335,625	19,513,125	12,766,250	11,011,875	6,898,125	109,525,000
	(55.96)	(18.49)	(30.31)	(24.89)	(30.24)	(34.15)
1982	54,847,500	16,178,750	11,572,500	10,276,250	5,000,000	97,875,000
	(51.73)	(15.33)	(27.47)	(23.25)	(21.92)	(30.52)
1985	52,578,750	15,987,500	11,053,125	9,678,125	4,993.75	94,291,250
	(49.59)	(15.15)	(26.24)	(21.90)	(21.89)	(29.40)
1988	50,251,250	14,808,125	10,777,500	9,143,750	4,896,250	89,876,875
	(47.39)	(14.03)	(25.59)	(20.69)	(21.46)	(28.03)
1989	50,138,750	14,741,250	10,764,375	9,125,000	4,866,625	89,635,625
	(47.29)	(13.97)	(25.55)	(20.65)	(21.33)	(27.95)
1991	48,214,375	13,624,375	10,385,000	8,405,625	4,806,875	85,436,250
	(45.47)	(12.91)	(24.65)	(19.02)	(21.07)	(26.64)
1993	47,019,375	13,420,625	10,234,375	8,005,000	4,771,250	83,450,625
	(44.35)	(12.72)	(24.30)	(18.11)	(20.91)	(26.02)
1995	46,178,701	13,290,417	10,180,105	7,784,105	4,744,797	82,178,161
	(43.55)	(12.59)	(24.17)	(17.61)	(20.80)	(25.62)
1998	45,660,552	13,114,979	10,030,609	7,578,113	4,691,867	81,076,120
	(43.06)	(12.43)	(23.81)	(17.15)	(20.57)	(25.28)
Total area	106,027,680	105,533,958	42,124,189	44,196,992	22,814,063	320,696,882

Source: Royal Forest Department, Bangkok, 2000.

Note:
Figures in parentheses are percentages of forest area in the total regional area. The *rai* is the usual unit of measurement of land area in Thailand. 1 *rai* = 0.16 hectare; 6.25 *rai* = 1 hectare.

their ecological and social functions, including regulation of stream flows, soil and water conservation, microclimate regulation, carbon sequestration, tourism, education, recreation, and as a store of the future wealth which could come from biodiversity. Forests are increasingly viewed as important sources of genetic resources, some currently being used but with the vast majority waiting for their potential to be actualized.

Much of the poor performance cited above is a result of outdated policies and institutions. Forestry policies and agencies are often centralized and bureaucratic and are oriented towards production. The current forest policies and institutions still reflect the old economic values that were placed on forests. Thai forest policy was designed to protect public timber

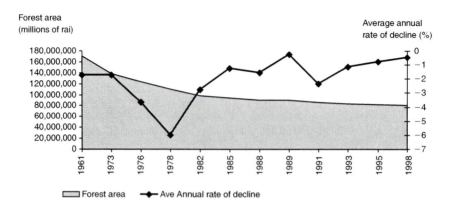

Figure 11.1 Forest area and the rate of forest land decline, 1961 to 1998 (source: Royal Forest Department, Bangkok, 2002).

revenues and public land. Most of the government budget was used for planting trees on public land rather than to understand the value of their ecological functions and then optimize these values for each watershed in order to maximize social gains.

The Royal Forest Department was first established over a century ago as a revenue generating, and not a conservation, department. The management of timber revenue was the major function of the RFD until 1989, when the logging ban was put in place. This shift in emphasis of the main mission of the RFD to forest protection forced the RFD to shoulder responsibilities for which it had no expertise – the management of the

Table 11.2 Forest situations before and after the logging ban (unit: millions of *rai*)

Description	Forested area
Before the logging ban	
1982	97.8
1989 (logging ban declared)	89.6
Forest cover lost before the logging ban, 1982–89 (%)	8.2
Average forest cover loss per year (%)	1.2
After the logging ban	
1989 (logging ban declared)	89.6
1995	82.2
Forest cover lost after the logging ban, 1989–95 (%)	7.4
Average forest cover loss per year (%)	1.2

Source: TDRI estimates, 1997.

Note
Definition of rai, see Table 11.1.

Area (millions of rai)

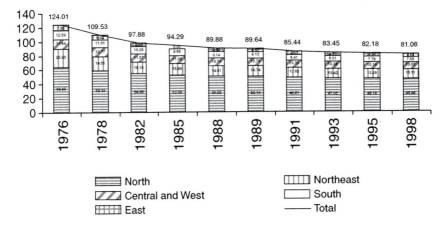

Area (millions of rai)

North
Central and West
East

Northeast
South
Total

Figure 11.2 National forest area by region, 1976 to 1998 (source: Royal Forest Department, Bangkok, 2002).

forest inhabitants. This is important, as protected forest areas are not necessarily areas of pure wilderness. They are often inhabited by communities who have traditionally relied on forest resources for their livelihood. The modern legal instruments used by the state to create protected areas have often neglected the rights of these traditional users, depriving local communities of their usual sources of sustenance and resulting in bitter, and at times violent, conflicts between the state and local communities.

As for watershed protection, attempts to replace shifting cultivation with sedentary agriculture in the highlands has led to soil erosion, agricultural chemicals discharge and residues, and competition for water between highland and the lowland users. Moreover, protected areas are also valued for tourism purposes. The number of tourists and the accompanying wastes that they generate have transformed forest rangers in some famous national parks into tourist and traffic managers and diverted them from their actual duties and responsibilities. Unable to cope with multiple-use conflicts between agencies and the public, between different agencies, and between highlanders and lowlanders, Thai forests continue to deteriorate despite increased budgets and numbers of personnel assigned to their protection.

Land resources

Thailand has always enjoyed a relative abundance of land, and when compared with the rest of Asia, it is currently the second most land abundant country in the region. It is also predicted to be the most land abundant country in the near future (Table 11.3). In fact, the amount of arable land per head continued to increase until the 1970s, when it began a continuous decline, from 2.5 *rai* per person in 1983 to 2.2 *rai* per person by 1993. Unfortunately, the increases in the amount of arable land have come as a result of deforestation. Agricultural production has increased as a result of increases in the amount of area under cultivation, rather than increasing yields per unit area. The Green Revolution has made only a relatively small contribution to agriculture in Thailand, where producers have tended to favour crops of higher eating quality over the modified and high-yield varieties of the Green Revolution. As a result, rice yields are very low, lower than those of Laos, Myanmar or Vietnam.

Further complicating matters is that much of the most recently cleared agricultural land is located in less favourable environments. These lands produce less and also tend to degrade most rapidly and, because they are usually located on land cleared from conservation forests by poor subsistence farmers who do not have title to the land, there are few resources or incentives available to conserve or improve the land's condition. Losses in

Table 11.3 Arable land scarcity index (ha per capita) in Asia, 1961, 1990 and 2025

Economy	Year		
	1961	1990	2025
East Asia			
China, Peoples Rep. of	0.16	0.08	0.06
Japan	0.06	0.004	0.04
Korea, Rep. of	0.08	0.05	0.04
Southeast Asia			
Cambodia	0.43	0.35	0.16
Indonesia	0.18	0.12	0.08
Lao PDR	0.38	0.2	0.09
Malaysia	0.49	0.27	0.15
Myanmar	0.47	0.27	0.13
Philippines	0.24	0.13	0.08
Thailand	0.43	0.41	0.31
Vietnam	0.17	0.1	0.05
South Asia			
Afghanistan	0.71	0.54	0.18
Bangladesh	0.17	0.09	0.05
India	0.36	0.2	0.12
Nepal	0.19	0.14	0.07
Pakistan	0.34	0.17	0.07
Sri Lanka	0.16	0.11	0.08

Source: Engelman and LeRoy (1995).

actual production due to land degradation in these less favourable environments are not likely to be very large in terms of total national output. Degraded lands are, however, generally in areas already stricken by poverty, and therefore losses in crop productivity due to land degradation deprive a significant portion of income from the poorer, if not the poorest, segments of the society.

The lack of well-defined land use rights can lead to a lack of incentives to improve and invest in the land or to engage in land, soil, and water conservation. The process of providing title deeds to farmers has been going on for several decades. Increasingly, the government is turning land outside of protected and fragile headwater areas over to local inhabitants. The remaining contentious issue is how to deal with settlements in headwaters and fragile ecosystems. Even in a land-abundant country such as Thailand, the removal of settlements from such areas is usually met with strong resistance. This is compounded by the difficulty of locating new sites that are appropriate for resettlement.

If the highland inhabitants are to be allowed to remain in less fragile ecosystems, some form of land security needs to be given as this directly affects conservation behaviour. Currently, the government's policy is not to give land ownership. In the highlands, where land tenure security is mostly absent, farmers lack incentives for the adoption of erosion control practices. Discussions on community usufruct rights (Knok *et al.* 1994) have been proposed but no decisions have been made so far. The types of rights that need to be given are those that harmonize the goals of increased conservation efforts and productivity, but prevent the agricultural extensification that has led to so much of the deforestation. Other policies are needed to complement land policies, such as non-farm employment and education for the younger generation designed to create more non-farm employment options.

In the lowlands, successive governments have initiated various projects to deal with the people inhabiting forest areas. The two most famous are the allocation of land to poor people in degraded forest reserve areas (*Khor Jor Kor*) and the usufruct right (*Sor Thor Kor*) projects. They illustrate how public land policy can interfere with, or even usurp, the role of forest policy.

The *Khor Jor Kor* Project had as its objective the relocation of people from conservation forest areas into degraded forest areas. The initial size of the project was about 1 million *rai* (160,000 hectares), and was to be implemented first in the northeast, where deforestation was greatest. Its implementation brought widespread discontent for numerous reasons, not least that the land where people were being resettled was often already inhabited. Claims were made by some of those already inhabiting the areas designated for resettlement that they were forced to reduce the size of the land they already held. Similar claims exist that some of those people who had been relocated lost land as well, being moved onto smaller amounts of land than they had originally held.

The amount of land allocated to the resettled people, 15 *rai*, often proved to be inadequate for subsistence living, especially where the relocated people were now living on less fertile land. In other cases, the infrastructure or utilities that had been prepared in the resettlement areas were inadequate, causing hardships to the people concerned. There were also allegations that the military used force in some cases to move and resettle people. Amid widespread protests and resistance, the government, under the leadership of Prime Minister Anand Panyarachun, decided to abandon the project entirely in July 1992.

The *Sor Thor Kor* Project was part of the plan to allocate land to people in degraded forest areas. It was approved by the Cabinet in 1979 and implemented in 1982. The objective was to provide some kind of a usufruct right to those people already inhabiting and using the degraded forest areas. Following several years of implementation, the *Sor Thor Kor* Project had often been criticized for not achieving its intended results. One reason cited for its failure is that the land document that is granted, the *Sor Thor Kor* document, does not confer land ownership. These documents are of limited economic value as they cannot be mortgaged for capital that can then be invested in the land. Despite the fact that the usufruct right is granted on the condition that it cannot be sold or transferred, it has been found that land speculation on areas covered by *Sor Thor Kor* documents is widespread, and the prices for these lands depend on their potential economic, not solely agricultural, use.

Before the economic collapse of 1997, land speculation was rampant and the failure to curb windfall gains either through capital gains tax or taxes on non-utilized land encouraged land sales and forest encroachment. Appropriate tax instruments are therefore needed to reduce the pressure to open new land while non-used lands are still available.

Water resources

Thailand is not currently experiencing a water shortage, but competition for water is increasingly intense. Water availability per capita is slightly over 1,800 cubic metres per person per year, while countries considered to be experiencing water stress generally have less than 1,700 cubic metres. Moreover, Thailand is actually the country in the Greater Mekong sub-region least endowed with water, having much less water per capita than neighbours Vietnam and Myanmar (Table 11.4). The lack of water is in fact a constraint for Thai agriculture, particularly rice.

The ratio of annual internal renewable water resources per capita in Thailand is lower than the Asian average. River basins with low water per capita ratios that are expected to face shortages in the future include the

Table 11.4 Water resources of Asia

Country	Annual internal renewable water resource[a]			Annual river flows		Annual withdrawals[b]	
	Total (cubic km)	Per capita (cubic metres)	From other countries (cubic km)	Volume (cubic km)	Percentage of water from from internal sources (%)	Including external (%)	Per capita (cubic metres)
East Asia							
PRC	2,812.4	2,201	17.2	525.5	19	19	439
Japan	430.0	3,393	0.0	91.4	21	21	735
Rep. of Korea	64.9	1,384	4.9	23.7	36	34	531
Mongolia	34.8	13,073	n.a.	0.4	1	1	182
Southeast Asia							
Cambodia	120.6	10,795	355.6	0.5	0	0	66
Indonesia	2,838.0	13,380	0.0	73.4	3	3	407
Lao PDR	190.4	35,049	91.2	1.0	1	0	260
Malaysia	580.0	26,074	n.a.	12.7	2	2	633
Myanmar	880.6	19,306	128.2	4.0	0	0	102
Philippines	479.0	6,305	0.0	55.4	12	12	811
Thailand	210.0	3,420	199.9	33.1	16	8	596
Vietnam	366.5	4,591	524.7	54.3	15	6	815
South Asia							
Afghanistan	55.0	2,421	10.0	26.1	47	40	1,846
Bangladesh	105.0	813	1,105.6	14.6	14	1	134
Bhutan	95.0	44,728	n.a.	0.0	0	0	13
India	1,260.6	1,244	647.2	500.0	40	26	588
Nepal	198.2	8,282	12.0	29.0	15	14	1,397
Pakistan	84.7	541	170.3	155.6	184	61	1,269
Sri Lanka	50.0	2,656	n.a.	9.8	20	20	573

Source: World Resources Institute 2000–01.

Notes:
a Annual internal renewable water excludes river flows from other countries.
b Water withdrawal includes all water used for irrigation, industry, and agriculture (including watering of animals). It is not the same as water consumption.
0 = zero or less than half of the unit measured. n.a. means not available.

Sakaekrang, Pasak, Thachin, Chi, Wang and Yom. There are multiple-use conflicts between water users, such as those between manufacturing industries, agriculture, and services, as well as between upstream and downstream river residents.

To date, there have been few rigorous studies on the potential of ground water. Over-pumping in large cities, especially Bangkok, has caused land subsidence, seawater intrusion, and the contamination of ground water with chemicals and waste water from agricultural and industrial activities, as well as from residential communities.

Almost 90 per cent of Thailand's water usage occurs in agriculture. In recent years, the rapid growth of the non-farm sector and urbanization have placed a much greater demand on the water supply. As urbanization and industrialization in the lower Chao Praya delta intensified, seasonal shortages arose and competition for water between different sectors – urban versus rural, industrial versus personal, upstream versus downstream, and so forth – took place. Thus, in comparison with other countries in Southeast Asia, except Singapore, water allocation is a more serious concern in Thailand. Population and economic growth in the Northern basins have resulted in greater water use there as well. Even within the agricultural sector, there is competition for water among dry season users between the different stakeholders, and the resulting conflicts have become more intense and at times even violent. Although the water situation is not severe, it is fast becoming evident that the present water institutions are unable to cope with rising demand and the social conflicts that result.

Water policy and institutions are generally shaped by the supply and demand situation in a country. In water-abundant countries, water is often under an open access regime. As the demand for water increases and multiple-use conflicts heighten, national governments invariably feel the need to adapt the old institutions and design new ones to meet the changing and ever-increasing demands for water.

Unlike forestry, Thailand did not have a national water policy until the announcement of the long term Natural Resources and Environment Policy and Plan in 1997. Past government directions had been aimed at developing water resources in order to secure a greater supply. The national directives on water resource management were referred to in a general, not specific, manner in the National Economic and Social Development Plans, which provided very broad outlines only – such as encouraging a holistic approach to basin development in Plan 6, and sustainable development in Plan 8. In late 1996, as part of the long-term Natural Resources and Environment Policy and Plan, covering 1997–2016, a water resource policy was announced with the aim of systematically developing water supplies and of conserving and restoring both surface and underground water resources in all basins in order to have adequate and sustainable water use and a suitable level of water quality.

The emphasis of water policy is focused on the provision of water and supply side management. There are no clear policies and rules on water allocation, despite the fact that water is becoming scarce. Until recently, the elected governments have been formed by unstable coalitions, which has prevented them from taking bold steps in demand-side management, such as water pricing. At the same time, the construction of new dams has become more expensive, not only financially but also socially and environmentally, given that the best locations have already been dammed. As a result, the water institutions at all levels can be said to be under stress. In general, under the present open access regime, water belongs to those who are wealthy and who have access to advanced technology for water extraction and political power. This situation raises questions of efficiency and equity. Since water for irrigation is essentially free, for example, farmers in the irrigation systems (normally the richer groups) benefit at the expense of the tax-paying public who are left to foot the bill, and who also include the poorer rain-fed farmers.

Water institutions are fragmented, overlapping, and lack coordination. Surface water is under an open access system. It is considered available for general use under the Civil and Commercial Code. Water for irrigation is under the control of the Royal Irrigation Department (RID), which is empowered to charge (nominal) water fees to users but has hardly ever exercised this power. Water for hydro power dams is controlled by the Electricity Generating Authority of Thailand (EGAT), a state enterprise. Underground water is under the jurisdiction of the Department of Minerals in the Ministry of Industry, which charges relatively high fees to users and the fees bear no relationship to the fees charged for irrigated water. Water in the people's irrigation systems is controlled by the water user groups, which charge some fees, normally much higher than those allowed for under the irrigation law of the Royal Irrigation Department.

At the policy level, Thailand has a number of coordinating bodies with the mandate of recommending or setting of a national policy relating to water resource development, management and conservation. All these bodies are composed differently, as they were established under different laws and regulations and for various purposes, but some of their functions and mandates overlap, especially those concerning water quality and water resource development. Yet, there is no one law that explicitly identifies the exact rights and entitlements to water of the different stakeholders when water shortages occur.

Water resource development management and planning is currently done on a project basis, although attempts are being made to convert this to a river basin approach. At present, water resource planning and management is undertaken in the context of administrative regions rather than the traditional hydrologic unit, the catchment basin. As a result, the projects from different departments may be overlapping, and compete or even conflict over the same source of water.

In addition, existing water resource planning and management has been almost exclusively undertaken by the ministries from their central offices in Bangkok. This centralization of decision-making has been exacerbated by the rapid urbanization of Bangkok and the need to protect the people and the wealth of Bangkok from water shortages and from floods. Hence, development has tended to emphasize the problems of the lower Chao Phraya Basin at the expense of other water-related activities outside of this immediate area.

At the village level, where communities are in charge of people's irrigation, water management is threatened by declining membership as the youth tends to opt for urban rather than agricultural occupations. Innovations such as water pricing and other market instruments have been introduced. Villagers have hired irrigation managers and, in some cases, paid for water in cash rather than in kind. However, local communities have no legal rights to the water they use. Non-contributing individuals, such as the operators of land owned by absentee landlords, may pump water from the community sources without providing any compensation.

There are no charges for surface water, although water charges were explicitly encouraged as early as the Fifth National Economic and Social Development Plan of 1972–77. In the Eighth Plan (1996–2001), charges for raw water for household consumption and all economic sectors were recommended. In addition, it was suggested during a revision of the price structure for household and industrial water consumption that it should reflect the costs of acquisition, production, distribution, and wastewater treatment. At present, there is no legal basis for charging water fees for surface water outside irrigation project areas.

According to the State Irrigation Act, the RID is authorized to charge farmers up to 0.50 baht per *rai* of land farmed and non-farmers 0.50 baht per cubic metre of water used. In addition, the Dykes and Ditches Act of 1962 and the 1974 Agricultural Land Consolidation Act allow the RID to collect Operation and Maintenance charges (including capital costs) from land owners and water users. Revenues from surface charges have been negligible, totalling about 23 million baht in 1996.

Economic instruments for controlling the use of groundwater were not installed until 1984, when the Department of Mineral Resources (DMR) imposed a user charge of 1 baht (then about US$0.04) per cubic metre. As land subsidence due to the over-extraction of groundwater continued, this user charge was raised to 3.5 baht (US$0.14) per cubic metre in 1995. In areas where an alternative piped water supply is not available, a 25 per cent discount is applied. User charges apply only to commercial businesses, industry, and farming. Households are exempted.

The single most important weakness of current water institutions is that the relationship between underground water, irrigated water, and surface water has not been recognized, and hence water prices are fixed in an unrelated manner. For example, the ceiling price of irrigated water is only one-seventh that of groundwater, while surface water is available free of charge. The consequence of this water pricing system is the wasteful and inefficient use of water, creating unnecessary water logging, and sub-optimal levels of wastewater.

The implementation of groundwater user charges faces two limitations: a lack of enforcement and the inability to control the volume of water extracted. When the volume of extraction is not closely monitored, the user charge imposed will not be appropriate. Users may lower their water bills simply by reporting lower than actual levels of use and hence reduce the effectiveness of the user charge.

The Groundwater Act requires that anyone desiring to drill for, or extract, groundwater must apply for permission. This may seem to indicate that the government has firm control over the regulation of groundwater use, and would be able to induce the proper allocation, management, and conservation of it. It is doubtful, however, that the existing legislation really is capable of assisting the government in achieving such a goal. For instance, all government agencies and state enterprises are actually not subject to this law, and the issue of the simultaneous use of groundwater and surface water is not addressed.

Although the Polluter-Pays Principle was adopted 1992, and the 1992 Environment Act had a provision to raise waste treatment charges, wastewater treatment fees have not been enforced in Bangkok, one of the few places where some capacity for treatment actually exists. Wastewater charges are now controlled by the industrial estates. The method of costing is called 'average cost pricing'. Outside of Bangkok, charges for wastewater treatment are implemented in Patong Beach in the Province of Phuket and in Pattaya in Chonburi Province, where the treatment is financed by the Environment Fund. So far, there have been no charges for wastewater treatment by the treatment centres established by the Department of Public Works, which is financed from the central government's budget.

Water resources management problems can be summarized as follows. No acceptable mechanism currently exists for water allocation in times of shortages. The state has emphasized supply management and engineering solutions. Other instruments, such as demand side management tools, have yet to be developed. The enforcement of regulations concerning underground water resources is inadequate. Local governments lack rules and procedures for flood control, especially in flood-prone areas.

Some appropriate strategies for the future management of water resources are the following:

1   Management should be organized at the basin-level unit and include representatives from local water users.
2   Economic, legislative, regulatory, and social instruments should be utilized so as to reflect changes and trends in the demand and supply of water.
3   Recharge areas should be identified and protected. A monitoring system for ground water use should be established.
4   Water resource development should include a cost–benefit analysis that takes into account the valuation of damage to natural resources and the environment using methods that are acceptable to all stakeholders.

Coastal and fisheries resources

Thailand has been one of the world's top ten fishing nations since 1972, and is currently the world's largest producer and exporter of edible fish and fish products. Commercial aquaculture has grown rapidly, particularly shrimp, of which Thailand has been the largest producer and exporter since 1993. As the result of decades of over-fishing, tourism, industry, human occupation, commercial agriculture and aquaculture, the coastal areas have undergone tremendous changes. The stocks of economically important species of fish have been depleted. Coastal ecosystems, such as mangroves, coral reefs, and sea-grass beds, have been destroyed or degraded, and land-based pollution has been intense (see Figure 11.3). A number of estimates have indicated that approximately one-third of Thailand's mangroves have been destroyed for shrimp farming. Fortunately, increased scientific understanding has confirmed that mangroves are not suitable areas for this, which has decreased the commercial demand for mangroves as a source of land for shrimp farming.

One of the biggest challenges faced in addressing these problems is that there is not much useful information on the status of coastal and ocean resources in Thailand, and the collection of realistic and accurate information therefore needs to be a priority. Nevertheless, there is little doubt that the extent of the degradation to coastal and ocean resources has been severe. Examples of this include the rapidly declining catch rates, as measured by catch per unit effort, which are currently only 7 per cent of what they were in the early 1960s and the high percentage (up to 40 per cent) of trashfish (economically unimportant bycatch species) in marine landings. Shrimp farming is subject to frequent disease outbreaks, making its sustainable development doubtful. As a result of these problems, the share of fisheries in GDP halved between 1970 and 1996.

The major reason behind these high levels of degradation and depletion of coastal and ocean resources is the fact that they have been exploited as open-access resources, with poorly defined or undefined user

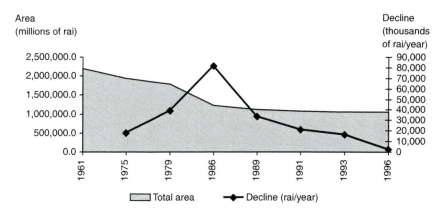

Figure 11.3 Mangrove forest area and decline per year, 1961 to 1996 (source: Royal Forest Department, Bangkok, 1996).

rights and restrictions. This essentially means that anyone who wishes to have access to these resources can do so, and they are only limited in what they can remove by their own extractive abilities. It is therefore not surprising that Thailand has an overcapacity of fishing vessels.

According to the Fisheries Act, a 3,000 m near-shore zone has been reserved for small-scale artisanal fisherfolk, yet the commercial trawlers and push-netters, which use relatively destructive fishing gear, routinely fish there illegally. This has caused numerous conflicts between the small-scale artisanal fishery establishments – which constitute 78 per cent of fishing establishments yet account for less than a fifth of total catch by value and only 5–6 per cent by volume – and the large-scale commercial fishery establishments.

Thailand's policies on coastal and ocean resources can be described as production-oriented. However, those policies, designed during times of abundant resources, have been slow to respond to changes in the supply situation. Moreover, the enforcement of conservation regulations on fishing and aquaculture has been very lax. There are also many government agencies involved with coastal and marine resources but the political will to create effective laws and institutions is lacking. The National Marine Rehabilitation Board was formed as an inter-agency arm to enable integrated planning for the fisheries sector, but currently it is virtually not functioning, due to financial constraints and administrative bungling.

Existing economic incentives in the fisheries sector also tend to favour overexploitation, in the form of very low licence fees or fees that bear no relationship to the extractive capacity of the fishing gear to be used. The fishmeal sector, which relies on fish caught by methods that are damaging to the environment, is promoted through surcharges and tariffs. As a result, there is greater incentive for extraction than conservation.

One reason behind the lack of political will to enforce marine conservation measures and regulations is that, unlike other resources, such as forestry, the depletion of marine resources is much less readily apparent. It is not visible, like degraded lands or degraded forests, nor does it tend to have direct effects on people, such as the landslides that can result from deforestation. It is also more difficult to measure for institutions; satellite photography cannot reveal the extent of the depletion of aquatic resources as it can the extent of deforestation. Research and data collection related to fishery and aquatic resources are both difficult and expensive, and as a result scientific knowledge of these sectors is much more limited than that for agriculture, livestock and forestry, for example. Thus, both official and public awareness about the severity of the issue is not as high as that for the forest sector. There is a great need to educate not only the public, but government agencies and institutions as well.

Environmental degradation

Urbanization

Between 1995 and 2001, the proportion of Thais living in urban areas increased from 18 to 29 per cent (National Economic and Social Development Board 2002). These numbers are considered low, even when compared with countries at a similar level of development. The growth of the urban population has exceeded that of the rural population, and is predicted to continue to do so, with the urban population set to grow by 2.6 per cent annually over 1995–2015 (United Nations Development Programme 1998). Much of this shift is due to rural to urban migration, and it explains how, in the future (2020), the rural population will actually begin to decline (World Resources Institute 1998 and Chapter 10 of this volume).

Urbanization concentrates human population and therefore the wastes that they produce. About 73 per cent of water pollution, measured in terms of Biochemical Oxygen Demand (BOD) loading, is generated by households, 21 per cent by industry and about 5 per cent by agriculture (Thailand Development Research Institute 1999). Solid waste management, on the other hand, has become the greatest challenge for city management. In 1996, the country produced about 13 million tons of solid waste. By 2000, Thailand will be producing as much solid waste as rice, the main staple crop. This amount is considerable considering that Thailand is the world's largest exporter of rice.

Human waste is generally disposed of untreated through waterways in Thailand, which means that urbanization has adverse effects on water resources. When these waterways are rivers, this means that the down-stream users of water normally receive water that is more polluted. Solid wastes and other wastes are generally stored in poorly constructed and managed landfills, degrading the land, potentially seeping into and degrading the water table, and causing deforestation as forests are often cleared to create landfills. These effects can extend beyond the confines of the landfill. Many major cities are facing serious problems in their search for appropriate landfills. Cities also generate increased air pollution, not only from industry but also from other forms of human activity, especially transportation. Poor public transportation infrastructures in Thai cities have spurred the adoption of personal transportation, cars and motorcycles, which further aggravates the situation. Therefore, although cities themselves suffer from the environmental degradation they engender, they also damage the environment in areas well removed from them.

Urban growth has also been uneven, with much in just one city. Bangkok accounted for 55 per cent of Thailand's urban population in 2000, with an estimated population of 5.7 million. In addition to magnifying all of the problems normally associated with urbanization, Bangkok's location has resulted in the creation of certain problems of its own. Situated in the country's largest and most important river basin, the Chao Phraya, and in the middle of its most productive agricultural land, Bangkok is located in a position where it can degrade some of the most important natural resources in the country. The wastes produced by Bangkok have heavily polluted the Chao Phraya River, which feeds into the Gulf of Thailand only 100 km from Bangkok. Therefore, in addition to the damage done to the Chao Phraya itself, wastes from Bangkok have severely degraded coastal and aquatic resources in the Gulf of Thailand. Also, the amount of water Bangkok demands has placed great stress on the local groundwater, resulting in severe land subsidence.

Bangkok exemplifies the principal problems of the process of urbanization throughout Thailand. The most glaring is that of poor city planning. Town plans and zoning laws have been formulated and updated for many cities, especially Bangkok, yet they have never been seriously enforced, such that cities have not been developing in any organized or predictable manner. This means, among other things, that city populations are poorly distributed, industry located haphazardly, and areas beneficial in ecological and social terms, such as green spaces, are inadequate. This is also one of the principal causes of transportation problems within the cities. In addition, because urban growth has been the result of rural migration, large proportions of city populations, especially in Bangkok, come from various parts of the country. This diversity in the composition of cities, both physical and social, is in itself an extra problem, as it creates further complications for city planning and management.

Industrialization

The transformation of Thailand into an industrial society only really began a few decades ago. The changes in the structure of industry, from simple production (mostly agricultural processing) to large-scale production (including high technology), have led to increases in the use of chemicals and hazardous substances and the production of both industrial pollution and hazardous wastes (Mingsarn and Pornpen 1998). Between 1988 and 2000, the use of chemicals and chemical compounds increased almost ninefold (Table 11.5), and according to a joint study by the Department of Industry and the Department of Pollution Control, hazardous wastes were estimated to increase from 0.9 million tons in 1991 to 1.6 million tons in 1996. Since the cost of hazardous waste treatment is high, a sizeable proportion of the wastes is left untreated and is stored in factories, released into the atmosphere, or dumped into waterways or the forest reserve.

The process of economic development in Thailand also took on a particularly damaging form, in that it relied on the accelerated depletion of its natural resources and viewed the environment as no more than a waste sink, causing not only environmental degradation but also negative impacts on human health. In the last decade, pollution and its effects have greatly increased, requiring increased attention and funding. According to projections done by the Asia Development Bank, the level of pollution in Thailand in 2000 was 2.5 times that of 1990 (Weatherly 1994), giving it the second most severe pollution problems in Asia, following South Korea. Unfortunately, as previously discussed, in most cases the institutions cur-

Table 11.5 Imports, production, and estimated use of chemicals and chemical compounds, 1988 to 1996 (unit: millions of tons)

Year	Import	Production	Estimated use[a]
1988	1.31	0.70	2.01
1989	1.37	1.19	2.56
1990	1.75	1.23	2.98
1991	1.76	1.44	3.20
1992	2.26	2.40	4.66
1993	2.79	2.74	5.53
1994	3.01	5.88	8.89
1995	3.23	6.61	9.84
1996	3.40	8.84	12.24

Sources: Customs Department, Industrial Works Department, and Industrial Estates. Authority of Thailand.

Note:
a These figures show the maximum estimates because no adjustment has been made for exported amounts.

rently in place to deal with the environment do not have the ability, funds, or sometimes even the mandate, that would enable them to deal with this problem.

The Thai government has a clear policy on industrial pollution, having adopted the Polluter-Pays principle, unlike its policy regarding the management of natural resources. Enforcement, however, is lax for various reasons. First, the Ministry of Industry, which has direct responsibility for the control of factory-generated pollution, tends to regard growth objectives as more important than environmental objectives. In other words, the Ministry considers factory owners its main constituency rather than the general public. It is generally felt that the mandate of the Ministry is to promote industry and not to increase production costs, making Thai industry less competitive. Secondly, the Ministry does not have the expertise, the manpower, or the budget to implement regular pollution control.

Rising social conflicts

As resources become more scarce, degraded, and are used by a greater number of people for an increasing number of uses, they inevitably lead to social conflicts. Such conflicts have become so commonplace that they appear routinely in the mass media.

The greatest conflicts are due to competition over water, especially in places where allocation priorities for times of shortages are not in place. In Chom Thong district, Chiang Mai Province, lowland-farmers' groups organized a series of protests against highland farmers, who they accused of using up all the water. In June 1999, small-scale fisherfolk in 13 southern provinces organized protests against the Department of Fisheries and demanded that the government revoke the permission granted to commercial fishing fleets to use small-size mesh nets and luring lights for anchovy fishing, claiming that these practices are damaging to the livelihood of artisanal day fishers and the long-term stability of the resource system. In recent years, conflicts between user groups have become more frequent and, at times, violent. Voluntary monitoring of the trawler-free zone by local communities in the Province of Phang-Gna has already resulted in one death.

Conflicts between the people and government agencies are also mounting. The establishment of protected areas has deprived local communities of their traditional livelihood, as the National Park Law prohibits the extraction of any products or natural objects from protected areas. The development of water resource projects, such as dams and reservoirs, provides benefits to lowland farmers but takes land away from upland farmers. Compensation is often inadequate and does not allow for the lost opportunities related to the harvest of non-timber forest products.

For example, 1995 saw a conflict between local villagers and government authorities over the proposed construction of a dam in Phrae Province. The dam's construction would create a large-scale reservoir, called *Kaeng Sua Ten*, which would have inundated several villages. The hostility of these villagers finally found expression in their throwing stones at the representatives of the World Bank, which was to fund the project. Although the Thai government decided to proceed with the project, it has been delayed by the actions of two of the government agencies involved, again demonstrating the lack of clear objectives and understanding of economic and environmental tradeoffs. The Royal Irrigation Department, which would carry out the project, requires the approval of its feasibility study and environmental impact assessment by the National Environment Board. This approval had not been forthcoming, leading the Royal Irrigation Department to accuse the National Environment Board of causing the delay.

Conflicts are also emerging between production-oriented and protection-oriented government agencies. Conflicts are frequent in the case of the Royal Forest Department (RFD) and the Department of Mineral Resources (DMR), which sides with groups that want to mine in the upper watersheds where development is not allowed. In the area of coastal resources, the RFD prohibits fishing in protected areas while the aim of the Department of Fisheries is to maximize fishery production. Fishing lobby groups often place pressure on provincial governors who are the final arbiters over the Fisheries law to open fishing areas in or near protected areas.

The above conflicts arose for two major reasons. First, the government relies heavily on a command and control regime for management and lacks an adequate variety of tools to deal with multiple-use conflicts. Second, rigorous evaluations of the costs and benefits to stakeholders involved, including damage to the environment, are rarely undertaken. Thus, the government does not appreciate the true value of the project or the plight of the affected stakeholders and does not therefore compensate them adequately. As a result, many large public projects have met with public protest and are unable to advance.

When efforts are made to value natural resources and the environment, the results can be very revealing and useful for public policy purposes. For example, the *Khao Yai* National Park, Thailand's first and most popular national park, provides many environmental benefits, but deprived the 200 neighbouring villagers of an estimated 10,000 to 20,000 baht (US$400–800 at pre-1997 exchange rates) of income annually on a per household basis from products they would otherwise have extracted from it (Mingsarn *et al.* 1995). The net present value of the income lost by these villages has been estimated at between 1,650–3,300 million baht (US$66–132 million). However, the willingness to pay for the park's protection by those who value its establishment was also measured, and it amounted to 30,000 million baht (US$1,200 million). This helped to send a clear signal to policy makers on the value of a conservation project and how the affected stakeholders should be treated. Another example of a proper valuation is the cost and benefit study of the *Kaeng Sua Ten* Dam (see above) prepared for submission to the World Bank. It found that the project was not economically worthwhile even before mitigation costs were included (Thailand Development Research Institute 1999). Moreover, the inclusion of preliminary estimates of environmental damage suggested a net economic loss, measured in terms of net present value, of 1.1 billion baht (US$37 million).

A valuation study of an upstream–downstream water competition problem revealed that the revenues to downstream farmers could be real and substantial. In the Mae Taeng watershed in Northern Thailand, the expansion of irrigated agriculture in the upper catchment has deprived water from lowland farmers (Vincent *et al.* 1995). After taking into account the variability of temperature, water from the upper catchment has been reduced by 3 million cubic metres per year as a result. This has been translated into a loss in potential revenue of up to two and a half million dollars to lowland farmers. In this case, a more innovative mechanism of water allocation is needed.

Institutional stress

The examples mentioned above in forest, water, and land use policies exemplify the most common theme related to Thailand's environmental and social problems: the weakness of its institutions. It has been repeatedly observed that failures to protect the country's natural resources and environment have occurred despite the government's passing of a number of environmental laws and regulations during the 1990s. The first environmental protection legislation was enacted in 1975, long before most other Asian countries enacted such laws. It was further amended in 1992. However, numerous natural resource management laws have existed for over a century as each ministry has its own laws backing its own responsibilities and functions. Earlier policies and laws in fact encouraged the increased utilization of natural resources. These institutions were therefore not conceived with the purpose of conserving resources but rather to facilitate their extraction, and they have yet to adapt to the new situation of increased resource scarcity. Currently, most natural resources are managed by a number of line ministries. For instance, there are at least 30, mostly unrelated, laws governing water and water resources.

In practice, the laws passed have proved impotent, for various reasons. First, the effectiveness of the nation's rules and regulations are constrained by executive and political powers. The small Thai electoral constituency enables local power to be transformed into national political might. When influential provincial representatives to Parliament muster enough support from other local MPs they can negotiate their way into a ministerial posting, especially under weak coalition governments. Moreover, Thai laws are normally short and vague and assign substantial powers to the executive through the use of Ministerial Regulations and announcements. Thus, the executive has the power to direct the application of rules and, if it cannot influence the regulations, it can still influence those overseeing the regulations.

Second, overlapping mandates are believed to prevent some authorities from enforcing a law for fear of offending or overstepping another's jurisdiction. When mandates are conflicting, there are no clear boundaries marking jurisdiction and the final decision depends on the political strength of individual ministers. Coordination is attempted through interministerial committees, but if the Chairman of the committee is not high ranking enough conflicts are not easily resolved. When the Chairman of the committee is very important, such as the Prime Minister or Deputy Prime Minister, the committee is rarely even convened.

The above discussion also implies that the management of natural resources and environment in Thailand is under a sectoral approach. One advantage of the sectoral approach to natural resources management is specialization. However, the holistic nature of an ecosystem requires integrated management, since one sector's activities will affect another's. The sectoral approach is not compatible with the management of multiple-use conflicts either.

Although a number of conservation-oriented laws were passed in the 1990s, they were highly centralized in nature and some of them followed western models, which are radically different from local Thai conditions. As indicated earlier, the National Park Act is only concerned with nature and neglects the fact that the livelihoods of many rural communities depended on non-forest timber products and ignores the rural rules and regulations that local communities have crafted to ensure the sustained use of such products. Moreover, the lack of personnel, monitoring capabilities, and the lack of people's participation in the management of local resources mean that important natural resources for the most part continue to remain under *de facto* if not *de jure* open access. This has clearly led to the abuse of forest, water, and aquatic resources.

The government is also handicapped in its pursuit of environmental protection as it only has experience with a few management tools in this regard. Rules and regulations have so far been the primary instruments used in environmental conservation. These have been clearly insufficient, yet there are a few other options available, including the most potentially effective instruments, which are economic in nature. The National Environmental Quality Enhancement Act of 1992 does not contain any reference to economic instruments for environmental management except for fines and charges. There is no basis for environmental taxation in current laws, therefore the Ministry of Finance relies on the excise tax to perform this function.

The above diagnosis of deficiencies in policies and management tools is not unknown to policy makers and administrators. National and sectoral plans have proposed policy and legal reforms as well as innovative economic instruments. However, these plans are recognized for their importance as a budget reference, meaning that those projects that are not consistent with the plan will not get funding from the Budget Bureau. It is not surprising that the plans have become effective only as guidelines for investment. Engineering solutions, requiring construction, are normally implemented while reform measures, especially those that will create political pressures, are left untouched.

In addition to the way in which they are used, the institutions themselves tend to have inadequate human resources attached to them. Despite efforts to build up these resources, training has not been continuously done and is often not effective, as promotion is not tied to performance-based evaluations. The patronage system within the civil service prevents the rise of effective personnel, and in fact more often succeeds in protecting the ineffective ones. Also, as wages tend to be low, many able staff were lost to the private sector during the economic boom, creating effectiveness and morale problems for those remaining. Planning and policy making therefore suffered because institutions were unable to supply staff with the relevant information.

Government institutions have also been reluctant to support adequately NGO institutions that could complement and increase the value of their work. Although there was an increase in the number of Thai environmental NGOs during the 1990s, Thailand's rapidly improving economy led many donor countries to decrease their financial assistance while support from the Thai government remained low. Government funding for these NGOs is essential as, to date, private donations have been insufficient to support them. Perhaps this is because they have yet to devise a method that demonstrates their contribution to society. Moreover, transparency and accountability within small NGOs are still lacking. Furthermore, past experiences have created a lack of trust between NGOs and government agencies, which has created little desire on the part of government agencies to provide support to NGOs, either in the form of information, training, or capacity building.

Finally, one reason why politicians tend to be accountable to special interests and not the general public is that the general public is often not sufficiently aware of the situation to want to hold the government to account itself. Increased environmental awareness can also be effective in getting the general public to adopt more environmentally friendly behaviour itself. The methods used by the government to spread such information have not been coordinated between different government agencies for the achievement of common goals. As a result, the dissemination of information has often been used as a public relations tool instead of an effective means of creating public awareness and improving communication between the government and the public.

Conclusions: Thailand's environmental future

If the current pattern and rates of consumption are allowed to continue without appropriate changes to the managing institutions, Thailand is likely to see ever more natural resource sectors ceasing to be economic assets and turning instead into social liabilities. This is exemplified by the rise and fall of the forest sector over the last quarter century. In the coming decade, the coastal resource sector is likely to be lost, followed closely by the collapse of the fishery sector. According to estimates made before the economic crisis, Thailand will be spending public funds, depending on the method of treatment adopted, of between 143 billion baht (US$5.72 billion at pre-1997 exchange rates) and 433 billion baht (US$17.3 billion) for wastewater treatment and between 17 billion baht (US$0.7 billion) and 77 billion baht (US$3 billion) for solid waste disposal in order to have sufficient capacity up to 2015 (Direk *et al.* 1996). In urban areas, the amount of solid waste and water pollution generated is likely to double, thus competing for public funds, which are also in high demand for poverty alleviation, technology transfers, education, and health care. While pollution abatement costs associated with production and consumption are unavoidable and expected, a great deal of public funds could be saved through prudent management.

Environment policy is currently based on the single principle of polluter-pays. Policy makers have to be made aware of other principles for environmental protection apart from the polluter-pays principle. Other principles, such as the beneficiary-pays principle, the precautionary approach, and appropriate resource cost pricing, need to be examined as well as the use of preventative as opposed to corrective measures, which are needed to ensure effective environmental protection in the future. Moreover, multiple use conflicts will have to be managed by a variety of tools and not by relying solely on legal instruments. Legal instruments tend to be corrective and punitive, but many forms of environmental damages are irreversible and therefore must be prevented from occurring at all. Participatory management in the various agencies and other stakeholder organizations should be organized at an ecosystem level, such as river basins, rather than according to administrative boundaries. Considerable political will is required in order to address the institutional issues that are at the root of the problems in natural resource management and to implement economic instruments such as taxation measures.

Public participation and awareness need to be incorporated into government efforts in environmental conservation. The public should have the right to participate in the decision-making process on large-scale projects that have serious environmental consequences. The ability to develop and present reliable and neutral public information, which can form the basis of discussion, should be fostered. The counter-balancing of political and executive powers will be possible only when the public is given sufficient knowledge and opportunity to do so.

At the same time, the public needs to be reminded that it also has responsibilities of its own and not just the right to a decent environment. In the end, it is the activities of the population as a whole that will determine the fate of the environment, not just those of the government. But it is the government's responsibility to educate the public on the choices that are available and the consequences of its actions.

The 1997 economic crisis made expensive technical and engineering solutions more difficult to adopt. Therefore, the crisis should be seen as an opportunity to probe into the institutional reforms necessary to save Thailand's environment. Above all, it must be remembered that some environmental damage, unlike economic damage, is irreversible.

Note

1 The *rai* is the usual unit of measurement of land area in Thailand. 1 *rai* = 0.16 hectare = 0.395 acres. 6.25 *rai* = 1 hectare; 2.53 *rai* = 1 acre.

References

Direk Patmasiriwat, Sanchai Sutiphanwiharn, Wallaya Suphatchai, Sombat Sae Hae and Prinyarat Liangcharoen (1996) *Investment Allocation for Environmental Management: Concepts and Criteria for Budget Allocation*, Bangkok: Thailand Development Research Institute.

Engelman, R. and LeRoy, P. (1995) *Conserving Land: Population and Sustainable Food Production. Population and Environment Program*, Washington, DC: Population Action International.

Knok Rerkasem, Benjavan Rekasem, Mingsarn Kaosa-ard, Chaiwat Roonruangsee, Jesdapipat, S., Shinawatra, S. and Wijukprasert, P. (1994) *Sustainability of Highland Agriculture*, Bangkok: Thailand Development Research Institute.

Mingsarn Kaosa-ard, Direk Patmasiriwat, Supachit Manopimoke, Pornpen Wijukprasert, Jiraporn Plangpraphan, Sombat Saehae, Ukrit Uparasit, Arnel B. Rala and Sunil Pednekar (1995) *Green Finance: A Case Study of Khao Yai*, Bangkok: Thailand Development Research Institute.

Mingsarn Santikarn Kaosa-ard and Benjavan Rerkasem (1999) The growth and sustainability of agriculture in Asia. ADB Theme Paper No. 2 Manila: Asian Development Bank.

Mingsarn Kaosa-ard and Pornpen Wijukprasert (eds) (1998) *Thailand's Natural*

Resources and Environment: A Decade of Change, Bangkok: Thailand Development Research Institute.

National Economic and Social Development Board (2002) *Population Data Online.* Available at http://www.nesdb.go.th/main_menu/hum_soc/data/population/03POP-M.xls. (accessed 26 November 2002).

Thailand Development Research Institute (1999) *Review of the Suitability and the Feasibility of the Kaeng Sua Ten Project, Phrae Province*, Bangkok: Thailand Development Research Institute.

United Nations Development Programme (1998) *Human Development Report 1998.* New York: Oxford University Press.

Vincent, J.R., Mingsarn Kaosa-ard, Laxmi Worachi, Eric Y. Azumi, Nipon Tangtham and Arnel B. Rala (1995) *The Economics of Watershed Management: A Case Study of Mae Taeng*, Thailand Development Research Institute. Bangkok.

Weatherly, Paul (1994) Major environmental problems and costs of abatement, in: G.M. Owens (ed.) *Financing Environmentally Sound Development*, Manila: Asian Development Bank, pp. 25–100.

World Resources Institute (1998) *World Resources 1998–1999: A Guide to Global Environment*, Washington DC: World Resources Institute.

Index

Page references include tables where appropriate. When information occurs in a table and is not referred to in the text on that page, the reference is shown in *italic*.